THE
BAKING
BOOK

Good Housekeeping

THE
BAKING
BOOK

THE ULTIMATE BAKER'S COMPANION

COLLINS & BROWN

First published in Great Britain in 2011
by Collins & Brown
10 Southcombe Street
London W14 0RA

An imprint of Anova Books Company Ltd.

The Good Housekeeping website is
www.allaboutyou.com/goodhousekeeping

10 9 8 7 6 5 4 3 2

ISBN 978-1-84340-636-5

A catalogue record for this book is available from the British
Library.

Reproduction by Dot Gradations Ltd, UK
Printed and bound by Toppan Leefung, China

This book can be ordered direct from the publisher at
www.anovabooks.com

NOTES

- Both metric and imperial measures are given for the recipes. Follow either set of measures, not a mixture of both, as they are not interchangeable.

- All spoon measures are level.
  1 tsp = 5ml spoon; 1 tbsp = 15ml spoon.

- Ovens and grills must be preheated to the specified temperature.

- Use sea salt and freshly ground black pepper unless otherwise suggested.

- Fresh herbs should be used unless dried herbs are specified in a recipe.

- Medium eggs should be used except where otherwise specified. Free-range eggs are recommended.

DIETARY GUIDELINES

- Note that some recipes contain raw or lightly cooked eggs. The young, elderly, pregnant women and anyone with an immune-deficiency disease should avoid these, because of the slight risk of salmonella.

- Note that some recipes contain alcohol. Check the ingredients list before serving to children.

CONTENTS

Foreword 6

FOREWORD

Baking has always had a welcome place in people's hearts. It promises not only a house filled with tantalising aromas, but also the satisfaction of feeding those you love with irresistible sweet treats – not to mention yourself! With the rise of the patisserie outlet and excellent shop-bought cakes, there's always the threat of 'the easy way out' but, good though these shop-bought cakes and bakes may be, they are not homemade.

For me, this self-madeness shows you care and it's hard not to feel a nibbling of pride when you're surrounded by munching sounds of delight. On the flip side, if a little mishap does occur and, say, your scones have not risen to the heavens, you'll know they still taste good.

In my experience, baking is what hooks most people into enjoying their kitchen – and with good reason, it's fun! Even if you haven't started at a tender age, stamping out dinosaur biscuits, there's always time to learn and to be rewarded with the huge sense of satisfaction of seeing something cooling on a wire rack.

Baking involves a delicate – scientific, even – balance, where a small change in an ingredient can have a large effect on the finished result. It's hard to 'wing it' when baking. But fear not, baking is very simple if you follow a good recipe closely – and Good Housekeeping recipes are not only excellent, but have also been triple-tested in our dedicated kitchens, so you are sure to succeed.

I hope you enjoy this book – it's filled with sweet promise.

Meike

Meike Beck
Cookery Editor
Good Housekeeping

CAKES

THE PERFECT VICTORIA SPONGE

Preparation: 20 minutes

Cooking time: about 25 minutes, plus cooling

175g (6oz) unsalted butter at room
   temperature, plus extra to grease
175g (6oz) golden caster sugar
3 medium eggs
175g (6oz) self-raising flour, sifted
3–4 tbsp jam
a little icing sugar to dust

PER SLICE

445 cals; 21g fat (of which 11g saturates);
30g carbohydrate; 0.8g salt

1 Grease two 18cm (7 inch) sandwich tins and base-line with greaseproof paper. Preheat the oven to 190°C (170°C fan oven) mark 5.

2 Put the butter and caster sugar into a large bowl and, using a hand-held electric whisk, beat together until pale and fluffy. Add the eggs, one at a time, beating well after each addition and adding a spoonful of flour to the mixture if it looks as if it's about to curdle. Using a large metal spoon, fold in the remaining flour.

3 Divide the mixture evenly between the prepared tins and level the surface with a palette knife. Bake in the centre of the oven for 20–25 minutes until the cakes are well risen and spring back when lightly pressed in the centre. Loosen the edges with a palette knife and leave in the tins for 5 minutes.

4 Turn out, remove the lining paper and leave to cool on a wire rack. Sandwich the two cakes together with jam and dust icing sugar over the top. Slice and serve.

TO STORE
Store in an airtight container. It will keep for up to three days. If stored in the fridge it will keep for up to one week.

CHOCOLATE VICTORIA SANDWICH

Preparation: 20 minutes
Cooking time: 20 minutes, plus cooling

175g (6oz) unsalted butter at room
    temperature, plus extra to grease
3 tbsp cocoa powder
175g (6oz) golden caster sugar
3 medium eggs, beaten
160g (5½oz) self-raising flour, sifted
golden caster sugar to dredge

CHOCOLATE
BUTTERCREAM

1 tbsp cocoa powder
75g (3oz) unsalted butter, softened
175g (6oz) icing sugar, sifted
a few drops of vanilla extract
1–2 tbsp milk or water

PER SLICE

520 cals; 30g fat (of which 19g saturates);
62g carbohydrate; 1g salt

1 Preheat the oven to 190°C (170°C fan oven) mark 5.
   Grease two 18cm (7 inch) sandwich tins and base-line
   with baking parchment. Blend the cocoa powder with
   3 tbsp hot water to make a smooth paste, then leave
   to cool.
2 Using a freestanding mixer or hand-held electric whisk,
   cream the butter and sugar together until pale and
   fluffy. Add the cooled cocoa mixture and beat until
   evenly blended.
3 Add the beaten eggs, a little at a time, beating well
   after each addition. Using a metal spoon or large
   spatula, fold in half the flour, then carefully fold in the
   rest. Divide the mixture evenly between the tins and
   level the surface.
4 Bake both cakes on the middle shelf of the oven for
   about 20 minutes until well risen, springy to the touch
   and beginning to shrink away from the sides of the
   tins. Cool in the tins for 5 minutes, then turn out on to
   a wire rack and leave to cool completely.

5 To make the chocolate buttercream, blend the cocoa
   powder with 3 tbsp boiling water and set aside to
   cool. Put the butter into a bowl and beat with a
   wooden spoon until light and fluffy. Gradually stir in
   the icing sugar. Add the blended cocoa, vanilla extract
   and milk or water and beat well until light and smooth.
6 When the cakes are cool, sandwich them together
   with the chocolate buttercream and sprinkle the top
   with caster sugar.

TO STORE
Store in an airtight container in a cool place. It will keep
well for up to one week.

WHISKED SPONGE

Preparation: 25 minutes
Cooking time: 20–25 minutes, plus cooling

butter to grease
90g (3oz) plain flour, plus extra
   to dust
3 large eggs
125g (4oz) golden caster sugar

TO ASSEMBLE
3–4 tbsp strawberry, raspberry or
   apricot jam
125ml (4fl oz) whipping cream,
   whipped (optional)
caster or icing sugar to dust

PER SLICE (WITHOUT CREAM)
215–160 cals; 4–3g fat (of which 0.9–0.7g
saturates); 30–24g carbohydrate; 0.1g salt

1 Preheat the oven to 190°C (170°C fan oven) mark 5. Grease and base-line two 18cm (7 inch) sandwich tins and dust the sides with a little flour or with a mixture of flour and caster sugar.

2 Put the eggs and sugar into a large heatproof bowl and, using a hand-held electric whisk, whisk until well blended. Put the bowl over a pan of hot water and whisk until pale and creamy and thick enough to leave a trail on the surface when the whisk is lifted. Remove the bowl from the pan and whisk until cool and thick.

3 Sift half the flour over the mixture and, using a large metal spoon or plastic-bladed spatula, fold it in very lightly. Sift in the remaining flour and fold in gently until evenly incorporated.

4 Pour the mixture into the prepared tins, tilting the tins to spread the mixture evenly. Bake in the middle of the oven for 20–25 minutes until well risen and springy to the touch when lightly pressed in the centre. Turn out on to a wire rack and leave to cool.

5 Sandwich the cakes together with jam, and cream, if you like. Dust with caster or icing sugar to serve.

VARIATION
Chocolate whisked sponge: Replace 1½ tbsp of the flour with 1½ tbsp cocoa powder. Sandwich the cake layers together with vanilla or chocolate buttercream (see page 321). Dust with icing sugar.

NOTE
This classic fatless sponge does not keep well and is best eaten on the day it is made.

SWISS ROLL

CUTS INTO 8 SLICES

Preparation: 25 minutes
Cooking time: 10–12 minutes, plus cooling

butter to grease
125g (4oz) golden caster sugar, plus extra to dust
125g (4oz) plain flour, plus extra to dust
3 large eggs

TO ASSEMBLE
caster sugar to sprinkle
125g (4oz) jam, warmed

PER SLICE
200 cals; 3g fat (of which 0.7g saturates); 41g carbohydrate; 0.9g salt

1 Grease and line a 33 × 23cm (13 × 9 inch) Swiss roll tin (see page 294). Grease the paper, then dust with caster sugar and flour. Preheat the oven to 200°C (180°C fan oven) mark 6.

2 Put the eggs and sugar into a large heatproof bowl and, using a hand-held electric whisk, whisk until well blended. Put the bowl over a pan of hot water and whisk until the mixture is pale and creamy and thick enough to leave a trail on the surface when the whisk is lifted. Remove the bowl from the pan and whisk until cool and thick.

3 Sift half the flour over the mixture and fold it in very lightly, using a large metal spoon or spatula. Sift in the remaining flour and gently fold in until evenly incorporated. Carefully fold in 1 tbsp hot water.

4 Pour into the prepared tin and tilt the tin backwards and forwards to spread the mixture evenly. Bake for 10–12 minutes until pale golden, risen and springy to the touch.

5 Meanwhile, put a sheet of greaseproof paper on a damp teatowel. Dredge the paper with caster sugar.

6 Quickly turn out the cake on to the paper and remove the lining paper. Trim off the crusty edges and spread the cake with jam.

7 Using the greaseproof paper to help, roll up the cake from a short side. Make the first turn firmly so that the cake will roll evenly and have a good shape when finished, but roll more lightly after this turn. Put seam-side down on a wire rack and sprinkle with sugar to serve.

VARIATION
Chocolate Swiss roll: Replace 1 tbsp flour with cocoa powder. Turn out and trim the sponge as above, then cover with a sheet of greaseproof paper and roll with the paper inside. When cold, unroll and remove the paper. Spread with whipped cream or buttercream (see page 321) and re-roll. Dust with icing sugar.

CARROT CAKE

Preparation: 15 minutes

Cooking time: 40 minutes, plus cooling

250ml (9fl oz) sunflower oil, plus
   extra to grease
225g (8oz) light muscovado sugar
3 large eggs
225g (8oz) self-raising flour
large pinch of salt
½ tsp each ground mixed spice,
   ground nutmeg and ground
   cinnamon
250g (9oz) carrots, peeled and
   coarsely grated

FROSTING

50g (2oz) butter, preferably unsalted,
   at room temperature
225g pack cream cheese
25g (1oz) golden icing sugar
½ tsp vanilla extract
8 pecan halves, roughly chopped

PER SLICE

383 cals; 32g fat (of which 10g saturates);
24g carbohydrate; 0.3g salt

1 Preheat the oven to 180°C (160°C fan oven) mark 4. Grease two 18cm (7 inch) sandwich tins and base-line with greaseproof paper.

2 Using a hand-held electric whisk, whisk the oil and muscovado sugar together to combine, then whisk in the eggs, one at a time.

3 Sift the flour, salt and spices together over the mixture, then gently fold in, using a large metal spoon. Tip the carrots into the bowl and fold in.

4 Divide the cake mixture between the prepared tins and bake for 30–40 minutes until golden and a skewer inserted into the centre comes out clean. Remove from the oven and leave in the tins for 10 minutes, then turn out on to a wire rack and leave to cool completely.

5 To make the frosting, beat the butter and cream cheese together in a bowl until light and fluffy. Sift in the icing sugar, add the vanilla extract and beat well until smooth. Spread one-third of the frosting over one cake and sandwich together with the other cake. Spread the remaining frosting on top and sprinkle with the pecans.

TO STORE

Store in an airtight container. Eat within two days. Alternatively, the cake will keep for up to one week in an airtight container if it is stored before the frosting is applied.

ALMOND AND APRICOT CAKE

CUTS INTO 12 SLICES

Preparation: 15 minutes

Cooking time: 15 minutes, plus cooling

175g (6oz) unsalted butter, softened,
  plus extra to grease
125g (4oz) caster sugar
4 medium eggs
175g (6oz) self-raising flour
75g (3oz) ground almonds
finely grated zest and juice of
  1 lemon

ICING AND FILLING

250g tub mascarpone cheese
40g (1½oz) icing sugar, plus extra
  to dust
4 tbsp apricot compote

PER SLICE

325 cals; 21g fat (of which 11g saturates);
30g carbohydrate; 0.3g salt

1 Preheat the oven to 200°C (180°C fan oven) mark 6. Grease two 18cm
   (7 inch) round sandwich tins and line with greaseproof paper.
2 Beat the butter and caster sugar together until fluffy. Then beat in the eggs,
   one at a time, until combined. Using a metal spoon, gently fold in the flour,
   ground almonds, lemon zest and juice and stir until smooth.
3 Divide the mixture between the tins, level the surface and bake for
   15 minutes or until golden and a skewer inserted into the centre comes
   out clean. Cool in the tins for 5 minutes, then turn out on to a wire rack
   and leave to cool completely.
4 For the icing, beat the mascarpone and icing sugar together in a bowl.
   Spread over one of the cakes. Spoon the apricot compote evenly over
   the cheese mixture and put the other cake on top. Dust with icing sugar
   to serve.

TO STORE

Store in an airtight container in a cool place. It will keep for up to two days.

FREEZING TIP

To freeze, complete the recipe
to the end of step 3. Wrap
each cake in greaseproof
paper and clingfilm. Freeze for
up to one month. To use, thaw
overnight at cool room
temperature and complete
the recipe.

MADEIRA CAKE

CUTS INTO 12 SLICES

Preparation: 20 minutes

Cooking time: about 50 minutes, plus cooling

175g (6oz) butter, softened, plus
    extra to grease
125g (4oz) plain flour
125g (4oz) self-raising flour
175g (6oz) golden caster sugar
1 tsp vanilla extract
3 large eggs, beaten
1–2 tbsp milk (optional)
2–3 thin slices citron peel

PER SLICE

260 cals; 14g fat (of which 8g saturates);
31g carbohydrate; 0.4g salt

1 Preheat the oven to 180°C (160°C fan oven) mark 4. Grease and line a deep 18cm (7 inch) round cake tin. Sift the plain and self-raising flours together.

2 Cream the butter and sugar together in a bowl until pale and fluffy, then beat in the vanilla extract. Add the eggs, a little at a time, beating well after each addition.

3 Using a metal spoon, fold in the sifted flours, adding a little milk if necessary to give a dropping consistency.

4 Spoon the mixture into the prepared tin and level the surface. Bake for 20 minutes. Lay the citron peel on the cake and bake for a further 30 minutes or until a skewer inserted into the centre comes out clean. Turn out on to a wire rack and leave to cool. This cake can be made up to one week in advance (store in an airtight tin) or frozen for up to one month.

VARIATION

Add the grated zest of 1 lemon at stage 2. Add the juice of the lemon instead of the milk at stage 3.

QUANTITIES AND SIZES FOR MADEIRA CAKES

To make a Madeira sponge cake follow the method above, choosing your tin size and corresponding ingredient amounts from the chart below:

Square tin size	Round tin size	Makes	Baking time	Ingredients
12.5cm (5 inch)	15cm (6 inch)	8–10 slices	1–1¼ hours	125g (4oz) each of softened unsalted butter and golden caster sugar; 2 medium eggs; 125g (4oz) sifted self-raising flour; 50g (2oz) sifted plain flour; grated zest and juice of ½ lemon
15cm (6 inch)	18cm (7 inch)	20 slices	1¼ hours	225g (8oz) each of softened unsalted butter and golden caster sugar; 4 medium eggs; 225g (8oz) sifted self-raising flour; 100g (3½oz) sifted plain flour; grated zest and juice of 1 lemon
23cm (9 inch)	25.5cm (10 inch)	28 slices	1 hour 20–30 minutes	350g (12oz) each of softened unsalted butter and golden caster sugar; 6 medium eggs; 350g (12oz) sifted self-raising flour; 175g (6oz) sifted plain flour; grated zest and juice of 1½ lemons

ORANGE SYRUP CAKE

Preparation: 20 minutes, plus soaking

Cooking time: 30–40 minutes, plus cooling

175g (6oz) unsalted butter, plus extra
   to grease
225g (8oz) caster sugar
2 medium eggs, beaten
200g (7oz) rice flour
2 tsp baking powder
75g (3oz) ground almonds
grated zest and juice of 1 large
   orange
250ml carton orange juice
2 tbsp lemon juice
2 large oranges, peeled and thickly
   sliced
blueberries to serve

PER SLICE

291 cals; 20g fat (of which 10g saturates);
27g carbohydrate; 0.4g salt

1 Preheat the oven to 190°C (170°C fan oven) mark 5. Grease a shallow 20.5cm (8 inch) round tin and base-line with baking parchment.

2 Cream the butter and 75g (3oz) sugar together. Gradually beat in the eggs. Fold in the rice flour, baking powder and ground almonds. Stir in the zest and juice of the orange and 8 tbsp orange juice. The mixture should be of a soft, dropping consistency. Spoon the mixture into the prepared tin and level the surface.

3 Bake for 40 minutes or until firm. Cool in the tin for 10 minutes, then turn out on to a wire rack and leave to cool completely.

4 Just before serving, combine the remaining sugar and orange juice plus the lemon juice in a small pan. Add the orange slices, bring to the boil and cook for 1–2 minutes. Take the pan off the heat and leave to cool for 5 minutes. Remove the orange slices from the syrup and set aside. Put the cake on a serving plate and, with a cocktail stick, prick the cake in a number of places. Drizzle with the syrup and leave to soak in for 30 minutes.

5 Serve with the orange slices and blueberries.

FREEZING TIP
To freeze, complete the recipe to the end of step 3, wrap and freeze. To use, thaw at cool room temperature for 2–3 hours. Complete the recipe.

SWEET PUMPKIN CAKE WITH TOFFEE SAUCE

Preparation: 25 minutes

Cooking time: 1½ hours, plus cooling

butter to grease

225g (8oz) self-raising flour, plus extra to dust

550g (1¼lb) pumpkin or butternut squash, cut into wedges

250ml (9fl oz) sunflower oil

275g (10oz) light muscovado sugar, plus extra to sprinkle

3 large eggs

1 tsp bicarbonate of soda

2 tsp ground ginger

1 tsp ground cinnamon

1 tsp ground nutmeg

pinch of ground cloves

pinch of ground allspice

Toffee Sauce (see right) to serve

PER SLICE

440 cals; 24g fat (of which 9g saturates); 55g carbohydrate; 0.3g salt

1 Preheat the oven to 200°C (180°C fan oven) mark 6. Grease a 23cm (9 inch) kugelhopf tin generously with butter and dust with flour.

2 Put the pumpkin on a baking sheet and roast for 40 minutes or until tender. Leave to cool for 15 minutes.

3 Lower the oven setting to 180°C (160°C fan oven) mark 4. Spoon out 250g (9oz) pumpkin flesh, put into a blender and whiz to a purée.

4 Put the oil and sugar into a freestanding mixer and whisk for 2 minutes (or use a hand-held electric whisk), then whisk in the eggs, one at a time. Sift the flour, bicarbonate of soda and spices on to the mixture and fold in. Add the pumpkin purée and stir in gently. Pour the mixture into the prepared tin.

5 Bake for 40–45 minutes until risen, springy to the touch and shrinking away from the sides of the tin. Cool in the tin for 10 minutes, then turn out on to a wire rack and leave to cool completely.

6 To serve, drizzle the toffee sauce over the cake and sprinkle with muscovado sugar.

TOFFEE SAUCE

Put 300g (11oz) light muscovado sugar, 300ml (½ pint) double cream and 50g (2oz) unsalted butter into a small heavy-based pan. Heat gently to dissolve the sugar, then simmer and stir for 3 minutes to thicken slightly. Pour into a jug.

RICH FRUIT CAKE

Preparation: 30 minutes

Cooking time: 2½ hours, plus cooling

175g (6oz) unsalted butter, cubed,
plus extra to grease
1kg (2¼lb) mixed dried fruit
100g (3½oz) ready-to-eat dried
prunes, roughly chopped
50g (2oz) ready-to-eat dried figs,
roughly chopped
100g (3½oz) dried cranberries
2 balls preserved stem ginger in
syrup, grated and syrup reserved
grated zest and juice of 1 orange
175ml (6fl oz) brandy
2 splashes Angostura bitters
175g (6oz) dark muscovado sugar
200g (7oz) self-raising flour
½ tsp ground cinnamon
½ tsp freshly grated nutmeg
½ tsp ground cloves
4 medium eggs, beaten

PER SLICE

277 cals; 11g fat (of which 6g saturates);
38g carbohydrate; 0.2g salt

1 Preheat the oven to 150°C (130°C fan oven) mark 2. Grease a 20.5cm
(8 inch) round, deep cake tin and line base and sides with greaseproof paper.

2 Put all the dried fruit into a very large pan and add the ginger, 1 tbsp
reserved ginger syrup, the orange zest and juice, brandy and Angostura
bitters. Bring to the boil, then simmer for 5 minutes. Add the butter and
sugar and heat gently to melt. Stir occasionally until the sugar dissolves.
Take the pan off the heat and leave to cool for a couple of minutes.

3 Add the flour, spices and beaten eggs and mix well. Pour the mixture into
the prepared tin and level the surface. Wrap the outside of the tin in
brown paper and secure with string to protect the cake during cooking.
Bake for 2–2½ hours – cover with greaseproof paper after about
1½ hours – until the cake is firm to the touch and a skewer inserted into
the centre comes out clean.

4 Cool in the tin for 2–3 hours, then remove from the tin, leaving the
greaseproof paper on, transfer to a wire rack and leave to cool completely.
Wrap the cake in a layer of clingfilm, then in foil.

TO STORE

Store in an airtight container. It will keep for up to three months. If you like,
after the cake has matured for two weeks, prick it all over with a metal
skewer and sprinkle with 1 tbsp brandy. Leave to soak in, then rewrap and
store as before.

QUANTITIES AND SIZES FOR RICH FRUIT CAKES

To make a formal cake for a birthday, wedding or anniversary, the following chart will show you the amount of ingredients required to fill the chosen cake tin or tins, whether round or square.

NOTE

When baking large cakes, 25.5cm (10 inch) and upwards, it is advisable to reduce the oven heat to 130°C (110°C fan) mark 1 after two-thirds of the cooking time. The amounts of Almond Paste quoted in this chart will give a thin covering. The quantities of Royal Icing should be enough for two coats. If using ready-to-roll fondant icing, use the quantities suggested for Royal Icing as a rough guide.

Size	Square tin size	Round tin size	Cooking time (approx.)	Weight when cooked	Ingredients	Almond Paste	Royal Icing
Size 1	12.5cm (5 inch)	15cm (6 inch)	2½–3 hours	1.1kg (2½lb)	225g (8oz) currants, 125g (4oz) each sultanas and raisins, 50g (2oz) glacé cherries, 25g (1oz) each mixed peel and flaked almonds, a little lemon zest, 175g (6oz) plain flour, 4 tsp each mixed spice and cinnamon, 150g (5oz) each softened butter and soft brown sugar, 2½ medium eggs, beaten, 1 tbsp brandy	350g (12oz)	450g (1lb)
Size 2	15cm (6 inch)	18cm (7 inch)	3 hours	1.6kg (3½lb)	350g (12oz) currants, 125g (4oz) each sultanas and raisins, 75g (3oz) glacé cherries, 50g (2oz) each mixed peel and flaked almonds, a little lemon zest, 200g (7oz) plain flour, ½ tsp each mixed spice and cinnamon, 175g (6oz) each softened butter and soft brown sugar, 3 medium eggs, beaten, 1 tbsp brandy	450g (1lb)	550g (1¼lb)
Size 3	20.5cm (8 inch)	23cm (9 inch)	4 hours	2.7kg (6lb)	625g (1lb 6oz) currants, 225g (8oz) each sultanas and raisins, 175g (6oz) glacé cherries, 125g (4oz) each mixed peel and flaked almonds, zest of ¼ lemon, 400g (14oz) plain flour, 1 tsp each cinnamon and mixed spice, 350g (12oz) each softened butter and soft brown sugar, 6 medium eggs, beaten, 2 tbsp brandy	800g (1¾lb)	900g (2lb)
Size 4	23cm (9 inch)	25.5cm (10 inch)	6 hours	4kg (9lb)	800g (1¾lb) currants, 375g (13oz) each sultanas and raisins, 250g (9oz) glacé cherries, 150g (5oz) each mixed peel and flaked almonds, zest of ¼–½ lemon, 600g (1lb 5oz) plain flour, 1 tsp each mixed spice and cinnamon, 500g (1lb 2oz) each softened butter and soft brown sugar, 9 medium eggs, beaten, 2–3 tbsp brandy	900g (2lb)	1kg (2¼lb)
Size 5	28cm (11 inch)	30.5cm (12 inch)	8 hours	6.7kg (14¾lb)	1.5kg (3lb 2oz) currants, 525g (1lb 3oz) each sultanas and raisins, 350g (12oz) glacé cherries, 250g (9oz) each mixed peel and flaked almonds, zest of ½ lemon, 825g (1lb 13oz) plain flour, 2½ tsp each mixed spice and cinnamon, 800g (1¾lb) each softened butter and soft brown sugar, 14 medium eggs, beaten, 4 tbsp brandy	1.1kg (2½lb)	1.4kg (3lb)
Size 6	30.5cm (12 inch)	33cm (13 inch)	8½ hours	7.7kg (17lb)	1.7kg (3lb 12oz) currants, 625g (1lb 6oz) each sultanas and raisins, 425g (15oz) glacé cherries, 275g (10oz) each mixed peel and flaked almonds, zest of 1 lemon, 1kg (2¼lb) plain flour, 2½ tsp each mixed spice and cinnamon, 950g (2lb 2oz) each softened butter and soft brown sugar, 17 medium eggs, beaten, 6 tbsp brandy	1.4kg (3lb)	1.6kg (3½lb)

DUNDEE CAKE

Preparation: 20 minutes

Cooking time: about 2 hours, plus cooling

225g (8oz) butter or margarine,
    softened, plus extra to grease
125g (4oz) currants
125g (4oz) raisins
50g (2oz) blanched almonds,
    chopped
125g (4oz) chopped mixed
    candied peel
300g (11oz) plain flour
225g (8oz) light muscovado sugar
finely grated zest of 1 lemon
4 large eggs, beaten
75g (3oz) split almonds to finish

PER SLICE

350 cals; 18g fat (of which 8g saturates);
45g carbohydrate; 0.4g salt

TO STORE

Store in an airtight container. It will
keep for up to one week.

1 Preheat the oven to 170°C (150°C fan oven) mark 3. Grease and line a deep 20cm (8 inch) round cake tin with greaseproof paper. Wrap a double thickness of paper around the outside and secure with string (see step 2, page 276).

2 Combine the dried fruit, chopped nuts and peel in a bowl. Sift in a little flour and stir to coat the fruit.

3 Cream the butter and sugar together in a bowl until pale and fluffy, then beat in the lemon zest. Add the eggs, a little at a time, beating well after each addition.

4 Sift in the remaining flour and fold in lightly, using a metal spoon, then fold in the fruit and nut mixture.

5 Turn the mixture into the prepared tin and, using the back of a metal spoon, make a slight hollow in the centre. Arrange the split almonds on top.

6 Bake on the centre shelf of the oven for 2 hours or until a skewer inserted into the centre comes out clean. Loosely cover the top of the cake with foil if it appears to be browning too quickly. Leave in the tin for 15 minutes, then turn out on to a wire rack and leave to cool completely. Wrap in greaseproof paper and foil and leave to mature for at least a week before cutting.

STICKY LEMON POLENTA CAKE

Preparation: 10 minutes

Cooking time: 1 hour, plus cooling

50g (2oz) unsalted butter, softened,
    plus extra to grease
3 lemons
250g (9oz) golden caster sugar
250g (9oz) instant polenta
1 tsp wheat-free baking powder
2 large eggs
50ml (2fl oz) semi-skimmed milk
2 tbsp natural yogurt
2 tbsp poppy seeds

PER SLICE

220 cals; 7g fat (of which 3g saturates);

37g carbohydrate; 0.1g salt

1 Preheat the oven to 180°C (160°C fan oven) mark 4. Lightly grease a 900g (2lb) loaf tin and base-line with greaseproof paper.

2 Grate the zest of 1 lemon and put into a food processor with the butter, 200g (7oz) sugar, the polenta, baking powder, eggs, milk, yogurt and poppy seeds, then whiz until smooth. Spoon the mixture into the prepared tin and level the surface. Bake for 55 minutes–1 hour until a skewer inserted into the centre comes out clean. Leave to cool in the tin for 10 minutes.

3 Next, make a syrup. Squeeze the juice from the zested lemon plus 1 more lemon. Thinly slice the third lemon. Put the lemon juice into a pan with the remaining sugar and 150ml (¼ pint) water. Add the lemon slices, bring to the boil and bubble for about 10 minutes until syrupy. Take the pan off the heat and leave to cool for 5 minutes. Remove the lemon slices from the syrup and set aside.

4 Slide a knife around the edge of the cake and turn out on to a serving plate. Pierce the cake in several places with a skewer, spoon the syrup over it and decorate with the lemon slices.

TO STORE
Wrap in clingfilm and store in an airtight container. It will keep for up to three days.

LEMON DRIZZLE LOAF

CUTS INTO 8–10 SLICES

Preparation: 20 minutes

Cooking time: about 50 minutes, plus cooling

175g (6oz) unsalted butter, softened,
    plus extra to grease
175g (6oz) caster sugar
4 medium eggs, lightly beaten
3 lemons
125g (4oz) gluten-free self-raising
    flour
50g (2oz) ground almonds
75g (3oz) sugar cubes

PER SLICE
424 cals; 25g fat (of which 13g saturates);
46g carbohydrate; 0.6g salt

1 Preheat the oven to 180°C (160°C fan oven) mark 4.
   Grease and line a 900g (2lb) loaf tin with parchment
   paper.
2 In a large bowl, beat together the butter and caster
   sugar with a hand-held electric whisk until pale and
   fluffy, about 5 minutes. Gradually beat in the eggs,
   followed by the finely grated zest of 2 of the lemons
   and the juice of ½ a lemon.
3 Fold the flour and ground almonds into the butter
   mixture, then spoon into the prepared tin and bake
   for 40–50 minutes or until a skewer inserted into the
   centre comes out clean. Cool in the tin for 10 minutes,
   then turn out on to a wire rack and leave to cool
   until warm.

4 Meanwhile, put the sugar cubes into a small bowl with
   the juice of 1½ lemons and the pared zest of 1 lemon
   (you should have 1 un-juiced lemon left over). Soak for
   5 minutes, then use the back of a spoon to roughly
   crush the cubes. Spoon over the warm cake and leave
   to cool completely before serving in slices.

TO STORE
Store in an airtight container. It will keep for up to
four days.

BANANA AND BUTTERSCOTCH LOAF

**MAKES I LOAF –
CUTS INTO 15 SLICES**

Preparation: 20 minutes
Cooking time: 1 hour, plus cooling

butter to grease
175g (6oz) plain flour, sifted
2 tsp baking powder
½ tsp bicarbonate of soda
½ tsp salt
175g (6oz) light muscovado sugar
2 large eggs
3 medium-size ripe bananas, peeled
    and mashed
150g carton natural yogurt
150g bar butterscotch chocolate,
    roughly chopped
100g (3½oz) pecan nuts, chopped
1–2 tbsp demerara sugar

PER SLICE
221 cals; 9g fat (of which 2g saturates);
34g carbohydrate; 0.2g salt

1 Preheat the oven to 170°C (150°C fan oven) mark 3. Grease a 1.4kg (3lb) loaf tin and line with greaseproof paper.

2 Put the flour, baking powder, bicarbonate of soda and salt into a large bowl and mix together.

3 In a separate bowl, beat the muscovado sugar and eggs together with a hand-held electric whisk until pale and fluffy. Carefully stir in the bananas, yogurt, chocolate and 50g (2oz) pecan nuts, followed by the flour mixture.

4 Spoon the mixture into the prepared tin and level the surface. Sprinkle with the remaining chopped pecan nuts and the demerara sugar. Bake for 1 hour or until a skewer inserted into the centre comes out clean. Leave to cool in the tin on a wire rack, then turn out and slice.

TO STORE
Store in an airtight container. It will keep for up to two days.

VARIATION
If you can't find butterscotch chocolate, use a bar of plain dark chocolate instead.

SPICED PECAN, APPLE AND CRANBERRY CAKE

Preparation: 20 minutes

Cooking time: about 1 hour

175g (6oz) unsalted butter, softened,
   plus extra to grease
150g (5oz) caster sugar
3 medium eggs
1 tsp vanilla extract
150g (5oz) plain flour
1 tsp baking powder
2 tbsp milk
½ tsp ground cinnamon
3 Braeburn apples, peeled, cored and
   cut into 1cm (½ inch) cubes
50g (2oz) fresh cranberries,
   defrosted if frozen
75g (3oz) pecan nuts, roughly
   chopped
2–3 tbsp apricot jam

PER SLICE

436 cals; 28g fat (of which 13g saturates);
44g carbohydrate; 0.5g salt

1 Preheat the oven to 180°C (160°C fan oven) mark 4. Grease a 20.5cm (8 inch) springform cake tin and line with baking parchment.

2 Using a freestanding mixer or hand-held electric whisk, beat 150g (5oz) butter with the sugar, eggs, vanilla extract, flour, baking powder and milk until pale and fluffy – about 5 minutes. Spoon into the prepared tin and level the surface. Bake for 10 minutes.

3 Meanwhile, heat the remaining butter in a large frying pan until foaming. Stir in the cinnamon and apples and cook for 3 minutes until almost tender. Take off the heat and stir in the cranberries and pecan nuts.

4 Carefully take the part-baked cake out of the oven and sprinkle the apple mixture over the surface. Return to the oven and bake for a further 40–50 minutes until a skewer inserted into the centre comes out clean.

5 Leave the cake to cool in tin for 5 minutes, then remove from the tin and peel off the paper. Transfer to a serving plate. Gently warm the jam in a small pan to loosen, then brush over the top of the cake. Serve the cake warm or at room temperature.

TO STORE

Store in an airtight container. It will keep for up to two days.

APPLE AND BLUEBERRY CAKE

Preparation: 20 minutes

Cooking time: 1 hour, plus cooling

125g (4oz) unsalted butter, diced, plus extra to grease
225g (8oz) self-raising flour, sifted
½ tsp salt
175g (6oz) granulated sugar, golden if possible
2 large eggs, beaten
2 large Granny Smith apples, peeled, cored and sliced
140g (4½oz) fresh blueberries
175g (6oz) apricot jam
1 tbsp lemon juice

PER SLICE

396 calories; 15g fat (of which 9g saturates); 65g carbohydrate; 0.6g salt

1 Preheat the oven to 190°C (170°C fan oven) mark 5. Grease a 20.5cm (8 inch) springform cake tin with butter and base-line with baking parchment.
2 Put the flour and salt into a large mixing bowl, add the diced butter and rub in the flour until the mixture resembles fine breadcrumbs. Add 140g (4½oz) sugar and the beaten eggs and stir well.

FREEZING TIP

To freeze, complete the recipe to the end of step 4. Wrap the cake in a freezer bag and freeze for up to one month. To use, thaw for 3 hours at cool room temperature, then complete the recipe.
To serve warm, heat individual cake slices in the microwave on full power for 1 minute per slice.

3 Spread half the mixture in a thin layer in the tin, then layer the sliced apples and the blueberries evenly over the surface, setting aside a little of the fruit for the top of the cake. Sprinkle with the remaining sugar, then spoon in the rest of the cake mixture. Add the remaining apple slices and blueberries, pressing them down slightly into the mixture.
4 Bake for 45–55 minutes until risen and firm to the touch and a skewer inserted into the centre comes out clean. Cool in the tin for 10 minutes, then turn out on to a wire rack and leave to cool completely.
5 Warm the jam and lemon juice in a small pan until evenly combined. Sieve the mixture and, while it's still warm, brush it over the top of the cake. Serve immediately.

RASPBERRY AND PEACH CAKE

Preparation: 15 minutes

Cooking time: 1–1¼ hours, plus cooling

200g (7oz) unsalted butter, melted,
    plus extra to grease
250g (9oz) self-raising flour, sifted
100g (3½oz) golden caster sugar
4 medium eggs, beaten
125g (4oz) raspberries
2 large, almost-ripe peaches or
    nectarines, halved, stoned and
    sliced
4 tbsp apricot jam
juice of ½ lemon

PER SLICE

405 cals; 24g fat (of which 14g saturates);
44g carbohydrate; 0.8g salt

1 Preheat the oven to 190°C (170°C fan oven) mark 5. Grease a 20.5cm (8 inch) springform cake tin and base-line with baking parchment.
2 Put the flour and sugar into a large bowl. Make a well in the centre and add the melted butter and the eggs. Mix well.
3 Spread half the mixture over the bottom of the cake tin and add half the raspberries and sliced peaches or nectarines. Spoon on the remaining cake mixture, smooth over, then add the remaining raspberries and peaches or nectarines, pressing them down into the mixture slightly.
4 Bake for 1–1¼ hours until risen and golden and a skewer inserted into the centre comes out clean. Remove from the oven and leave in the tin to cool for 10 minutes.
5 Warm the jam and the lemon juice together in a small pan and brush over the cake to glaze. Serve warm or at room temperature.

TO STORE
Store in an airtight container. It will keep for up to one week.

FRUITY TEACAKE

Preparation: 20 minutes, plus soaking

Cooking time: 1 hour, plus cooling

150ml (¼ pint) hot black tea, made
with 2 Earl Grey tea bags
200g (7oz) sultanas
75g (3oz) ready-to-eat dried figs,
roughly chopped
75g (3oz) ready-to-eat dried prunes,
roughly chopped
a little vegetable oil
125g (4oz) dark muscovado sugar
2 medium eggs, beaten
225g (8oz) gluten-free flour
2 tsp wheat-free baking powder
2 tsp ground mixed spice
butter to serve (optional)

PER SLICE

185 cals; 1g fat (of which trace saturates);
42g carbohydrate; 0.1g salt

1 Pour the tea into a bowl and add all the dried fruit. Leave to soak for
30 minutes.
2 Preheat the oven to 190°C (170°C fan oven) mark 5. Oil a 900g (2lb) loaf
tin and base-line with greaseproof paper.
3 Beat the sugar and eggs together in a large bowl until pale and slightly
thickened. Add the flour, baking powder, mixed spice and soaked dried fruit
and tea, then mix together well. Spoon the mixture into the prepared tin
and level the surface.
4 Bake on the middle shelf of the oven for 45 minutes–1 hour. Leave to cool
in the tin.
5 Serve sliced, with a little butter if you like.

TO STORE

Wrap in clingfilm and store in an airtight container. It will keep for up to
five days.

STICKY GINGER RING

Preparation: 15 minutes

Cooking time: 1 hour, plus cooling and setting

100g (3½oz) unsalted butter, diced,
  plus extra to grease
100g (3½oz) light brown soft sugar
3 tbsp black treacle
100ml (3½fl oz) milk
2 tbsp brandy
1 large egg, beaten
150g (5oz) plain flour
2 tsp ground ginger
2 tsp ground cinnamon
1 tsp bicarbonate of soda
75g (3oz) ready-to-eat dried prunes,
  coarsely chopped

DECORATION

225g (8oz) icing sugar, sifted
2 pieces preserved stem ginger,
  drained of syrup and roughly
  chopped

PER SLICE

375 cals; 12g fat (of which 7g saturates);
64g carbohydrate; 0.3g salt

FREEZING TIP
To freeze, complete the recipe
to the end of step 4, then
wrap the cake in clingfilm and
foil. Freeze for up to one
month. To use, thaw for
3 hours and complete the
recipe.

1 Preheat the oven to 150°C (130°C fan oven) mark 2. Generously grease
  a 21cm (8½ inch), 600ml (1 pint) round ring mould with butter.
2 Put the butter, brown sugar and treacle into a pan and heat gently until
  melted, stirring all the time. Add the milk and brandy and leave to cool,
  then beat in the egg.
3 Sift the flour, spices and bicarbonate of soda into a large mixing bowl. Make
  a well in the centre, pour in the treacle mixture and stir until all the flour
  has been combined – it should be of a soft, dropping consistency. Stir in the
  chopped prunes. Pour the mixture into the prepared ring mould and level
  the surface.
4 Bake for 1 hour or until the cake is firm to the touch and a skewer
  inserted into the centre comes out clean. Cool in the tin for 10 minutes,
  then loosen the sides of the cake, turn out on to a wire rack and leave to
  cool completely.
5 To make the icing, mix the icing sugar with about 2 tbsp hot water to
  create a coating consistency. Drizzle over the cake and down the sides,
  then decorate with the stem ginger. Leave to set

GINGER AND FRUIT TEABREAD

Preparation: 15 minutes, plus soaking

Cooking time: 1 hour, plus cooling

125g (4oz) each dried apricots,
   apples and pitted prunes, chopped
300ml (½ pint) strong fruit tea
a little butter to grease
25g (1oz) preserved stem ginger in
   syrup, chopped
225g (8oz) wholemeal flour
2 tsp baking powder
125g (4oz) dark muscovado sugar
1 medium egg, beaten

PER SLICE

145 cals; 1g fat (of which trace saturates);
33g carbohydrate; 0g salt

1 Put the dried fruit into a large bowl, add the tea and leave to soak for
2 hours.
2 Preheat the oven to 180°C (160°C fan oven) mark 4. Grease a 900g (2lb)
loaf tin and base-line with baking parchment.
3 Add the remaining ingredients to the soaked fruit and mix thoroughly.
Spoon into the prepared tin and brush with 2 tbsp cold water. Bake for
1 hour or until a skewer inserted into the centre comes out clean.
4 Cool in the tin for 10–15 minutes, then turn out on to a wire rack and
leave to cool completely.

TO STORE
Wrap in clingfilm and store in an airtight container. It will keep for up to
three days.

STICKY GINGERBREAD

BREAD MACHINE RECIPE

CUTS INTO 10 SLICES

Preparation: 15 minutes

Cooking time: 1 hour 10 minutes, plus cooling

125g (4oz) unsalted butter, plus extra
   to grease
125g (4oz) light muscovado sugar
75g (3oz) black treacle
200g (7oz) golden syrup
250g (9oz) plain flour
2 tsp ground mixed spice
65g (2½oz) preserved stem ginger,
   finely chopped
2 large eggs
100ml (3½fl oz) milk
1 tsp bicarbonate of soda
extra treacle or golden syrup to glaze
   (optional)

PER SLICE

341 cals; 12g fat (of which 7g saturates);
58g carbohydrate; 0.7g salt

1 Put the butter, sugar, treacle and golden syrup in a saucepan and heat gently until the butter has melted. Leave to cool for 5 minutes. Grease and line the bread maker bucket with baking parchment, if specified in the manual.

2 Sift the flour and mixed spice together into a bowl. Add the syrup mixture, chopped ginger, eggs and milk and stir well until combined.

3 In a cup, mix the bicarbonate of soda with 2 tbsp hot water, then add to the bowl. Stir the mixture well and pour into the bread maker bucket.

4 Fit the bucket into the bread maker and set to the cake or bake only programme. Select 1 hour 10 minutes on the timer and choose a light crust. Press start.

5 To check whether the cake is done, pierce the centre with a skewer; it should come out fairly clean. If necessary, re-set the timer for a little longer.

6 Remove the bucket from the machine, leave the cake in it for 5 minutes, then turn out on to a wire rack. Brush the top of the cake with the treacle or syrup to glaze, if you like, and leave to cool.

TO STORE
Wrap and store in an airtight container. It will keep for up to one week.

BRAZIL NUT AND CLEMENTINE CAKES

MAKES 8

Preparation: 30 minutes
Cooking time: 1¼ hours, plus cooling

butter to grease
1 lemon
10 clementines
150g (5oz) brazil nuts
100ml (3½fl oz) mild olive oil
3 medium eggs
275g (10oz) golden caster sugar
1 tsp baking powder
2 tbsp brandy

DECORATION
mint sprigs
icing sugar

PER CAKE
413 cals; 26g fat (of which 5g saturates); 41g carbohydrate; 0.1g salt

1 Grease eight 150ml (¼ pint) ramekin dishes and base-line with greaseproof paper. Wash the lemon and 4 clementines and put into a pan. Cover with boiling water, reduce the heat to a gentle simmer and cook for 30 minutes or until the clementines are tender.

2 Remove the clementines with a slotted spoon and set aside. Cook the lemon for a further 10 minutes or until tender. Drain, reserving 200ml (7fl oz) liquid, and cool slightly. Halve the fruit, remove the pips and roughly chop.

3 Preheat the oven to 180°C (160°C fan oven) mark 4. Grind the nuts in a food processor until finely chopped, then tip out and set aside. There's no need to wash the jug – add the cooked fruit and blend to a purée.

4 Put the oil, eggs and 125g (4oz) caster sugar into a mixing bowl and whisk until slightly thick and foamy. Stir in the ground nuts, fruit purée and baking powder. Divide among the ramekins and put on a baking sheet. Bake for 25 minutes or until slightly risen and firm to the touch. Leave to cool in the ramekins.

5 Peel the remaining clementines, remove the pips and divide into segments, then skin each segment. Heat the remaining sugar in a small pan with 150ml (¼ pint) of the reserved cooking liquid until the sugar dissolves. Bring to the boil and cook until a pale caramel in colour. Dip the base of the pan into cold water to stop the caramel cooking. Stir in the remaining liquid and the brandy. Return to the heat, stirring until the caramel has dissolved. Stir in the clementine segments.

6 Loosen the edges of the cakes, turn out on to individual plates and remove the paper lining. Pile the fruit segments on top and spoon the caramel over them. Decorate each with a mint sprig and a dusting of icing sugar.

ROCK BUNS

Preparation: 5 minutes
Cooking time: 20 minutes, plus cooling

125g (4oz) butter or margarine, plus
    extra to grease
225g (8oz) plain flour
pinch of salt
2 tsp baking powder
75g (3oz) demerara sugar
75g (3oz) mixed dried fruit
zest of ½ lemon
1 medium egg
milk

PER BUN

192 calories; 9g fat (of which 6g saturates);
26g carbohydrate; 0.5g salt

1   Preheat the oven to 200°C (180°C fan oven) mark 6.
    Lightly grease two baking sheets.
2   Sift together the flour, salt and baking powder. Rub
    in the butter until the mixture resembles fine
    breadcrumbs. Add the sugar, fruit and lemon zest
    and mix together thoroughly.
3   Using a fork, mix to a moist but stiff dough with the
    beaten egg and a little milk.
4   Using two forks, shape into really rocky heaps on the
    baking sheets. Bake for about 20 minutes until golden
    brown. Transfer to a wire rack and leave to cool.
    Rock buns are best eaten on the day they are made.

NOTE
Use a food processor to whiz the flour and butter
together if you prefer.

MADELEINES

Preparation: 20 minutes, plus chilling

Cooking time: 10–12 minutes, plus cooling

125g (4oz) unsalted butter, melted
    and cooled until tepid
125g (4oz) plain flour, plus extra to
    dust
4 medium eggs
125g (4oz) golden caster sugar
finely grated zest of 1 lemon
1 tsp baking powder
pinch of salt
icing sugar to dust

PER CAKE

90 cals; 5g fat (of which 2g saturates);
10g carbohydrate; 0.2g salt

1 Brush two Madeleine trays with a little of the melted butter. Leave to set, then dust with flour, shaking out any excess.

2 Using a hand-held electric whisk, beat the eggs, sugar and lemon zest together in a bowl, until the mixture is pale, creamy and thick enough to leave a trail when the whisk is lifted.

3 Sift in half the flour, together with the baking powder and salt. Carefully pour in half the melted butter around the edge of the bowl and gently fold in until evenly incorporated. Repeat with the remaining flour and butter. Cover and chill the mixture in the fridge for 45 minutes. Preheat the oven to 220°C (200°C fan oven) mark 7.

4 Two-thirds fill the Madeleine moulds with the mixture and bake for 10–12 minutes until well risen and golden. Ease out of the tins, transfer to a wire rack and leave to cool. Serve dusted with icing sugar.

NOTES

• Resting the sponge mixture before baking gives the Madeleines their characteristic dense texture.

• If you have only one Madeleine tray, then bake in two batches.

CHOCOLATE WHOOPIE PIES

Preparation: 30 minutes
Cooking time: 12 minutes

1 large egg
150g (5oz) caster sugar
75g (3oz) butter, melted
150g (5oz) crème fraîche
1 tsp vanilla extract
1½–2 tbsp milk
200g (7oz) plain flour
75g (3oz) cocoa powder
½ tsp bicarbonate soda

FILLING
115g (3¾oz) unsalted butter,
   softened
200g (7oz) icing sugar, sifted
1 tsp vanilla extract
milk (optional)

PER PIE
365 cals; 14g fat (of which 8g saturates); 59g
carbohydrate; 0.3g salt

1 Preheat the oven to 180°C (160°C fan oven) mark 4. Line two large baking sheets with baking parchment.
2 Whisk the egg and caster sugar together until thick and light in colour. Beat in the melted butter, crème fraîche, vanilla extract and milk.
3 Sift together the flour, cocoa powder and bicarbonate of soda. Beat into the egg mixture until smooth – it will make a very thick mixture but should be pipable. Add a drop more milk if necessary.
4 Fill a piping bag fitted with a large nozzle with the mixture and pipe walnut-sized balls on to the baking sheets, spacing well apart. Bake for 10–12 minutes until golden and risen. Cool on the baking sheet for 1–2 minutes until firm, then transfer to a wire rack and leave to cool completely.
5 To make the filling, cream together the butter and icing sugar until fluffy. Beat in the vanilla extract. Beat in a little milk, if necessary, to make the icing a spreadable consistency. Sandwich the whoopie halves together with the buttercream.

BLACK FOREST ROULADE

Preparation: 35 minutes

Cooking time: 20 minutes, plus cooling and chilling

4 large eggs, separated

125g (4oz) golden caster sugar, plus extra to dust

125g (4oz) plain chocolate (at least 70% cocoa solids), broken into pieces, melted (see page 326) and left to cool a little

cocoa powder and icing sugar to dust

chocolate curls (see page 327) to decorate (optional)

FILLING

140ml (4½ fl oz) whipping cream

1 tsp icing sugar

75g (3oz) Greek-style yogurt

2 × 425g cans morello cherries, drained, pitted and halved

PER SLICE

248 cals; 12g fat (of which 7g saturates); 33g carbohydrate; 0.1g salt

1 Preheat the oven to 180°C (160°C fan oven) mark 4. Line a 33 × 23cm (13 × 9 inch) Swiss roll tin with baking parchment.

2 Whisk the egg yolks with the sugar in a large bowl until thick and creamy. Whisk in the melted chocolate. Whisk the egg whites in a clean, grease-free bowl until stiff peaks form. Fold into the chocolate mixture. Pour into the prepared tin, level the surface and bake for 20 minutes or until firm to the touch. Leave to cool in the tin for 10–15 minutes.

3 Put a sheet of baking parchment on the worksurface and dust with caster sugar. Carefully turn out the roulade on to the parchment and peel off the lining parchment. Cover with a damp cloth and leave to cool for 30 minutes.

4 To make the filling, lightly whip the cream with the icing sugar, then fold in the yogurt. Spread over the cold roulade and scatter the cherries on top. Using the baking parchment to help, roll up the roulade from one of the narrow ends. Chill for 30 minutes. Dust with cocoa powder and icing sugar, decorate with chocolate curls, if you like, and serve sliced.

DECADENT CHOCOLATE CAKE

Preparation: 30 minutes

Cooking time: 1 ½ hours, plus cooling
and setting

225g (8oz) unsalted butter, softened,
  plus extra to grease
300g (11oz) plain chocolate, broken
  into pieces
225g (8oz) golden caster sugar
225g (8oz) ground almonds
8 large eggs, separated
125g (4oz) fresh brown breadcrumbs
4 tbsp apricot jam (optional)
cream to serve (optional)

GANACHE
175g (6oz) plain chocolate, broken
  into pieces
75g (3oz) butter, softened
4 tbsp double cream

PER SLICE
687 cals; 49g fat (of which 23g saturates);
54g carbohydrate; 0.7g salt

1 Preheat the oven to 180°C (160°C fan oven) mark 4.
   Grease a 23cm (9 inch) springform cake tin and line
   with greaseproof paper.
2 Melt the chocolate in a heatproof bowl set over a pan
   of gently simmering water, making sure the base of the
   bowl doesn't touch the water. Remove the bowl from
   the pan.
3 Put the butter and sugar into a large bowl and beat
   until light and creamy. Add the almonds, egg yolks and
   breadcrumbs. Beat well until thoroughly mixed. Slowly
   add the chocolate and carefully stir it in. Do not over-
   mix, as the chocolate may seize up and become
   unworkable.
4 Put the egg whites into a clean, grease-free bowl and
   whisk until stiff peaks form. Add half the whites to the
   chocolate mixture and, using a large metal spoon, fold in
   lightly. Carefully fold in the remainder. Pour into the
   prepared tin and level the surface.

5 Bake for 1 hour 20 minutes or until the cake is firm to
   the touch and a skewer inserted into the centre
   comes out clean. Cool in the tin for 5 minutes, then
   transfer to a wire rack and leave for 2–3 hours to
   cool completely.
6 Put the jam, if using, into a pan and melt over a low
   heat. Brush jam over the top and sides of the cake.
7 Melt the chocolate, butter and cream in a heatproof
   bowl set over a pan of gently simmering water, making
   sure the base of the bowl doesn't touch the water.
   Stir just once until smooth. Either raise the cake off
   the worksurface on the upturned tin or put it (still on
   the rack) on a tray to catch the drips. Pour the
   ganache into the centre and tip the cake to let it run
   down the sides evenly, or spread it with a palette
   knife. Leave to set then serve with cream, if you like.

CARDAMOM AND MANGO CAKE

Preparation: 45 minutes

Cooking time: 25–30 minutes, plus cooling and chilling

50g (2oz) unsalted butter, plus extra to grease
4 green cardamom pods, split and seeds removed
a good pinch of saffron strands
4 large eggs
125g (4oz) caster sugar
100g (3½oz) plain flour

FILLING, MANGO SAUCE AND DECORATION

2 large, ripe mangoes
150ml (¼ pint) double cream
150g (5oz) Greek-style yogurt
3 tbsp icing sugar, plus extra to dust
4 tbsp orange juice
orange segments

PER SLICE

274 cals; 16g fat (of which 9g saturates); 31g carbohydrate; 0.2g salt

1 Preheat the oven to 180°C (160°C fan oven) mark 4. Grease two 18cm (7 inch) sandwich tins, or one deep 18cm (7 inch) round cake tin, and base-line with baking parchment.

2 Crush the cardamom seeds to a powder together with the saffron. Put the butter into a pan and heat gently until melted, then remove from the heat and leave to cool for a few minutes until beginning to thicken.

3 Put the eggs and caster sugar into a large heatproof bowl. Using a hand-held electric whisk, whisk until evenly blended. Put the bowl over a pan of hot water and whisk until pale and thick enough to leave a trail on the surface when the whisk is lifted. Remove the bowl from the pan and whisk until cool and thick.

4 Sift the spices and flour together. Using a large metal spoon or plastic spatula, fold half into the whisked mixture. Pour the cooled butter around the edge of the mixture, leaving the sediment behind. Gradually fold it in very lightly, cutting through the mixture until it is all incorporated. Carefully fold in the remaining flour as lightly as possible. Pour into the prepared tins.

5 Bake for 25–30 minutes until well risen and the cakes spring back when lightly pressed. Run a small knife around the cake edge to loosen and leave in the tins for 5 minutes, then turn out on to a wire rack and leave to cool completely.

6 To make the filling, peel the mangoes, then cut one of them into slices. Whip the cream until it holds its shape. Stir in the yogurt with 2 tbsp icing sugar. Sandwich the cakes with the cream mixture and mango slices. Chill for 2–3 hours.

7 To make the mango sauce, put the remaining mango flesh, 1 tbsp icing sugar and the orange juice into a blender and whiz to a purée. Pass the purée through a nylon sieve to remove all the fibres. Cover and chill.

8 Just before serving, decorate the cake with orange segments and dust with icing sugar. Serve with the mango sauce.

BLACK FOREST GATEAU

SERVES 12

Preparation: 30 minutes

Cooking time: about 50 minutes, plus cooling

125g (4oz) unsalted butter, melted

200g (7oz) plain flour

50g (2oz) cornflour

50g (2oz) cocoa powder, plus extra
  to dust

2 tsp espresso instant coffee powder

1 tsp baking powder

4 large eggs, separated

300g (11oz) golden caster sugar

2 x 300g jars morello cherries in
  syrup

2 tbsp Kirsch

200ml (7fl oz) double cream

2 tbsp icing sugar, sifted

fresh cherries and chocolate curls
  (see page 327) to decorate

PER SERVING

440 cals; 22g fat (of which 12g saturates);
59g carbohydrate; 0.8g salt

1 Preheat the oven to 180°C (160°C fan oven) mark 4. Brush a little of the melted butter over the base and sides of a 20.5cm (8 inch) round x 9cm (3½ inch) deep cake tin. Line the base and sides with baking parchment.

2 Sift the flour, cornflour, cocoa powder, coffee powder and baking powder together three times – this helps to add air and makes sure the ingredients are well mixed.

3 Put the egg yolks, caster sugar and 100ml (3½fl oz) cold water into a freestanding mixer and whisk for 8 minutes until the mixture leaves a trail for 3 seconds when the whisk is lifted.

4 Add the rest of the melted butter, pouring it around the edge of the bowl so that the mixture doesn't lose any air, then quickly fold it in, followed by the sifted flour mixture in two batches.

5 In another bowl, whisk the egg whites until stiff peaks form, then fold a spoonful into the cake mixture to loosen. Carefully fold in the rest of the egg whites, making sure there are no white blobs left. Pour into the prepared tin and bake in the oven for 45–50 minutes until a skewer inserted into the centre comes out clean. Leave in the tin for 10 minutes, then turn out on to a wire rack to cool completely.

6 When the cake is cold, trim the top to make a flat surface. Turn the cake over so that the top becomes the base. Using a long serrated bread knife, carefully cut into three horizontally. Drain the cherries, reserving 250ml (9fl oz) of the syrup. Put the syrup into a pan and simmer to reduce by half. Stir in the Kirsch. Brush the hot syrup on to each layer of the cake – including the top – using up all the liquid.

7 Lightly whip the cream with the icing sugar. Spread one-third over the bottom layer of cake and cover with half the cherries. Top with the next cake layer and repeat with another third of the cream and the remaining cherries. Top with the final cake layer and spread the remaining cream over. Decorate with fresh cherries, chocolate curls and a dusting of cocoa powder.

NOTE
Make the gateau up to two hours ahead to allow the flavours to mingle and the syrup to moisten the cake.

BEST-EVER LEMON GATEAU

OVERNIGHT PREPARATION NEEDED

CUTS INTO 8 SLICES

Preparation: 35 minutes

Cooking time: about 20 minutes, plus cooling and chilling

butter to grease
2½ tbsp semolina, plus extra to dust
6 large eggs, separated
150g (5oz) caster sugar
2 large lemons
40g (1½oz) ground almonds
3 tbsp plain flour
3 gelatine leaves
150ml (¼ pint) double cream
icing sugar to dust

PER SLICE

276 cals; 17g fat (of which 7g saturates);
28g carbohydrate; 0.2g salt

1 Preheat the oven to 180°C (160°C fan oven) mark 4. Grease an 8cm (3¼ inch) deep, 20.5cm (8 inch) loose-based round tin. Base-line with baking parchment and dust the sides with semolina.

2 Put 3 egg yolks, 50g (2oz) sugar and the zest of 1 lemon into a bowl and beat for 5 minutes. Fold in the semolina, almonds and flour.

3 Put 3 egg whites into a clean, grease-free bowl and whisk until stiff. Add 25g (1oz) sugar and beat for a few seconds. Fold 1 tbsp into the cake mixture, then fold in the rest. Spoon into the prepared tin and level the surface. Bake for 15–20 minutes. Leave to cool in the tin.

4 Remove the sides of the tin and slide the cake on to a board, leaving the parchment in place. Slice the cake in half horizontally. Regrease and reline the sides of the tin with baking parchment, then put the cake half with the paper attached into the tin, paper side down.

5 Put the gelatine into a bowl and cover with cold water. Leave for 5 minutes. Heat the juice of 1 lemon until simmering. Squeeze the excess water from the gelatine, then whisk into the lemon juice. Leave to cool. Whisk the remaining yolks and sugar with the zest of the other lemon until mousse-like. Fold the gelatine mixture into the sugar and lemon mixture.

6 Put the remaining egg whites into a clean, grease-free bowl and whisk until stiff. Whip the cream until it just holds its shape. Fold the cream into the yolk mix, then fold in the egg whites. Pour into the tin, cover and chill for 2 hours. Put the second cake layer over the mousse, cut-side down. Cover and chill overnight.

7 Turn out the cake and peel off the paper. Dust with icing sugar. Heat a metal skewer in a gas flame and score lines on the top.

CREAMY COFFEE AND PRALINE GATEAU

CUTS INTO 8 SLICES

Preparation: 45 minutes

Cooking time: 25 minutes, plus cooling

50g (2oz) unsalted butter, melted,
   plus extra to grease
125g (4oz) plain flour, sifted, plus
   extra to dust
4 large eggs, separated
125g (4oz) caster sugar
1 tbsp coffee granules, dissolved in
   2 tsp boiling water

PRALINE
50g (2oz) whole blanched hazelnuts
150g (5oz) caster sugar

FILLING
500g (1lb 2oz) mascarpone cheese
250g (9oz) icing sugar, sifted
2 tbsp coffee granules, dissolved in
   1 tbsp boiling water

PER SLICE
548 cals; 21g fat (of which 10g saturates);
83g carbohydrate; 0.2g salt

1 Preheat the oven to 190°C (170°C fan oven) mark 5. Grease two 18cm (7 inch) loose-based sandwich tins. Dust lightly with flour and tip out the excess.

2 Put the egg whites into a clean, grease-free bowl and whisk until soft peaks form. Whisk in 1 egg yolk; repeat with the other 3 yolks. Add the sugar, 1 tbsp at a time, and continue to whisk. The mixture should be thick enough to leave a trail when the whisk is lifted. Using a large metal spoon, fold half the flour into the mixture.

3 Mix the coffee into the melted butter, then pour around the edge of the egg mixture. Add the remaining flour and gradually fold in. Divide the mixture between the prepared tins and bake for 25 minutes or until risen and firm to the touch. Turn out on to a wire rack and leave to cool completely.

4 To make the praline, line a baking sheet with non-stick baking parchment and scatter the nuts on it. Dissolve the sugar in a heavy-based pan over a low heat, shaking the pan once or twice to help it dissolve evenly. Cook until it forms a dark golden-brown caramel. Pour over the nuts and leave to cool.

5 To make the filling, put the mascarpone and icing sugar into a large bowl, add the coffee and mix with a hand-held electric whisk. Slice each cake in half horizontally. Put one cake layer on a plate and spread with a quarter of the filling. Continue layering in this way, finishing with a layer of mascarpone filling.

6 Break the praline into two or three pieces and put into a plastic bag. Using a rolling pin, smash it into smaller pieces. Use to decorate the top of the cake.

TROPICAL FRUIT CAKE

Preparation: 40 minutes

Cooking time: 1 hour 20 minutes, plus cooling

125g (4oz) unsalted butter, softened, plus extra to grease

125g (4oz) caster sugar

grated zest of 1 orange and 3 tbsp juice

2 large eggs, lightly beaten

pinch of salt

125g (4oz) semolina

125g (4oz) desiccated coconut

200g (7oz) ground almonds

1 tsp baking powder

300ml (½ pint) double cream

icing sugar and vanilla extract to taste

1 mango, 1 papaya or pineapple,

1 star fruit and 1 banana, peeled and sliced

6 lychees, peeled and stones removed

50g (2oz) coconut slices (see notes)

CITRUS SYRUP

pared zest of 1 orange and juice of 2 oranges

pared zest of 1 lemon and juice of 3 lemons

125g (4oz) caster sugar

PER SLICE

857 cals; 60g fat (of which 32g saturates); 74g carbohydrate; 0.3g salt

1 Preheat the oven to 170°C (150°C fan oven) mark 3. Grease a 23cm (9 inch) springform cake tin and base-line with baking parchment.

2 To make the cake, whisk the butter and sugar together in a food processor (or use a hand-held electric whisk) until pale and fluffy. Beat the orange zest, eggs and salt together, then beat into the butter mixture, a spoonful at a time. Using a large metal spoon, fold in the semolina, desiccated coconut, ground almonds, baking powder and orange juice. Spoon the mixture into the prepared tin and level the surface.

3 Bake for 45–50 minutes until a skewer inserted into the centre comes out clean. Cool in the tin for 15 minutes, then turn out on to a wire rack and leave to cool completely.

4 Put the orange and lemon zests and juice, sugar and 450ml (¾ pint) water into a pan. Bring to the boil and bubble for 15–20 minutes until syrupy. Set aside to cool.

5 Cut about 1cm (½ inch) from the centre of the cake, crumble and keep the crumbs to one side. Prick the cake with a fine skewer – without piercing right through, or the syrup will run through – and spoon the syrup over it. Set aside 3 tbsp of the syrup.

6 Whip the cream until soft peaks form, then add the icing sugar and vanilla extract to taste. Carefully fold in the reserved cake crumbs, one-third of the prepared fruit and the reserved syrup. Stir gently to combine, taking care not to mash the fruit. Spoon on to the cake. Decorate with the remaining fruit and coconut slices.

NOTES

- For fresh coconut slices, use a vegetable peeler to pare off thin slices, sprinkle with caster sugar and grill until lightly browned.

- For a spun sugar topping, see page 330.

GLUTEN-FREE CHOCOLATE CAKE

Preparation: 30 minutes

Cooking time: 45 minutes–1 hour, plus cooling

125g (4oz) unsalted butter, softened, plus extra to grease

200g (7oz) light muscovado sugar

2 large eggs, lightly beaten

125g (4oz) gluten-free plain chocolate, broken into pieces, melted (see page 326) and left to cool slightly

100g (3½oz) natural yogurt

a few drops of vanilla extract

200g (7oz) brown rice flour

½ tsp wheat-free baking powder

1 tsp bicarbonate of soda

ICING

150g (5oz) gluten-free plain chocolate, broken into pieces

150ml (¼ pint) double cream

large milk and plain or white chocolate buttons (gluten-free) to decorate

PER SLICE

476 cals; 28g fat (of which 16g saturates); 60g carbohydrate; 0.3g salt

1 Preheat the oven to 180°C (160°C fan oven) mark 4. Grease a deep 18cm (7 inch) square cake tin and line with greaseproof paper.

2 Cream the butter and sugar together until light and fluffy. Gradually beat in the eggs, then the melted chocolate, yogurt and vanilla extract. Sift the rice flour, baking powder and bicarbonate of soda together, then beat into the mixture a little at a time. Pour into the prepared tin and bake for 45 minutes–1 hour or until a skewer inserted into the centre comes out clean. Cool in the tin for 10 minutes, then turn out on to a wire rack and leave to cool completely.

3 To make the icing, put the chocolate into a heatproof bowl. Heat the cream to just below boiling point. Pour on to the chocolate and leave for 5 minutes, then beat until the chocolate has melted and the mixture is smooth. Cool until thickened, then, using a palette knife, spread all over the cake. Decorate the top and sides with alternate milk and plain or white chocolate buttons to create a polka-dot effect.

TO STORE

Store in an airtight container. It will keep for up to three days.

TOASTED HAZELNUT MERINGUE CAKE

Preparation: 10 minutes

Cooking time: about 30 minutes, plus cooling

oil to grease
175g (6oz) skinned hazelnuts, toasted
3 large egg whites
175g (6oz) golden caster sugar
250g carton mascarpone cheese
285ml (9½fl oz) double cream
3 tbsp Bailey's Irish Cream liqueur, plus extra to serve
140g (4½oz) frozen raspberries
340g jar redcurrant jelly

PER SLICE

598 cals; 38g fat (of which 16g saturates); 57g carbohydrate; 0.1g salt

1 Preheat the oven to 190°C (170°C fan oven) mark 5. Lightly oil two 18cm (7 inch) sandwich tins and base-line with baking parchment. Whiz the hazelnuts in a food processor until finely chopped.

2 Put the egg whites into a clean, grease-free bowl and whisk until stiff peaks form. Whisk in the sugar, a spoonful at a time. Using a metal spoon, fold in half the nuts. Divide the mixture between the tins and spread evenly. Bake in the middle of the oven for about 30 minutes, then leave to cool in the tins for 30 minutes.

3 To make the filling, put the mascarpone cheese into a bowl. Beat in the cream and liqueur until smooth. Put the raspberries and redcurrant jelly into a pan and heat gently until the jelly has melted. Sieve, then cool.

4 Use a palette knife to loosen the edges of the meringues, then turn out on to a wire rack. Peel off the baking parchment and discard. Put a large sheet of baking parchment on a board and sit one meringue on top, flat-side down. Spread one-third of the mascarpone mixture over the meringue, then drizzle with raspberry purée. Top with the other meringue, then cover the whole cake with the rest of the mascarpone mixture. Sprinkle with the remaining hazelnuts. Carefully put the cake on to a serving plate and drizzle with more liqueur, if you like.

FREEZING TIP

Freezing the meringue makes it slightly softer but no less tasty. Complete the recipe to the end of step 4, but don't put on a serving plate or drizzle with more liqueur. Using the paper, lift the cake into the freezer, then freeze until solid. Once solid, store in a sturdy container in the freezer for up to one month. To use, thaw overnight in the fridge, then complete the recipe.

EASTER CHOCOLATE FUDGE CAKE

Preparation: 30 minutes

Cooking time: about 50 minutes, plus cooling

175g (6oz) unsalted butter, softened, plus extra to grease
150g (5oz) plain flour
50g (2oz) cocoa powder
1 tsp baking powder
pinch of salt
150g (5oz) light muscovado sugar
3 medium eggs, beaten
250ml (9fl oz) soured cream
1 tsp vanilla extract

ICING AND DECORATION
100g (3½oz) plain chocolate, finely chopped
150g (5oz) unsalted butter, softened
125g (4oz) cream cheese
175g (6oz) icing sugar, sifted
50g (2oz) chocolate curls, lightly crushed (see page 327)
foil-covered chocolate eggs

PER SLICE
590 cals; 42g fat (of which 25g saturates); 50g carbohydrate; 0.7g salt

1 Preheat the oven to 180°C (160°C fan oven) mark 4. Grease and line a 20.5cm (8 inch) springform tin with greaseproof paper. Sift the flour, cocoa powder, baking powder and salt into a large bowl.

2 Using an electric mixer or electric beaters, mix the butter and muscovado sugar in a separate bowl until pale and fluffy – about 5 minutes. Gradually add the beaten eggs, mixing well after each addition. Add a little of the flour mixture if the butter mixture looks like curdling. In one go, add the remaining flour mixture, the soured cream and vanilla extract, then fold everything together gently with a metal spoon. Spoon into the prepared tin and bake for 40–50 minutes until a skewer inserted into centre comes out clean. Cool in the tin.

3 To make the icing, melt the chocolate in a heatproof bowl set over a pan of barely simmering water, making sure the base of the bowl doesn't touch the water. Leave to cool for 15 minutes. In a separate bowl, beat the butter and cream cheese with a wooden spoon until combined. Beat in the icing sugar, then the cooled chocolate. Take care not to over-beat the mixture – it should be fudgey, not stiff.

4 Remove the cake from the tin, cut in half horizontally and use some icing to sandwich the layers together. Transfer to a cake stand, then ice the top and sides, smoothing with a palette knife. Decorate with crushed curls and chocolate eggs.

CAPPUCCINO AND WALNUT CAKE

Preparation: 30 minutes

Cooking time: about 45 minutes, plus cooling

65g (2½oz) unsalted butter, melted and cooled, plus extra
    to grease
100g (3½oz) plain flour
1 tsp baking powder
4 medium eggs
125g (4oz) caster sugar
1 tbsp chicory and coffee essence
75g (3oz) walnuts, toasted, cooled and finely chopped

DECORATION

50g (2oz) walnuts
1 tbsp granulated sugar
¼ tsp ground cinnamon

ICING

200g (7oz) good-quality white chocolate
4 tsp chicory and coffee essence
2 x 250g tubs mascarpone cheese
fresh unsprayed violets to decorate (optional)

PER SLICE

449 cals; 30g fat (of which 13g saturates); 36g carbohydrate; 0.3g salt

1 Preheat the oven to 190°C (170°C fan oven) mark 5. Grease two 20.5 x 4cm deep (8 x 1½ inch deep) round cake tins and base-line each with a circle of greased greaseproof paper. Sift the flour and baking powder together twice.

2 Using an electric mixer, whisk the eggs and caster sugar in a large heatproof bowl set over a pan of barely simmering water for 3–4 minutes until light, thick and fluffy. Remove the bowl from the heat and continue whisking until the mixture has cooled and the whisk leaves a ribbon trail for 8 seconds when lifted out of the bowl.

3 Fold in the butter, coffee essence and chopped walnuts. Sift half the flour over the mixture, then fold in carefully but quickly with a metal spoon. Sift and fold in the rest, taking care not to knock out too much air. Pour into the prepared tins and tap them lightly on the worksurface. Bake for 20–25 minutes until the tops feel springy. Cool in the tins for 10 minutes, then turn out on to a wire rack and leave to cool completely.

4 To make the decoration, whiz the walnuts in a food processor or blender with the granulated sugar and cinnamon until finely chopped. Take care not to overprocess the nuts or they'll become oily. Set aside.

5 To make the icing, break up the chocolate and put into a heatproof bowl set over a pan of gently simmering water, making sure the base of the bowl doesn't touch the water. Allow to melt slowly without stirring. In another bowl, add the coffee essence to the mascarpone and beat until smooth, then slowly beat in the melted chocolate.

6 Spread one-third of the icing on top of one cake, then sandwich with the other half. Smooth the remaining icing over the top and sides. Lift the cake on to a large piece of greaseproof paper and scatter the chopped nuts all around it. Then lift the greaseproof up to press nuts on to the sides. Transfer to a plate and decorate with the violets, if you like.

TO STORE

Store in an airtight container in the fridge. It will keep for up to two days.

WHITE CHOCOLATE CAPPUCCINO CAKE

CUTS INTO 10 SLICES

Preparation: 45 minutes
Cooking time: about 50 minutes, plus cooling

300g (11oz) unsalted butter, at room
  temperature, plus extra to grease
250g (9oz) self-raising flour, plus extra to dust
200g (7oz) caster sugar
3 large eggs, at room temperature, beaten
1½ tsp baking powder
50ml (2fl oz) milk
1 tsp vanilla extract
125g (4oz) white chocolate
125ml (4fl oz) double cream
1½–2 tbsp espresso coffee, cooled
75g (3oz) icing sugar, sifted, plus extra to dust
50g (2oz) plain chocolate, grated
40g (1½oz) hazelnuts, roasted and chopped
small roses to decorate

PER SLICE

659 cals; 45g fat (of which 25g saturates);
60g carbohydrate; 0.3g salt

1 Preheat the oven to 180°C (160°C fan oven) mark 4. Grease a deep non-stick 20.5cm (8 inch) cake tin and dust with flour.

2 Beat together the caster sugar and 175g (6oz) butter until pale and creamy. Gradually add the eggs, beating well after each addition. Add 1 tbsp flour if the mix looks like curdling. Fold in the remaining flour and the baking powder, followed by the milk and vanilla extract. Spoon into the prepared tin and level the surface. Bake for 40–50 minutes until a skewer inserted into the centre comes out clean. Cool in the tin for 5 minutes, then turn out on to a wire rack and leave to cool completely.

3 Cut the cake in half horizontally. Grate 25g (1oz) white chocolate, then beat together with the cream and coffee until the mixture holds its shape. Use to sandwich the two cake halves together.

4 Melt the remaining white chocolate in a bowl set over a pan of simmering water (see page 326). Leave to cool for 10 minutes. Beat together the remaining butter and the icing sugar until pale and creamy. Beat in the cooled white chocolate, then spread over the sides and top of the cake.

5 Mix the plain chocolate with the nuts and press around the side of the cake. Decorate with small roses dusted with icing sugar.

NOTE
For convenience, prepare ahead. Make to the end of step 2 up to 24 hours ahead. Return to the tin when cool and wrap in clingfilm. Complete the recipe to serve.

EGG-FREE CHOCOLATE CAKE

Preparation: 30 minutes, plus cooling

Cooking time: 1–1¼ hours, plus cooling

150ml (¼ pint) sunflower oil, plus extra to
  grease
75g (3oz) creamed coconut
25g (1oz) plain chocolate, broken into pieces
50g (2oz) cocoa powder
350g (12oz) self-raising flour
1 tsp baking powder
pinch of salt
175g (6oz) light muscovado sugar

ICING

350g (12oz) plain chocolate, broken into
  small pieces
150ml (¼ pint) double cream
white and milk chocolate Maltesers to decorate

PER SLICE

515 cals; 31g fat (of which 15g saturates);
59g carbohydrate; 0.4g salt

1　Grease a 1.7 litre (3 pint), 30.5 x 10cm (12 x 4 inch) loaf tin and line with greaseproof paper. Put the coconut into a heatproof bowl, pour on 425ml (14½fl oz) boiling water and stir to dissolve. Set aside to cool for 30 minutes.

2　Melt the chocolate in a heatproof bowl set over a pan of gently simmering water, making sure the base of the bowl doesn't touch the water. Stir until smooth, then remove the bowl from the pan and leave to cool slightly. Preheat the oven to 180°C (160°C fan oven) mark 4.

3　Sift the cocoa powder, flour, baking powder and salt into a bowl. Stir in the sugar and make a well in the middle. Add the coconut mixture, melted chocolate and oil and beat to make a smooth batter. Pour the cake batter into the prepared tin.

4　Bake for 1–1¼ hours or until risen and just firm to the touch (if necessary, after about 40 minutes, lightly cover the top of the cake with foil if it appears to be browning too quickly. Leave in the tin for 10 minutes, then transfer to a wire rack and leave to cool completely. When cold, trim to neaten the edges.

5　To make the icing, put the chocolate into a heatproof bowl. Heat the cream to just below boiling point. Pour on to the chocolate and stir until melted. Leave to cool, beating occasionally, until thick – pop into the fridge for 30 minutes to help thicken, if necessary.

6　Cut the cold cake in half horizontally and sandwich the layers together with one-third of the icing. Spread the rest evenly over the top and sides of the cake. Decorate the top of the cake with alternate rows of milk and white Maltesers. Lay an edging of alternate milk and white Maltesers around the base of the cake to decorate.

BANOFFEE CAKE

Preparation: 25 minutes
Cooking time: about 55 minutes, plus cooling

200g (7oz) unsalted butter, softened,
    plus extra to grease
200g (7oz) light soft brown sugar
4 large eggs, beaten
2 ripe bananas, peeled and broken
    into chunks
75g (3oz) walnuts, chopped
200g (7oz) self-raising flour

ICING
150g (5oz) butter, softened
250g (9oz) icing sugar, sifted
3 tbsp dulce de leche toffee sauce
40g (1½oz) fudge chunks

PER SLICE
653 cals; 39g fat (of which 20g saturates);
73g carbohydrate; 0.9g salt

1 Preheat the oven to 180°C (160°C fan oven) mark 4. Grease and line a 20.5cm (8 inch) deep cake tin with parchment paper.

2 In a large bowl, beat together the butter and brown sugar with a hand-held electric whisk until pale and fluffy, about 5 minutes. Gradually beat in the eggs, then whisk in the bananas until smooth (if you don't have electric beaters, mash the bananas with a fork and fold into the mixture). The mixture might look a little curdled, but don't worry.

3 Using a large metal spoon, fold in the walnuts and flour. Spoon into the prepared tin and bake for 50–55 minutes until a skewer inserted into the centre comes out clean. Cool in the tin for 5 minutes, then turn out on to a wire rack and leave to cool completely.

4 Meanwhile, make the icing. In a large bowl, beat the butter, icing sugar and dulce de leche together until smooth and creamy. Thinly spread over the top and sides of the cake, then scatter the fudge chunks over.

TO STORE
Store in the fridge. It will keep for up to two days. Allow to reach room temperature before serving.

RED VELVET CAKE

Preparation: 20 minutes

Cooking time: about 1 hour 10 minutes,

plus cooling

200g (7oz) unsalted butter, softened,
    plus extra to grease
250g (9oz) plain flour
40g (1½oz) cocoa powder
1½ tsp baking powder
225g (8oz) caster sugar
2 large eggs, beaten
250ml (9fl oz) soured cream
1 tbsp white wine vinegar
1 tsp bicarbonate of soda
¼ tsp red food colouring paste

FROSTING
400g (14oz) cream cheese
125g (4oz) unsalted butter, softened
125g (4oz) icing sugar
red sugar sprinkles to decorate
    (optional)

PER SLICE
724 cals, 53g fat (of which 33g saturates);
58g carbohydrate; 1.4g salt

1 Preheat the oven to 180°C (160°C fan oven) mark 4. Grease and line a 20.5cm (8 inch) deep cake tin with parchment paper.

2 Sift the flour, cocoa powder and baking powder into a medium bowl. In a separate large bowl, beat together the butter and caster sugar with a hand-held electric whisk until pale and fluffy, about 5 minutes. Gradually beat in the eggs, until combined.

3 Alternately beat the flour mixture and the soured cream into the butter bowl until completely combined. Beat in the vinegar, bicarbonate of soda and food colouring. Spoon the mixture into the tin, level the surface and bake for 1 hour–1 hour 10 minutes until a skewer inserted into the centre comes out clean. Cool in the tin for 10 minutes, then turn out on to a wire rack and leave to cool completely.

4 To make the frosting, put the cream cheese and butter into a large bowl and beat together until combined. Sift in the icing sugar and mix well. Halve the cooled cake, then sandwich back together using half of the icing. Spread the remaining icing over the top of the cake, decorate with sugar sprinkles, if you like, and serve in slices.

TO STORE
Store the finished cake in the fridge. It will keep for up to two days. Allow to reach room temperature before serving.

SPICED CARROT MUFFINS

Preparation: 30 minutes
Cooking time: 20–25 minutes, plus cooling

125g (4oz) unsalted butter, softened
125g (4oz) light muscovado sugar
3 pieces preserved stem ginger, drained and chopped
150g (5oz) self-raising flour, sifted
1½ tsp baking powder
1 tbsp ground mixed spice
25g (1oz) ground almonds
3 medium eggs
finely grated zest of ½ orange
150g (5oz) carrots, peeled and grated
50g (2oz) pecan nuts, chopped
50g (2oz) sultanas
3 tbsp white rum or orange liqueur (optional)

TOPPING AND DECORATION

200g (7oz) cream cheese
75g (3oz) icing sugar
1 tsp lemon juice
12 unsprayed rose petals (optional)

PER MUFFIN

333 cals; 22g fat (of which 11g saturates); 31g carbohydrate; 0.5g salt

1 Preheat the oven to 180°C (160°C fan oven) mark 4.
   Line a 12-hole bun tin or muffin tin with paper muffin
   cases.
2 Beat the butter, muscovado sugar and stem ginger
   together until pale and creamy. Add the flour, baking
   powder, spice, ground almonds, eggs and orange zest
   and beat well until combined. Stir in the carrots, pecan
   nuts and sultanas. Divide the mixture equally among
   the paper cases.
3 Bake for 20–25 minutes until risen and just firm.
   A skewer inserted into the centre should come out
   clean. Transfer to a wire rack and leave to cool
   completely.
4 For the topping, beat the cream cheese in a bowl until
   softened. Beat in the icing sugar and lemon juice to
   give a smooth icing that just holds its shape.

5 Drizzle each cake with a little liqueur, if you like. Using
   a small palette knife, spread a little icing over each cake.
   Decorate with a rose petal, if you like.

TO STORE

Store in an airtight container. They will keep for up to
one week.

FREEZING TIP

To freeze, complete the recipe to the end of step
3. Once the muffins are cold, pack, seal and freeze.
To use, thaw at cool room temperature and
complete the recipe.

BLUEBERRY MUFFINS

MAKES 12

Preparation: 10 minutes
Cooking time: 20–25 minutes, plus cooling

2 medium eggs
250ml (9fl oz) semi-skimmed milk
250g (9oz) golden granulated sugar
2 tsp vanilla extract
350g (12oz) plain flour
4 tsp baking powder
250g (9oz) blueberries, frozen
finely grated zest of 2 lemons

PER MUFFIN
218 cals; 2g fat (of which trace saturates); 49g carbohydrate; 0.5g salt

VARIATION
Double chocolate chip muffins: Omit the blueberries and lemon zest. Replace 40g (1½oz) of the flour with cocoa powder, then add 150g (5oz) chopped dark chocolate to the dry ingredients in step 3.

1 Preheat the oven to 200°C (180°C fan oven) mark 6. Line a 12-hole bun tin or muffin tin with paper muffin cases.
2 Put the eggs, milk, sugar and vanilla extract into a bowl and mix well.
3 In another bowl, sift the flour and baking powder together, then add the blueberries and lemon zest. Toss together and make a well in the centre.
4 Pour the egg mixture into the flour and blueberries and mix in gently – over-beating will make the muffins tough. Divide the mixture equally among the cases.
5 Bake for 20–25 minutes until risen and just firm. Transfer to a wire rack and leave to cool completely. These are best eaten on the day they are made.

FREEZING TIP
To freeze, complete the recipe. Once the muffins are cold, pack, seal and freeze. To use, thaw at cool room temperature.

BRAN AND APPLE MUFFINS

Preparation: 20 minutes
Cooking time: 30 minutes, plus cooling

250ml (9fl oz) semi-skimmed milk
2 tbsp orange juice
50g (2oz) All Bran
9 ready-to-eat dried prunes
100g (3½oz) light muscovado sugar
2 medium egg whites
1 tbsp golden syrup
150g (5oz) plain flour, sifted
1 tsp baking powder
1 tsp ground cinnamon
1 eating apple, peeled and grated
demerara sugar to sprinkle

PER MUFFIN
137 cals; 1g fat (of which trace saturates);
31g carbohydrate; 0.3g salt

1 Preheat the oven to 190°C (170°C fan oven) mark 5. Line a bun tin or muffin tin with 10 paper muffin cases.
2 Put the milk, orange juice and All Bran into a bowl and stir to mix. Put to one side for 10 minutes.

3 Put the prunes into a food processor or blender with 100ml (3½fl oz) water and whiz for 2–3 minutes to make a purée, then add the muscovado sugar and whiz briefly to mix.
4 Put the egg whites into a clean, grease-free bowl and whisk until soft peaks form. Add the whites to the milk mixture with the syrup, flour, baking powder, cinnamon, grated apple and prune mixture. Fold all the ingredients together gently – don't over-mix. Spoon the mixture equally into the muffin cases.
5 Bake for 30 minutes or until well risen and golden brown. Transfer to a wire rack and leave to cool completely. Sprinkle with demerara sugar just before serving. These are best eaten on the day they are made.

FREEZING TIP
To freeze, complete the recipe, but don't sprinkle with the sugar topping. Once the muffins are cold, pack, seal and freeze. To use, thaw at cool room temperature. Sprinkle with the sugar to serve.

BROWN SUGAR MUFFINS

MAKES 6

Preparation: 10 minutes
Cooking time: 30–35 minutes, plus cooling

12 brown sugar cubes
150g (5oz) plain flour
1½ tsp baking powder
¼ tsp salt
1 medium egg, beaten
40g (1½oz) golden caster sugar
50g (2oz) unsalted butter, melted
½ tsp vanilla extract
100ml (3½fl oz) milk

PER MUFFIN

233 cals; 8g fat (of which 5g saturates); 38g carbohydrate; 0.4g salt

VARIATIONS

Apple and cinnamon muffins: Fold 5 tbsp ready-made chunky apple sauce and 1 tsp ground cinnamon into the mixture with the flour.

Maple syrup and pecan muffins: Lightly toast 50g (2oz) pecan nuts and roughly chop. Fold half the nuts and 3 tbsp maple syrup into the mixture. Mix the remaining nuts with the crushed sugar and sprinkle over the muffins before baking. Drizzle with maple syrup to serve.

1 Preheat the oven to 200°C (180°C fan oven) mark 6. Line a 6-hole bun tin or muffin tin with paper muffin cases.
2 Roughly crush the sugar cubes and put to one side. Sift the flour, baking powder and salt together.
3 Put the beaten egg, caster sugar, melted butter, vanilla extract and milk into a large bowl and stir to combine. Gently fold in the sifted flour. Spoon the mixture equally into the paper cases and sprinkle with the crushed sugar.
4 Bake for 30–35 minutes until golden. Transfer to a wire rack and leave to cool completely. These are best eaten on the day they are made.

FREEZING TIP
To freeze, complete the recipe. Once the muffins are cold, pack, seal and freeze. To use, thaw at cool room temperature.

DOUBLE CHOCOLATE MUFFINS

MAKES 12

Preparation: 20 minutes
Cooking time: about 25 minutes, plus cooling

125g (4oz) unsalted butter
100g (3½oz) plain chocolate
225g (8oz) plain flour
1 tsp bicarbonate of soda
40g (1½oz) cocoa powder, sifted
175g (6oz) golden caster sugar
200g (7oz) white chocolate, chopped
pinch of salt
1 medium egg
200ml (7fl oz) milk
150g carton natural yogurt
1 tsp vanilla extract

PER MUFFIN

368 cals; 19g fat (of which 11g saturates);
47g carbohydrate; 0.8g salt

1 Preheat the oven to 190°C (170°C fan oven) mark 5. Line a 12-hole muffin tin with paper cases.
2 Melt the butter and plain chocolate in a heatproof bowl set over a pan of barely simmering water, making sure the base of the bowl doesn't touch the water. Mix together very gently and leave to cool a little.
3 Meanwhile, put the flour into a large bowl. Add the bicarbonate of soda, cocoa powder, caster sugar, white chocolate and salt. Stir everything together. Put the egg, milk, yogurt and vanilla extract in a jug and beat together.
4 Pour both the egg mixture and the chocolate mixture on to the dry ingredients, then roughly fold together. Be careful not to over-mix, or the muffins won't rise properly.
5 Divide the mixture equally among the paper cases. Bake for 20–25 minutes until well risen and springy. Take each muffin out of the tin and cool on a wire rack before serving.

TO STORE

If not serving immediately, store the muffins in an airtight container. They will keep for up to three days.

WHOLEMEAL BANANA MUFFINS

Preparation: 15 minutes, plus soaking

Cooking time: 20–25 minutes

50g (2oz) raisins

finely grated zest and juice of
    1 orange

125g (4oz) wholemeal flour

25g (1oz) wheatgerm

3 tbsp caster sugar

2 tsp baking powder

pinch of salt

1 large egg, beaten

50ml (2fl oz) milk

50ml (2fl oz) sunflower oil

2 medium-sized ripe bananas, about
    225g (8oz) when peeled, roughly
    mashed

TOPPING

5 tbsp orange marmalade

50g (2oz) banana chips, roughly
    chopped

50g (2oz) walnuts, roughly chopped

PER MUFFIN

341 cals; 13g fat (of which 2g saturates);
51g carbohydrate; 0.6g salt

1 Preheat the oven to 200°C (180°C fan oven) mark 6. Line a 6-hole bun tin or muffin tin with paper muffin cases. Put the raisins into a bowl, pour the orange juice over them and leave to soak for 1 hour.

2 Put the orange zest into a bowl with the flour, wheatgerm, sugar, baking powder and salt and mix together. Make a well in the centre.

3 In a separate bowl, mix the egg, milk and oil, then pour into the flour mixture and stir until just blended.

4 Drain the raisins, reserving 1 tbsp juice, and stir into the mixture with the bananas. Don't over-mix. Fill each muffin case two-thirds full.

5 Bake for 20–25 minutes until a skewer inserted into the centre comes out clean. Transfer to a wire rack and leave to cool slightly.

6 For the topping, gently heat the marmalade with the reserved orange juice until melted. Simmer for 1 minute, then add the banana chips and walnuts. Spoon on top of the muffins. Serve while still warm.

FREEZING NOTE

To freeze, complete the recipe to the end of step 4. Once the muffins are cold, pack, seal and freeze. To use, thaw at cool room temperature. Complete the recipe.

HONEY AND YOGURT MUFFINS

Preparation: 15 minutes
Cooking time: 17–20 minutes

225g (8oz) plain white flour
1½ tsp baking powder
1 tsp bicarbonate of soda
½ tsp each ground mixed spice and
    ground nutmeg
pinch of salt
50g (2oz) ground oatmeal
50g (2oz) light muscovado sugar
225g (8oz) Greek-style yogurt
125ml (4fl oz) milk
1 medium egg
50g (2oz) butter, melted and cooled
4 tbsp runny honey

PER MUFFIN
180 cals; 6g fat (of which 4g saturates);
27g carbohydrate; 0.1g salt

1 Preheat the oven to 200°C (180°C fan oven) mark 6. Line a 12-hole bun tin or muffin tin with paper muffin cases.
2 Sift the flour, baking powder, bicarbonate of soda, mixed spice, nutmeg and salt into a bowl. Stir in the oatmeal and sugar.

3 Mix the yogurt with the milk in a bowl, then beat in the egg, butter and honey. Pour on to the dry ingredients and stir in quickly until just blended – don't over-mix. Divide the mixture equally among the paper cases.
4 Bake for 17–20 minutes until the muffins are well risen and just firm. Cool in the tin for 5 minutes, then transfer to a wire rack. Serve warm or cold. These are best eaten on the day they are made.

FREEZING TIP
To freeze, complete the recipe. Once the muffins are cold, pack, seal and freeze. To use, thaw at cool room temperature.

FAIRY CAKES

Preparation: 20 minutes

Cooking time: 10–15 minutes, plus cooling and setting

125g (4oz) self-raising flour, sifted
1 tsp baking powder
125g (4oz) caster sugar
125g (4oz) unsalted butter, very soft
2 medium eggs
1 tbsp milk

ICING AND DECORATION
225g (8oz) icing sugar, sifted
assorted food colourings (optional)
sweets, sprinkles or coloured sugar

PER CAKE
160 cals; 6g fat (of which 4g saturates); 26g carbohydrate; 0.2g salt

1 Preheat the oven to 200°C (180°C fan oven) mark 6. Put paper cases into 18 of the holes in two bun tins.
2 Put the flour, baking powder, sugar, butter, eggs and milk into a mixing bowl and beat with a hand-held electric whisk for 2 minutes or until the mixture is pale and very soft. Half-fill each paper case with the mixture.
3 Bake for 10–15 minutes until golden brown. Transfer to a wire rack and leave to cool completely.
4 Put the icing sugar into a bowl and gradually blend in 2–3 tbsp warm water until the icing is fairly stiff, but spreadable. Add a couple of drops of food colouring, if you like.
5 When the cakes are cold, spread the tops with the icing and decorate. Leave to set.

FREEZING TIP
To freeze, complete the recipe to the end of step 3. Open-freeze, then wrap and freeze. To use, thaw for about 1 hour, then complete the recipe.

TO STORE
Store in an airtight container. They will keep for 3–5 days.

VARIATION
Chocolate fairy cakes: Replace 2 tbsp of the flour with the same amount of cocoa powder. Stir 50g (2oz) chocolate drops, sultanas or chopped dried apricots into the mixture at the end of step 1. Complete the recipe.

CHOCOLATE CUPCAKES

Preparation: 15 minutes

Cooking time: 20 minutes, plus cooling and setting

125g (4oz) unsalted butter, softened

125g (4oz) light muscovado sugar

2 medium eggs, beaten

15g (½oz) cocoa powder

100g (3½oz) self-raising flour

100g (3½oz) plain chocolate (at least 70% cocoa solids), roughly chopped

TOPPING

150ml (¼ pint) double cream

100g (3½oz) plain chocolate (at least 70% cocoa solids), broken up

PER CUPCAKE

203 cals; 14g fat (of which 8g saturates); 19g carbohydrate; 0.2g salt

1 Preheat the oven to 190°C (170°C fan oven) mark 5. Line a 12-hole and a 6-hole bun tin or muffin tin with paper muffin cases.

2 Beat the butter and sugar together until light and fluffy. Gradually beat in the eggs. Sift the cocoa powder with the flour and fold into the creamed mixture with the chopped chocolate. Divide the mixture among the paper cases and lightly flatten the surface with the back of a spoon.

3 Bake for 20 minutes, then transfer to a wire rack and leave to cool completely.

4 For the topping, put the cream and chocolate into a heavy-based pan over a low heat and heat until melted, then allow to cool and thicken slightly. Spoon on to the cooled cakes, then stand the cakes upright on the wire rack and leave for 30 minutes to set.

TO STORE

Store in an airtight container in the fridge. They will keep for 2–3 days.

FREEZING TIP

To freeze, complete the recipe to the end of step 3. Open-freeze, then wrap and freeze. To use, thaw for about 1 hour, then complete the recipe.

RASPBERRY RIPPLE CUPCAKES

Preparation: 30 minutes
Cooking time: 20 minutes, plus cooling

50g (2oz) seedless raspberry jam
50g (2oz) fresh raspberries
125g (4oz) unsalted butter, softened
100g (3½oz) caster sugar
2 medium eggs
1 tbsp milk
150g (5oz) self-raising flour, sifted

TOPPING AND DECORATION
150g (5oz) fresh raspberries
300ml (½ pint) whipping cream
50g (2oz) icing sugar, sifted

PER CUPCAKE
385 cals; 26g fat (of which 16g saturates); 36g carbohydrate; 0.5g salt

1 Preheat the oven to 190°C (170°C fan oven) mark 5. Line a 12-hole muffin tin with 9 paper muffin cases.
2 Mix the raspberry jam with the 50g (2oz) raspberries, lightly crushing the raspberries. Set aside.
3 Using a hand-held electric whisk, whisk the butter and caster sugar in a bowl, or beat with a wooden spoon, until pale and creamy. Gradually whisk in the eggs and milk until just combined. Using a metal spoon, fold in the flour until just combined, then carefully fold in the raspberry jam mixture until just marbled, being careful not to over-mix. Divide the mixture equally among the paper cases.

4 Bake for 20 minutes or until golden and risen. Cool in the tin for 5 minutes, then transfer to a wire rack and leave to cool completely.
5 For the decoration, reserve 9 raspberries. Mash the remaining raspberries in a bowl with a fork. Pass through a sieve into a bowl to remove the seeds. Using a hand-held electric whisk, whip the cream and icing sugar together until stiff peaks form. Mix the raspberry purée into the cream until combined.
6 Insert a star nozzle into a piping bag, then fill the bag with the cream and pipe a swirl on to the top of each cake. Decorate each with a raspberry.

TO STORE
Store in an airtight container in the fridge. They will keep for up to two days.

FREEZING TIP
To freeze, complete the recipe to the end of step 4. Open-freeze, then wrap and freeze. To use, thaw for about 1 hour, then complete the recipe.

THE ULTIMATE CARROT CUPCAKES

Preparation: 30 minutes
Cooking time: 20 minutes, plus cooling

150g (5oz) carrots, peeled
50g (2oz) raisins
175g (6oz) self-raising flour, sifted
½ tsp bicarbonate of soda
150g (5oz) light soft brown sugar
zest of 1 orange
½ tsp ground mixed spice
3 medium eggs
100ml (3½fl oz) sunflower oil
75ml (2½fl oz) buttermilk

TOPPING AND DECORATION

50g (2oz) icing sugar, sifted
250g (9oz) mascarpone cheese
100g (3½oz) quark cheese
juice of ½ orange
red, yellow and green ready-made
    fondant icing (optional)

PER CUPCAKE

255 cals; 12g fat (of which 4g saturates);
34g carbohydrate; 0.3g salt

1 Preheat the oven to 190°C (170°C fan oven) mark 5. Line a 12-hole muffin tin with paper muffin cases.
2 Coarsely grate the carrots and put into a large bowl. Add the raisins, flour, bicarbonate of soda, brown sugar, orange zest and mixed spice. Put the eggs, oil and buttermilk into a jug and lightly beat together until combined. Pour the egg mixture into the flour and stir with a spatula until just combined. Divide the mixture equally among the paper cases.
3 Bake for 20 minutes or until lightly golden and risen. Cool in the tin for 5 minutes, then transfer to a wire rack and leave to cool completely.
4 For the topping, mix the icing sugar with the mascarpone, quark and orange juice to a smooth icing. Using a small palette knife, spread a little of the icing over each cake. Use the coloured fondant to make small carrots, if you like, and decorate the cakes with them.

TO STORE
Store in an airtight container in the fridge. They will keep for up to two days.

FREEZING TIP
To freeze, complete the recipe to the end of step 3. Open-freeze, then wrap and freeze. To use, thaw for about 1 hour, then complete the recipe.

LAVENDER AND HONEY CUPCAKES

Preparation: 35 minutes
Cooking time: 15–20 minutes, plus cooling and setting

125g (4oz) unsalted butter, softened
125g (4oz) runny honey
2 medium eggs
125g (4oz) self-raising flour, sifted
1 tsp baking powder

ICING AND DECORATION
3 honey and lavender tea bags
2 tsp unsalted butter
250g (9oz) icing sugar, sifted
red and blue food colouring
purple sugar stars
edible silver dust (optional)

PER CUPCAKE
316 cals; 13g fat (of which 8g saturates); 50g carbohydrate; 0.3g salt

FREEZING TIP
To freeze, complete the recipe to the end of step 3. Open-freeze, then wrap and freeze. To use, thaw for about 1 hour, then complete the recipe.

1 Preheat the oven to 190°C (170°C fan oven) mark 5. Line a 12-hole muffin tin with 9 paper muffin cases.
2 Using a hand-held electric whisk, whisk the butter and honey in a bowl, or beat with a wooden spoon, until combined. Gradually whisk in the eggs until just combined. Using a metal spoon, fold in the flour and baking powder until combined. Divide the mixture equally among the paper cases.
3 Bake for 15–20 minutes until golden and risen. Cool in the tin for 5 minutes, then transfer to a wire rack and leave to cool completely.
4 For the icing, infuse the tea bags in 50ml (2fl oz) boiling water in a small bowl for 5 minutes. Remove the tea bags and squeeze out the excess water into the bowl. Stir in the butter until melted. Put the icing sugar into a large bowl, add the infused tea mixture and stir to make a smooth icing. Add a few drops of red and blue food colouring until it is lilac in colour.
5 Spoon a little icing on top of each cake, to flood the tops, then sprinkle with stars. Stand the cakes upright on the wire rack and leave for about 1 hour to set. Dust with edible dust, if you like, when set.

TO STORE
Store in an airtight container. They will keep for 3–5 days.

CHERRY BAKEWELL CUPCAKES

Preparation: 30 minutes, plus chilling

Cooking time: 25 minutes, plus cooling and setting

175g (6oz) unsalted butter, softened
175g (6oz) caster sugar
3 medium eggs
150g (5oz) self-raising flour, sifted
1 tsp baking powder
75g (3oz) ground almonds
1 tsp almond extract
75g (3oz) glacé cherries, finely chopped

TOPPING AND DECORATION

1 tbsp custard powder
100ml (3½fl oz) milk
50g (2oz) unsalted butter, softened
250g (9oz) icing sugar, sifted
red sugar sprinkles

PER CUPCAKE

405 cals; 21g fat (of which 11g saturates); 53g carbohydrate; 0.4g salt

1 Preheat the oven to 190°C (170°C fan oven) mark 5. Line a 12-hole muffin tin with paper muffin cases.

2 Using a hand-held electric whisk, whisk the butter and caster sugar in a bowl, or beat with a wooden spoon, until pale and creamy. Gradually whisk in the eggs until just combined. Using a metal spoon, fold in the flour, baking powder, ground almonds, almond extract and cherries until combined. Divide the mixture equally among the paper cases.

3 Bake for 20 minutes or until golden and risen. Cool in the tin for 5 minutes, then transfer to a wire rack and leave to cool completely.

4 For the topping, put the custard powder into a jug and add a little of the milk to make a smooth paste. Put the remaining milk into a saucepan and bring just to the boil. Pour the hot milk on to the custard paste and stir. Return to the milk pan and heat gently for 1–2 minutes until it thickens. Remove from the heat, cover with dampened greaseproof paper to prevent a skin forming and cool completely.

5 Put the custard into a bowl and, using a hand-held electric whisk, whisk in the butter. Chill for 30 minutes.

6 Gradually whisk the icing sugar into the chilled custard mixture until you have a smooth, thick icing. Using a small palette knife, spread a little custard cream over the top of each cake, then decorate with sugar sprinkles. Stand the cakes upright on the wire rack and leave for about 1 hour to set.

TO STORE

Store in an airtight container in the fridge. They will keep for 2–3 days.

FREEZING TIP

To freeze, complete the recipe to the end of step 3. Open-freeze, then wrap and freeze. To use, thaw for about 1 hour, then complete the recipe.

MINI GREEN TEA CUPCAKES

MAKES 12

Preparation: 40 minutes

Cooking time: 25 minutes, plus cooling and infusing

100ml (3½fl oz) milk
2 tsp loose green tea leaves
100g (3½oz) unsalted butter, softened
125g (4oz) caster sugar
2 medium eggs
150g (5oz) self-raising flour, sifted
¼ tsp baking powder

TOPPING AND DECORATION
3 tsp loose green tea leaves
about 75ml (2½fl oz) boiling water
75g (3oz) unsalted butter, softened
250g (9oz) icing sugar, sifted
ready-made sugar flowers

PER CUPCAKE
282 cals; 13g fat (of which 8g saturates); 41g carbohydrate; 0.3g salt

1 Preheat the oven to 190°C (170°C fan oven) mark 5. Line a 12-hole muffin tin with paper fairy cake or bun cases.
2 Put the milk into a small saucepan and bring to the boil. Add the green tea leaves and leave to infuse for 30 minutes.
3 Using a hand-held electric whisk, whisk the butter and caster sugar in a bowl, or beat with a wooden spoon, until pale and creamy. Gradually whisk in the eggs until just combined. Pass the green tea milk through a sieve into the bowl, then discard the tea. Using a metal spoon, fold in the flour and baking powder until combined. Divide the mixture equally among the paper cases.
4 Bake for 18–20 minutes until golden and risen. Cool in the tin for 5 minutes, then transfer to a wire rack and leave to cool completely.
5 For the topping, put the green tea leaves into a jug, add about 75ml (2½fl oz) boiling water and leave to infuse for 5 minutes.

6 Put the butter into a bowl and whisk until fluffy. Gradually add the icing sugar and whisk until combined. Pass the green tea through a sieve into the bowl, then discard the tea. Continue to whisk until light and fluffy.
7 Insert a star nozzle into a piping bag, then fill the bag with the buttercream and pipe a swirl on to the top of each cake. Decorate each with a sugar flower.

TO STORE
Store in an airtight container. They will keep for 3–5 days.

FREEZING TIP
To freeze, complete the recipe to the end of step 4. Open-freeze, then wrap and freeze. To use, thaw for about 1 hour, then complete the recipe.

PINK CUPCAKES

MAKES 12

Preparation: 35 minutes
Cooking time: 20 minutes, plus cooling

150g (5oz) raw beetroot, peeled and
    finely grated
200g (7oz) self-raising flour, sifted
½ tsp bicarbonate of soda
150g (5oz) caster sugar
zest of 1 orange
2 medium eggs
100ml (3½fl oz) sunflower oil
125ml (4fl oz) buttermilk

TOPPING AND DECORATION

100g (3½oz) unsalted butter, softened
350g (12oz) icing sugar, sifted
50ml (2fl oz) milk
pink food colouring
ready-made pink or red sugar flowers
    (optional)

PER CUPCAKE

361 cals; 14g fat (of which 6g saturates);
58g carbohydrate; 0.2g salt

1 Preheat the oven to 190°C (170°C fan oven) mark 5. Line a 12-hole muffin tin with paper muffin cases.
2 Put the beetroot, flour, bicarbonate of soda, caster sugar and orange zest into a bowl. Put the eggs, oil and buttermilk into a jug and lightly beat together until combined. Pour the egg mixture into the flour and stir with a spatula until just combined. Divide the mixture equally among the paper cases.
3 Bake for 20 minutes or until lightly golden and risen. Cool in the tin for 5 minutes, then transfer to a wire rack and leave to cool completely.
4 For the topping, put the butter into a bowl and whisk until fluffy. Gradually whisk in half the icing sugar, then add the milk, a little pink food colouring and the remaining icing sugar and whisk until light and fluffy.
5 Insert a star nozzle into a piping bag, then fill the bag with the buttercream and pipe small swirls all the way around the top of each cake. Decorate with the sugar flowers, if you like.

FREEZING TIP

To freeze, complete the recipe to the end of step 3. Open-freeze, then wrap and freeze. To use, thaw for about 1 hour, then complete the recipe.

NOTES

Store in an airtight container. They will keep for 3–5 days.

COCONUT AND LIME CUPCAKES

MAKES 12

Preparation: 30 minutes
Cooking time: 18–20 minutes, plus cooling and setting

275g (10oz) plain flour, sifted
1 tbsp baking powder
100g (3½oz) caster sugar
zest of 1 lime
50g (2oz) desiccated coconut
2 medium eggs
100ml (3½fl oz) sunflower oil
225ml (8fl oz) natural yogurt
50ml (2fl oz) milk

TOPPING

150g (5oz) icing sugar, sifted
juice of 1 lime
1–2 tsp boiling water
50g (2oz) desiccated coconut

PER CUPCAKE

291 cals; 13g fat (of which 6g saturates); 42g carbohydrate; 0.1g salt

1 Preheat the oven to 200°C (180°C fan oven) mark 6. Line a 12-hole muffin tin with paper muffin cases.
2 Put the flour, baking powder, caster sugar, lime zest and coconut into a large bowl. Put the eggs, oil, yogurt and milk into a jug and lightly beat together until combined. Pour the yogurt mixture into the flour and stir with a spatula until just combined. Divide the mixture equally among the paper cases.
3 Bake for 18–20 minutes until lightly golden and risen. Cool in the tin for 5 minutes, then transfer to a wire rack and leave to cool completely.
4 For the decoration, mix the icing sugar with the lime juice and enough boiling water to make a thick, smooth icing. Put the coconut into a shallow bowl. Dip each cake top into the icing until coated, allowing the excess to drip off, then carefully dip into the coconut until coated. Stand the cakes upright on the wire rack and leave for about 1 hour to set.

FREEZING TIP

To freeze, complete the recipe to the end of step 3. Open-freeze, then wrap and freeze. To use, thaw for about 1 hour, then complete the recipe.

NOTES

Store in an airtight container. They will keep for 3–5 days.

HONEYCOMB CREAM CUPCAKES

Preparation: 30 minutes

Cooking time: 20 minutes, plus cooling

125g (4oz) unsalted butter, softened
50g (2oz) caster sugar
2 medium eggs
75g (3oz) runny honey
125g (4oz) self-raising flour, sifted
50g (2oz) rolled oats
½ tsp baking powder
1 tbsp milk

TOPPING AND DECORATION

125g (4oz) unsalted butter, softened
300g (11oz) golden icing sugar, sifted
2 tbsp milk
1 Crunchie bar, thinly sliced

PER CUPCAKE

480 cals; 25g fat (of which 15g saturates); 65g carbohydrate; 0.6g salt

TO STORE

Store in an airtight container. They will keep for 2–3 days.

FREEZING TIP
To freeze, complete the recipe to the end of step 3. Open-freeze, then wrap and freeze. To use, thaw for about 1 hour, then complete the recipe.

1 Preheat the oven to 190°C (170°C fan oven) mark 5. Line a 12-hole muffin tin with 9 paper muffin cases.
2 Using a hand-held electric whisk, whisk the butter and caster sugar in a bowl, or beat with a wooden spoon, until pale and creamy. Gradually whisk in the eggs and honey until just combined. Using a metal spoon, fold in the flour, oats, baking powder and milk until combined. Divide the mixture equally among the paper cases.
3 Bake for 20 minutes or until golden and risen. Cool in the tin for 5 minutes, then transfer to a wire rack and leave to cool completely.
4 For the topping, put the butter into a bowl and whisk until fluffy. Gradually whisk in half the icing sugar, then add the milk and the remaining icing sugar and whisk until light and fluffy.
5 Insert a star nozzle into a piping bag, then fill the bag with the buttercream and pipe a swirl on to the top of each cake. When ready to serve, decorate each with a few slices of Crunchie.

BANOFFEE CUPCAKES

Preparation: 30 minutes

Cooking time: 20 minutes, plus cooling

175g (6oz) self-raising flour, sifted
½ tsp bicarbonate of soda
150g (5oz) light soft brown sugar
1 banana (about 150g/5oz), peeled
3 medium eggs
100g (3½oz) unsalted butter, melted
75ml (2½fl oz) buttermilk

TOPPING AND DECORATION
150g (5oz) dulce de leche toffee sauce
75g (3oz) unsalted butter, softened
250g (9oz) golden icing sugar, sifted
mini fudge chunks (optional)

PER CUPCAKE
404 cals; 16g fat (of which 10g saturates); 63g carbohydrate; 0.4g salt

TO STORE
Store in an airtight container. They will keep for 2–3 days.

FREEZING TIP
To freeze, complete the recipe to the end of step 3.
Open-freeze, then wrap and freeze. To use, thaw for
about 1 hour, then complete the recipe.

1 Preheat the oven to 190°C (170°C fan oven) mark 5.
   Line a 12-hole muffin tin with paper muffin cases.
2 Put the flour, bicarbonate of soda and brown sugar
   into a large bowl. Mash the banana with a fork in a
   small bowl. Put the eggs, melted butter and buttermilk
   into a jug and lightly beat together until combined.
   Pour into the flour mixture along with the mashed
   banana and stir with a spatula until just combined.
   Divide the mixture equally among the paper cases.
3 Bake for 18–20 minutes until lightly golden and risen.
   Cool in the tin for 5 minutes, then transfer to a wire
   rack and leave to cool completely.
4 For the decoration, whisk together the dulce de leche
   and butter in a bowl until combined. Gradually whisk
   in the icing sugar until light and fluffy. Use a palette
   knife to spread the buttercream on to the top of each
   cake. Decorate with the mini fudge chunks, if you like.

GLUTEN-FREE PISTACHIO AND POLENTA CUPCAKES

Preparation: 35 minutes
Cooking time: 25 minutes, plus cooling

150g (5oz) shelled pistachio nuts
175g (6oz) unsalted butter, softened
175g (6oz) caster sugar
3 medium eggs
200g (7oz) fine polenta
½ tsp baking powder
150g (5oz) ground almonds
zest of 2 lemons
2 tbsp milk

ICING

75g (3oz) unsalted butter, softened
300g (11oz) icing sugar, sifted
juice of 2 lemons

PER CUPCAKE

542 cals; 33g fat (of which 13g saturates);
56g carbohydrate; 0.6g salt

1 Preheat the oven to 180°C (160°C fan oven) mark 4. Line a 12-hole muffin tin with paper muffin cases.
2 Whiz the pistachio nuts in a food processor until really finely chopped.
3 Using a hand-held electric whisk, whisk the butter and caster sugar in a bowl, or beat with a wooden spoon, until pale and creamy. Gradually whisk in the eggs until just combined. Using a metal spoon, fold in the polenta, baking powder, ground almonds, lemon zest, milk and 100g (3½oz) ground pistachio nuts until combined. Divide the mixture equally among the paper cases.
4 Bake for 25 minutes or until golden and risen. Cool in the tin for 5 minutes, then transfer to a wire rack and leave to cool completely.

5 For the icing, put the butter into a bowl and whisk until fluffy. Gradually whisk in half the icing sugar, then add the lemon juice and the remaining icing sugar, whisking until light and fluffy. Using a small palette knife, spread a little of the buttercream over the top of each cake, then sprinkle each with a little of the remaining chopped pistachio nuts.

TO STORE

Store in an airtight container. They will keep for 3–5 days.

FREEZING TIP

To freeze, complete the recipe to the end of step 4. Open-freeze, then wrap and freeze. To use, thaw for about 1 hour, then complete the recipe.

TOAST AND MARMALADE CUPCAKES

Preparation: 30 minutes

Cooking time: 20–25 minutes, plus cooling and setting

150g (5oz) low-fat olive oil spread
200g (7oz) wholemeal self-raising
  flour, sifted
150g (5oz) light soft brown sugar
3 medium eggs
50g (2oz) marmalade
100ml (3½fl oz) milk
zest of 1 orange
50g (2oz) fresh wholemeal
  breadcrumbs

ICING AND DECORATION
125g (4oz) marmalade
300g (11oz) icing sugar, sifted

PER CUPCAKE
336 cals; 10g fat (of which 2g saturates);
57g carbohydrate; 1.5g salt

1 Preheat the oven to 180°C (160°C fan oven) mark 4. Line a 12-hole muffin tin with paper muffin cases.

2 Put the low-fat spread, flour, brown sugar, eggs, marmalade, milk, orange zest and breadcrumbs into a large bowl. Using a hand-held electric whisk, whisk together until pale and creamy. Divide the mixture equally among the paper cases.

3 Bake for 20–25 minutes until golden and risen. Cool in the tin for 5 minutes, then transfer to a wire rack and leave to cool completely.

4 For the icing, pass the marmalade through a sieve into a bowl to remove the rind. Reserve the rind. Mix the icing sugar with the sieved marmalade in a bowl until it forms a smooth icing. Spoon a little icing on to each cake to flood the top, then scatter on the reserved rind. Stand the cakes upright on the wire rack and leave for about 1 hour to set.

TO STORE
Store in an airtight container. They will keep for 3–5 days.

FREEZING TIP
To freeze, complete the recipe to the end of step 3. Open-freeze, then wrap and freeze. To use, thaw for about 1 hour, then complete the recipe.

TRAYBAKES BISCUITS AND COOKIES

APRICOT AND ALMOND TRAYBAKE

CUTS INTO 18 BARS

Preparation: 20 minutes

Cooking time: 30–40 minutes, plus cooling

250g (9oz) unsalted butter, softened,
 plus extra to grease
225g (8oz) golden caster sugar
275g (10oz) self-raising flour, sifted
2 tsp baking powder
finely grated zest of 1 orange and
 2 tbsp orange juice
75g (3oz) ground almonds
5 medium eggs, lightly beaten
225g (8oz) ready-to-eat dried
 apricots, roughly chopped
25g (1oz) flaked almonds
icing sugar to dust (optional)

PER BAR

277 cals; 16g fat (of which 8g saturates);
30g carbohydrate; 0.4g salt

1 Preheat the oven to 180°C (160°C fan oven) mark 4. Grease a 33 × 20.5cm (13 × 8 inch) baking tin and base-line with baking parchment.

2 Put the butter, caster sugar, flour, baking powder, orange zest, ground almonds and eggs into the bowl of a large freestanding mixer. Mix on a low setting for 30 seconds, then increase the speed and mix for 1 minute or until thoroughly combined. (Alternatively, mix well, using a wooden spoon.)

3 Remove the bowl from the mixer. Using a large metal spoon, fold in the apricots. Spoon the mixture into the prepared tin, level the surface and sprinkle the flaked almonds over the top.

4 Bake for 30–40 minutes until risen and golden brown and a skewer inserted into the centre comes out clean. Leave to cool in the tin.

5 Cut into 18 bars. Dust with icing sugar, if you like.

TO STORE

Wrap in clingfilm and store in an airtight container. They will keep for up to three days.

QUICK CHOCOLATE SLICES

Preparation: 10 minutes

Cooking time: 2 minutes, plus chilling

225g (8oz) unsalted butter or olive
   oil spread, plus extra to grease
50g (2oz) cocoa powder, sifted
3 tbsp golden syrup
300g pack digestive biscuits, crushed
400g (14oz) plain chocolate (at least
   70% cocoa solids), broken into
   pieces

PER SLICE

137 cals; 9g fat (of which 6g saturates);
13g carbohydrate; 0.3g salt

1 Grease a 25.5 x 16.5cm (10 x 6½ inch) tin. Put the butter or olive oil
   spread into a heatproof bowl, add the cocoa powder and syrup and melt
   over a pan of gently simmering water. Mix everything together.

2 Remove from the heat and stir in the biscuits. Mix well until thoroughly
   coated in chocolate, crushing any large pieces of biscuit. Turn into the
   prepared tin and leave to cool, then cover and chill for 20 minutes.

3 Melt the chocolate in a heatproof bowl in a 900W microwave oven on full
   power for 1 minute 40 seconds, stirring twice. (Alternatively, put into a
   heatproof bowl set over a pan of gently simmering water, making sure the
   base of the bowl doesn't touch the water.) Stir once more and pour over
   the chocolate biscuit base, then chill for 20 minutes.

4 Cut in half lengthways. Cut each half into 20 rectangular slices.

TO STORE

Store in an airtight container. They will keep for up to one week.

BLACKBERRY TRAYBAKE

CUTS INTO 24 SQUARES

Preparation: 20 minutes

Cooking time: about 45 minutes, plus cooling
and setting

275g (10oz) unsalted butter,
    softened, plus extra to grease
275g (10oz) golden caster sugar
400g (14oz) self-raising flour
1½ tsp baking powder
5 medium eggs, beaten
finely grated zest of 1 large orange
1 tbsp vanilla extract
4–5 tbsp milk
250g (9oz) blackberries
40g (1½oz) flaked almonds

ICING

150g (5oz) icing sugar
1 tsp vanilla extract
about 2 tbsp orange juice

PER SQUARE

239 cals; 12g fat (of which 7g saturates);
32g carbohydrate; 0.4g salt

1 Preheat the oven to 190°C (170°C fan oven) mark 5. Grease a shallow 30.5 x 20.5cm (12 x 8 inch) baking tin and line with greaseproof paper.

2 Put the butter and caster sugar into a large bowl. Sift in the flour and baking powder, then add the eggs, orange zest and juice, vanilla extract and milk and beat together until light and fluffy.

3 Using a metal spoon, fold in half the blackberries. Spoon into the prepared tin and dot with the remaining blackberries, then the almonds.

4 Bake for 40–45 minutes until springy to the touch. Cool in the tin for 5 minutes, then turn out on to a wire rack and leave to cool completely.

5 When the cake is cool, make the icing. Sift the icing sugar into a bowl, then add the vanilla extract and orange juice, mixing as you go, until smooth and runny. Drizzle over the cake and leave for 30 minutes to set. Cut into 24 squares to serve.

TO STORE

Wrap in clingfilm and store in an airtight container. It will keep for up to four days.

FREEZING TIP
To freeze, complete the recipe to the end of step 4. Leave to cool completely, keeping the cake in its greaseproof paper, then wrap in clingfilm. Freeze for up to one month. To use, thaw overnight at cool room temperature. Complete the recipe.

CARROT TRAYBAKE

Preparation: 30 minutes

Cooking time: 50 minutes–1 hour 5 minutes, plus cooling

100g (3½oz) unsalted butter, chopped, plus extra to grease
140g (4½oz) carrots, peeled and grated
100g (3½oz) sultanas
100g (3½oz) dried dates, chopped
50g (2oz) tenderised coconut
1 tsp ground cinnamon
½ tsp freshly grated nutmeg
330g bottle maple syrup
150ml (¼ pint) apple juice
zest and juice of 2 oranges
225g (8oz) wholemeal self-raising flour, sifted
2 tsp bicarbonate of soda
125g (4oz) walnut pieces

TOPPING

pared zest from ½–1 orange
200g (7oz) cream cheese
200g (7oz) crème fraîche
2 tbsp icing sugar
1 tsp vanilla extract

PER SQUARE

399 cals; 25g fat (of which 13g saturates);
41g carbohydrate; 0.4g salt

1 Preheat the oven to 190°C (170°C fan oven) mark 5. Grease a 23cm (9 inch) square cake tin and line with greaseproof paper.
2 Put the butter, carrots, sultanas, dates, coconut, spices, syrup, apple juice and orange zest and juice into a large pan. Cover and bring to the boil, then cook for 5 minutes. Tip into a bowl and leave to cool.
3 Put the flour, bicarbonate of soda and walnuts into a large bowl and stir together. Add the cooled carrot mixture and stir well. Spoon the mixture into the prepared tin and level the surface.
4 Bake for 45 minutes–1 hour until firm. Cool in the tin for 10 minutes, then turn out on to a wire rack and leave to cool completely.
5 To make the topping, finely slice the orange zest and put to one side. Put the cream cheese, crème fraîche, icing sugar and vanilla extract into a bowl and stir with a spatula. Spread over the cake and top with the zest. Cut into 15 squares to serve.

TO STORE

Store in an airtight container in the fridge. It will keep for up to two weeks.

CHOCOLATE PECAN BARS

Preparation: 15 minutes

Cooking time: 1¼ hours, plus cooling

200g (7oz) unsalted butter, softened,
    plus extra to grease
125g (4oz) plain flour, sifted
25g (1oz) icing sugar
1 large egg yolk and 2 large eggs
125g (4oz) self-raising flour
1 tsp baking powder
125g (4oz) caster sugar
3–4 drops vanilla extract
150g (5oz) milk chocolate chips
75g (3oz) pecan nuts, chopped
6 tbsp chocolate and hazelnut spread

PER BAR

189 cals; 13g fat (of which 6g saturates); 18g
carbohydrate; 0.2g salt

1 Preheat the oven to 200°C (180°C fan oven) mark 6.
Grease a 25.5 x 15cm (10 x 6 inch) shallow baking tin
and base-line with baking parchment.

2 Put the plain flour and icing sugar into a food
processor with 75g (3oz) roughly chopped butter and
whiz until crumb-like in texture. (Alternatively, rub the
butter into the dry ingredients in a large bowl by hand
or using a pastry cutter.) Add the egg yolk and whiz
for 10–15 seconds, or add to the bowl with the dry
ingredients and stir until the mixture begins to come
together. Turn into the tin and press into a thin layer.
Bake for 15 minutes or until golden.

3 Meanwhile, put the self-raising flour, baking powder,
caster sugar, vanilla extract and the remaining eggs into
the food processor with the remaining softened butter
and blend for 15 seconds or until smooth (or put the
ingredients into a bowl and mix well with a wooden
spoon). Remove the blade and fold in the chocolate
chips and pecan nuts. Set aside.

4 Spread the chocolate and hazelnut spread over the
cooked base and top with the cake mixture. Lower
the oven setting to 180°C (160°C fan oven) mark 4
and bake for 45–50 minutes until golden – cover the
top of the cake with foil if it appears to be browning
too quickly. Cool in the tin for about 10 minutes, then
turn out on to a wire rack and leave to cool
completely. Cut into 25 pieces.

TO STORE

Store in an airtight container. They will keep for up to
two days.

APPLE CRUMBLE BARS

CUTS INTO 10 BARS

Preparation: 20 minutes, plus chilling

Cooking time: about 45 minutes, plus cooling

200g (7oz) butter
125g (4oz) caster sugar
200g (7oz) plain flour
pinch of salt
3 dessert apples, peeled, cored and diced
 into 5mm (¼ inch) cubes
1 tsp ground cinnamon
2 tbsp lemon juice
1 tbsp cornflour
4 tbsp raspberry jam

TOPPING

50g (2oz) pecan nuts, roughly chopped
40g (1½oz) gingernut biscuits, crushed
icing sugar to dust

PER BAR

355 cals, 21g fat (of which 11g saturates);
42g carbohydrate; 0.5g salt

1 Whiz 175g (6oz) butter in a food processor with 75g (3oz) caster sugar for 1 minute. Add the flour and salt and whiz until the mixture just comes together. Wrap the dough in clingfilm and chill for 30 minutes.
2 Preheat the oven to 190°C (170°C fan oven) mark 5 and line an 18cm (7 inch) square baking tin with parchment paper. Push the dough evenly into the bottom of the tin, then prick all over with a fork. Bake for 20–25 minutes until lightly golden, then take out of the oven.
3 Meanwhile, put the remaining butter and caster sugar into a pan with the apples and cinnamon and cook over a gentle heat for 5 minutes or until the apples are softening. In a small bowl, mix the lemon juice with the cornflour, then add this mixture to the apples. Continue to cook, stirring constantly, for 2–3 minutes until the sauce has thickened. Set aside.
4 Warm the jam in a small saucepan, then spread over the shortbread. Top with the apple mixture, then sprinkle the pecan nuts and crushed biscuits over the apples. Bake for 10 minutes, then leave to cool completely in tin before dusting with icing sugar and cutting into 10 bars.

NOTE
For convenience, complete the recipe to the end of step 3 up to one day ahead. Transfer the apple mixture to a bowl and store, covered, in fridge. Store the shortbread in a tin, covered, at room temperature. Complete the recipe to serve.

TO STORE
Store in an airtight container. It will keep for up to four days.

TRADITIONAL FLAPJACKS

Preparation: 10 minutes

Cooking time: about 20 minutes, plus cooling

200g (7oz) butter, plus extra
    to grease
150g (5oz) demerara sugar
4 tbsp golden syrup
1 tsp ground cinnamon
finely grated zest of ½–1 orange
400g (14oz) jumbo oats
100g (3½oz) raisins or sultanas

PER FLAPJACK

354 cals; 17g fat (of which 9g saturates);
50g carbohydrate; 0.4g salt

1 Preheat the oven to 190°C (170°C fan oven) mark 5. Grease and line a
   20.5cm (8 inch) square baking tin with parchment paper.
2 Melt the butter in a large pan and add the sugar, syrup, cinnamon and
   orange zest. Heat gently until the sugar dissolves.
3 Remove the pan from the heat and stir in the oats and raisins or sultanas.
   Press the mixture into the tin and bake for 17–20 minutes until lightly
   golden. Leave to cool before cutting into squares.

TO STORE
Store in an airtight container. They will keep for up to three days.

HAZELNUT AND CHOCOLATE FLAPJACKS

Preparation: 10 minutes

Cooking time: 30 minutes, plus cooling

125g (4oz) unsalted butter, plus extra
   to grease
125g (4oz) light muscovado sugar
1 tbsp golden syrup
50g (2oz) hazelnuts, roughly chopped
175g (6oz) jumbo or porridge oats
50g (2oz) plain chocolate such as
   Bournville, roughly chopped

PER FLAPJACK

229 cals; 14g fat (of which 6g saturates);
26g carbohydrate; 0.2g salt

1 Preheat the oven to 180°C (160°C fan oven) mark 4. Lightly grease a shallow 28 × 18cm (11 × 7 inch) baking tin.

2 Put the butter, sugar and syrup into a pan and melt together over a low heat. Stir in the hazelnuts and oats. Leave the mixture to cool slightly, then stir in the chopped chocolate. Spoon the mixture into the prepared tin and level the surface.

3 Bake for about 30 minutes until golden and firm. Cool in the tin for a few minutes, then cut into 12 pieces. Turn out on to a wire rack and leave to cool completely.

TO STORE

Store in an airtight container. They will keep for up to one week.

VARIATIONS

Tropical fruit and coconut flapjacks: Replace the hazelnuts and chocolate with mixed dried tropical fruits, chopped into pieces. Replace 50g (2oz) of the oats with desiccated coconut.

Apricot and mixed seed flapjacks: Replace the hazelnuts with 50g (2oz) mixed seeds (such as pumpkin, sunflower, linseed and sesame). Reduce the oats to 125g (4oz). Replace the chocolate with 100g (3½oz) chopped dried apricots.

STICKY GINGER FLAPJACKS

Preparation: 10 minutes

Cooking time: 40 minutes, plus cooling

350g (12oz) unsalted butter, plus
    extra to grease
275g (10oz) caster sugar
225g (8oz) golden syrup
450g (1lb) rolled oats
1 tbsp ground ginger

PER FLAPJACK

259 cals; 14g fat (of which 8g saturates);
33g carbohydrate; 0.3g salt

1 Preheat the oven to 180°C (160°C fan oven) mark 4. Grease a 28 × 18cm (11 × 7 inch) shallow cake tin and base-line with baking parchment.

2 Put the butter, sugar and syrup into a large pan and heat gently until melted. Mix in the rolled oats and ground ginger until they are thoroughly combined. Pour the mixture into the tin and level the surface.

3 Bake for 30–35 minutes until golden brown around the edges. Leave to cool in the tin for 15 minutes.

4 While still warm, score into 24 pieces with a sharp knife. Leave in the tin to cool completely, then turn out and cut out the pieces.

TO STORE
Store in an airtight container. They will keep for up to one week.

NOTE
Don't over-cook the flapjacks or they will be hard and dry. When they are cooked, they should still be sticky and slightly soft when you press them in the middle.

DOUBLE-CHOCOLATE BROWNIES

CUTS INTO 16 BROWNIES

Preparation: 15 minutes

Cooking time: 20–25 minutes, plus cooling

250g (9oz) butter, plus extra to grease

250g (9oz) plain chocolate (at least 50% cocoa solids),
    broken into pieces

100g (3½oz) white chocolate, broken into pieces

4 medium eggs

175g (6oz) light muscovado sugar

1 tsp vanilla extract

75g (3oz) plain flour, sifted

¼ tsp baking powder

1 tbsp cocoa powder, sifted, plus extra to dust

100g (3½oz) pecan nuts, chopped

pinch of salt

a little icing sugar to dust

PER BROWNIE

352 cals; 25g fat (of which 13g saturates); 29g carbohydrate; 0.3g salt

1 Preheat the oven to 200°C (180°C fan oven) mark 6. Grease a 20.5cm (8 inch) square shallow tin and base-line with baking parchment. Melt the butter and plain chocolate in a heatproof bowl set over a pan of gently simmering water, making sure the base of the bowl doesn't touch the water. Remove the bowl from the pan and put to one side.

2 In a separate bowl, melt the white chocolate over a pan of gently simmering water, making sure the base of the bowl doesn't touch the water. Remove the bowl from the pan and put to one side.

3 Put the eggs into a separate large bowl. Add the muscovado sugar and vanilla extract and whisk until the mixture is pale and thick. Add the flour, baking powder, cocoa powder, nuts and salt to the bowl, then pour in the dark chocolate mixture. Using a large metal spoon, gently fold the ingredients together to make a smooth batter – if you fold too roughly, the chocolate will seize up and become unusable.

4 Pour the brownie mixture into the prepared tin. Spoon dollops of the white chocolate over the top, then swirl a skewer through it several times to create a marbled effect. Bake for 20–25 minutes. The brownie should be fudgy inside and the top should be cracked and crispy. Leave to cool in the tin.

5 Transfer the brownies to a board and cut into 16 individual brownies. To serve, dust with a little icing sugar and cocoa powder.

TO STORE

For convenience, complete the recipe to the end of step 5, then store in an airtight container. It will keep for up to one week. Complete the recipe to serve.

VARIATION

Try making these brownies without butter – believe it or not, this recipe will still work. But you'll need to eat them within an hour of taking them out of the oven – fat is what makes cakes moist and allows them to be stored.

WHITE CHOCOLATE AND NUT BROWNIES

Preparation: 20 minutes

Cooking time: 30–35 minutes, plus cooling

75g (3oz) unsalted butter, plus extra
   to grease
500g (1lb 2oz) white chocolate,
   roughly chopped
3 large eggs
175g (6oz) golden caster sugar
175g (6oz) self-raising flour
pinch of salt
175g (6oz) macadamia nuts, roughly
   chopped
1 tsp vanilla extract

PER BROWNIE

502 cals; 31g fat (of which 13g saturates);
52g carbohydrate; 0.4g salt

1 Preheat the oven to 190°C (170°C fan oven) mark 5. Grease a 25.5 × 20.5cm (10 × 8 inch) baking tin and base-line with baking parchment.

2 Melt 125g (4oz) white chocolate with the butter in a heatproof bowl set over a pan of gently simmering water, making sure the base of the bowl doesn't touch the water, stirring occasionally. Remove the bowl from the pan and leave to cool slightly.

3 Whisk the eggs and sugar together in a large bowl until smooth, then gradually beat in the melted chocolate mixture – the consistency will become quite firm. Sift the flour and salt over the mixture, then fold in with the nuts, the remaining chopped chocolate and the vanilla extract. Turn the mixture into the prepared tin and level the surface.

4 Bake for 30–35 minutes until risen and golden and the centre is just firm to the touch – the mixture will still be soft under the crust; it firms up on cooling. Leave to cool in the tin.

5 Turn out and cut into 12 individual brownies.

TO STORE

Store in an airtight container. They will keep for up to one week.

RASPBERRY AND CREAM CHEESE CHOCOLATE BROWNIES

Preparation: 20 minutes

Cooking time: about 35 minutes, plus cooling

200g (7oz) unsalted butter, plus extra
  to grease
150g (5oz) each dark chocolate and
  plain chocolate (at least 70% cocoa
  solids), chopped
4 medium eggs
150g (5oz) light muscovado sugar
125g (4oz) plus 1 tbsp self-raising
  flour, sifted
125g (4oz) curd cheese or cream
  cheese
2 tbsp raspberry jam
crème fraîche to serve

PER BROWNIE

465 cals; 32g fat (of which 20g saturates);
41g carbohydrate; 0.7g salt

1   Preheat the oven to 200°C (180°C fan oven) mark 6. Grease a 23cm (9 inch) square tin and line with greaseproof paper. Put both chocolates and the butter into a heatproof bowl set over a pan of simmering water and stir to combine. When they have melted, take off the heat and set aside to cool.

2   Put 3 of the eggs and all but 1 tsp sugar into a bowl and whisk together with a hand-held electric whisk until thick and mousse-like. Fold in the cooled chocolate mixture and all but 1 tbsp flour, then pour into the prepared tin.

3   Put the cheese into a bowl with the remaining egg and the reserved 1 tsp sugar and 1 tbsp flour. Mix well to combine.

4   Place dollops of the cheese mixture randomly over the surface, then top each with a teaspoonful of the raspberry jam. Use a skewer to marble the cheese, jam and brownie mixture together.

5   Bake for 25–30 minutes. Remove from the oven and cool in the tin for 10 minutes, then turn out on to a wire rack and leave to cool completely. Cut into 9 individual brownies and serve with a dollop of crème fraîche.

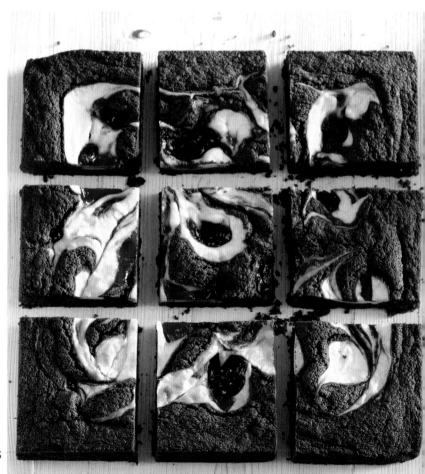

LAMINGTONS

CUTS INTO 16 SQUARES

Preparation: 40 minutes

Cooking time: 30 minutes, plus cooling and setting

125g (4oz) unsalted butter, softened, plus extra to grease

125g (4oz) golden caster sugar

2 medium eggs

125g (4oz) self-raising flour, sifted

1 tsp baking powder

2 tsp vanilla extract

COATING

200g (7oz) icing sugar

50g (2oz) cocoa powder

25g (1oz) unsalted butter, cubed

5 tbsp milk

200g (7oz) desiccated coconut

PER SQUARE

273 cals; 17g fat (of which 12g saturates); 29g carbohydrate; 0.4g salt

1 Preheat the oven to 180°C (160°C fan oven) mark 4. Grease a 15cm (6 inch) square cake tin and base-line with baking parchment.

2 Put the butter, caster sugar, eggs, flour, baking powder and vanilla extract into a bowl and beat with a hand-held electric whisk until creamy. Turn the mixture into the prepared tin and level the surface.

3 Bake for about 30 minutes until just firm to the touch and a skewer inserted into the centre comes out clean. Transfer to a wire rack and leave to cool completely. Wrap and store, preferably overnight, so that the cake is easier to slice.

NOTE

If, towards the end of coating the cakes, the chocolate topping mixture has thickened, carefully stir in a drop of water to thin it down.

4 To make the topping, sift the icing sugar and cocoa powder into a bowl. Put the butter and milk into a small pan and heat until the butter has just melted. Pour over the icing sugar and stir until smooth, adding 2–3 tbsp water if necessary, so that the icing thickly coats the back of a spoon.

5 Trim the side crusts from the cake and cut into 16 squares. Place a sheet of greaseproof paper under a wire rack to catch the drips. Scatter the coconut on to a large plate. Pierce a piece of cake through the top crust and dip into the icing until coated, turning the cake gently. Transfer to the wire rack. Once you've coated half the pieces, roll them in the coconut and transfer to a plate. Repeat with the remainder and leave to set for a couple of hours before serving.

THE ULTIMATE CHOCOLATE CHIP COOKIE

MAKES ABOUT 25

Preparation: 15 minutes

Cooking time: about 12 minutes, plus cooling

225g (8oz) unsalted butter, very soft
125g (4oz) caster sugar
150g (5oz) light muscovado sugar
1½ tbsp golden syrup
1 tsp vanilla extract
2 large eggs, beaten
375g (13oz) plain flour
1 tsp bicarbonate of soda
¼ tsp salt
350g (12oz) milk chocolate, cut into
    large chunks

PER COOKIE

223 cals; 11g fat (of which 7g saturates);
28g carbohydrate; 0.9g salt

1 Preheat the oven to 200°C (180°C fan oven) mark 6. Line three baking sheets with baking parchment.

2 Put the butter, caster and muscovado sugars, golden syrup and vanilla extract into a bowl and, using a hand-held electric whisk or freestanding mixer, beat until pale and fluffy – this should take about 5 minutes.

3 Gradually beat in the eggs, adding 2 tbsp flour if the mixture looks as if it's about to curdle. Sift in the remaining flour, the bicarbonate of soda and salt all at once and beat in quickly for a few seconds. Using a large metal spoon, mix in the milk chocolate chunks.

4 Spoon heaped teaspoonfuls of the mixture on to the baking sheets, spacing them well apart. Don't press the mixture down – the mounds will spread during baking. For a chewy biscuit, bake for 10 minutes until pale and golden; for a crisper version, bake for 12 minutes. Transfer the cookies from the trays on to wire racks and leave to cool.

TO STORE

Store in an airtight container. They will keep for up to one week.

CHOCOLATE CHIP OAT COOKIES

Preparation: 15 minutes

Cooking time: 12–15 minutes, plus cooling

125g (4oz) unsalted butter, softened,
   plus extra to grease
125g (4oz) golden caster sugar
1 medium egg
1 tsp vanilla extract
125g (4oz) porridge oats
150g (5oz) plain flour
½ tsp baking powder
200g (7oz) plain chocolate (at least
   70% cocoa solids), cut into 1cm
   (½ inch) chunks

PER COOKIE

197 cals; 10g fat (of which 6g saturates);
26g carbohydrate; 0.2g salt

1 Preheat the oven to 180°C (160°C fan oven) mark 4.
   Lightly grease two baking sheets.
2 Cream the butter and sugar together in a bowl until
   pale and creamy.
   Add the egg, vanilla extract and oats. Sift the flour and
   baking powder together over the mixture and mix
   until evenly combined. Stir in the chocolate chunks.

3 Put dessertspoonfuls of the mixture on to the
   prepared baking sheets, spacing them well apart to
   allow room for spreading. Flatten each one slightly
   with the back of a fork.
4 Bake for 12–15 minutes or until risen and turning
   golden, but still quite soft. Leave on the baking sheet
   for 5 minutes, then transfer to a wire rack and leave
   to cool completely.

TO STORE
Store in an airtight container. They will keep for up to
one week.

FREEZING TIP
To freeze, complete the recipe and allow the
cookies to cool. Wrap, seal, label and freeze. To
use, thaw the cookies individually, as needed, at
room temperature for 1–2 hours.

PEANUT AND RAISIN COOKIES

Preparation: 10 minutes
Cooking time: 15 minutes, plus cooling

125g (4oz) unsalted butter, softened,
   plus extra to grease
150g (5oz) caster sugar
1 medium egg
150g (5oz) plain flour, sifted
½ tsp baking powder
½ tsp salt
125g (4oz) crunchy peanut butter
175g (6oz) raisins

PER COOKIE

111 cals; 6g fat (of which 3g saturates); 14g
carbohydrate; 0.2g salt

1 Preheat the oven to 190°C (170°C fan oven) mark 5
   and grease two baking sheets.
2 Beat together all the ingredients except the raisins,
   until well blended. Stir in the raisins.
3 Spoon large teaspoonfuls of the mixture, spaced well
   apart, on to the prepared baking sheets, leaving room
   for the mixture to spread.
4 Bake for about 15 minutes until golden brown around
   the edges. Leave to cool slightly, then transfer to a wire
   rack and leave to cool completely.

TO STORE
Store in an airtight container. They will keep for up to
three days.

VARIATIONS
Chocolate nut cookies: Omit the peanut
butter and raisins and add 1 tsp vanilla extract.
Stir in 175g (6oz) roughly chopped chocolate
and 75g (3oz) roughly chopped walnuts.

Coconut and cherry cookies: Omit the
peanut butter and raisins, reduce the sugar to
75g (3oz) and stir in 50g (2oz) desiccated
coconut and 125g (4oz) rinsed, roughly
chopped glacé cherries.

Oat and cinnamon cookies: Omit the
peanut butter and raisins and add 1 tsp vanilla
extract. Stir in 1 tsp ground cinnamon and 75g
(3oz) rolled oats.

SULTANA AND PECAN COOKIES

MAKES 20

Preparation: 15 minutes

Cooking time: 12–15 minutes, plus cooling

225g (8oz) unsalted butter, at room
    temperature, plus extra to grease

175g (6oz) light muscovado sugar

2 medium eggs, lightly beaten

225g (8oz) pecan nut halves

300g (11oz) self-raising flour, sifted

¼ tsp baking powder

125g (4oz) sultanas

2 tbsp maple syrup

PER COOKIE

276 cals; 18g fat (of which 7g saturates);
27g carbohydrate; 0.2g salt

1 Preheat the oven to 190°C (170°C fan oven) mark 5. Lightly grease four baking sheets.

2 Cream the butter and sugar together until the mixture is pale and fluffy. Gradually beat in the eggs until thoroughly combined.

3 Put 20 pecan nut halves to one side, then roughly chop the rest and fold into the mixture with the flour, baking powder, sultanas and syrup.

4 Roll the mixture into 20 balls and place them, spaced well apart, on the prepared baking sheets. Using a dampened palette knife, flatten the cookies and top each with a piece of pecan nut.

5 Bake for 12–15 minutes until pale golden. Leave on the baking sheets for 5 minutes, then transfer to a wire rack and leave to cool completely.

TO STORE
Store in an airtight container. They will keep for up to one week.

FREEZING TIP
To freeze, complete the recipe to the end of step 4, then open-freeze a tray of unbaked cookies. When frozen, pack into bags or containers.
To use, cook from frozen for 18–20 minutes.

ALMOND MACAROONS

Preparation: 10 minutes

Cooking time: 12–15 minutes, plus cooling

2 medium egg whites
125g (4oz) caster sugar
125g (4oz) ground almonds
¼ tsp almond extract
22 blanched almonds

PER MACAROON

86 cals; 6g fat (of which 1g saturates);
7g carbohydrate; 0g salt

1 Preheat the oven to 180°C (fan oven 160°C) mark 4. Line baking trays with baking parchment.

2 Whisk the egg whites in a clean, grease-free bowl until stiff peaks form. Gradually whisk in the sugar, a little at a time, until thick and glossy. Gently stir in the ground almonds and almond extract.

3 Spoon teaspoonfuls of the mixture on to the prepared baking trays, spacing them slightly apart. Press an almond into the centre of each one and bake in the oven for 12–15 minutes until just golden and firm to the touch.

4 Leave on the baking sheets for 10 minutes, then transfer to wire rack and leave to cool completely. On cooling, these biscuits have a soft, chewy centre; they harden up after a few days.

TO STORE
Store in airtight containers. They will keep for up to one week.

FLORENTINES

MAKES 18

Preparation: 15 minutes

Cooking time: 16–20 minutes, plus cooling and setting

65g (2½oz) unsalted butter, plus extra to grease

50g (2oz) golden caster sugar

2 tbsp double cream

25g (1oz) sunflower seeds

20g (¾oz) chopped mixed candied peel

20g (¾oz) sultanas

25g (1oz) natural glacé cherries, roughly chopped

40g (1½oz) flaked almonds, lightly crushed

15g (½oz) plain flour

125g (4oz) plain chocolate (at least 70% cocoa solids), broken into pieces

PER BISCUIT

115 cals; 8g fat (of which 4g saturates); 11g carbohydrate; 0.1g salt

1 Preheat the oven to 180°C (160°C fan oven) mark 4. Lightly grease two large baking sheets.

2 Melt the butter in a small heavy-based pan. Add the sugar and heat gently until dissolved, then bring to the boil. Take off the heat and stir in the cream, seeds, peel, sultanas, cherries, almonds and flour. Mix until evenly combined. Put heaped teaspoonfuls on to the prepared baking sheets, spaced well apart to allow for spreading.

3 Bake one sheet at a time, for 6–8 minutes, until the biscuits have spread considerably and the edges are golden brown. Using a large plain metal biscuit cutter, push the edges into the centre to create neat rounds. Bake for a further 2 minutes or until deep golden. Leave on the baking sheet for 2 minutes, then transfer to a wire rack and leave to cool completely.

4 Melt the chocolate in a heatproof bowl set over a pan of gently simmering water, making sure the base of the bowl doesn't touch the water, stirring occasionally. Spread on the underside of each Florentine and mark wavy lines with a fork. Put, chocolate-side up, on a sheet of baking parchment and leave to set.

TO STORE

Store in an airtight container. They will keep for up to two weeks.

ORANGE TUILE BISCUITS

MAKE 24

Preparation: 10 minutes, plus chilling

Cooking time: 12 minutes per batch, plus
cooling

3 large egg whites
100g (3½oz) icing sugar, sifted
100g (3½oz) plain flour
finely grated zest of 1 orange
75g (3oz) unsalted butter, melted

PER BISCUIT
55 cals; 3g fat (of which 2g saturates);
8g carbohydrate; 0.1g salt

1   Put the egg whites into a clean, grease-free bowl, add the sugar and whisk lightly. Stir in the flour, orange zest and melted butter, then cover and chill for 30 minutes.
2   Preheat the oven to 200°C (180°C fan oven) mark 6. Line a baking sheet with baking parchment.
3   Put 3 teaspoonfuls of the mixture, spaced well apart, on the prepared baking sheet and spread out into 9cm (3½ inch) circles.
4   Bake for 12 minutes or until just brown around the edges. Remove from the oven and, while still warm, shape each biscuit over a rolling pin to curl. Repeat with the remaining mixture. Leave on a wire rack to cool completely.

TO STORE
Store in an airtight container. They will keep for up to one week.

CHRISTMAS COOKIES

Preparation: 25 minutes, plus chilling

Cooking time: about 15 minutes, plus cooling

75g (3oz) unsalted butter, softened

100g (3½oz) caster sugar

1 medium egg

½ tsp vanilla extract

250g (9oz) plain flour, plus extra to
   dust

½ tsp baking powder

a selection of coloured ready-to-roll
   fondant icings, royal icing, food
   colourings and edible decorations

PER COOKIE

94 cals; 3g fat (of which 2g saturates);
16.5g carbohydrate; 0.1g salt

1 Using a wooden spoon, cream the butter and sugar together in a large
   bowl until smooth. Beat in the egg and vanilla extract. Sift the flour and
   baking powder into the bowl and stir until combined. Tip out on to a lightly
   floured surface and knead gently to make a soft dough. Shape into a disc
   and wrap in clingfilm, then chill for 1 hour until firm.

2 Preheat the oven to 180°C (160°C fan oven) mark 4. Roll out the dough
   on a lightly floured surface until 5mm (¼ inch) thick. Using Christmas
   cookie cutters, stamp out shapes, re-rolling the trimmings if necessary.
   If the cookies are to be hung as decorations, use a skewer to make a 5mm
   (¼ inch) hole in each one. Place on two non-stick baking trays and bake
   for 10–15 minutes until pale golden and risen. Leave to cool on the sheets
   for 3 minutes to harden, then transfer to a wire rack to cool completely.

3 When the cookies are completely cool, decorate with different coloured
   fondant icings or royal icing and edible decorations.

TO STORE

Store in an airtight container. They will keep for up to two weeks.

GINGER BISCUITS

Preparation: 15 minutes

Cooking time: about 12 minutes, plus cooling

50g (2oz) butter, plus extra to grease
125g (4oz) golden syrup
50g (2oz) dark muscovado sugar
finely grated zest of 1 orange
2 tbsp orange juice
175g (6oz) self-raising flour
1 tsp ground ginger

PER BISCUIT

55 cals; 2g fat (of which 1g saturates);
10g carbohydrate; 0.1g salt

1 Preheat the oven to 180°C (160°C fan oven) mark 4. Lightly grease two large baking sheets.
2 Put the butter, golden syrup, sugar, orange zest and juice into a heavy-based pan and heat very gently until melted and evenly blended.
3 Leave the mixture to cool slightly, then sift in the flour with the ginger. Mix thoroughly until smooth. Put small spoonfuls of the mixture on the baking sheets, spacing them well apart to allow room for spreading.
4 Bake for 12 minutes or until the biscuits are golden brown. Leave on the baking sheets for 1 minute, then carefully transfer to a wire rack and leave to cool.

TO STORE
Store in an airtight container. They will keep for up to five days.

CHOCOLATE FUDGE SHORTBREAD

Preparation: 30 minutes

Cooking time: 20 minutes, plus cooling
and setting

175g (6oz) unsalted butter, at room
   temperature, diced, plus extra to
   grease
250g (9oz) plain flour, plus extra to
   dust
75g (3oz) golden caster sugar

TOPPING

2 x 397g cans sweetened condensed
   milk
100g (3½oz) light muscovado sugar
100g (3½oz) butter
250g (9oz) plain chocolate (at least
   70% cocoa solids), broken into
   pieces

PER SQUARE

369 cals; 19g fat (of which 12g saturates);
48g carbohydrate; 0.4g salt

1 Preheat the oven to 180°C (160°C fan oven) mark 4. Grease a 33 × 23cm (13 × 9 inch) Swiss roll tin and line with baking parchment.

2 Put the flour, caster sugar and butter into a food processor and blend until the mixture forms crumbs, then pulse a little more until it forms a ball. Turn out on to a lightly floured surface and knead lightly to combine. Press the mixture into the prepared tin.

3 Bake for 20 minutes or until firm to the touch and a very pale brown.

4 To make the topping, put the condensed milk, muscovado sugar and butter into a non-stick pan and cook over a medium heat, stirring continuously until a fudge-like consistency. (Alternatively, melt in a heatproof bowl in a 900W microwave oven on full power for 12 minutes or until the mixture is thick and fudgy, beating with a whisk every 2–3 minutes.) Spoon the caramel on to the shortbread, smooth over and leave to cool.

5 To finish, melt the chocolate in a heatproof bowl set over a pan of gently simmering water, making sure the base of the bowl doesn't touch the water, then pour over the caramel layer. Leave to set at room temperature, then cut into 20 squares to serve.

TO STORE

Store in an airtight container. They will keep for up to one week.

SHORTBREAD

MAKES 18–20

Preparation: 20 minutes, plus chilling

Cooking time: 15–20 minutes, plus cooling

225g (8oz) butter, at room
    temperature
125g (4oz) golden caster sugar
225g (8oz) plain flour
125g (4oz) rice flour
pinch of salt
golden or coloured granulated sugar
    to coat
caster sugar to sprinkle

PER PIECE

190–170 cals; 10–9g fat (of which 7–6g
saturates); 23–21g carbohydrate;
0.3–0.2g salt

1 Cream the butter and sugar together in a bowl until pale and fluffy. Sift the flours and salt together on to the creamed mixture and stir in, using a wooden spoon, until the mixture resembles breadcrumbs.

2 Gather the dough together with your hand and turn on to a clean surface. Knead very lightly until it forms a ball, then lightly roll into a sausage, about 5cm (2 inch) thick. Wrap in clingfilm and chill in the fridge until firm.

3 Preheat the oven to 190°C (170°C fan oven) mark 5. Line two baking sheets with greaseproof paper. Remove the clingfilm and slice the dough into discs, 7–10mm (⅓–½ inch) thick. Pour some granulated sugar on to a plate and roll the edge of each disc in the sugar. Put the shortbread, cut-side up, on the baking sheets.

4 Bake the shortbread for 15–20 minutes, depending on thickness, until very pale golden. On removing from the oven, sprinkle with caster sugar. Leave on the baking sheets for 10 minutes, then transfer to a wire rack and leave to cool.

TO STORE

Store in an airtight container. They will keep for up to two weeks.

APPLE SHORTIES

Preparation: 20 minutes

Cooking time: 30 minutes, plus cooling

75g (3oz) unsalted butter, softened,
plus extra to grease

40g (1½oz) caster sugar

75g (3oz) plain flour, sifted

40g (1½oz) fine semolina

1 cooking apple, about 175g (6oz),
peeled and grated

125g (4oz) sultanas

½ tsp mixed spice

2 tbsp light muscovado sugar

1 tsp lemon juice

PER SQUARE

100 cals; 4g fat (of which 3g saturates);
17g carbohydrate; 0.1g salt

1 Preheat the oven to 190°C (170°C fan oven) mark 5. Grease an 18cm (7 inch) square shallow cake tin.

2 Beat the butter, caster sugar, flour and semolina together until the mixture is blended. Press the mixture into the prepared tin and level the surface. Bake for 15 minutes.

3 Meanwhile, mix the apple with the remaining ingredients. Spoon evenly over the shortbread and put back in the oven for a further 15 minutes.

4 Cool in the tin for a few minutes, then cut into 16 squares. Leave to cool completely, then remove from the tin.

TO STORE

Store in an airtight container. They will keep for up to three days.

AMARETTI BISCUITS

Preparation: 5 minutes
Cooking time: 20 minutes, plus cooling

125g (4oz) ground almonds
15g (½oz) ground rice
225g (8oz) caster sugar
2 medium egg whites
½ tsp almond flavouring
about 24 split almonds

PER BISCUIT

79 calories; 4g fat (of which 0.3g saturates);
11g carbohydrate; 0.1g salt

1 Preheat the oven to 180°C (160°C fan oven) mark 4. Line two baking
   sheets with rice paper.
2 Mix together the ground almonds, ground rice and sugar. Add the egg
   whites and almond flavouring and beat together until smooth.
3 Put the mixture into a piping bag fitted with a 1cm (½ inch) plain nozzle.
   Pipe small rounds about 2.5cm (1 inch) in diameter on to the paper, leaving
   plenty of room for spreading. Top each biscuit with a split almond.
4 Bake in the oven for about 20 minutes until pale golden brown. Transfer to
   a wire rack and leave to cool. Remove the rice paper from around each
   Amaretti before serving.

TO STORE
Store in an airtight container. They will keep for up to two weeks.

HAZELNUT AND CHOCOLATE BISCOTTI

Preparation: 10 minutes

Cooking time: 35–40 minutes, plus cooling

125g (4oz) plain flour, sifted, plus
    extra to dust
75g (3oz) golden caster sugar
¼ tsp baking powder
pinch of cinnamon
pinch of salt
1 large egg, beaten
1 tbsp milk
¼ tsp vanilla extract
25g (1oz) hazelnuts
25g (1oz) plain chocolate chips

PER BISCUIT

50 cals; 1g fat (of which trace saturates);
9g carbohydrate; 0g salt

1 Preheat the oven to 200°C (180°C fan oven) mark 6. Put the flour into a large bowl. Stir in the sugar, baking powder, cinnamon and salt. Make a well in the centre and, using a fork, stir in the beaten egg, milk, vanilla extract, hazelnuts and chocolate chips to form a sticky dough.

2 Turn out the dough on to a lightly floured surface and gently knead into a ball. Roll into a 28cm (11 inch) log shape. Put on a non-stick baking sheet and flatten slightly. Bake for 20–25 minutes until pale golden.

3 Lower the oven setting to 150°C (130°C fan oven) mark 2. Transfer the biscotti log on to a chopping board and slice diagonally with a bread knife at 1cm (½ inch) intervals. Arrange the slices on the baking sheet and put back into the oven for 15 minutes or until golden and dry. Transfer to a wire rack and leave to cool completely.

TO STORE

Store in an airtight container. They will keep for up to one month.

NOTES

To enjoy Italian-style, dunk in coffee or dessert wine.

To make as gifts, divide the biscuits among four large squares of cellophane, then draw up the edges and tie with ribbon. Label the packages with storage information and an eat-by date.

CHOCOLATE AND PISTACHIO BISCOTTI

Preparation: 15 minutes
Cooking time: about 1 hour, plus cooling

300g (11oz) plain flour, sifted, plus
    extra for dusting
75g (3oz) cocoa powder, sifted
1 tsp baking powder
150g (5oz) plain chocolate chips
150g (5oz) shelled pistachio nuts
pinch of salt
75g (3oz) unsalted butter, softened
225g (8oz) granulated sugar
2 large eggs, beaten
1 tbsp icing sugar

PER BISCUIT
152 cals; 7g fat (of which 3g saturates);
20g carbohydrate; 0.2g salt

1 Preheat the oven to 180°C (160°C fan oven) mark 4. Line a large baking sheet with baking parchment.
2 Mix the flour with the cocoa powder, baking powder, chocolate chips, pistachio nuts and salt. Using a hand-held electric whisk, beat the butter and granulated sugar together until light and fluffy. Gradually whisk in the eggs.
3 Stir the dry ingredients into the mixture until it forms a stiff dough. With floured hands, shape the dough into two slightly flattened logs, each about 30.5 × 5cm (12 × 2 inch). Sprinkle with icing sugar. Put the logs on to the prepared baking sheet and bake for 40–45 minutes until they are slightly firm to the touch.
4 Leave the logs on the baking sheet for 10 minutes, then cut diagonally into 15 slices, 2cm (¾ inch) thick. Arrange them, cut-side down, on the baking sheet and bake again for 15 minutes or until crisp. Transfer to a wire rack and leave to cool.

TO STORE
Store in an airtight container. They will keep for up to one month.

VARIATION
Cranberry, hazelnut and orange biscotti: Increase the flour to 375g (13oz), omit the cocoa powder and add the grated zest of 1 orange. Replace the chocolate chips with dried cranberries and the pistachios with chopped blanched hazelnuts.

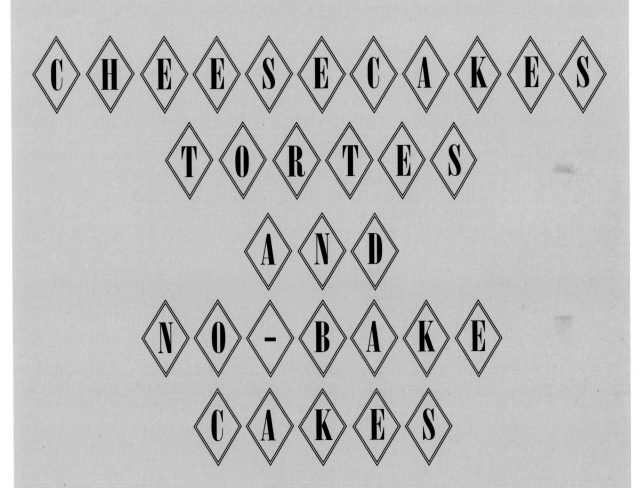

CHEESECAKES
TORTES
AND
NO-BAKE
CAKES

CLASSIC BAKED CHEESECAKE

LONG CHILLING REQUIRED

Preparation: 30 minutes, plus chilling
Cooking time: 55 minutes, plus cooling
and chilling

BASE
125g (4oz) unsalted butter, melted,
   plus extra to grease
250g pack digestive biscuits, finely
   crushed (see page 298)

FILLING
1 large lemon
2 x 250g cartons curd cheese
142ml carton soured cream
2 medium eggs
175g (6oz) golden caster sugar
1½ tsp vanilla extract
1 tbsp cornflour
50g (2oz) sultanas

PER SLICE
340 cals; 19g fat (of which 11g saturates);
36g carbohydrate; 1g salt

1 Grease a 20.5cm (8 inch) springform cake tin. Put the biscuits into a bowl, add the melted butter and mix until well combined. Tip the crumb mixture into the prepared tin and press evenly on to the bottom, using the back of a metal spoon to level the surface. Chill for 1 hour or until firm.

2 Preheat the oven to 180°C (160°C fan oven) mark 4. To make the filling, grate the zest from the lemon and set aside. Halve the lemon, cut 3 very thin slices from one half and put to one side. Squeeze the juice from the rest of the lemon.

3 Put the lemon zest, lemon juice, curd cheese, soured cream, eggs, sugar, vanilla extract and cornflour into a large bowl. Using a hand-held electric whisk, beat together until thick and smooth, then fold in the sultanas. Pour the mixture into the tin and shake gently to level the surface.

4 Bake for 30 minutes. Put the lemon slices, overlapping, on top. Bake for a further 20–25 minutes until the cheesecake is just set and golden brown. Turn off the oven and leave the cheesecake inside, with the door ajar, until it is cool, then chill for at least 2 hours or overnight.

5 Remove the cheesecake from the fridge about 30 minutes before serving. Run a knife around the edge, release the clasp on the tin and remove the cake. Cut the cheesecake into slices to serve.

RHUBARB AND GINGER CHEESECAKE

CUTS INTO 8 SLICES

Preparation: 30 minutes, plus chilling

Cooking time: about 2 hours, plus cooling and chilling

450g (1lb) rhubarb, cut into chunks
4 tbsp caster sugar
2 balls preserved stem ginger, syrup reserved
175g (6oz) ginger nuts, finely crushed (see page 298)
60g (2½oz) unsalted butter, melted
450g (1lb) cream cheese
3 medium eggs
1 tsp vanilla extract
4 tbsp icing sugar
½ tsp arrowroot

PER SLICE

530 cals; 39g fat (of which 23g saturates);
40g carbohydrate; 0.9g salt

1 Put 225g (8oz) rhubarb chunks into a pan with the caster sugar, 3 tbsp ginger syrup and 2 tbsp cold water. Simmer for 5–10 minutes until tender. Transfer to a food processor and whiz until smooth, then set aside to cool.

2 Finely chop the stem ginger and combine with the ginger nuts and butter. Press into the bottom of an 18cm (7 inch) round springform cake tin. Chill until firm.

3 Preheat the oven to 150°C (130°C fan oven) mark 2. Whisk together the cream cheese, eggs, vanilla extract and 3 tbsp icing sugar. Fold in two-thirds of the rhubarb purée. Pour into the cake tin. Stir the remainder of the purée through the filling, making swirls and ripples. Bake for 1½ hours until just set, then leave in the oven with the door ajar until cool. Chill, preferably overnight.

4 Put the remaining rhubarb into a pan with 150ml (¼ pint) cold water, the remaining icing sugar and 2 tbsp ginger syrup. Gently poach for 5–10 minutes until just tender. Remove the rhubarb and put to one side, then strain the liquid into a bowl and return it to the rinsed-out pan. Mix 1 tbsp of the liquid with the arrowroot until smooth, then add to the rest. Bring to the boil, then remove from the heat as soon as it is slightly thickened. Leave to cool.

5 To serve, remove the cheesecake from its tin and top with the poached rhubarb. Slice and drizzle with sauce.

NOTE
For convenience, prepare ahead. Complete the recipe to the end of step 4. Keep the cheesecake in the tin, cover with clingfilm and chill. Put the poached rhubarb in an airtight container and chill. Complete the recipe to serve.

ORANGE AND CHOCOLATE CHEESECAKE

LONG CHILLING REQUIRED

CUTS INTO 12 SLICES

Preparation: 45 minutes
Cooking time: 2–2¼ hours, plus cooling and chilling

225g (8oz) chilled unsalted butter, plus extra to grease
250g (9oz) plain flour, sifted
150g (5oz) light muscovado sugar
3 tbsp cocoa powder
chocolate curls to decorate (see page 327, optional)

TOPPING

2 oranges
800g (1lb 12oz) cream cheese
250g (9oz) mascarpone cheese
4 large eggs
225g (8oz) golden caster sugar
2 tbsp cornflour
½ tsp vanilla extract
1 vanilla pod

PER SLICE

767 cals; 60g fat (of which 37g saturates);
53g carbohydrate; 1.2g salt

1 Preheat the oven to 180°C (160°C fan oven) mark 4. Grease a 23cm (9 inch) springform cake tin and base-line with baking parchment.

2 Cut 175g (6oz) butter into cubes. Melt the remaining butter and set aside. Put the flour and cubed butter into a food processor with the sugar and cocoa powder. Whiz until the texture of fine breadcrumbs. (Alternatively, rub the butter into the flour in a large bowl by hand or using a pastry cutter. Stir in the sugar and cocoa powder.) Pour in the melted butter and pulse, or stir with a fork, until the mixture comes together.

3 Tip the crumb mixture into the prepared tin and press evenly on to the bottom, using the back of a metal spoon to level the surface. Bake for 35–40 minutes until lightly puffed; avoid over-browning or the biscuit base will have a bitter flavour. Remove from the oven and leave to cool. Lower the oven setting to 150°C (130°C fan oven) mark 2.

4 Meanwhile, make the topping. Grate the zest from the oranges, then squeeze the juice – you will need 150ml (¼ pint). Put the cream cheese, mascarpone, eggs, sugar, cornflour, grated orange zest and vanilla extract into a large bowl. Using a hand-held electric whisk, beat the ingredients together thoroughly until well combined.

5 Split the vanilla pod in half lengthways and, using the tip of a sharp knife, scrape out the seeds and add them to the cheese mixture. Beat in the orange juice and continue whisking until the mixture is smooth.

6 Pour the cheese mixture over the cooled biscuit base. Bake for about 1½ hours until pale golden on top, slightly risen and just set around the edge. The cheesecake should still be slightly wobbly in the middle; it will set as it cools. Turn off the oven and leave the cheesecake inside, with the door ajar, to cool for 1 hour. Remove and allow to cool completely (about 3 hours), then chill.

7 Just before serving, unclip the tin and transfer the cheesecake to a plate. Scatter chocolate curls on top to decorate, if you like.

BLUEBERRY CHEESECAKE

LONG CHILLING REQUIRED

CUTS INTO 8 SLICES

Preparation: 15 minutes

Cooking time: 45 minutes, plus cooling
and chilling

1 large sponge flan case, 23–25.5cm
   (9–10 inch) diameter
butter to grease
300g (11oz) cream cheese
1 tsp vanilla extract
100g (3½oz) golden caster sugar
150ml (¼ pint) soured cream
2 medium eggs
2 tbsp cornflour

TOPPING
150g (5oz) blueberries
2 tbsp redcurrant jelly

PER SLICE
376 cals; 24g fat (of which 14g saturates);
36g carbohydrate; 0.4g salt

1 Preheat the oven to 180°C (160°C fan oven) mark 4. Use the base of a 20.5cm (8 inch) springform cake tin to cut out a circle from the flan case, discarding the edges. Grease the tin and base-line with greaseproof paper, then put the flan base into it. Press down with your fingers.

2 Put the cream cheese, vanilla extract, sugar, soured cream, eggs and cornflour into a food processor and whiz until evenly combined. Pour the mixture over the flan base and shake gently to level the surface. Bake for 45 minutes or until just set and pale golden. Turn off the oven and leave the cheesecake inside, with the door ajar, for about 30 minutes. Leave to cool, then chill for at least 2 hours.

3 To serve, put the blueberries into a pan with the redcurrant jelly and heat through until the jelly has melted and the blueberries have softened slightly (or place in a heatproof bowl and cook in a 900W microwave oven on full power for 1 minute). Spoon them over the top of the cheesecake. Cool and chill for 15 minutes before serving.

VARIATION
Use raspberries or other soft berries instead of blueberries.

RASPBERRY CHEESECAKE

LONG CHILLING REQUIRED

CUTS INTO 10 SLICES

Preparation: 25 minutes, plus chilling

Cooking time: 5 minutes, plus cooling
and chilling

100g (3½oz) unsalted butter, melted,
    plus extra to grease
25g (1oz) blanched almonds, lightly
    toasted, then finely chopped
225g (8oz) almond butter biscuits,
    finely crushed (see page 298)
a few drops of almond extract
450g (1lb) raspberries
300g (11oz) Greek-style yogurt
150g (5oz) low-fat cream cheese
1 tbsp powdered gelatine
2 medium egg whites
50g (2oz) icing sugar

PER SLICE

270 cals; 19g fat (of which 10g saturates);
20g carbohydrate; 0.5g salt

1 Grease a 20.5cm (8 inch) round springform cake tin. Mix the almonds with the crushed biscuits and melted butter and add the almond extract. Tip the crumb mixture into the prepared tin and press evenly on to the bottom, using the back of a metal spoon to level the surface. Chill for 1 hour or until firm.

2 To make the filling, purée 225g (8oz) raspberries in a blender, then press through a sieve. Put three-quarters of the purée to one side and return the rest to the blender. Add the yogurt and cheese, then whiz to blend. Transfer to a bowl. Sprinkle the gelatine over 2 tbsp cold water in a heatproof bowl and leave to soak for 2–3 minutes. Put the bowl over a pan of simmering water until the gelatine has dissolved. Leave to cool.

3 Whisk the egg whites with the sugar until thick and shiny. Fold into the cheese mixture. Add the cooled gelatine. Arrange half the remaining berries over the biscuit base, then pour the cheese mixture over the berries. Add the reserved purée and swirl with a knife to marble. Top with the remaining berries and chill for 3–4 hours.

CHOCOLATE TORTE

Preparation: 15 minutes, plus chilling

Cooking time: 5 minutes, plus cooling

200g (7oz) plain chocolate, broken
    into pieces
25g (1oz) butter, melted, plus extra
    to grease
1½ tbsp golden syrup
125g (4oz) butter biscuits, finely
    crushed (see page 298)
40g (1½oz) icing sugar
300ml (½ pint) double cream, at
    room temperature
2–3 tbsp amaretto (optional)
crème fraîche to serve

TO DECORATE
plain chocolate, grated
raspberries
icing sugar to dust

PER SERVING
383 cals; 27g fat (of which 16g saturates);
31g carbohydrate; 0.2g salt

1 Melt the chocolate pieces in a heatproof bowl set
    over a pan of barely simmering water, making sure the
    base of the bowl doesn't touch the water. Put to one
    side to cool for 10 minutes. Grease a 20.5cm (8 inch)
    loose-bottomed cake tin and line the sides with
    greaseproof paper.

2 In a medium bowl, mix together the butter, golden
    syrup and crushed biscuits. Press the mixture into the
    bottom of the prepared tin.

3 Sift the icing sugar into a separate bowl. Pour in the
    cream and amaretto, if you like, and whip until the
    cream just holds its shape. Using a metal spoon, fold
    the cooled chocolate into the cream mixture. Spoon
    the chocolate mixture into the cake tin, level the
    surface, cover and chill until ready to serve.

4 Transfer the torte to a serving plate and peel off the
    paper. Scatter grated chocolate over the top, dot a few
    raspberries over and lightly dust with icing sugar.
    Serve in slices with crème fraîche.

NOTE
For convenience, prepare ahead. Complete the recipe to
the end of step 3 up to one day ahead. Complete the recipe
to serve.

CHOCOLATE AND RASPBERRY TORTE

CUTS INTO 20 SLICES

Preparation: 30 minutes, plus chilling

Cooking time: 5 minutes

5 x 100g bars good-quality dark
 chocolate
50g (2oz) golden syrup or liquid
 glucose
50ml (2fl oz) amaretto (optional)
100g (3½oz) brandy snaps, crushed
600ml carton double cream
75g (3oz) icing sugar, sifted
200g (7oz) raspberries

PER SLICE

427 cals; 37g fat (of which 21g saturates);
24g carbohydrate; 0.1g salt

1 Put the chocolate and golden syrup or glucose into a heatproof bowl with the amaretto, if you like. Set the bowl over a pan of gently simmering water, making sure the base of the bowl doesn't touch the water. Allow the chocolate to melt without stirring – otherwise it might seize up and become unworkable. Remove the bowl from the pan and cool until the chocolate is just warm.

2 Line the base and sides of a 20.5cm (8 inch) round tin with baking parchment. Sprinkle the brandy snap pieces over the bottom of the tin.

3 In a large bowl, whip the cream and icing sugar until the mixture just holds its shape. Using a metal spoon, gently fold the chocolate into the cream – do this in two stages.

4 Spoon half the mixture into the tin and level the surface. Sprinkle the raspberries over, cover with the remaining chocolate and cream mixture and smooth the top. Chill for 4 hours (see note).

5 Half an hour before serving, take the torte out of the fridge. Remove from the tin, peel off the parchment and put on a cake stand to serve.

NOTE
The texture of the torte becomes firmer the further ahead you make it. If you prefer a soft, moussey texture, make and chill no more than 1½ hours before serving.

ALMOND AND ORANGE TORTE

Preparation: 30 minutes
Cooking time: 1 hour 50 minutes, plus cooling

oil to grease
plain flour to dust
1 medium orange
3 medium eggs
225g (8oz) golden caster sugar
250g (9oz) ground almonds
½ tsp baking powder
icing sugar to dust
crème fraîche to serve

PER WEDGE

223 cals; 13g fat (of which 1g saturates);
22g carbohydrate; 0.1g salt

1 Oil and line, then oil and flour a 20.5cm (8 inch) springform cake tin. Put the whole orange into a small pan and cover with water. Bring to the boil, then cover and simmer for at least 1 hour or until tender (see notes). Remove from the water and leave to cool.

2 Cut the orange in half and remove the pips. Whiz in a food processor or blender to make a smooth purée.

3 Preheat the oven to 180°C (160°C fan oven) mark 4. Put the eggs and caster sugar into a bowl and whisk together until thick and pale. Fold in the almonds, baking powder and orange purée. Pour the mixture into the prepared tin.

4 Bake for 40–50 minutes until a skewer inserted into the centre comes out clean. Leave to cool in the tin.

5 Release the clasp on the tin and remove the cake. Carefully peel off the lining paper and put the cake on a serving plate. Dust with icing sugar, then cut into 12 wedges. Serve with crème fraîche.

TO STORE

Store in an airtight container. It will keep for up to three days.

NOTE

To save time, you can microwave the orange. Put it into a small heatproof bowl, cover with 100ml (3½fl oz) water and cook in a 900W microwave oven on full power for 10–12 minutes until soft.

LUXURY CHOCOLATE ORANGE TORTE

CUTS INTO 12 SLICES

Preparation: 30 minutes
Cooking time: 55 minutes–1 hour 5 minutes,
plus cooling

75g (3oz) unsalted butter, diced, plus
    extra to grease
100g (3½oz) plain chocolate (at least
    70% cocoa solids), broken into
    pieces
6 medium eggs
225g (8oz) golden caster sugar
150g (5oz) ground almonds, sifted
grated zest and juice of 1 orange
strawberries and raspberries to serve

PER SLICE
231 cals; 12g fat (of which 3g saturates);
25g carbohydrate; 0.1g salt

1 Preheat the oven to 190°C (170°C fan oven) mark 5.
  Grease a 20.5cm (8 inch) springform cake tin and line
  with greaseproof paper.

2 Melt the butter and chocolate in a heatproof bowl set
  over a pan of gently simmering water, making sure the
  base of the bowl doesn't touch the water. Remove the
  bowl from the pan and set aside to cool a little.

3 Put the eggs and sugar into a large bowl and mix
  with a hand-held electric whisk until the volume has
  tripled and the mixture is thick and foamy – it will take
  5–10 minutes. Add the ground almonds, orange zest
  and juice to the egg mixture, then gently fold together
  with a metal spoon.

4 Pour about two-thirds of the mixture into the
  prepared tin. Add the melted chocolate and butter to
  the remaining mixture and fold together. Add to the
  tin and swirl around just once or twice to create a
  marbled effect. Bake for 50 minutes–1 hour. Leave to
  cool in the tin.

5 Carefully remove the cake from the tin and slice.
  Serve with strawberries and raspberries.

TO STORE
Store in an airtight container. It will keep for up to
three days.

TIRAMISÙ TORTE

LONG CHILLING REQUIRED

Preparation: 40 minutes, plus chilling

Cooking time: 45 minutes, plus cooling and chilling

275g (10oz) amaretti biscuits, ratafias or macaroons
75g (3oz) unsalted butter, melted
700g (1½lb) mascarpone or cream cheese (at room temperature)
150g (5oz) caster sugar
3 medium eggs, separated
25g (1oz) plain flour, sifted
3 tbsp dark rum
½ tsp vanilla extract
175g (6oz) plain chocolate (at least 50% cocoa solids)
1 tbsp finely ground coffee
3 tbsp Tia Maria or other coffee liqueur

PER SLICE
682 cals; 50g fat (of which 30g saturates); 51g carbohydrate; 0.9g salt

1　Put the biscuits into a food processor and whiz until finely ground. Add the melted butter and stir until well mixed. Tip the crumb mixture into a 23cm (9 inch) springform cake tin and, using the back of a metal spoon, press evenly over the bottom and 4cm (1½ inch) up the sides to form a shell. Chill for about 1 hour until firm.

2　Preheat the oven to 200°C (180°C fan oven) mark 6. Using a wooden spoon or a hand-held electric whisk, beat the cheese until smooth. Add the sugar and beat again until smooth, then beat in the egg yolks. Transfer half of the mixture to another bowl and stir in the flour, rum and vanilla extract.

3　Melt the chocolate in a heatproof bowl set over a pan of gently simmering water, making sure the base of the bowl doesn't touch the water. Remove the bowl from the pan and cool slightly, then stir in the coffee and coffee liqueur. Stir into the remaining half of the cheese mixture.

4　Put the egg whites into a clean, grease-free bowl and whisk until soft peaks form, then fold half the egg whites into each flavoured cheese mixture. Spoon alternate mounds of the two mixtures into the biscuit case until it is full. Using a knife, swirl them together for a marbled effect.

5　Bake for 45 minutes. If necessary, lightly cover the top of the cake with foil if it appears to be browning too quickly. At this stage the torte will be soft in the middle.

6　Turn off the oven and leave the torte inside, with the door slightly ajar, until cool; it will firm up during this time. Chill for several hours.

SACHERTORTE

Preparation: 35 minutes

Cooking time: 45–55 minutes, plus cooling
and setting

175g (6oz) unsalted butter, at room
    temperature, plus extra to grease
175g (6oz) golden caster sugar
5 medium eggs, lightly beaten
3 tbsp cocoa powder
125g (4oz) self-raising flour
225g (8oz) plain chocolate (at least
    70% cocoa solids), broken into
    pieces, melted (see page 326) and
    cooled for 5 minutes
4 tbsp brandy
1 x quantity warm Rich Chocolate
    Ganache (see below)
12 lilac sugar-coated almonds, or
    50g (2oz) milk chocolate, melted

PER SLICE

496 cals; 33g fat (of which 20g saturates);
45g carbohydrate; 0.7g salt

1 Preheat the oven to 190°C (170°C fan oven) mark 5.
   Grease a 20.5cm (8 inch) springform cake tin and line
   with baking parchment.
2 Cream together the butter and sugar until pale and
   fluffy. Gradually beat in two-thirds of the beaten eggs –
   don't worry if the mixture curdles. Sift in the cocoa
   powder and 3 tbsp flour, then gradually beat in the
   remaining eggs. Fold in the remaining flour. Fold in the
   melted chocolate until evenly incorporated. Stir in
   2 tbsp brandy. Pour the mixture into the prepared tin.
3 Bake for 45 minutes. If necessary, loosely cover the top
   of the cake with foil if it appears to be browning too
   quickly. To test if done, insert a skewer into the centre
   of the cake – it should come out clean. Cool in the tin
   for 30 minutes, then turn out on to a wire rack and
   leave to cool completely.

4 Drizzle with the remaining brandy, then position the
   wire rack over a tray. Ladle the ganache over the top
   of the cake, letting it trickle down the sides. Using a
   palette knife, spread it evenly over the cake. Decorate
   with almonds or melted milk chocolate and leave for
   about 1 hour to set.

RICH CHOCOLATE GANACHE

Melt 175g (6oz) plain chocolate (at least 70% cocoa
solids), broken into pieces, with 75g (3oz) butter and
4 tbsp warmed double cream in a heatproof bowl set
over a pan of gently simmering water, making sure the
base of the bowl doesn't touch the water, stirring
occasionally. Stir the ganache until smooth.

TO STORE

Store in an airtight container. It will keep for up to
one week.

WHITE CHOCOLATE TORTE

LONG
CHILLING
REQUIRED

Preparation: about 50 minutes, plus chilling
and freezing
Cooking time: about 2 minutes, plus cooling

125g (4oz) unsalted butter
225g (8oz) ginger snaps or digestive
  biscuits, roughly broken
750g (1lb 11oz) white chocolate
568ml carton double cream
white Maltesers to decorate

PER SERVING
563 cals; 44g fat (of which 26g saturates);
40g carbohydrate; 0.5g salt

1 Line the base and sides of a 20.5 x 6.5cm (8 x 2½ inch) springform tin with non-stick baking parchment or greaseproof paper. Melt the butter in a pan. Whiz the biscuits in a food processor until finely crushed. Tip the crumbs into a bowl and stir in the melted butter. Spread evenly over the base of the prepared tin and press down. Chill for 15 minutes to set.

2 Chop 700g (1½lb) chocolate and combine with half the cream in a bowl set over a pan of barely simmering water, making sure the base of the bowl doesn't touch the water. Leave the chocolate to melt, but don't stir it – this might take as long as 30 minutes. Once melted, remove from the heat and stir until smooth, then leave to cool for 15 minutes or until just beginning to thicken, stirring occasionally. Don't allow it to cool completely or the cream won't fold in evenly.

3 In a separate bowl, whip the remaining cream until soft peaks form, then fold into the chocolate mixture. Pour over the biscuit base and chill for 3 hours.

4 Pull a vegetable peeler across the remaining white chocolate to make rough curls and scatter them over the torte, then arrange the Maltesers on top. Freeze for 15 minutes, then remove from the tin and serve.

FREEZING TIP
To freeze, complete the recipe up to one month ahead, then freeze the torte in its tin. When frozen, remove the torte from the tin and carefully wrap in clingfilm before returning to the freezer. To use, thaw overnight in the fridge, then put back in the freezer for 15 minutes before serving to make sure it's chilled.

REFRIGERATOR CAKE

Preparation: 10 minutes, plus chilling

Cooking time: 4 minutes

175g (6oz) unsalted butter, cut into
  8 pieces, plus extra to grease
200g (7oz) natural glacé cherries,
  halved
2 tbsp Kirsch
150g (5oz) dark chocolate with fruit,
  broken into pieces
200g (7oz) plain chocolate, broken
  into pieces
100g (3½oz) golden syrup
200g (7oz) digestive biscuits, roughly
  crushed (see page 298)

PER SLICE

411 cals; 24g fat (of which 14g saturates); 48g
carbohydrate; 0.6g salt

1 Grease a 20.5cm (8 inch) round tin and base-line with
   greaseproof paper. Put the cherries into a bowl, add
   the Kirsch and leave to soak.
2 Put all the chocolate, the butter and syrup into a large
   heatproof bowl and melt in a 900W microwave oven
   on medium for 2 minutes. Stir and cook for a further
   2 minutes or until the chocolate has melted.
   (Alternatively, put into a heatproof bowl set over a pan
   of simmering water, making sure the base of the bowl
   doesn't touch the water, and leave until melted.)

3 Add half the soaked cherries and all the biscuits to the
   chocolate, then stir together. Spoon into the prepared
   tin and level the surface.
4 Arrange the remaining cherries around the edge of
   the cake and chill for at least 15 minutes.
5 Cut into slices to serve.

TO STORE

Cover and store in the fridge. It will keep for up to
two weeks.

ITALIAN ICE CREAM CAKE

CUTS INTO 10 SLICES

Preparation: 30 minutes, plus freezing and softening

400g (14oz) fresh cherries, pitted and
  quartered
4 tbsp Amaretto liqueur
150ml (¼ pint) crème de cacao liqueur
200g (7oz) Savoiardi biscuits or sponge
  fingers
5 medium egg yolks
150g (5oz) golden caster sugar
450ml (¾ pint) double cream, lightly whipped
1 tbsp vanilla extract
75g (3oz) pistachio nuts or hazelnuts, roughly
  chopped
75g (3oz) plain chocolate (at least 70% cocoa
  solids), roughly chopped
2–3 tbsp cocoa powder
2–3 tbsp golden icing sugar

PER SLICE

522 cals; 33g fat (of which 15g saturates);
46g carbohydrate; 0.2g salt

1 Put the cherries and Amaretto into a bowl, stir, cover with clingfilm and put to one side. Pour the crème de cacao into a shallow dish. Quickly dip a sponge finger into the liqueur on one side only, then cut in half lengthways to separate the sugary side from the base. Repeat with each biscuit.

2 Double-line a deep 24 x 4cm (9½ x 1½ inch) round tin with clingfilm. Arrange the sugar-coated sponge finger halves, sugar-side down, on the bottom of the tin. Drizzle with any remaining crème de cacao.

3 Put the egg yolks and caster sugar into a bowl and whisk until pale, light and fluffy. Fold in the cream, vanilla extract, nuts, chocolate and cherries with Amaretto. Spoon on top of the sponge fingers in the tin and cover with the remaining sponge finger halves, cut-side down. Cover with clingfilm and freeze for at least 5 hours.

4 Upturn the cake on to a serving plate and remove the clingfilm. Sift cocoa powder and icing sugar over the cake and cut into slices. Before serving, leave at room temperature for 20 minutes if the weather is warm, 40 minutes at cool room temperature, or 1 hour in the fridge, to allow the cherries to thaw and the ice cream to become mousse-like.

NOTE
For a decorative top, use the tin to cut a template circle of greaseproof paper, then fold to make eight triangles. Cut these out. Put four on the cake and dust the uncovered cake with cocoa powder. Remove the triangles. Cover the cocoa with four triangles and dust the uncovered cake with icing sugar.

CHOCOLATE ICED MILLE FEUILLES

SERVES 12

Preparation: 45 minutes, plus chilling
and freezing
Cooking time: about 10 minutes, plus cooling

200g (7oz) plain chocolate, broken
   into pieces
300g (11oz) white chocolate, broken
   into pieces
450ml (¾ pint) double cream
2 tsp vanilla extract
2 medium egg whites
25g (1oz) icing sugar
sifted cocoa powder to dust

PER SERVING
430 cals; 32g fat (of which 20g saturates);
28g carbohydrate; 0.1g salt

1. Use a little water to dampen a 900g (2lb) loaf tin. Line with a double layer of clingfilm. Melt the plain chocolate in a bowl set over a pan of simmering water, making sure the base of the bowl doesn't touch the water. Cut out two sheets of baking parchment, each 45.5 x 33cm (18 x 13 inch). Spoon half the chocolate on to one sheet and spread it to the edges in a thin layer. Repeat with the remaining chocolate and baking parchment. Lift on to baking sheets and chill for 30 minutes to set.

2. Put the white chocolate into another bowl with 150ml (¼ pint) cream, then melt slowly over a pan of simmering water, as above. Leave to cool. In a separate bowl, whip the remaining cream with the vanilla extract until just holding its shape. Fold into the melted white chocolate.

3. Whisk the egg whites in a clean, grease-free bowl and gradually whisk in the icing sugar. Fold the egg whites into the white chocolate mixture.

4. Peel the plain chocolate from the paper and break into large pieces. Put a quarter into a freezerproof container for decoration and freeze overnight.

5. Spoon a quarter of the cream mixture into the lined tin and layer with a third of the remaining plain chocolate pieces. Repeat, finishing with the cream mixture. Cover with clingfilm and freeze overnight.

6. Transfer the torte and reserved chocolate to the fridge for 1 hour before serving. Turn out on to a serving plate and peel away the clingfilm. Break the reserved chocolate into smaller jagged pieces and arrange on top. Dust with cocoa powder and serve.

FREEZING TIP
To freeze, complete the recipe to the end of step 5 up to one month ahead. To use, complete the recipe.

BASIC PASTRY RECIPES

Shortcrust Pastry

MAKES 225G (8OZ)

Preparation: 10 minutes, plus chilling

225g (8oz) plain flour, plus extra to dust
pinch of salt
125g (4oz) unsalted butter, or half white vegetable fat and
  half butter, cut into pieces

PER 25G (1OZ)

110 cals; 6g fat (of which 3g saturates); 12g carbohydrate; 0.6g salt

1 Sift the flour and salt into a bowl, add the fat and mix
   lightly. Using your fingertips, rub the fat into the flour
   until the mixture resembles fine breadcrumbs.
2 Sprinkle 3–4 tbsp cold water evenly over the surface
   and stir with a round-bladed knife until the mixture
   begins to stick together in large lumps. If the dough
   seems dry, add a little extra water. With one hand,
   collect the dough together to form a ball.
3 Knead lightly on a lightly floured surface for a few
   seconds to form a smooth, firm dough; do not over-
   work. Form the pastry into a ball, wrap tightly in
   clingfilm and leave to rest in the fridge for at least
   30 minutes before rolling out. (This allows the pastry
   to 'relax' and prevents shrinkage when it is baked.)

NOTES

• To make the pastry in a food processor, put the flour
  and salt in the processor bowl with the butter. Whiz
  until the mixture resembles fine crumbs, then add the
  water. Process briefly, using the pulse button, until the
  mixture just comes together in a ball. Continue from
  step 3.

• Shortcrust pastry can be stored in the fridge for up to
  three days, or frozen.

VARIATIONS

Wholemeal pastry: Replace half the white flour with
wholemeal flour. A little extra water may be needed to
mix the dough.

Nut pastry: Replace 50g (2oz) flour with finely chopped
or ground walnuts, hazelnuts or almonds, adding them to
the rubbed-in mixture just before the cold water.

Cheese pastry: Stir in 3–4 tbsp freshly grated Parmesan
or 75g (3oz) finely grated Cheddar cheese and a small
pinch of mustard powder before adding the water.

Herb pastry: Stir in 3 tbsp finely chopped fresh herbs,
such as parsley, sage, thyme or rosemary, before adding
the water.

Sweet Shortcrust Pastry

MAKES 125G (4OZ)

Preparation: 10 minutes, plus chilling

125g (4oz) plain flour, plus extra to dust
pinch of salt
50g (2oz) unsalted butter, at room temperature, cut into
  pieces
2 medium egg yolks
50g (2oz) caster sugar

PER 25G (1OZ)

110 cals; 6g fat (of which 4g saturates); 14g carbohydrate; 0.5g salt

1 Sift the flour and salt into a mound on a clean surface.
   Make a large well in the centre and add the butter, egg
   yolks and sugar.
2 Using the fingertips of one hand, work the sugar,
   butter and egg yolks together until well blended.
3 Gradually work in all the flour to bind the mixture
   together.
4 Knead the dough gently on a lightly floured surface
   until smooth, then wrap in clingfilm and leave to rest in
   the fridge for at least 30 minutes before rolling out.

NOTE

This pastry can be stored in the fridge for up to three
days, or frozen.

Rich Shortcrust Pastry

MAKES 225G (8OZ)

Preparation: 10 minutes, plus chilling

125g (4oz) plain flour, plus extra to dust
pinch of salt
75g (3oz) unsalted butter or block margarine and lard, diced
1 tsp caster sugar
1 medium egg, beaten

PER 25G (1OZ)

120 cals; 5g fat (of which 2g saturates); 13g carbohydrate; 0.5g salt

1 Put the flour and salt into a bowl. Rub the fat into the flour until the mixture resembles fine breadcrumbs. Stir in the sugar.
2 Add the egg, stirring with a round-bladed knife until the ingredients begin to stick together in large lumps.
3 With one hand, collect the mixture together and knead lightly for a few seconds to give a firm, smooth dough. Form into a ball, wrap tightly in clingfilm and chill for 1 hour before using. Roll out the pastry on a lightly floured surface to make a sheet at least 5cm (2inch) larger than the tart tin or pie dish.
4 Bake at 200°C (180°C fan oven) mark 6, unless otherwise stated, until lightly browned.

Flaky (Rough Puff) Pastry

MAKES 225G (8OZ)

Preparation: 25 minutes, plus chilling

225g (8oz) plain flour, plus extra to dust
pinch of salt
175g (6oz) unsalted butter, chilled
1 tsp lemon juice

PER 25G (1OZ)

100 cals; 7g fat (of which 4g saturates); 9g carbohydrate; 0.6g salt

1 Sift the flour and salt together into a bowl. Cut the butter into 2cm (¾ inch) cubes and add to the flour. Mix lightly to coat the pieces of butter with flour.
2 Using a round-bladed knife, stir in 100ml (3½fl oz) chilled water together with the lemon juice to make a soft elastic dough. If the pastry is too dry, add a little extra water.
3 Turn out on to a lightly floured surface and lightly knead the dough until smooth.
4 Roll the pastry out to a neat rectangle, measuring 30.5 x 10cm (12 x 4 inch). Mark off three equal sections from top to bottom.
5 Fold the bottom third up and the top third down, then give the pastry a quarter turn, so that the folded edges are at the sides. Press the edges with a rolling pin to seal. Wrap in clingfilm and leave to rest in the fridge for 15 minutes.
6 Put the pastry on a lightly floured surface with the folded edges to the sides. Repeat the rolling, folding and turning sequence four more times. Wrap in clingfilm and leave to rest in the fridge for 30 minutes before rolling out.
7 Shape the rough puff pastry as required, then rest in the fridge for 30 minutes before baking.

NOTE
Rough puff pastry has the buttery flakiness of puff pastry, although it won't rise as much.

Puff Pastry

MAKES 450G (1LB)

Preparation: 40 minutes, plus chilling

450g (1lb) strong plain (bread) flour, plus extra to dust
pinch of salt
450g (1lb) unsalted butter, chilled
1 tbsp lemon juice

PER 25G (1OZ)
100 cals; 8g fat (of which 4g saturates); 7g carbohydrate; 0.6g salt

1 Sift the flour and salt together into a bowl. Cut off 50g (2oz) butter and flatten the remaining large block with a rolling pin to a slab, about 2cm (¾ inch) thick; put to one side.
2 Cut the 50g (2oz) butter into small pieces and rub into the flour, using your fingertips.
3 Using a round-bladed knife, stir in the lemon juice and enough chilled water – you will need about 300ml (½ pint) – to make a soft elastic dough.
4 Turn out on to a lightly floured surface and quickly knead the dough until smooth. Cut a cross through half the depth, then open out to form a star.
5 Roll out, keeping the centre four times as thick as the flaps. Put the slab of butter in the centre of the dough. Fold the flaps over the dough, envelope-style.
6 Press gently with a rolling pin and roll out to a rectangle, measuring 40.5 x 20.5cm (16 x 8 inch).
7 Fold the bottom third up and the top third down, keeping the edges straight. Wrap in clingfilm and leave to rest in the fridge for 30 minutes.
8 Put the pastry on a lightly floured surface with the folded edges to the sides. Repeat the rolling, folding, resting and turning sequence five times.
9 Shape the puff pastry as required, then rest in the fridge for about 30 minutes before baking.

NOTES

• If possible, the pastry should be made the day before it is to be used. It is not practical to make less than a 450g (1lb) flour weight quantity.

• Ready-made puff pastry is available fresh and frozen, so use this for convenience, if you prefer. Two 375g (13oz) packs would be roughly equivalent to this home-made quantity.

Hot Water Crust Pastry

MAKES 300G (11OZ)

Preparation: 10 minutes, plus resting

300g (11oz) plain flour
¼ tsp salt
65g (2½oz) white vegetable fat

PER 25G (1OZ)
80 cals; 3g fat (of which 1g saturates); 10g carbohydrate; 0.5g salt

1 Sift the flour and salt into a bowl and make a well in the middle.
2 Put the fat and 150ml (¼ pint) water in a small pan and heat slowly until the fat melts, then increase the heat and bring to the boil.
3 Pour the hot liquid into the flour well. Gradually lap the flour into the liquid, then beat together.
4 Lightly knead against the side of the bowl until smooth. Wrap the dough in a teatowel and leave to rest in a warm place for 20 minutes. Use the pastry while it is still warm and pliable.

NOTE

Any pastry not in use must be kept covered with a damp teatowel in a warm place (if exposed to air it will become dry and impossible to use).

Choux Pastry

MAKES A 2-EGG QUANTITY

Preparation: 10 minutes

65g (2½oz) plain flour
pinch of salt
50g (2oz) unsalted butter
2 medium eggs, lightly beaten

PER 25G (1OZ)

50 cals; 4g fat (of which 2g saturates); 3g carbohydrate; 0.4g salt

1 Sift the flour and salt on to a large sheet of greaseproof paper.
2 Pour 150ml (¼ pint) cold water into a medium pan, add the butter and melt over a low heat. Increase the heat and bring to a rolling boil.
3 Take off the heat, immediately tip in all the flour and beat vigorously, using a wooden spoon. Continue beating until the mixture is smooth and leaves the sides of the pan to form a ball; do not over-beat. Leave to cool slightly, for 1–2 minutes.
4 Gradually add the eggs, beating well between each addition, adding just enough to give a smooth dropping consistency. The choux pastry should be smooth and shiny. Use as required.

NOTE
For a sweeter pastry, add 1 tsp caster sugar with the flour and salt.

Pizza Base Dough

MAKES 1 LARGE OR 2 SMALL PIZZA BASES

Preparation: 5 minutes, plus rising

225g (8oz) strong plain (bread) flour, plus extra to dust
½ tsp sea salt
1 tsp fast-action dried yeast
1 tbsp extra virgin olive oil, plus extra to grease

PER 25G (1OZ)

60 cals; 1g fat (of which 0.3g saturates); 11g carbohydrate; 0.8g salt

1 Sift the flour and salt into a bowl and stir in the dried yeast. Make a well in the centre and gradually work in 150ml (¼ pint) warm water and the olive oil to form a soft dough.
2 Turn the pizza dough out on to a lightly floured surface and knead well for 8–10 minutes until smooth and elastic. (Alternatively, use a large food mixer fitted with a dough hook.)
3 Put into an oiled bowl, turn the dough once to coat the surface with oil and cover the bowl with clingfilm. Leave to rise in a warm place for about 1 hour until doubled in size.
4 Knock back the dough and shape as required.

NOTE
If preferred, use 15g (½oz) fresh yeast instead of fast-action dried yeast. Mix with 2 tbsp of the flour, a pinch of sugar and the warm water. Leave in a warm place for 10 minutes until frothy, then add to the rest of the flour and salt. Mix to a dough and continue as above.

TOPPINGS
Scatter one or two of the following on top of a basic cheese and tomato pizza:

- Bacon or pancetta bits, or slices of prosciutto
- Rocket leaves
- Dried chilli flakes
- Capers
- Sliced sun-dried tomatoes
- Pepperoni slices
- Roasted peppers
- Artichoke hearts, drained and quartered
- Sliced mushrooms

SPINACH AND FETA PIE

Preparation: 40 minutes

Cooking time: 45 minutes, plus cooling

1 tbsp vegetable oil

1 onion, peeled and finely chopped

1 garlic clove, peeled and crushed

1 tbsp cumin seeds

400g (14oz) baby leaf spinach

1.1kg (2½lb) waxy potatoes, such as
  Desirée, boiled in their skins until
  tender, cooled, peeled and sliced

2 x 200g packs vegetarian feta
  cheese, crumbled

2 medium eggs, beaten

50g (2oz) butter, melted, plus extra
  for greasing

200g pack filo pastry, thawed if
  frozen

salt and ground black pepper

PER SERVING

311 cals; 15g fat (of which 9g saturates);
33g carbohydrate; 1.7g salt

1 Heat the oil in a large pan and cook the onion for 10 minutes or until soft. Add the garlic and cumin and cook for 1–2 minutes. Add the spinach, cover and cook until the spinach has just wilted – 1–2 minutes. Tip into a bowl and leave to cool. Add the potatoes, cheese and eggs. Season and mix.

2 Preheat the oven to 200°C (180°C fan oven) mark 6. Lightly grease a 28cm (11 inch) tart tin with butter. Unroll the pastry and cut the sheets lengthways into three. Work with one-third of the strips at a time and cover the remainder with clingfilm. Lay a strip on the tin, starting from the middle so that half covers the tin and half hangs over the edge. Brush with melted butter, then lay another strip next to it, slightly overlapping, and brush again. Repeat, working quickly around the tin in a cartwheel shape.

3 Add the filling and level the surface. Fold in the overhanging pastry to cover the mixture, filling any gaps with leftover pastry. Drizzle with the remaining melted butter, then cook for 45 minutes or until golden.

NOTE
If you don't eat all the pie, it's just as delicious cold the next day or, if you prefer, warm it in the oven at 200°C (180°C fan oven) mark 6 for 15–20 minutes. Cover with foil if it starts to over-brown.

SALMON AND ASPARAGUS PIE

SERVES 6

Preparation: 40 minutes, plus 1½ hours chilling

Cooking time: 1 hour 10 minutes, plus cooling

275g (10oz) plain flour, plus extra to dust
200g (7oz) chilled butter, cubed
pinch of salt
1 large egg, beaten, plus 1 large egg, beaten, to glaze

FILLING

2 large eggs and 2 large yolks, beaten
200ml (7fl oz) crème fraîche
3 tbsp freshly chopped dill
450g (1lb) fresh salmon fillet, cut into wide strips,
    10cm (4 inch) long
200g (7oz) button mushrooms, sliced and fried in 25g (1oz)
    butter for 1–2 minutes, then cooled
150g (5oz) thick asparagus tips, blanched, drained and
    refreshed in iced water
salt and ground black pepper

PER SERVING

782 cals; 59g fat (of which 32g saturates); 37g carbohydrate; 0.8g salt

1 Whiz the flour, butter and salt in a food processor until the mixture resembles breadcrumbs. Add 1 egg and 2 tbsp cold water and pulse until the mixture just comes together. Knead lightly on a floured surface. Cut off one-third, wrap both pieces and chill for 30 minutes.

2 Preheat the oven to 200°C (180°C fan oven) mark 6. Roll out the larger piece of pastry to a 28cm (11 inch) round and line a 20.5cm (8 inch) loose-based deep tin. Bake the pastry case blind (see page 311) for 25 minutes at the first stage and then 5–10 minutes, using a little of the remaining egg to seal the pastry case

3 Remove from the oven and leave to cool. Put a baking tray in the oven to heat up.

4 To make the filling, mix the eggs and yolks, crème fraîche and dill, and season. Put half the fish in the pie case, arrange the vegetables on top and season. Top with the remaining fish and pour the crème fraîche mixture over to within 1cm (½ inch) of the top. Brush the rim with beaten egg. Cut the remaining pastry into a 25.5cm (10 inch) round, place on top and seal the edges. Brush with egg and make a steam hole. Bake the pie on the hot tray for 40 minutes or until golden and the filling is cooked.

NOTE

To check the pie is cooked, insert a skewer into the centre for 30 seconds – it should feel hot when you pull it out. Cool the pie in the tin for 1 hour to serve warm, or 3 hours to serve at room temperature.

CHICKEN AND MUSHROOM PIES

Preparation: 20 minutes, plus chilling

Cooking time: 55 minutes–1 hour 5 minutes, plus cooling

2 tbsp olive oil

1 leek, about 200g (7oz), finely sliced

2–3 garlic cloves, peeled and crushed

350g (12oz) boneless, skinless
   chicken thighs, cut into
   2.5cm (1 inch) cubes

200g (7oz) chestnut mushrooms,
   sliced

150ml (¼ pint) double cream

2 tbsp freshly chopped thyme

500g pack puff pastry, thawed if
   frozen

plain flour to dust

1 medium egg, beaten

salt and ground black pepper

PER SERVING

805 cals; 58g fat (of which 14g saturates);
49g carbohydrate; 1.2g salt

1 Heat the oil in a pan and fry the leek over a medium heat for 5 minutes to soften. Add the garlic and cook for 1 minute. Add the chicken pieces and continue to cook for 8–10 minutes. Add the mushrooms and cook for 5 minutes or until all the juices have disappeared.

2 Pour the cream into the pan and bring to the boil. Cook for 5 minutes to make a thick sauce. Add the thyme, then season well with salt and pepper. Tip into a bowl and leave to cool.

3 Roll out the pastry on a lightly floured surface until it measures 33 x 33cm (13 x 13 inch). Cut into four squares. Brush the edges with water and spoon the chicken mixture into the middle of each square. Bring each corner of the square up to the middle to make a parcel. Crimp the edges to seal, leaving a small hole in the middle. Brush the pies with beaten egg, put on a baking sheet and chill for 20 minutes.

4 Preheat the oven to 200°C (180°C fan oven) mark 6. Cook the pies for 30–40 minutes until golden.

VARIATION
For a vegetarian alternative, replace the chicken with 200g (7oz) cooked, peeled (or vacuum-packed) chestnuts, roughly chopped. Add another leek and increase the quantity of mushrooms to 300g (11oz).

CHICKEN AND BACON PIE

Preparation: 30 minutes

Cooking time: about 55 minutes

1 tbsp olive oil
4 chicken breasts, cut into 2.5cm (1 inch)
    cubes
1 medium onion, peeled and sliced
1 carrot, peeled and roughly chopped
50g (2oz) smoked streaky bacon, chopped
1 tbsp flour
200ml (7fl oz) chicken stock
100ml (3½fl oz) double cream
25g (1oz) frozen peas
1½ tsp wholegrain mustard
1 tbsp freshly chopped tarragon
175g (6oz) puff pastry, thawed if frozen
plain flour to dust
1 medium egg, beaten
salt and ground black pepper

PER SERVING

554 cals; 34g fat (of which 6g saturates);
24g carbohydrate; 1.3g salt

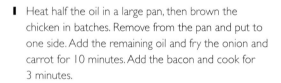

NOTE

For convenience, prepare ahead. Assemble the pie,
then cover and chill for up to two days. Brush with
beaten egg and complete the recipe.

1 Heat half the oil in a large pan, then brown the
chicken in batches. Remove from the pan and put to
one side. Add the remaining oil and fry the onion and
carrot for 10 minutes. Add the bacon and cook for
3 minutes.

2 Stir in the flour and cook for 1 minute. Gradually add
the stock, stirring well. Add the cream and return
the chicken and any juices to the pan. Simmer for
5 minutes or until the chicken is cooked.

3 Add the peas, mustard and tarragon, then check the
seasoning. Leave to cool a little.

4 Preheat the oven to 200°C (180°C fan oven) mark 6.
Put a pie funnel, if you have one, in the centre of a
1 litre (1¾ pint) pie dish or ovenproof casserole and
tip in the filling. Roll out the pastry on a lightly floured
surface to make a lid (make a slit for the pie funnel).
Brush the pastry edges with the egg, then lay the
pastry over the dish and trim with a sharp knife.
Seal and brush with beaten egg and cook for 25–30
minutes until golden.

STEAK AND KIDNEY PIE

Preparation: 40 minutes

Cooking time: about 1½ hours, plus cooling

700g (1½lb) stewing steak, cubed and seasoned
2 tbsp plain flour, plus extra to dust
3 tbsp vegetable oil
25g (1oz) butter
1 small onion, peeled and finely chopped
175g (6oz) ox kidney, cut into small pieces
150g (5oz) flat mushrooms, cut into large chunks
small pinch of cayenne pepper
1 tsp anchovy essence
350g (12oz) puff pastry, thawed if frozen
1 large egg, beaten with pinch of salt, to glaze
salt and ground black pepper

PER SERVING

565 cals; 36g fat (of which 8g saturates); 26g carbohydrate; 0.9g salt

1 Preheat the oven to 170°C (150°C fan oven) mark 3. Toss half the steak with half the flour. Heat the oil in a flameproof, non-stick casserole and add the butter. Fry the steak in batches until brown, remove and put to one side. Repeat with the remaining steak.

2 Add the onion and cook gently until soft. Return the steak to the casserole with 200ml (7fl oz) water, the kidney, mushrooms, cayenne and anchovy essence. Bring to the boil, then reduce the heat, cover and simmer for 5 minutes.

FREEZING TIP

To freeze, complete the recipe but do not glaze or bake. Wrap the uncooked pie and freeze. To use, thaw at cool room temperature overnight. Glaze the pastry and add 5–10 minutes to the cooking time, covering the pie with foil if the top starts to turn too brown.

3 Transfer to the oven and cook for 1 hour or until tender. The sauce should be syrupy. If not, transfer the casserole to the hob, remove the lid, bring to the boil and bubble for 5 minutes to reduce the liquid. Leave the steak mixture to cool.

4 Preheat the oven to 200°C (180°C fan oven) mark 6. Put the steak and kidney mixture into a 900ml (1½ pint) pie dish. Pile it high to support the pastry.

5 Roll out the pastry on a lightly floured surface to 5mm (¼ inch) thick. Cut off four to six strips, 1cm (½ inch) wide. Dampen the edge of the dish with cold water, then press the pastry strips on to the edge. Dampen the pastry rim and lay the sheet of pastry on top. Press the surfaces together, trim the edge and press down with the back of a knife to seal. Brush the pastry with the glaze and score with the back of a knife. Put the pie dish on a baking sheet and cook for 30 minutes or until the pastry is golden brown and the filling is hot to the centre.

WILD MUSHROOM PITHIVIERS

Preparation: 1 hour, plus chilling

Cooking time: about 1 hour, plus cooling

450g (1lb) wild mushrooms
300ml (½ pint) milk
200ml (7fl oz) double cream
2 garlic cloves, peeled and crushed
450g (1lb) floury potatoes, peeled and thinly sliced
freshly grated nutmeg
50g (2oz) butter
2 tsp freshly chopped thyme, plus fresh sprigs to
 garnish
2 x 500g packs puff pastry, thawed if frozen
plain flour to dust
1 large egg, beaten
salt and ground black pepper

PER SERVING

710 cals; 51g fat (of which 12g saturates); 58g carbohydrate;
1.2g salt

1 Rinse the mushrooms in cold running water to remove any grit, then pat dry with kitchen paper. Roughly slice.
2 Pour the milk and cream into a large heavy-based pan and add the garlic. Bring to the boil, then add the potatoes. Bring back to the boil, then reduce the heat and simmer gently, stirring occasionally, for 15–20 minutes until the potatoes are tender. Season with salt, pepper and nutmeg. Leave to cool.
3 Melt the butter in a large frying pan. When it's sizzling, add the mushrooms and cook over a high heat, stirring all the time, for 5–10 minutes until the mushrooms are cooked and the juices have evaporated completely. Season. Stir in the chopped thyme, then set aside to cool.

NOTE
For convenience, complete the recipe to the end of step 4, then cover and chill in the fridge overnight until ready to cook.

4 Roll out the pastry thinly on a lightly floured surface. Cut into eight rounds, approximately 12.5cm (5 inch) in diameter, for the tops, and eight rounds, approximately 11.5cm (4½ inch) in diameter, for the bases. Put the smaller pastry rounds on baking sheets and brush the edges with beaten egg. Put a large spoonful of the cooled potato mixture in the centre of each round, leaving a 1cm (½ inch) border around the edge. Top with a spoonful of the mushroom mixture, then cover with the pastry tops. Press the edges together well to seal. Chill for 30 minutes–1 hour.
5 Meanwhile, preheat the oven to 220°C (200°C fan oven) mark 7 and put two baking trays in to heat up. Use the back of a knife to scallop the edges of the pastry and brush the top with the remaining beaten egg. If you like, use a knife to decorate the tops of the pithiviers.
6 Put the pithiviers, on their baking sheets, on the preheated baking trays. Cook for 15–20 minutes until deep golden brown, swapping the trays around in the oven halfway through cooking. Serve immediately, garnished with thyme sprigs.

MOROCCAN FILO PIE

Preparation: 20 minutes

Cooking time: about 55 minutes

2 tbsp olive oil, plus extra to grease

1 medium onion, peeled and finely
    chopped

3 tsp ras el hanout spice

400g (14oz) spinach leaves, roughly
    chopped

2 x 400g tins green lentils, drained
    and rinsed

50g (2oz) pine nuts, toasted

300g (11oz) vegetarian feta,
    crumbled

2 tbsp each chopped fresh flat-leafed
    parsley and coriander

2 large eggs, beaten

270g pack filo pastry

PER SERVING

581 cals; 27g fat (of which 9g saturates);

57g carbohydrate; 0.7g salt

1 Heat 1 tbsp oil in a large pan over a low heat. Gently fry the onion and
   spice for 10 minutes until softened.

2 Add the spinach to the pan with a splash of water and cover. Cook for
   1–2 minutes until wilted. Stir in the lentils, then tip into a bowl to cool.

3 Preheat the oven to 180°C (160°C fan oven) mark 4 and put in a heavy
   baking sheet to heat up. Stir the pine nuts, feta, herbs and beaten eggs into
   the lentil mixture.

4 Lightly oil a 20.5 x 28cm (8 x 11 inch) dish. Cut the filo sheets to fit the
   dish. Brush a sheet of filo with oil and put in the bottom of the dish. Repeat
   with four more sheets. Cover with the lentil mixture. Lightly brush the
   remaining filo sheets with oil, then scrunch up and arrange on top. Put the
   dish on the hot baking sheet and bake for 30–40 minutes until golden. Take
   to the table and serve straight from the dish.

LEEK AND HAM GALETTE

Preparation: 30 minutes, plus chilling

Cooking time: 40 minutes, plus cooling

25g (1oz) butter, plus extra to grease

350g (12oz) medium leeks, trimmed and cut into
2cm (¾ inch) thick slices

25g (1oz) plain flour, plus extra to dust

50ml (2fl oz) milk

1 tbsp freshly chopped marjoram

50g (2oz) Gruyère cheese, cubed, plus 2 tbsp, grated

150g (5oz) cooked sliced ham, thickly shredded

225g (8oz) puff pastry, thawed if frozen

½ medium egg, beaten with a pinch of salt

salt and freshly ground black pepper

PER SERVING

395 cals; 25g fat (of which 6g saturates); 29g carbohydrate; 2g salt

1 Preheat the oven to 220°C (200°C fan oven) mark 7.
Grease a baking sheet. Cook the leeks in lightly salted
boiling water for 2–3 minutes until just beginning to
soften. Drain, keeping the cooking liquid to one side.
Plunge the leeks into cold water, drain and dry well on
kitchen paper.

2 Melt the butter in a pan, remove from the heat and
mix in the flour to form a smooth paste. Add 225ml
(8fl oz) leek water and the milk and stir until smooth.
Bring to the boil, then reduce the heat and simmer for
1–2 minutes. Remove from the heat, cover and leave
to cool for 20 minutes or until cold. Add the
marjoram, leeks, cubed cheese and ham and season.

3 Roll out the pastry on a lightly floured surface to a
30.5 x 33cm (12 x 13 inch) rectangle. Cut into two
rectangles, one 15 × 30.5cm (6 × 12 inch) and the
other 18 x 30.5cm (7 x 12 inch). Put the smaller piece
on to the baking sheet. Spoon on the ham mixture,
leaving a 2cm (¾ inch) border all the way around.
Brush the border with beaten egg. Cover the filling
with the larger pastry rectangle and press the edges
together. Cut slashes in the top of the pastry to
prevent the filling seeping out. Crimp the edges to seal,
then cover and freeze for 20 minutes or until firm.
Remove from the freezer, brush again with the beaten
egg and sprinkle with the grated cheese. Bake for
20–30 minutes until brown and crisp. Serve hot.

FREEZING TIP

To freeze, cover the uncooked galette in clingfilm
and freeze on the baking sheet. When firm,
remove from the baking tray. Wrap in baking
parchment, and then in clingfilm. To use, thaw for
3 hours at cool room temperature on baking
parchment. Preheat the oven to 220°C (200°C
fan oven) mark 7 and put a baking tray in the
oven to heat. Brush the galette with beaten egg
and sprinkle with cheese. Put the galette on the
hot tray (this will keep the pastry base crisp) and
bake for 40 minutes.

GOAT'S CHEESE PARCELS

Preparation: 45 minutes, plus chilling

Cooking time: 10 minutes, plus cooling

125g (4oz) fresh spinach leaves

2 tbsp sunflower oil

1 onion, peeled and finely chopped

1 large garlic clove, peeled and
  chopped

250g (9oz) soft goat's cheese

275g (10oz) filo pastry, thawed if
  frozen

50g (2oz) butter, melted

sesame seeds to sprinkle

salt and ground black pepper

**PER SERVING (2 PARCELS PER
SERVING)**

345 cals; 22g fat (of which 12g saturates);
26g carbohydrate; 0.8g salt

1 Plunge the spinach into a pan of boiling water, bring back to the boil for 1 minute, then drain and refresh under very cold water. Squeeze out all the excess liquid and chop finely.

2 Heat the oil in a pan, add the onion and garlic and cook until translucent, then leave to cool. Combine the spinach, onion mixture and goat's cheese in a bowl and season generously.

3 Cut the pastry into twenty-four 12.5cm (5 inch) squares. Brush one square with melted butter, cover with a second square and brush with more butter. Put to one side and cover with a damp teatowel. Repeat with the remaining squares, to make twelve sets.

4 Put a dessertspoonful of the filling on each square and join up the corners to form a parcel. Brush with a little more butter, sprinkle with sesame seeds and chill for 20 minutes. Meanwhile, preheat the oven to 220°C (200°C fan oven) mark 7. Bake the parcels for about 5 minutes until the pastry is crisp and browned.

CHESTNUT AND BUTTERNUT FILO PARCELS

SERVES 4

Preparation: 40 minutes

Cooking time: 45–50 minutes, plus cooling

½ tbsp olive oil, plus extra to grease

75g (3oz) butter

½ onion, peeled and finely chopped

5 fresh rosemary sprigs

½ small butternut squash, peeled and
    finely chopped

1 celery stalk, finely chopped

½ firm pear, peeled, cored and finely
    chopped

100g (3½oz) cooked, peeled (or
    vacuum-packed) chestnuts, roughly
    chopped

1 slice walnut bread, about 50g (2oz),
    cut into small cubes

8 sheets filo pastry, about 30.5 x
    20.5cm (12 x 8 inch) each

50g (2oz) cream cheese

salt and ground black pepper

PER SERVING

408 cals; 22g fat (of which 13g saturates); 49g
carbohydrate; 0.5g salt

1 Heat the oil and 15g (½oz) butter in a medium pan, add the onion and fry gently for 10 minutes. Finely chop 1 rosemary sprig and add to the pan, along with the squash. Continue to cook for 5 minutes or until everything is soft and golden. Add the celery and pear and cook for 1–2 minutes. Add the chestnuts, season and mix well. Add the bread to the pan, mix everything together, then set aside to cool.

2 Preheat the oven to 200°C (180°C fan oven) mark 6. Lightly grease a baking sheet. Melt the remaining butter in a pan. Brush one sheet of filo pastry with the melted butter and layer another sheet of pastry on top, diagonally. Put a quarter of the chestnut mixture in the centre of the pastry and dot with a quarter of the cream cheese. Brush the edges of the pastry with a little more butter, bring the edges up and over the filling and pinch together tightly to make a parcel. Repeat to make three more parcels.

3 Put the parcels on the baking sheet and cook for 25–30 minutes until the pastry is golden and the filling is piping hot; 5 minutes before the end of the cooking time, put a rosemary sprig into the top of each parcel. Serve hot.

FREEZING TIP
To freeze, complete the recipe to the end of step 2, put the parcels in a freezerproof container and freeze for up to one month. To use, put the frozen parcels on a lightly greased baking sheet and complete the recipe.

SAUSAGE ROLLS

MAKES 28

Preparation: 25 minutes

Cooking time: 30 minutes

450g (1lb) puff pastry, thawed if
    frozen
plain flour to dust
450g (1lb) pork sausagemeat
milk to brush
beaten egg to glaze

PER SAUSAGE ROLL

119 cals; 9g fat (of which 2g saturates);
8g carbohydrate; 0.4g salt

VARIATION
Add 1 hot red chilli, deseeded
and finely chopped, 1 tbsp
freshly grated ginger and a
handful of chopped fresh
coriander leaves to the pork
sausagemeat.

1 Preheat the oven to 220°C (200°C fan oven) mark 7. Roll out half the
  pastry on a lightly floured surface to a 40.5 x 20.5cm (16 x 8 inch)
  rectangle; cut lengthways into two strips.

2 Divide the sausagemeat into four, dust with flour and form two portions
  into rolls, the length of the pastry. Lay a sausagemeat roll on each strip of
  pastry. Brush the pastry edges with a little milk, fold one side of the pastry
  over and press the long edges together to seal. Repeat with the remaining
  pastry and sausagemeat. Trim the ends.

3 Brush the pastry with beaten egg to glaze and cut each roll into 5cm
  (2 inch) lengths. Make two or three slits in the top of each one.

4 Transfer to a baking sheet and cook for 15 minutes. Lower the oven setting
  to 180°C (160°C fan oven) mark 4 and cook for a further 15 minutes.
  Transfer to a wire rack. Serve hot or cold.

CORNISH PASTIES

Preparation: 30 minutes

Cooking time: 1¼ hours

450g (1lb) stewing steak, trimmed
   and cut into very small pieces
175g (6oz) potato, peeled and diced
175g (6oz) swede, peeled and diced
1 onion, peeled and chopped
1 tbsp freshly chopped thyme
1 tbsp freshly chopped parsley
1 tbsp Worcestershire sauce
Shortcrust Pastry (see page 126),
   made with 500g (1lb 2oz) plain
   flour and 250g (9oz) butter
plain flour to dust
25g (1oz) butter
1 medium egg, beaten, to glaze
salt and ground black pepper
lettuce and tomato salad to serve

PER SERVING

756 cals; 42g fat (of which 25g saturates);
74g carbohydrate; 1.1g salt

1 Preheat the oven to 220°C (200°C fan oven) mark 7. Put the meat into a bowl with the potato, swede and onion. Add the chopped herbs, Worcestershire sauce and seasoning, then mix well.

2 Divide the pastry into six and roll out each piece thinly on a lightly floured surface to a 20cm (8 inch) round. Spoon the filling on to one half of each round and top with a small knob of butter.

3 Brush the edges of the pastry with water, then fold the uncovered side over to make pasties. Press the edges firmly together to seal and crimp them. Make a slit in the top of each pasty. Put on a baking sheet.

4 Brush the pastry with beaten egg to glaze and bake for 15 minutes. Lower the oven setting to 170°C (150°C fan oven) mark 3 and bake for a further 1 hour to cook the filling. Serve the pasties warm or cold with a lettuce and tomato salad.

QUICK CARAMELISED ONION AND GOAT'S CHEESE TART

SERVES 4

Preparation: 20 minutes

Cooking time: about 50 minutes

200g (7oz) ready-made shortcrust pastry

plain flour to dust

1 tbsp olive oil

2 red onions and 1 medium white onion,
  peeled and finely chopped

1 tbsp balsamic vinegar

1 tbsp light muscovado sugar

1 tbsp fresh oregano leaves, finely chopped

50g (2oz) goat's cheese, roughly chopped

2 medium eggs, beaten

200ml (7fl oz) double cream

salt and ground black pepper

PER SERVING

627 cals; 34g fat (of which 17g saturates);

210g carbohydrate; 1g salt

1 Preheat the oven to 200°C (180°C fan oven) mark 6.
   Roll out the pastry on a lightly floured surface to the
   thickness of a £1 coin. Use to line a 20.5cm (8 inch)
   diameter, 2.5cm (1 inch) deep, fluted quiche tin and
   prick the base with a fork. Chill for 30 minutes. Bake
   blind (see page 311) for 10–12 minutes until pastry is
   set, then remove the beans and paper and bake for a
   further 10 minutes until the base feels sandy to the
   touch. Take out of the oven and set aside. Lower the
   oven setting to 150°C (130°C fan oven) mark 2.

NOTES

- Onions take a good 45 minutes to caramelise
  over a low heat, but chopping them finely and
  adding a touch of sugar and balsamic vinegar
  speeds up the process dramatically.

- You can make this recipe even faster by using a
  ready-cooked tart case.

FREEZING TIP

To freeze, complete the recipe and cool completely
in the tin. Wrap in clingfilm and freeze for up to
three months. To use, thaw in the fridge overnight,
then serve at room temperature, or heat for
25 minutes in an oven preheated to 150°C (130°C
fan oven) mark 2.

2 Meanwhile, heat the oil in a pan. Add the onions and
   fry gently for 10 minutes. Turn up the heat, add the
   vinegar and sugar and cook for 10 minutes, stirring
   until the onions are golden. Add a little water if the
   pan dries out. Stir in most of the oregano.

3 Spoon the onion mixture into the pastry case and dot
   the cheese on top. Lightly beat the eggs, cream and
   seasoning in a small bowl. Pour over the onions, then
   use a fork to lift some onions to the surface. Sprinkle
   the remaining oregano over the surface, then cook for
   30 minutes until just set. Serve warm or at room
   temperature.

ROASTED VEGETABLE AND ROCKET TARTLETS

Preparation: 15 minutes

Cooking time: 5–7 minutes

375g pack ready-rolled puff pastry
plain flour to dust
1 medium egg, beaten
2 tbsp coarse sea salt
300g (11oz) vegetable antipasti in
   olive oil (such as mixed roasted
   peppers, artichokes and onions)
a little olive oil, if needed
2 tbsp balsamic vinegar
190g tub red pepper hummus
50g (2oz) wild rocket
salt and ground black pepper

PER SERVING
371 cals; 26g fat (of which 1g saturates); 30g
carbohydrate; 1.1g salt

1 Preheat the oven to 220°C (200°C fan oven) mark 7. Unroll the puff pastry on a lightly floured surface and cut it into six equal-sized squares.

2 Put the pastry squares on a large baking sheet and prick each one all over with a fork. Brush all over with beaten egg and sprinkle the edges with sea salt. Cook for 5–7 minutes or until the pastry is golden brown and cooked through.

3 Pour off 4 tbsp olive oil from the antipasti into a bowl (top it up with a little more olive oil if there's not enough in the antipasti jar). Add the balsamic vinegar, season well with salt and pepper and mix well, then put to one side.

4 To serve, divide the hummus among the pastry bases, spreading it over each. Put the bases on individual plates and spoon the antipasti over each – there's no need to be neat.

5 Whisk the balsamic vinegar dressing together. Add the rocket leaves and toss to coat, then pile a small handful of leaves on top of each tartlet.

NOTE
For convenience, make the tartlets to the end of step 2. Cool on a wire rack, then store in an airtight container for up to two days. To use, complete the recipe.

PRAWN TARTLETS

Preparation: 50 minutes

Cooking time: 1¼–1½ hours, plus cooling

30 raw large prawns, shells on, about 400g (14oz) total
  weight
4 tbsp olive oil
2 shallots, peeled and finely chopped
2 garlic cloves, peeled and roughly chopped
1 bay leaf
150ml (¼ pint) brandy
150ml (¼ pint) white wine
400g can chopped tomatoes
2 tbsp freshly chopped tarragon
175g (6oz) celeriac, peeled and chopped
125g (4oz) carrots, peeled and chopped
175g (6oz) leeks (white part only), roughly chopped
2 tbsp vegetable oil
150ml (¼ pint) double cream
grated zest of ½ lemon
225g (8oz) puff pastry, thawed if frozen
plain flour to dust
salt and ground black pepper
fresh tarragon sprigs to garnish
celeriac and carrots, shredded, blanched and dressed with
  lemon juice and olive oil to serve

PER SERVING

489 cals; 34g fat (of which 10g saturates); 21g carbohydrate; 1.4g salt

NOTE

For convenience, prepare ahead. Complete the recipe
to the end of step 4. Cover the prawns, vegetables and
pastry separately and chill overnight. To use, complete
the recipe.

1 Cook the prawns in a pan of lightly salted boiling
   water for 1 minute until the shells are pink. Plunge into
   a bowl of cold water to cool. Remove the heads and
   shells and put to one side. Devein the prawns, then
   cover and chill.

2 Heat the olive oil in a large pan, add the shallots and
   cook gently for 5 minutes or until soft. Add the garlic,
   bay leaf and prawn heads and shells. Cook over a high
   heat for 1 minute, then add the brandy. (If you're
   cooking over gas, take care, as the brandy may ignite.)
   Allow the liquid to reduce by half, then add the wine.
   Bring to the boil and bubble until reduced by half, then
   add the tomatoes and season. Add 1 tbsp tarragon.
   Cook over a medium-low heat for 20 minutes. Put a
   colander over a large bowl, pour the contents of the
   pan into the colander and push through as much liquid
   as possible. Put the liquid to one side and discard the
   heads and shells.

3 Put the celeriac, carrots and leeks in a food processor
   and pulse until finely chopped. Heat the vegetable oil
   in a frying pan, add the vegetables and cook quickly for
   2 minutes (don't allow them to colour). Add the
   prawn and tomato liquid and the cream, bring to the
   boil and bubble for 10–15 minutes until thick. Season
   and stir in the remaining tarragon and the lemon zest.
   Leave to cool.

4 Preheat the oven to 200°C (180°C fan oven) mark 6.
   Roll out the pastry on a lightly floured surface and use
   to line six 4cm (1½ inch) diameter (at base) brioche
   tins. Bake blind (see page 311), then remove from the
   oven and leave to cool.

5 Divide the vegetable mixture among the pastry cases
   and top each with five prawns. Put back in the oven
   for 10–15 minutes until hot to the centre. Season with
   pepper; garnish with tarragon and serve with a salad of
   finely shredded celeriac and carrots.

FREEZING TIP
To freeze, complete the recipe to the end of step 4.
Pack the pastry, prawns and vegetables separately
and freeze for up to one month. To use, thaw at cool
room temperature then complete the recipe.

QUICHE LORRAINE

SERVES 8

Preparation: 35 minutes, plus chilling

Cooking time: 1 hour

Shortcrust Pastry (see page 126),
  made with 200g (7oz) plain flour,
  pinch of salt, 100g (3½oz) chilled
  butter and 1 large egg
plain flour to dust

FILLING
5 large eggs
225g (8oz) unsmoked streaky bacon,
  rind removed
40g (1½oz) butter
125g (4oz) shallots, onions or spring
  onions, peeled and finely chopped
400g (14oz) crème fraîche
100g (3½oz) Gruyère cheese, grated
salt and ground black pepper
crispy bacon and fried spring onions
  to garnish

PER SERVING
595 cals; 50g fat (of which 29g saturates);
22g carbohydrate; 1.5g salt

1   Preheat the oven to 200°C (180°C fan oven) mark 6.
    Roll out the pastry thinly on a lightly floured surface and
    use to line a 23cm (9 inch), 3cm (1¼ inch) deep, loose-
    based tart tin. Bake the pastry case blind (see page 311).
    Meanwhile, lightly whisk the eggs for the filling. Use a
    little to brush the inside of the pastry case and return it
    to the oven for 5 minutes to seal any cracks. Lower the
    oven setting to 190°C (170°C fan oven) mark 5.

2   Cut the bacon into 5mm (¼ inch) strips. Put the
    bacon in a pan of cold water and bring to the boil.
    Drain, then refresh under cold water and dry on
    kitchen paper.

3   Melt the butter in a frying pan, add the shallots or
    onions and cook for 1 minute. Add the bacon and
    cook, stirring, until brown.

4   Mix the eggs with the crème fraîche and cheese and
    season. Put the bacon mixture in the pastry case and
    spoon the crème fraîche mixture on top (see note).
    Cook for 30–35 minutes until golden and just set.
    Cool for 10 minutes before serving. Garnish with
    bacon and fried spring onions.

NOTE
Fill the pastry case as full as possible. You may find
you have a little mixture left, as flan tins vary in size.

BROCCOLI, GORGONZOLA AND WALNUT QUICHE

SERVES 6

Preparation: 15 minutes, plus chilling

Cooking time: about 1 hour

400g (14oz) shortcrust pastry
plain flour to dust
150g (5oz) broccoli florets
100g (3½oz) crumbled gorgonzola
2 medium eggs plus 1 egg yolk
300ml (½ pint) double cream
25g (1oz) roughly chopped walnut
   halves
salt and ground black pepper

PER SERVING

683 cals; 57g fat (of which 27g saturates);
33g carbohydrate; 0.9g salt

1 Preheat the oven to 200°C (180°C fan oven)
   mark 6. Roll out the pastry on a lightly floured surface
   until the thickness of a £1 coin, then use to line a
   23cm (9 inch) × 2.5cm (1 inch) deep fluted tart tin.
   Prick the base all over and chill for 15 minutes. Bake
   blind (see page 311) for 20 minutes, then remove the
   beans and paper and bake for the last 5 minutes of
   the cooking. Lower the oven setting to 150°C
   (130°C fan oven) mark 2.

2 Cook the broccoli in boiling water for 3 minutes, then
   drain and dry on kitchen paper. Arrange the broccoli
   in the pastry case and dot with the gorgonzola. Whisk
   together the eggs and egg yolk, cream and seasoning,
   then pour into the case. Scatter the walnut halves
   over the surface.

3 Cook the quiche for 40 minutes or until the filling is
   set. Serve warm or at room temperature.

FREEZING TIP
To freeze, complete the recipe up to one month in
advance. Cool in the tin, then wrap in clingfilm and
freeze. To serve, thaw completely, then serve
at room temperature, or gently reheat for
20 minutes in a preheated 150°C (130°C fan
oven) mark 2 oven.

RUSTIC BLACKBERRY AND APPLE PIE

SERVES 6

Preparation: 25 minutes

Cooking time: 40 minutes

500g (1lb 2oz) eating apples,
quartered, cored and cut into
chunky wedges

300g (11oz) blackberries

75g (3oz) golden caster sugar, plus
1 tbsp to sprinkle

¼ tsp ground cinnamon

juice of 1 small lemon

butter to grease

plain flour to dust

450g (1lb) ready-made shortcrust
pastry

PER SERVING

372 cals; 19g fat (of which 11g saturates);
49g carbohydrate; 0.4g salt

1 Preheat the oven to 200°C (180°C fan oven) mark 6. Put the apples, blackberries, 75g (3oz) sugar, the cinnamon and lemon juice into a bowl and toss together, making sure the sugar dissolves in the juice.

2 Grease a 25.5cm (10 inch) enamel or metal pie dish. Using a lightly floured rolling pin, roll out the pastry on a large sheet of baking parchment to a 30.5cm (12 inch) circle. Lift up the paper, upturn the pastry on to the pie dish and peel away the paper.

3 Put the prepared fruit in the centre of the pie dish and fold the pastry edges up and over the fruit. Sprinkle with the remaining sugar and bake for 40 minutes or until the fruit is tender and the pastry golden.

CLASSIC APPLE PIE

Preparation: 20 minutes

Cooking time: 35–40 minutes

900g (2lb) cooking apples, peeled, cored and sliced

50g (2oz) caster sugar, plus extra to sprinkle

Sweet Shortcrust Pastry (see page 126), made with 225g (8oz) plain flour, a pinch of salt, 100g (3½oz) chilled butter and 1 large egg

flour to dust

cream to serve

PER SERVING

268 cals; 11g fat (of which 4g saturates); 43g carbohydrate; 0.4g salt

1 Preheat the oven to 190°C (170°C fan oven) mark 7.

2 Layer the apples and sugar in a 1.1 litre (2 pint) pie dish. Sprinkle with 1 tbsp water.

3 Roll out the pastry on a lightly floured surface to a round 2.5cm (1 inch) larger than the pie dish. Cut off a strip the width of the rim of the dish, dampen the rim of the dish and press on the strip. Dampen the pastry strip and cover with the pastry circle, pressing the edges together well. Decorate the edge of the pastry and make a slit in the centre to allow steam to escape.

4 Bake for 35–40 minutes until the pastry is lightly browned. Sprinkle with caster sugar before serving with cream.

NOTE
Apple pie is also great served cold, with vanilla ice cream.

PLUM AND CARDAMOM PIE

SERVES 6

Preparation: 15 minutes
Cooking time: 30 minutes, plus cooling

250g (9oz) ready-rolled sweet
    shortcrust pastry
plain flour to dust
900g (2lb) mixed yellow and red
    plums, halved, stoned and
    quartered
2–3 green cardamom pods, split
    open, seeds removed and crushed
    or chopped
50–75g (2–3oz) caster sugar, plus
    extra to sprinkle
beaten egg or milk to glaze

PER SERVING
275 cals; 12g fat (of which 4g saturates);
41g carbohydrate; 0.4g salt

1 Preheat the oven at 220°C (200°C fan oven) mark 7 and put a flat baking sheet in to heat up. Roll out the pastry on a lightly floured surface a little thinner into a 30.5cm (12 inch) circle. Put it on a floured baking sheet, without a lip if possible.
2 Pile the fruit on to the pastry and sprinkle with the cardamom seeds and sugar (if the plums are tart you'll need all of it; less if they are ripe and sweet). Fold in the pastry edges and pleat together.
3 Brush the pastry with beaten egg or milk and sprinkle with sugar. Put on the preheated sheet and bake for 30 minutes or until the pastry is golden brown and the plums just tender. The juices will begin to bubble from the pie as it cooks.
4 Leave to cool for 10 minutes, then carefully loosen the pastry around the edges. Cool for another 20 minutes, then transfer very carefully to a serving plate. Sprinkle with a little sugar and serve warm.

RHUBARB AND CINNAMON PIE

Preparation: 15 minutes, plus chilling

Cooking time: 50 minutes

175g (6oz) plain flour, plus extra to
    dust
125g (4oz) butter, plus extra to
    grease
150g (5oz) golden caster sugar, plus
    extra to sprinkle
700g (1½lb) rhubarb, cut into bite-
    size chunks
2 tbsp cornflour
½ tsp ground cinnamon
a little milk to glaze

PER SERVING

379 cals; 14g fat (of which 11g saturates);
55g carbohydrate; 0.3g salt

1 Put the flour, butter and 25g (1oz) sugar into a food processor and whiz until the pastry comes together. (Alternatively, rub the butter into the flour in a large bowl by hand until it resembles fine crumbs. Stir in the sugar. Bring together and knead very briefly to form a ball.) If the dough is slightly sticky, roll it in some flour. Chill for 20 minutes.

2 Preheat the oven to 200°C (180°C fan oven) mark 6. Grease a 23cm (9 inch) round ovenproof dish with sides at least 5cm (2 inch) deep. Roll out the pastry on a lightly floured surface to a large circle, leaving the edges uneven. It should be large enough to line the dish and to allow the edges of the pastry to drape over the sides.

3 Toss the rhubarb in the remaining sugar, the cornflour and cinnamon and spoon into the dish. Bring the pastry edges up and over the fruit, leaving a gap in the centre. Glaze with milk and sprinkle with sugar.

4 Put on a baking sheet and bake for 50 minutes or until the pastry is golden brown and the juice is bubbling up. Serve hot.

VARIATION
Add the grated zest of 1 orange instead of the ground cinnamon.

SUGAR-CRUSTED FRUIT PIE

SERVES 4

Preparation: 30 minutes, plus chilling

Cooking time: about 40 minutes, plus cooling

75g (3oz) hazelnuts
350g (12oz) cherries, stoned
75g (3oz) caster sugar, plus 2 tbsp
175g (6oz) plain flour, plus extra
    to dust
125g (4oz) butter
275g (10oz) cooking apples, peeled,
    cored and quartered

PER SERVING

673 cals; 38g fat (of which 17g saturates);
79g carbohydrate; 0.5g salt

1 Spread the hazelnuts over a baking sheet. Toast under a hot grill until golden brown, turning them frequently. Put the hazelnuts in a clean teatowel and rub off the skins. Leave to cool. Put the cherries into a bowl with 25g (1oz) caster sugar. Cover and set aside.

2 For the hazelnut pastry, put 50g (2oz) hazelnuts into a food processor with the flour and pulse to a powder. Remove and set aside. In the food processor, whiz the butter with 50g (2oz) sugar. Add the flour mixture and pulse until it forms a dough. Turn out on to a lightly floured surface and knead lightly, then wrap and chill for 30 minutes. If the pastry cracks, just work it together.

3 Preheat the oven to 180°C (160°C fan oven) mark 4. Cut the apples into small chunks and put into a 900ml (1½ pint) oval pie dish. Spoon the cherries on top. Roll out the pastry on a lightly floured surface to about 5mm (¼ inch) thick. Cut into 1cm (½ inch) strips. Dampen the edge of the pie dish with a little water and press a few of the strips on to the rim to cover it. Dampen the pastry rim. Put the remaining strips over the cherries to create a lattice pattern.

4 Brush the pastry with water and sprinkle with the extra sugar. Bake for 30–35 minutes until the pastry is golden. Leave to cool for 15 minutes.

5 Chop the remaining toasted hazelnuts and sprinkle over the tart. Serve warm.

PECAN PIE

SERVES 8

Preparation: 25 minutes, plus chilling

Cooking time: 1 hour 10 minutes, plus cooling

Sweet Shortcrust Pastry (see page 126) made with 175g (6oz) plain flour, 75g (3oz) chilled butter, 50g (2oz) icing sugar and 1 medium egg in place of the egg yolks

plain flour to dust

ice cream to serve

FILLING

125g (4oz) butter

4 tbsp clear honey

25g (1oz) caster sugar

75g (3oz) dark soft brown sugar

3 tbsp double cream

grated zest of 1 small lemon

1 tsp vanilla extract

175g (6oz) pecan nuts

PER SERVING

549 cals; 40g fat (of which 16g saturates); 45g carbohydrate; 0.4g salt

1   Roll out the pastry on a lightly floured surface to a 30.5cm (12 inch) diameter circle and use to line a 20.5cm (8 inch) diameter, 2.5cm (1 inch) deep, loose-based fluted tart tin. Put the tin on a baking sheet and chill for 20 minutes. Meanwhile, preheat the oven to 200°C (180°C fan oven) mark 6. Line the pastry case with greaseproof paper and baking beans and bake for 15 minutes. Remove the paper and beans, then return the pastry case to the oven for a further 10 minutes. Lower the oven setting to 150°C (130°C fan oven) mark 2.

2   To make the filling, melt the butter with the honey and sugars over a low heat, bring to the boil without stirring and bubble for 2–3 minutes. Remove from the heat, stir in the cream, lemon zest, vanilla extract and pecan nuts and leave to cool for 15 minutes.

3   Pour the pecan mixture into the pastry case. Bake for 40 minutes or until the mixture begins to bubble in the middle (cover with foil if it appears to be browning too quickly). Serve warm with ice cream.

LEMON MERINGUE PIE

SERVES 8

Preparation: 30 minutes, plus chilling

Cooking time: about 1 hour, plus cooling and standing

Sweet Shortcrust Pastry (see page 126),
  made with 225g (8oz) plain flour, pinch
  of salt, 2 tbsp caster sugar, 150g (5oz)
  butter, cut into pieces, 1 medium egg yolk
  and 3 tbsp cold water
plain flour to dust
a little beaten egg to seal the pastry case

FILLING AND TOPPING

7 medium eggs, 4 separated, at room
  temperature
finely grated zest of 3 lemons
175ml (6fl oz) freshly squeezed lemon juice
  (about 4 lemons), strained
400g can condensed milk
150ml (¼ pint) double cream
225g (8oz) golden icing sugar

PER SERVING

692 cals; 36g fat (of which 21g saturates); 83g
carbohydrate; 0.6g salt

1 Roll out the pastry on a lightly floured surface and use to line a 23cm (9 inch), 4cm (1½ inch) deep, loose-based fluted tart tin. Prick the base with a fork and chill for 30 minutes. Meanwhile, preheat the oven to 190°C (170°C fan oven) mark 5.

2 Bake the pastry case blind (see page 311) for 10 minutes at each stage. Brush the inside with beaten egg and put back in the oven for 1 minute to seal. Increase the oven setting to 180°C (160°C fan oven) mark 4.

3 To make the filling, put 4 egg yolks into a bowl with the 3 whole eggs. Add the lemon zest and juice and whisk lightly. Mix in the condensed milk and cream.

4 Pour the filling into the pastry case and bake for 30 minutes or until just set in the centre. Set aside to cool while you prepare the meringue. Increase the oven setting to 200°C (180°C fan oven) mark 6.

5 For the meringue, whisk the egg whites and icing sugar together in a heatproof bowl set over a pan of gently simmering water, using a hand-held electric whisk, for 10 minutes or until shiny and thick. Take off the heat and continue to whisk at low speed for 5–10 minutes until the bowl is cool. Pile the meringue on to the filling and swirl to form peaks. Bake for 5–10 minutes until the meringue is tinged brown. Leave to stand for about 1 hour, then serve.

VARIATION
Use lime zest and juice instead of lemon.

BANOFFEE PIE

SERVES 14

Preparation: 15 minutes, plus chilling

Cooking time: 2–3 minutes

100g (3½oz) butter, melted, plus extra to
grease

200g (7oz) digestive biscuits, roughly broken

2 small bananas, peeled and sliced

8 tbsp dulce de leche toffee sauce

284ml carton double cream

1 tbsp cocoa powder to dust

PER SERVING

250 cals; 19g fat (of which 10g saturates);
18g carbohydrate; 0.4g salt

VARIATIONS

- Top with a handful of toasted
  flaked almonds instead of the
  cocoa powder.

- Whiz 25g (1oz) chopped pecan
  nuts into the biscuits with the
  butter.

- Scatter grated plain dark chocolate
  over the cream.

1 Grease the base and sides of a 23cm (9 inch) loose-based tart tin.
   Whiz the biscuits in a food processor until they resemble
   breadcrumbs. Pour in the melted butter and whiz briefly to
   combine. Press the mixture into the base and up the sides of the
   prepared tart tin, using the back of a metal spoon to level the
   surface, and leave to chill for 2 hours.
2 Arrange the banana slices evenly over the biscuit base and spoon
   the dulce de leche on top. Whip the cream until thick and spread it
   over the top. Dust with a sprinkling of cocoa powder and serve.

MINCE PIES

MAKES 24

Preparation: 15 minutes, plus chilling
Cooking time: 12–15 minutes, plus cooling

225g (8oz) plain flour, plus extra
   to dust
125g (4oz) unsalted butter, chilled
   and diced
100g (3½oz) cream cheese
1 egg yolk
finely grated zest of 1 orange
400g jar mincemeat (see notes)
1 egg, beaten
icing sugar to dust

PER PIE

150 cals; 8g fat (of which 4g saturates);
17g carbohydrate; 0.2g salt

1 Put the flour in a food processor. Add the butter, cream cheese, egg yolk and orange zest and whiz until the mixture just comes together. Tip the mixture into a large bowl and bring the dough together with your hands. Shape into a ball, wrap in clingfilm and put in the freezer for 5 minutes.

2 Preheat the oven to 220°C (200°C fan) mark 7. Cut off about one-third of the pastry dough and set aside. Roll out the remainder on a lightly floured surface to 5mm (¼ inch) thick. Stamp out circles with a 6.5cm (2½ inch) cutter to make 24 rounds, re-rolling the dough as necessary. Use the pastry circles to line two 12-hole patty tins. Roll out the reserved pastry and use a star cutter to stamp out the stars.

3 Put 1 tsp mincemeat into each pastry case, then top with pastry stars. Brush the tops with beaten egg, then bake for 12–15 minutes until golden. Remove from the tins and leave to cool on a wire rack. Serve warm or cold, dusted with icing sugar. Store in an airtight container for up to four days.

NOTES
- Improve the flavour of a jar of bought mincemeat by adding 2 tbsp brandy, the grated zest of 1 lemon and 25g (1oz) pecan nuts, chopped. Instead of the nuts, try a piece of preserved stem ginger, chopped.

- For vegetarians, make sure you use mincemeat made with vegetable suet rather than beef suet.

SUMMER FRUIT PARCELS

Preparation: 20 minutes

Cooking time: 30–35 minutes, plus cooling

2 oranges

200g (7oz) strawberries

250g (9oz) cherries, stoned and
halved

2 tbsp maple syrup

1 tbsp light olive oil

12 sheets filo pastry, each trimmed
into 18cm (7 inch) squares

sifted icing sugar to dust

PER SERVING

214 cals; 16g fat (of which 7g saturates);
13g carbohydrate; 0.1g salt

1 Use a small knife to segment the oranges: on a board,
cut the top and bottom off one orange, then cut
down around it to remove the peel and pith. Cut in
between each segment to release the pieces of
orange. Repeat with the other orange.

2 Put the strawberries, cherries, maple syrup and 50ml
(2fl oz) water into a pan. Simmer for 3 minutes. Take
off the heat and strain over a jug, reserving the juices.
Cool. Stir in the orange segments.

3 Preheat the oven to 200°C (180°C fan oven) mark 6.
Lightly oil six 200ml (7fl oz) ramekins. Brush one of
the filo squares with a little oil, then lay another square
on top and brush again. Turn the square over so that
the greased side is facing down, then gently push into
a ramekin. Repeat with the remaining pastry and
ramekins.

4 Divide the fruit among the ramekins. Gather up the
filo edges and push together lightly to seal. Transfer the
ramekins to a non-stick baking sheet and bake for
25–30 minutes until crisp and golden.

5 Meanwhile, put the reserved juice into a pan and
simmer until reduced by half. When the parcels are
cooked, remove from the ramekins and put on to
plates. Dust with icing sugar and serve with the
reduced juice poured over.

TARTE TATIN

CUTS INTO 6 SLICES

Preparation: 30 minutes, plus chilling

Cooking time: about 1 hour, plus cooling

Sweet Shortcrust Pastry (see page
  126), made with 225g (8oz) plain
  flour, ¼ tsp salt, 150g (5oz)
  unsalted butter, 50g (2oz) golden
  icing sugar, 1 medium egg in place
  of the egg yolks and 2–3 drops
  vanilla extract
plain flour to dust

FILLING

200g (7oz) golden caster sugar
125g (4oz) chilled unsalted butter
1.4–1.6kg (3–3½lb) crisp dessert
  apples, peeled and cored
juice of ½ lemon

PER SLICE

727 cals; 39g fat (of which 24g saturates);
94g carbohydrate; 0.7g salt

1 To make the filling, sprinkle the sugar over the bottom of a 20.5cm (8 inch)
   tarte tatin tin or ovenproof frying pan. Cut the butter into slivers and
   arrange on the sugar. Halve the apples and pack them tightly, cut-side up, on
   top of the butter.
2 Put the tin or pan on the hob and cook over a medium heat for 30 minutes
   (making sure it doesn't bubble over or catch on the bottom) or until the
   butter and sugar turn a dark golden brown (see note). Sprinkle with the
   lemon juice, then leave to cool for 15 minutes. Meanwhile, preheat the oven
   to 220°C (200°C fan oven) mark 7.
3 Put the pastry on a large sheet of lightly floured baking parchment. Roll out
   to make a round 2.5cm (1 inch) larger than the tin or pan. Prick several
   times with a fork. Lay the pastry over the apples, tucking the edges down the
   side of the tin. Bake for 25–30 minutes until golden brown. Leave in the tin
   for 10 minutes, then carefully upturn on to a serving plate. Serve warm.

NOTE
When caramelising the apples in step 2, be patient. Allow
the sauce to turn a dark golden brown – any paler and it will
be too sickly. Don't let it burn, though, as this will make the
caramel taste bitter.

PLUM AND ALMOND TART

Preparation: 30 minutes, plus chilling
Cooking time: 40 minutes, plus cooling
and setting

150g (5oz) unsalted butter, chilled
   and diced
175g (6oz) plain flour, plus extra
   to dust
7 tbsp soured cream

FILLING
50g (2oz) unsalted butter
50g (2oz) caster sugar, plus extra
   to dust
2 medium eggs, lightly beaten
100g (3½oz) ground almonds
1 tbsp Kirsch or 3–4 drops almond
   essence
900g (2lb) plums, stoned and
   quartered
50g (2oz) blanched almonds to
   decorate
175g (6oz) redcurrant jelly

PER SLICE
535 cals; 35g fat (of which 16g saturates);
50g carbohydrate; 0.5g salt

1 To make the pastry, put the butter and flour into a food processor and whiz for 1–2 seconds. Add the soured cream and process for a further 1–2 seconds until the dough just begins to come together. (Alternatively, rub the butter into the flour in a large bowl by hand or using a pastry cutter, then mix in the soured cream.) Turn out on to a lightly floured surface and knead lightly for about 30 seconds until the pastry just comes together. Wrap in clingfilm and chill for 30 minutes.

2 To make the filling, put the butter into a bowl and beat until soft, then add the sugar and beat until light and fluffy. Beat in the eggs, alternating with the ground almonds. Add the Kirsch or almond essence, cover and set aside.

3 Roll out the pastry on a lightly floured surface to a 30.5cm (12 inch) circle, then transfer to a baking sheet and prick all over with a fork. Spread the almond mixture over the pastry, leaving a 3cm (1¼ inch) border all round. Scatter the plums over the filling and fold the edges of the pastry up over the fruit. Dust with caster sugar, then chill for 20 minutes.

4 Preheat the oven to 220°C (200°C fan oven) mark 7 and put a baking tray in the oven to heat for 10 minutes. Put the tart, on its baking sheet, on top of the hot baking tray. Cook for 35–40 minutes until deep golden brown.

5 Leave the tart to cool for 10 minutes, then slide it on to a wire rack. Arrange the almonds among the fruit. Heat the redcurrant jelly gently in a pan, stirring until smooth, then brush generously over the tart. Leave to set.

PEAR, CRANBERRY AND FRANGIPANE TART

CUTS INTO 8 SLICES

Preparation: 30 minutes, plus chilling
Cooking time: 1 hour, plus cooling

150g (5oz) caster sugar
2 small ripe pears
150g (5oz) unsalted butter, softened, plus extra to grease
175g (6oz) Hobnob biscuits, finely crushed (see page 298)
100g (3½oz) ground almonds
2 tbsp plain flour
1 tsp cornflour
1 tsp baking powder
2 medium eggs, beaten
1 tsp vanilla extract
25g (1oz) dried cranberries
25g (1oz) flaked almonds
icing sugar to dust
crème fraîche to serve

PER SLICE

466 cals; 28g fat (of which 13g saturates); 48g carbohydrate; 0.6g salt

1 Put 50g (2oz) caster sugar in a pan with 500ml (18fl oz) water and dissolve over a gentle heat. Peel, halve and core the pears and add to the sugar syrup. Cover the pan with a lid and simmer gently for 5–8 minutes, turning once. Transfer the pears and liquid to a bowl and leave to cool.

2 Lightly grease a 20.5cm (8 inch) loose-based cake tin and line with greaseproof paper. Melt 25g (1oz) butter and mix in the crushed biscuits. Press into the bottom of the tin, using the back of a metal spoon to level the surface, and chill for about 1 hour.

3 Preheat the oven to 180°C (160°C fan oven) mark 4. Cream the remaining butter and sugar together in a freestanding mixer (or use a hand-held electric whisk) until light and fluffy. Add the ground almonds, flour, cornflour and baking powder and mix to combine. Add the eggs and vanilla extract and mix until smooth. Stir in the cranberries and flaked almonds. Spoon the mixture on top of the biscuit base and level the surface.

4 Remove the pears from the syrup and place on kitchen paper to soak up excess liquid. Slice one of the pear halves horizontally into 5mm (¼ inch) slices. Gently push down on the pear to fan out the slices slightly. Place on top of the frangipane filling. Repeat with the remaining pear halves, spacing them evenly apart on top of the filling.

5 Bake for 45–50 minutes until the frangipane is golden, puffed and firm to the touch. Dust with icing sugar and serve with crème fraîche.

FREEZING TIP
To freeze, complete the recipe to the end of step 4, then leave the tart, still in its tin, to cool completely. Once cool, wrap the entire tin in clingfilm, then freeze for up to one month. To use, thaw overnight in the fridge and serve as in step 5.

PINENUT AND HONEY TART

Preparation: 50 minutes, plus chilling

Cooking time: 1 hour, plus cooling

250g (9oz) plain flour, plus extra
    to dust
200g (7oz) unsalted butter, softened
40g (1½oz) icing sugar
4 large eggs
100g (3½oz) pinenuts
200g (7oz) muscovado sugar
100ml (3½fl oz) clear honey
150ml (¼ pint) double cream
ice cream to serve

PER SLICE

863 cals; 54g fat (of which 26g saturates);
88g carbohydrate; 0.6g salt

1 Put 225g (8oz) flour, 150g (5oz) butter and the icing sugar into a food processor and pulse until the mixture resembles fine crumbs. (Alternatively, rub the butter into the flour in a large bowl, by hand or using a pastry cutter, until it resembles fine crumbs. Stir in the icing sugar.) Add 1 egg. Pulse, or stir with a fork, until the mixture forms a ball. Wrap in clingfilm and chill for 30 minutes.

2 Preheat the oven to 200°C (180°C fan oven) mark 6. Roll out the pastry on a lightly floured surface and use to line a 23cm (9 inch) loose-based tart tin. Prick the base all over with a fork and bake blind (see page 311), using a little of the remaining eggs to seal the pastry case. Remove from the oven. Increase the oven setting to 190°C (170°C fan oven) mark 5.

3 Sprinkle 75g (3oz) pinenuts over the pastry base. Melt 25g (1oz) butter and whisk with 175g (6oz) muscovado sugar, the honey, remaining eggs and the cream. Pour into the pastry case and bake for 25–30 minutes.

4 Pulse the remaining pinenuts, flour, butter and sugar until the mixture forms a crumbly texture. (Alternatively, rub the butter into the flour in a large bowl and stir in the pinenuts and sugar.) When the tart is cooked, remove it from the oven, sprinkle with the crumble mixture and return to the oven for 8–10 minutes.

5 Remove from the oven and leave to cool slightly. Serve warm, with ice cream.

BRAMLEY APPLE AND CUSTARD TART

Preparation: 30 minutes, plus chilling
Cooking time: about 2 hours, plus cooling
and chilling

750g (1lb 11oz) Bramley apples,
    peeled, cored and roughly
    chopped
200g (7oz) golden caster sugar
500g shortcrust pastry, chilled
plain flour to dust
a little beaten egg to seal the
    pastry case
400ml (14fl oz) double cream
1 cinnamon stick
3 large egg yolks, plus 1 large egg,
    beaten together
2 dessert apples to decorate
Apple Sauce (see below) to serve

PER SLICE

472 cals; 32g fat (of which 15g saturates);
    46g carbohydrate; 0.5g salt

1   Cook the Bramley apples with 2 tbsp water over a
    low heat until soft. Add 50g (2oz) sugar and beat to
    make a purée. Leave to cool.

2   Roll out the pastry on a lightly floured surface and use
    to line a 20.5cm (8 inch), 4cm (1½ inch) deep, loose-
    based fluted flan tin. Cover and chill for 1 hour. Preheat
    the oven to 180°C (160°C fan oven) mark 4. Bake the
    pastry case blind (see page 311). Brush the inside with
    beaten egg and put back in the oven for 1 minute to
    seal. Remove from the oven.

3   Put the cream into a pan with 50g (2oz) sugar and the
    cinnamon stick. Bring slowly to the boil, then take off
    the heat and remove the cinnamon. Cool for 2–3
    minutes, then beat in the egg yolks and egg.

4   Lower the oven setting to 170°C (150°C fan oven)
    mark 3. Put the tart on a baking sheet, then spoon the
    apple purée over the pastry. Pour the cream mixture
    on top and bake for 1–1½ hours until the custard is
    set. Remove from the oven, cool in the tin, then chill.

5   To decorate, preheat the grill. Cut the dessert apples
    into 5mm (¼ inch) thick slices and lay them on a
    lipped baking sheet. Sprinkle with 50g (2oz) sugar and
    grill for 4–5 minutes until caramelised. Turn them over
    and repeat on the other side, then cool. Remove the
    tart from the tin and decorate with the apple slices.
    Serve with Apple Sauce.

APPLE SAUCE
Pour 300ml (½ pint) apple juice into a measuring jug.
Mix 2 tbsp of the apple juice with 1 tbsp arrowroot to
make a smooth paste. Pour the remaining apple juice into
a small pan and bring to a gentle simmer. Add the
arrowroot paste and continue to heat, stirring constantly,
for 2–3 minutes until the sauce has thickened slightly.

EXPRESS APPLE TART

Preparation: 10 minutes

Cooking time: 20 minutes

375g ready-rolled puff pastry
500g (1lb 2oz) dessert apples, such
    as Cox's Orange Pippins, cored
    and thinly sliced, then tossed in the
    juice of 1 lemon
golden icing sugar to dust

PER SLICE:
197 cals; 12g fat (of which 0g saturates);
24g carbohydrate; 0.4g salt

1 Preheat the oven to 200°C (180°C fan oven) mark 6. Unroll the pastry on
   to a 28 x 38cm (11 x 15 inch) baking sheet and lightly roll a rolling pin over
   it to smooth down the pastry. Score lightly around the edge, leaving a 3cm
   (1¼ inch) border.
2 Put the apple slices on top of the pastry, within the border. Turn the edge
   of the pastry inwards to reach the edge of the apples, pressing it down and
   using your fingers to crimp the edge.
3 Dust heavily with icing sugar. Bake for 20 minutes or until the pastry is
   cooked and the sugar has caramelised. Serve warm, dusted with more
   icing sugar.

NOTE
The pastry will be easier to unroll if you remove it from the
fridge 10–15 minutes beforehand.

CHOCOLATE ESPRESSO TART

Preparation: 30 minutes, plus chilling
Cooking time: 25 minutes, plus cooling
and chilling

175g (6oz) plain flour, plus extra
    to dust
pinch of salt
100g (3½oz) cold unsalted butter,
    diced
25g (1oz) caster sugar
1 medium egg, separated, plus a little
    beaten egg to seal the pastry case

FILLING
200g bar dark chocolate (at least
    64% cocoa solids), broken into
    squares
1 tbsp powdered espresso coffee
284ml carton double cream
cocoa powder and chocolate curls
    (see page 327) to decorate

PER SLICE
383 cals; 30g fat (of which 18g saturates);
30g carbohydrate; 0.2g salt

1 Sift the flour and salt into a bowl. Rub in the butter until it resembles fine breadcrumbs. Stir in the sugar.

2 Lightly beat the egg yolk with 2 tbsp ice-cold water. Using a flat-bladed knife, stir enough of this liquid into the flour mixture to make it clump together without being sticky or too dry. Bring together with your hands and knead lightly until smooth. Shape into a disc, wrap in clingfilm and chill for 30 minutes.

3 Roll out the pastry on a lightly floured surface to 3mm (⅛ inch) thick. Use to line a round 20.5cm (8 inch) tin, 2.5cm (1 inch) deep. Prick the base all over, then chill for 30 minutes. Meanwhile, preheat the oven to 200°C (180°C fan oven) mark 6 and put a baking sheet in the oven to heat up.

4 Bake the pastry case blind (see page 311) for 12–15 minutes at the first stage and then 5–10 minutes. Brush the inside with egg and put back in the oven for 1 minute. Transfer to a wire rack and leave to cool.

5 Melt the chocolate and coffee in a heatproof bowl set over a pan of gently simmering water, making sure the base of the bowl doesn't touch the water. Stir once or twice. Set aside to cool.

6 Put the egg white into a clean, grease-free bowl and whisk until stiff. Using a metal spoon, fold into the chocolate. Whip the cream until it just holds its shape, then fold into the chocolate mixture. Pour into the pastry case and chill until set.

7 Dust with cocoa powder and decorate with chocolate curls to serve.

CHOCOLATE ORANGE TART

Preparation: 30 minutes, plus chilling
Cooking time: about 1 hour, plus cooling

Sweet Shortcrust Pastry (see page
 126), made with 150g (5oz) plain
 flour, pinch of salt, 75g (3oz)
 unsalted butter, 50g (2oz) caster
 sugar, 25g (1oz) golden icing sugar,
 grated zest of 1 orange and 2 large
 egg yolks
plain flour to dust
a little beaten egg to seal the
 pastry case
icing sugar to dust

FILLING

175g (6oz) plain chocolate (at least
 50% cocoa solids), chopped
175ml (6fl oz) double cream
75g (3oz) light muscovado sugar
2 medium eggs
1 tbsp Grand Marnier or Cointreau

PER SLICE

441 cals; 28g fat (of which 17g saturates);
42g carbohydrate; 0.2g salt

1 Roll out the pastry on a lightly floured surface and use
 to line a 20.5cm (8 inch) loose-based tart tin. Prick
 the base all over with a fork, put the tin on a baking
 sheet and chill for 30 minutes. Preheat the oven to
 190°C (170°C fan oven) mark 5.
2 Bake the pastry case blind (see page 311). Brush the
 inside with egg and put back in the oven for 1 minute
 to seal. Remove from the oven. Lower the oven
 setting to 170°C (150°C fan oven) mark 3.
3 To make the filling, melt the chocolate in a heatproof
 bowl set over a pan of simmering water, making sure
 the base of the bowl doesn't touch the water. Remove
 the bowl from the pan and cool for 10 minutes.

4 Put the cream, muscovado sugar, eggs and liqueur into
 a bowl and stir, using a wooden spoon to mix
 thoroughly. Gradually stir in the chocolate, then pour
 into the pastry case and bake for 20 minutes or until
 just set.
5 Serve warm or cold, dusted liberally with icing sugar.

VARIATION
Omit the orange zest and replace the Grand
Marnier with crème de menthe.

LEMON TART

Preparation: 30 minutes, plus chilling

Cooking time: about 50 minutes

butter to grease

plain flour to dust

Sweet Shortcrust Pastry (see page 284), made with
150g (5oz) plain flour, 75g (3oz) unsalted butter,
50g (2oz) icing sugar and 2 large egg yolks

peach slices and fresh or frozen raspberries, thawed,
to decorate

icing sugar to dust

FOR THE FILLING

1 large egg, plus 4 large yolks

150g (5oz) caster sugar

grated zest of 4 lemons

150ml (¼ pint) freshly squeezed lemon juice (about
4 medium lemons)

150ml (¼ pint) double cream

PER SLICE

385 cals; 23g fat (of which 13g saturates); 42g carbohydrate; 0.2g salt

NOTE
Remember that ovens vary, so check the tart after 15 minutes of cooking. Turn round if cooking unevenly, otherwise the eggs might curdle.

1 Grease and flour a 23cm (9in), 2.5cm (1in) deep, loose-based flan tin. Roll out the pastry on a lightly floured worksurface into a circle – if the pastry sticks to the surface, gently ease a palette knife under it to loosen. Line the tin with the pastry and trim the excess. Prick the base all over with a fork. Chill for 30 minutes.

2 Preheat the oven to 190°C (170°C fan oven) mark 5. Put the tin on a baking sheet and bake the pastry case blind (see page 284). Remove from the oven, leaving the flan tin on the baking sheet. Reduce the oven temperature to 170°C (150°C fan oven) mark 3.

3 Meanwhile, to make the filling, put the whole egg, egg yolks and caster sugar into a bowl and beat together with a wooden spoon or balloon whisk until smooth. Carefully stir in the lemon zest, lemon juice and cream. Leave to stand for 5 minutes.

4 Ladle three-quarters of the filling into the pastry case, position the baking sheet on the oven shelf and ladle in the remainder. Bake for 25–30 minutes until the filling bounces back when touched lightly in the centre. Cool for 15 minutes to serve warm, or cool completely and chill. Decorate with peaches and raspberries and dust with icing sugar.

FREEZING TIP
To freeze, complete the recipe, then cool the tart, wrap carefully in foil and freeze for up to three months. When ready to use, thaw for 3 hours at room temperature.

STRAWBERRY TART

Preparation: 40 minutes, plus chilling

Cooking time: 35–40 minutes, plus cooling

Sweet Shortcrust Pastry (see page 126),
    made with 125g (4oz) plain flour, pinch
    of salt, 50g (2oz) caster sugar, 50g (2oz)
    unsalted butter and 2 medium egg yolks

plain flour to dust

a little beaten egg to seal the pastry case

CRÈME PÂTISSIÈRE

300ml (½ pint) milk

1 vanilla pod, split, seeds separated

2 medium egg yolks

50g (2oz) golden caster sugar

2 tbsp plain flour

2 tbsp cornflour

50ml (2fl oz) crème fraîche

TOPPING

450g (1lb) medium strawberries, hulled
    and halved

6 tbsp redcurrant jelly

PER SLICE

384 cals; 15g fat (of which 8g saturates);
57g carbohydrate; 0.2g salt

NOTE
Serve within 2 hours of putting the tart together,
otherwise the pastry will go soggy.

1 To make the crème pâtissière, pour the milk into a pan
   and add the vanilla pod and seeds. Heat gently to just
   below boiling, then remove from the heat. Put the egg
   yolks and sugar into a bowl and beat until pale, then
   stir in the flours. Discard the vanilla pod, then gradually
   mix the hot milk into the yolk mixture. Return to
   the pan and slowly bring to the boil, stirring for
   3–4 minutes until thick and smooth. Scrape into a
   bowl, cover with a circle of damp greaseproof paper
   and leave to cool.

2 Put the pastry between two sheets of lightly floured
   greaseproof paper and roll out thinly. Use to line a
   23cm (9 inch) loose-based flan tin. Prick with a fork,
   line with greaseproof paper and chill for 30 minutes.

3 Preheat the oven to 190°C (170°C fan oven) mark 5.
   Bake the pastry case blind (see page 311). Brush the
   inside with beaten egg and put back in the oven for
   1 minute to seal. Cool for 5 minutes, then remove
   from the tin and leave to cool completely.

4 Add the crème fraîche to the crème pâtissière and
   beat until smooth. Spread evenly in the pastry case.
   Arrange the strawberry halves on top, working from
   the outside edge into the centre.

5 Heat the redcurrant jelly in a pan until syrupy, whisking
   lightly. Using a pastry brush, cover the strawberries
   with jelly. Serve within 2 hours.

CHERRY AND ALMOND TART

Preparation: 35 minutes, plus chilling

Cooking time: 30 minutes

PASTRY

200g (7oz) plain flour, sifted, plus extra to dust

100g (3½oz) unsalted butter, chilled and cut into cubes

50g (2oz) ground almonds

25g (1oz) caster sugar

2–3 drops almond extract

1 large egg, beaten

FILLING

650g (1lb 7oz) fresh whole cherries (see notes)

3 tbsp morello cherry conserve

250g (9oz) mascarpone cheese

4 tbsp elderflower cordial (see tip)

75g (3oz) icing sugar, sifted

seeds scraped from 1 vanilla pod

250ml (9fl oz) double cream

PER SERVING

425 cals; 30g fat (of which 18g saturates); 35g carbohydrate; 0.2g salt

TIP

Elderflower Cordial: Pick 20 large young elderflower heads (shake to release any insects). Bring 1.2 litres (2 pints) water to the boil, add 2kg (4½lb) golden granulated sugar and stir until dissolved. Then add 80g (just over 3oz) citric acid and 2 medium lemons, sliced. Stir in the flower heads. Cover and leave overnight. In the morning strain the liquid. If you want it clearer, strain again through muslin or a coffee filter. Bottle and store in the fridge – it will last for months.

NOTE

If you don't have fresh cherries, use tinned. Drain them well – no need to poach. Simmer the conserve and water in a pan, without the cherries, until syrupy, then complete the recipe.

1 In a food processor, pulse the flour, butter and almonds until the mixture resembles fine breadcrumbs. Add the caster sugar and almond extract and pulse again to combine. Tip into a bowl. Add just enough egg to bind the mixture, stirring with a blunt-ended knife, then use your hands to bring the pastry together. Wrap in clingfilm and chill for 30 minutes.

2 Roll out the pastry on a lightly floured surface to the thickness of a £1 coin. Use to line a 23cm (9 inch) straight-sided, loose-based tart tin. Prick the base all over and chill for 30 minutes.

3 Preheat the oven to 190°C (170°C fan oven) mark 5. Bake the pastry case blind (see page 311) for 12–15 minutes, then remove the beans and paper and bake for a further 10–12 minutes until the base feels sandy. Cool in the tin on a wire rack.

4 Meanwhile, pit the cherries and put into a pan with the conserve and 125ml (4fl oz) water. Bring to a gentle simmer, then poach for 3 minutes or until the cherries are just starting to soften. Take out with a slotted spoon, then set aside to cool. Return the pan to the hob and simmer the liquid until syrupy and reduced by half. Strain and leave to cool.

5 Beat together the mascarpone, cordial, icing sugar and vanilla seeds until smooth. In a separate bowl, lightly whip the cream until soft peaks form. Fold the cream into the mascarpone mixture, then spoon into the cooked pastry case and level the surface. Up to 3 hours ahead, remove the filled pastry case from the tin and arrange the cooled cherries on top, then brush with syrup to glaze. Serve.

GLAZED CRANBERRY AND ORANGE TART

CUTS INTO 8 SLICES

Preparation: 15 minutes

Cooking time: 6 minutes

350g (12oz) fresh or frozen
    cranberries, thawed
grated zest and juice of 1 orange
125g (4oz) golden caster sugar
½ tbsp arrowroot
250g tub mascarpone cheese
200ml (7fl oz) ready-made fresh
    custard with real vanilla
20.5cm (8 inch) cooked shortcrust
    pastry case

PER SLICE

234 cals; 11g fat (of which 3g saturates);
29g carbohydrate; 0.2g salt

1 Tip the cranberries into a pan, add the orange zest, juice and sugar and bring to the boil. Reduce the heat and simmer for 5 minutes or until the cranberries are just softened and the syrup has reduced slightly. Using a slotted spoon, strain off the cranberries and set aside in a bowl, leaving the syrup in the pan.

2 Mix the arrowroot with 1 tbsp cold water, add to the pan and cook for 1 minute, stirring until the syrup has thickened. Pour over the cranberries and leave to cool.

3 Tip the mascarpone and custard into a bowl and, using a hand-held electric whisk, mix until smooth. Spoon into the pastry case, top with the cranberry mixture and serve.

NOTE
A shop-bought pastry case helps to cut corners but, if you prefer, you can make a pie crust using Sweet Shortcrust Pastry (see page 126).

SWEET RICOTTA TART

Preparation: 25 minutes, plus chilling

Cooking time: 1 hour, plus cooling

Sweet Shortcrust Pastry (see page
   126), made with 200g (7oz) plain
   flour, 75g (3oz) unsalted butter,
   50g (2oz) golden caster sugar and
   1 medium egg in place of the egg
   yolks
plain flour to dust
a little beaten egg to seal the
   pastry case
icing sugar to dust

FILLING

100g (3½oz) cracked wheat or
   bulgur wheat
200ml (7fl oz) milk
250g (9oz) ricotta cheese
150g (5oz) golden caster sugar
2 medium eggs
1 tbsp orange flower water
1 tsp vanilla extract
½ tsp ground cinnamon
1 piece – about 40g (1½oz) –
   candied peel, finely chopped

PER SLICE

404 cals; 15g fat (of which 9g saturates);
60g carbohydrate; 0.3g salt

1 To make the filling, put the wheat into a pan and add the milk, then cover
and bring to the boil. Reduce the heat and simmer for 5–8 minutes until
all the liquid has been absorbed and the wheat still has a slight bite. Leave
to cool.

2 Preheat the oven to 190°C (170°C fan oven) mark 5. Roll out the pastry
on a lightly floured surface and use to line a 20.5cm (8 inch) loose-based
sandwich tin. Prick the base all over with a fork. Cover and chill for
10 minutes. Knead together the trimmings, then wrap and chill. Bake the
pastry case blind (see page 311). Brush with beaten egg and put back in
the oven for 1 minute to seal. Remove from the oven.

3 Put the ricotta into a bowl and add the sugar, eggs, orange flower water,
vanilla extract and cinnamon. Beat well. Add the peel and wheat and mix.

4 Roll out the pastry trimmings. Cut out six strips, each measuring
1 × 20.5cm (½ × 8 inch). Pour the filling into the pastry case, then lay the
strips on top. Bake for 45 minutes. Leave in the tin for 10 minutes, then
turn out on to a wire rack and leave to cool completely. Dust with icing
sugar to serve.

CLASSIC CUSTARD TART

CUTS INTO 10 SLICES

Preparation: 25 minutes, plus chilling

Cooking time: 1¼ hours, plus cooling

Sweet Shortcrust Pastry (see page
     126), made with 225g (8oz) plain
     flour, 175g (6oz) unsalted butter,
     50g (2oz) golden caster sugar,
     finely grated zest of 1 lemon,
     1 medium egg yolk
plain flour to dust

FILLING
8 large egg yolks
75g (3oz) golden caster sugar
450ml (¾ pint) single cream
nutmeg to grate

PER SLICE
399 cals; 28g fat (of which 16g saturates);
32g carbohydrate; 0.4g salt

1 Roll out the pastry on a lightly floured surface to a 3mm (⅛ inch) thickness.
  Use to line a 23cm (9 inch) round, 4cm (1½ inch) deep flan tin. Prick the
  base all over with a fork and chill for 30 minutes.

2 Preheat the oven to 200°C (180°C fan oven) mark 6. Put the flan tin on a
  baking sheet and bake blind (see page 311). Remove from the oven. Lower
  the oven setting to 130°C (110°C fan oven) mark ½.

3 Using a wooden spoon, mix the egg yolks with the sugar. Gradually stir in
  the cream, then strain into a jug to remove any eggy strands. Pour the
  mixture into the pastry case and bake for 40–50 minutes until just set with
  a little wobble. Grate plenty of nutmeg over the top and cool in the tin on
  a wire rack. Serve at room temperature.

FREEZING TIP
Freeze the leftover egg whites in a clean container. They will
keep for up to three months. Use to make meringues.

TREACLE TART

Preparation: 25 minutes, plus chilling

Cooking time: 45–50 minutes, plus cooling

Sweet Shortcrust Pastry (see page
126), made with 225g (8oz) plain
flour, 150g (5oz) unsalted butter,
15g (½oz) golden caster sugar and
1 medium egg yolk

plain flour to dust

FILLING

700g (1½lb) golden syrup

175g (6oz) fresh white breadcrumbs

grated zest of 3 lemons

2 medium eggs, lightly beaten

PER SLICE

486 cals; 15g fat (of which 8g saturates);

88g carbohydrate; 1.1g salt

1 Preheat the oven to 180°C (160°C fan oven) mark 4. Roll out the pastry
on a lightly floured surface and use to line a 25.5cm (10 inch), 4cm
(1½ inch) deep, loose-based fluted tart tin. Prick the base all over with
a fork and chill for 30 minutes.

2 To make the filling, heat the syrup in a pan over a low heat until thinner in
consistency. Remove from the heat and mix in the breadcrumbs and lemon
zest. Stir in the beaten eggs.

3 Pour the filling into the pastry case and bake for 45–50 minutes until the
filling is lightly set and golden. Leave to cool slightly. Serve warm.

VARIATION

For the pastry, replace half the plain flour with wholemeal
flour. For the filling, use fresh wholemeal breadcrumbs
instead of white.

CARAMELISED ORANGE TART

Preparation: 15 minutes, plus chilling

Cooking time: 45 minutes, plus cooling

PASTRY

225g (8oz) plain flour, plus extra
   to dust
pinch of salt
125g (4oz) unsalted butter, diced
2 tbsp golden icing sugar
1 medium egg yolk, beaten

FILLING

juice of 1 lemon
juice of 1 orange
zest of 2 oranges
75g (3oz) unsalted butter
225g (8oz) golden granulated sugar
3 medium eggs, beaten
75g (3oz) ground almonds
2 tbsp orange liqueur
a few drops of orange food colouring
   (optional)

DECORATION

100g (3½oz) golden caster sugar
pared zest of 1 orange, cut into
   slivers

PER SLICE

556 cals; 29g fat (of which 14g saturates);
70g carbohydrate; 0.5g salt

1   To make the pastry, put the flour, salt, butter and icing sugar into a food processor and pulse until the mixture forms fine crumbs. (Alternatively, rub the fat into the flour, by hand or using a pastry cutter, then stir in the icing sugar.) Beat the egg yolk with 2 tbsp cold water and add to the flour mixture. Process (or stir) until the crumbs make a dough. Knead lightly, wrap and chill for 30 minutes.

2   To make the filling, put the juices, orange zest, butter, sugar and eggs into a heavy-based pan and heat gently, stirring until thickened. Stir in the almonds, liqueur and food colouring, if you like, then set aside.

3   Preheat the oven to 200°C (180°C fan oven) mark 6. Roll out the dough on a lightly floured surface and use to line a 23cm (9 inch) tin. Prick the base all over with a fork. Cover and chill for 10 minutes. Bake the pastry case blind (see page 311). Remove from the oven. Lower the oven setting to 180°C (160°C fan oven) mark 4. Pour the filling into the pastry case and bake for 20 minutes or until just firm. Cool in the tin.

4   To decorate, preheat the grill. Dissolve 50g (2oz) sugar in a pan with 300ml (½ pint) water. Add the orange zest and simmer for 10–15 minutes until the liquid has reduced and the zest is tender. Drain. Sprinkle the rest of the sugar over the tart. Caramelise under the hot grill, then leave to cool. Spoon the orange zest around the edge to serve.

CHOCOLATE, AMARETTI AND GINGER TART

CUTS 10 SLICES

Preparation: 30 minutes, plus chilling
Cooking time: about 55 minutes, plus cooling

PASTRY
225g (8oz) plain flour, sifted, plus extra to dust
125g (4oz) cold unsalted butter, diced
25g (1oz) caster sugar
1 large egg, beaten, plus a little beaten egg to seal
    the pastry case

FILLING
125g (4oz) dark chocolate, broken into pieces
100g (3½oz) milk chocolate, broken into pieces
125g (4oz) unsalted butter, cubed
75g (3oz) Amaretti biscuits, crushed into small
    pieces
40g (1½oz) preserved stem ginger, finely chopped
75g (3oz) caster sugar
2 large eggs
cocoa powder to dust (optional)

PER SLICE
485 cals, 31g fat (18g saturates); 48g carbohydrate; 0.5g salt

1 Put the flour and butter into a food processor and
   pulse until the mixture resembles fine breadcrumbs
   (alternatively, if you don't have a processor, rub the
   butter into the flour using your fingers). Add caster
   sugar and pulse to combine. Tip the mixture into a
   bowl, then add the egg and stir quickly with a blunt-
   ended knife. Bring the pastry together using your
   hands, then wrap it in clingfilm and chill for 30 minutes.
2 Roll out pastry on a lightly floured surface to thickness
   of a £1 coin. Use to line a 20.5cm (8 inch) straight-
   sided, 1½in (4cm) deep, loose-based tart tin. Prick the
   pastry base all over and chill for 15 minutes.
3 Preheat the oven to 190°C (170°C fan oven) mark 5.
   Bake the pastry case blind (see page 311) for 15–18
   minutes and then 10–12 minutes. Brush with egg and
   bake for 1 minute. Remove from the oven. Lower the
   oven setting to 150°C (130°C fan oven) mark 2.

4 Meanwhile, make the filling. Melt both chocolates and
   the butter in a heatproof bowl set over a pan of
   simmering water. Stir in the Amaretti biscuits and
   ginger and set aside.
5 In a separate large bowl, beat together the sugar and
   eggs with a hand-held electric whisk until pale and
   moussey. Fold in the chocolate mixture, then pour the
   filling into the cooked pastry case. Bake for 25 minutes
   or until just set. Leave to cool completely in the tin,
   then remove from tin, dust with cocoa powder, if you
   like, and serve in slices.

TO STORE
Store in the fridge. It will keep for up to five days. Allow
to reach room temperature before serving.

ALMOND BAKEWELL TARTS

Preparation: 25 minutes, plus chilling
Cooking time: 50 minutes, plus cooling

Sweet Shortcrust Pastry (see page 126), made with 200g
    (7oz) plain flour, 100g (3½oz) unsalted butter, 75g (3oz)
    caster sugar, 3 large egg yolks and ½ tsp vanilla extract
plain flour to dust
Plum Sauce (see below) to serve

FILLING
125g (4oz) unsalted butter, softened
125g (4oz) caster sugar
3 large eggs
125g (4oz) ground almonds
2–3 drops almond essence
6 tbsp redcurrant jelly

CRUMBLE TOPPING
25g (1oz) unsalted butter
75g (3oz) plain flour
25g (1oz) caster sugar

PER TART
931 cals; 52g fat (of which 24g saturates); 104g carbohydrate; 0.8g salt

1 Roll out the pastry thinly on a lightly floured surface
   and use to line six 10cm (4 inch), 3cm (1¼ inch) deep
   tartlet tins. Chill for 30 minutes. Preheat the oven to
   190°C (170°C fan oven) mark 5.
2 Bake the tartlet cases blind (see page 311). Remove
   from the oven and leave to cool.
3 To make the filling, beat the butter and sugar together
   until light and fluffy. Gradually beat in 2 eggs, then beat
   in the remaining egg with one-third of the ground
   almonds. Fold in the remaining almonds and the
   almond essence.
4 Melt the redcurrant jelly in a small pan and brush over
   the inside of each pastry case. Spoon in the almond
   filling. Put the tarts on a baking sheet and bake for
   20–25 minutes until golden and just firm. Leave in the
   tins for 10 minutes, then unmould on to a wire rack
   and leave to cool completely.

5 To make the crumble topping, rub the butter into the
   flour and add the sugar. Spread evenly on a baking
   sheet and grill until golden. Cool, then sprinkle over
   the tarts. Decorate with plums (see below) and serve
   with Plum Sauce.

PLUM SAUCE
Put 450g (1lb) halved and stoned ripe plums, 50–75g
(2–3oz) soft brown sugar and 150ml (¼ pint) sweet
white wine into a pan with 150ml (¼ pint) water. Bring
to the boil, then simmer until tender. Remove 3 plums to
decorate; slice and put to one side. Cook the remaining
plums for about 15 minutes until very soft. Put into a
food processor and whiz until smooth. Sieve, if you like,
adding more sugar to taste. Leave to cool.

RASPBERRY AND WHITE CHOCOLATE TARTS

LONG CHILLING REQUIRED

Preparation: 40 minutes, plus chilling

Cooking time: 40 minutes, plus cooling, chilling and thawing

225g (8oz) plain flour, plus extra to dust
150g (5oz) butter, cut into cubes
50g (2oz) icing sugar, plus extra to dust
2–3 drops of vanilla extract
1 large egg, lightly beaten
350–450g (12oz–1lb) raspberries
pouring cream to serve

FILLING

275g (10oz) good-quality white chocolate,
   broken into small pieces
300ml (½ pint) double cream
1 vanilla pod, split
2 large eggs, separated
2 tbsp Kirsch

PER TART

648 cals; 49g fat (of which 28g saturates); 52g carbohydrate;
0.6g salt

1 Put the flour, butter and icing sugar into a food processor and pulse until the mixture resembles fine crumbs. (Alternatively, rub the butter into the dry ingredients in a large bowl by hand or using a pastry cutter.) Add the vanilla extract and the beaten egg. Pulse, or stir with a fork, until the dough comes together to form a ball. Wrap in clingfilm and chill for at least 30 minutes.

2 Roll out the pastry thinly on a lightly floured surface. Cut out rounds and use to line eight 9cm (3½ inch), 3cm (1¼ inch) deep, loose-based tart tins. If the pastry cracks as you line the tins, just patch it together. Prick the base all over with a fork, then chill for 30 minutes.

3 Preheat the oven to 200°C (180°C fan oven) mark 6. Bake the pastry cases blind (see page 311). Remove from the oven and leave in the tins to cool slightly. Lower the oven setting to 190°C (170°C fan oven) mark 5.

4 To make the filling, put the chocolate into a bowl. Pour the cream into a small heavy-based pan, add the vanilla and bring just to the boil. Take off the heat and remove the vanilla. Slowly pour the cream on to the chocolate and stir until the chocolate is melted. Leave to cool.

5 Mix the egg yolks and Kirsch into the cooled chocolate mixture. Put the egg whites into a clean, grease-free bowl and whisk until soft peaks form, then fold carefully into the chocolate mixture until evenly incorporated. Pour the filling into the pastry cases.

6 Bake for 10–15 minutes until just set. If the filling appears to be colouring too quickly in the oven, cover with foil. Leave to cool in the tins. Don't worry if the filling seems very soft – it will become firmer on chilling. Chill for at least 5 hours or overnight.

7 Remove from the fridge 30 minutes before serving. Unmould on to plates. Arrange the raspberries on top, dust with icing sugar and serve with cream.

WHITE CHOCOLATE FRUIT TARTS

LONG CHILLING REQUIRED

MAKES 8

Preparation: 40 minutes, plus chilling

Cooking time: 40 minutes, plus cooling and chilling

Sweet Shortcrust Pastry (see page 126), made with
225g (8oz) plain flour, 150g (5oz) unsalted
butter, 50g (2oz) caster sugar, 50g (2oz) icing
sugar, 1 large egg instead of the egg yolks and
2–3 drops vanilla extract

plain flour to dust

450g (1lb) fresh mango, peeled, stoned and sliced

fresh mint sprigs to decorate

icing sugar to dust

FILLING

275g (10oz) white chocolate, chopped

300ml (½ pint) double cream

1 vanilla pod, split

2 large eggs, separated

2 tbsp Kirsch

PER TART

688 cals; 48g fat (of which 29g saturates); 58g carbohydrate;
0.5g salt

1 Roll out the pastry thinly on a lightly floured surface
   and use to line eight 9cm (3½ inch), 3cm (1¼ inch)
   deep, loose-based tartlet tins (see notes). Prick the
   bases all over with a fork and chill for 30 minutes.

2 Preheat the oven to 200°C (180°C fan oven) mark 6.
   Bake the tartlet cases blind (see page 311). Remove
   from the oven. Lower the oven setting to 190°C
   (170°C fan oven) mark 5.

3 To make the filling, put the chocolate into a heatproof
   bowl. Pour the cream into a small, heavy-based pan,
   add the vanilla pod and bring to the boil. Remove
   from the heat, lift out the vanilla pod and add the hot
   cream to the chocolate. Stir until the chocolate is
   completely melted. Leave to cool.

4 Mix the egg yolks and the Kirsch into the cooled
   chocolate and cream mixture. Put the egg whites into
   a clean, grease-free bowl and whisk until soft peaks
   form, then fold carefully into the chocolate mixture
   until well incorporated. Pour the mixture into the
   pastry cases and bake for 10–15 minutes until just
   set (see notes). Leave to cool in the tins and chill for
   5 hours or overnight. Don't worry if the filling seems
   very soft – it will become firmer as it chills.

5 Remove the tarts from the fridge 30 minutes before
   serving. Unmould the tarts and arrange the mango
   slices on top. Decorate with fresh mint sprigs and dust
   with icing sugar just before serving.

NOTES

- Don't worry if the pastry cracks when you're
  lining the tins – it's easy to patch together.

- If the filling starts to get too dark during
  cooking, cover it with foil.

CHOCOLATE CHOUX BUNS

Preparation: 25 minutes

Cooking time: 40–45 minutes, plus cooling

Choux Pastry (see page129)

FILLING
300ml (½ pint) double cream

1 tsp vanilla extract

1 tsp golden caster sugar

TOPPING
200g (7oz) plain chocolate, in pieces

75g (3oz) butter, at room
    temperature

PER BUN
475 cals; 40g fat (of which 25g saturates);

25g carbohydrate; 0.3g salt

VARIATION
Eclairs: Put the choux pastry into a piping bag
fitted with a medium plain nozzle and pipe 9cm
(3½ inch) long fingers on to the baking sheet.
Trim with a wet knife. Bake at 200°C (180°C fan
oven) mark 6 for about 35 minutes until crisp and
golden. Using a sharp, pointed knife, make a slit
down the side of each bun to release the steam,
then transfer to a wire rack and leave for 20–30
minutes to cool completely. Just before serving,
whip 300ml (½ pint) double cream until stiff and
use it to fill the éclairs. Break 125g (4oz) plain
chocolate into a bowl set over a pan of
simmering water, making sure the base of the
bowl doesn't touch the water. Stir until melted.
Pour into a wide shallow bowl and dip the top of
each filled éclair into it, drawing each one across
the surface of the chocolate. Leave to set.
Makes 12.

1 Preheat the oven to 220°C (200°C fan oven) mark 7.
   Sprinkle a non-stick baking sheet with a little water.
   Using two dampened tablespoons, spoon the choux
   paste into eight large mounds on the baking sheet,
   spacing them well apart to allow room for expansion.

2 Bake for about 30 minutes until risen and golden
   brown. Make a small hole in the side of each bun, then
   put back in the switched-off oven for 10–15 minutes
   to dry out. Transfer to a wire rack and leave to cool.

3 For the filling, whip the cream with the vanilla extract
   and sugar until soft peaks form. Split the choux buns
   and fill them with the cream.

4 For the topping, melt the chocolate with the butter in
   a heatproof bowl set over a pan of gently simmering
   water. Leave to cool until beginning to thicken. Top the
   choux buns with the warm melted chocolate to serve.

RASPBERRY MILLEFEUILLES

Preparation: 40 minutes, plus chilling

Cooking time: 40 minutes, plus cooling
and standing

550g (1¼lb) puff pastry, thawed if
   frozen
plain flour to dust
25g (1oz) caster sugar, plus 3 tbsp
50g (2oz) hazelnuts, toasted and
   chopped
225g (8oz) raspberries
1 tbsp lemon juice
1 x quantity Confectioner's Custard
   (see below)
300ml (½ pint) double cream
50g (2oz) icing sugar, sifted

PER SERVING

828 cals; 57g fat (of which 23g saturates);
65g carbohydrate; 1.4g salt

1 Cut the pastry into three and roll out each piece on a lightly floured
surface into an 18 x 35.5cm (7 x 14 inch) rectangle. Put each on a baking
sheet, prick and chill for 30 minutes.

2 Preheat the oven to 220°C (200°C fan oven) mark 7. Bake the pastry for
10 minutes, then turn the pieces over and cook for another 3 minutes.
Sprinkle each sheet with 1 tbsp caster sugar and one-third of the nuts.
Return to the oven for 8 minutes or until the sugar dissolves. Cool slightly,
then transfer to wire racks to cool.

3 Sprinkle the raspberries with 25g (1oz) caster sugar and the lemon juice.
Beat the custard until smooth and whip the cream until thick, then fold the
cream into the custard with the raspberries and juices. Cover and chill.

4 Put the icing sugar into a bowl, then stir in 2 tbsp water. Trim each pastry
sheet to 15 x 30.5cm (6 x 12 inch), then drizzle with the icing. Leave for
15 minutes.

5 Spoon half the custard over a sheet of pastry. Put another sheet on top
and spoon on the remaining custard. Top with the final sheet and press
down lightly. Leave for 30 minutes before slicing.

CONFECTIONER'S CUSTARD

Scrape the vanilla seeds from 1 vanilla pod into a pan. Add the pod and 450ml
(¾ pint) milk, bring to the boil, then set aside for 30 minutes. Remove the
vanilla pod. Whisk 4 large egg yolks and 75g (3oz) caster sugar until pale. Mix
in 50g (2oz) plain flour. Strain in a quarter of the infused milk, mix, then stir in
the remainder. Return to the pan and bring to the boil over a low heat, stirring.
Pour into a bowl, cover with clingfilm, cool and chill for 3–4 hours.

ECCLES CAKES

Preparation: 10 minutes, plus resting

Cooking time: 15 minutes, plus cooling

212g (7½oz) puff pastry, thawed
    if frozen
plain flour to dust
25g (1oz) butter, softened
25g (1oz) dark brown soft sugar
25g (1oz) fine chopped mixed peel
50g (2oz) currants
caster sugar to sprinkle

PER CAKE
126–158 calories; 7–9g fat (of which
1–2g saturates); 15–19g carbohydrate;
0.2–0.3g salt

1 Roll out the puff pastry on a lightly floured surface and cut into 9cm (3½ inch) rounds.
2 For the filling, mix the butter, sugar, mixed peel and currants in a bowl.
3 Place 1 tsp of the fruit and butter mixture in the centre of each pastry round. Draw up the edges of each pastry round to enclose the filling, brush the edges with water and pinch together firmly, then reshape. Turn each round over and roll lightly until the currants just show through. Prick the top of each with a fork. Leave to rest for about 10 minutes in a cool place. Preheat the oven to 230°C (210°C fan oven) mark 8.
4 Put the pastry rounds on a damp baking sheet and bake for about 15 minutes until golden. Transfer to a wire rack and leave to cool for 30 minutes. Sprinkle with caster sugar while still warm.

APPLE AND CRANBERRY STRUDEL

Preparation: 20 minutes
Cooking time: 40 minutes

700g (1½lb) red apples, quartered,
   cored and thickly sliced
1 tbsp lemon juice
2 tbsp golden caster sugar
100g (3½oz) dried cranberries
6 sheets of filo pastry, thawed
   if frozen
1 tbsp olive oil
crème fraîche or Greek-style yogurt
   to serve

PER SERVING
178 cals; 2g fat (of which trace saturates);
40g carbohydrate; 0g salt

1 Preheat the oven to 190°C (170°C fan oven) mark 5. Put the apples into a
   bowl and mix with the lemon juice, 1 tbsp sugar and the cranberries.
2 Lay three sheets of filo pastry side by side, overlapping the long edges.
   Brush with a little oil. Cover with three more sheets of filo and brush again.
   Tip the apple mixture on to the pastry, leaving a 2cm (¾ inch) border all
   round. Brush the border with a little water, then roll up the strudel from a
   long edge. Put on to a non-stick baking sheet, brush with the remaining oil
   and sprinkle with the remaining sugar.
3 Bake in the oven for 40 minutes or until the pastry is golden and the
   apples are soft. Serve with crème fraîche or yogurt.

PISTACHIO BAKLAVA

Preparation: 30 minutes

Cooking time: 40–45 minutes, plus cooling

175g (6oz) shelled, unsalted pistachio
    nuts

125g (4oz) pinenuts

1 tsp ground cinnamon

½ tsp ground cloves

pinch of freshly grated nutmeg

2 tbsp caster sugar

225g (8oz) filo pastry, thawed
    if frozen

75g (3oz) unsalted butter, melted

SYRUP

grated zest and juice of ½ lemon

225g (8oz) clear honey

2 cardamom pods, bruised

2 tbsp rosewater (optional)

PER SERVING

479 cals; 31g fat (of which 7g saturates);
45g carbohydrate; 0.4g salt

1   Preheat the oven to 180°C (160°C fan oven) mark 4. Put the pistachio nuts, pinenuts, cinnamon, cloves and nutmeg into a food processor and pulse briefly until coarsely ground. Stir in the sugar.

2   Brush a sheet of filo pastry with melted butter and press into an 18 x 25.5cm (7 x 10 inch) baking tin. Continue to brush and layer half the filo. Scatter the nut mixture over, then top with the remaining filo sheets, brushing each with butter. Score through the pastry in a diamond pattern. Drizzle with any remaining butter and bake for 20 minutes. Lower the oven setting to 170°C (150°C fan oven) mark 3 and bake for a further 20–25 minutes until crisp and golden.

3   To make the syrup, put the lemon zest and juice, honey, cardamom pods and 150ml (¼ pint) water into a pan and simmer gently for 5 minutes. Remove from the heat and stir in the rosewater, if you like. Pour half the honey syrup evenly over the hot baklava. Leave in the tin until completely cold. Cut into diamond shapes and drizzle with the remaining syrup.

CINNAMON WHIRLS

Preparation: 20 minutes, plus cooling

Cooking time: 20 minutes, plus cooling

3 tbsp golden caster sugar, plus extra
   to dust
375g ready-rolled puff pastry
1 tsp ground cinnamon
1 tsp ground mixed spice
1 medium egg, beaten

PER WHIRL

49 cals; 3g fat (of which 0g saturates);
6g carbohydrate; 0.1g salt

1 Preheat the oven to 200°C (180°C fan oven) mark 6. Sprinkle the worksurface with caster sugar in a rectangle measuring 35.5 x 23cm (14 x 9 inch). Unroll the pastry and lay it on top to fit the shape of the sugar rectangle. Trim the edges, then cut vertically down the middle to make two smaller rectangles.

2 Mix the cinnamon with the mixed spice and remaining sugar in a small bowl. Sprinkle half the spice mixture evenly over the pastry rectangles. Fold the top and bottom edges of the pastry pieces into the middle so they meet at the centre. Sprinkle the remaining spice mixture over the surface and repeat, folding the upper and lower folded edges in to meet in the centre. Finally, fold in half lengthways to make a log shape.

3 Turn each roll over so that the seam faces down, trim off the ragged ends, then cut into slices 1cm (½ inch) wide. Lay the slices flat, spaced well apart, on two non-stick baking sheets. Reshape them slightly if needed, but don't worry if the rolls look loose – as the pastry cooks, they'll puff up.

4 Lightly brush each pastry whirl with a little beaten egg, sprinkle with a dusting of sugar and bake for 20 minutes or until pale golden. Transfer to a wire rack and leave to cool before serving.

TO STORE
Store in an airtight container. They will keep for up to three days.

FREEZING TIP
To freeze, put the whirls into a freezerproof container and freeze for up to one month. To use, thaw overnight at cool room temperature.

DROP SCONES (SCOTCH PANCAKES)

Preparation: 10 minutes
Cooking time: 12–18 minutes

125g (4oz) self-raising flour
2 tbsp caster sugar
1 medium egg, beaten
150ml (¼ pint) milk
vegetable oil to grease
butter, or whipped cream and jam,
    to serve

PER SCONE
50–40 cals; 1g fat (of which 9–7g saturates);
9–7g carbohydrate; 0.1g salt

1 Mix the flour and sugar together in a bowl. Make a well in the centre and mix in the egg, with enough of the milk to make a batter the consistency of thick cream – working as quickly and lightly as possible.
2 Cook the mixture in batches: drop spoonfuls on to an oiled hot griddle or heavy-based frying pan. Keep the griddle at a steady heat and when bubbles rise to the surface of the scone and burst, after 2–3 minutes, turn over with a palette knife.
3 Cook for a further 2–3 minutes until golden brown on the other side.
4 Put the cooked drop scones on a clean teatowel and cover with another teatowel to keep them moist. Serve warm, with butter, or cream and jam.

WELSH CAKES

Preparation: 10 minutes

Cooking time: 3 minutes per batch,
plus cooling

oil to grease
225g (8oz) plain flour, plus extra to
    dust
1 tsp baking powder
pinch of salt
50g (2oz) butter or margarine
50g (2oz) lard
75g (3oz) caster sugar
50g (2oz) currants
1 medium egg, beaten
about 2 tbsp milk

PER CAKE

123 calories; 6g fat (of which 3g saturates);
18g carbohydrate; 0.2g salt

VARIATION

Griddle scones: Use the same quantity of self-
raising flour (instead of plain flour) with 1 tsp baking
powder, pinch of salt and ½ tsp freshly grated
nutmeg. Omit the lard. Use 50g (2oz) golden caster
sugar. Omit the currants. You may need 3–4 tbsp
milk. Roll out to 1cm (½ inch) thick and cut into
triangles or rounds. Cook for about 5 minutes on
each side. Serve the scones warm, split in half and
spread with butter.

1 Lightly oil a griddle or heavy-based frying pan.
2 Sift together the flour, baking powder and salt. Rub in
   the fats until the mixture resembles fine breadcrumbs.
   Add the sugar and currants.
3 Make a well in the centre, then add the beaten egg
   and enough milk to make a stiff paste similar to
   shortcrust pastry.
4 Roll the paste out on a lightly floured surface until
   5mm (¼ inch) thick and then, using a 7.5cm (3 inch)
   cutter, cut into rounds.
5 Cook the cakes slowly on the griddle for about
   3 minutes on each side until golden brown. Cool on
   a wire rack. Eat on the day they are made.

OVEN SCONES

Preparation: 15 minutes

Cooking time: 10 minutes, plus cooling

40g (1½oz) butter, diced, plus extra to grease
225g (8oz) self-raising flour, plus extra to dust
pinch of salt
1 tsp baking powder
about 150ml (¼ pint) milk
beaten egg or milk to glaze
whipped cream, or butter and jam to serve

PER SCONE

140 cals; 5g fat (of which 3g saturates); 22g carbohydrate; 0.7g salt

NOTE
To ensure a good rise, avoid heavy handling and make sure the rolled-out dough is at least 2cm (¾ inch) thick.

1 Preheat the oven to 220°C (200°C fan oven) mark 7. Grease a baking sheet. Sift the flour, salt and baking powder together into a bowl. Rub in the butter until the mixture resembles fine breadcrumbs. Using a knife to stir it in, add enough milk to give a fairly soft dough.
2 Gently roll or pat out the dough on a lightly floured surface to a 2cm (¾ inch) thickness and then, using a 6cm (2½ inch) plain cutter, cut out rounds.
3 Put on the baking sheet and brush the tops with beaten egg or milk. Bake for about 10 minutes until golden brown and well risen. Transfer to a wire rack and leave to cool.
4 Serve warm, split and filled with cream, or butter and jam.

VARIATIONS
Wholemeal scones: Replace half the white flour with wholemeal flour.

Fruit scones: Add 50g (2oz) currants, sultanas, raisins or chopped dates (or a mixture) to the dry ingredients.

Buttermilk scones: Increase the flour to 300g (11oz) and the butter to 50g (2oz). Replace the milk with 284ml carton buttermilk and add 25g (1oz) golden caster sugar. Bake for 12–15 minutes, then cool a little. Beat 250g (9oz) mascarpone in a bowl to soften. Add the seeds from 1 vanilla pod and beat well to combine. Serve the warm scones split and sandwiched together with the vanilla mascarpone and blueberry jam.

Cheese and herb scones: Sift 1 tsp mustard powder with the dry ingredients. Stir 50g (2oz) finely grated Cheddar cheese into the mixture before adding the milk. After glazing, sprinkle the tops with a little cheese.

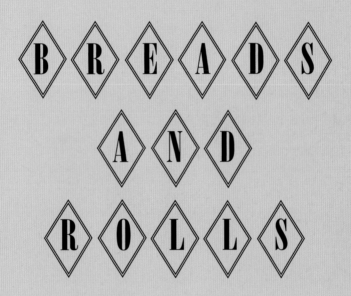

BREADS AND ROLLS

WHITE FARMHOUSE LOAF

MAKES I LOAF – CUTS INTO 12 SLICES

Preparation: 10 minutes, plus kneading

Cooking time: as per your machine, plus cooling

1 tsp easy-blend dried yeast
500g (1lb 2oz) strong white bread
    flour, plus extra to sprinkle
1 tbsp caster sugar
2 tbsp milk powder
1 1/2 tsp salt
25g (1oz) butter
350ml (12fl oz) water

PER SLICE
180 cals; 3g fat (of which 1g saturates); 34g carbohydrate; 0.9g salt

1 Put the ingredients into the bread maker bucket, following the order and method specified in the manual.
2 Fit the bucket into the bread maker and set to the Basic programme with a crust of your choice. Press start.
3 Just before baking starts, brush the top of the dough with water and sprinkle with flour. If preferred, slash the top of the bread lengthways with a sharp knife, taking care not to scratch the bucket.
4 After baking, remove the bread from the machine and shake out on to a wire rack to cool.

BROWN LOAF

**MAKES 1 LOAF –
CUTS INTO 16 SLICES**

Preparation: 25 minutes, plus sponging
and rising
Cooking time: 45–50 minutes, plus cooling

300g (11oz) strong plain white flour,
   sifted, plus extra to dust
200g (7oz) strong plain wholemeal
   flour
15g (½oz) fresh yeast or 1 tsp
   traditional dried yeast
2 tsp salt
vegetable oil to grease

PER SLICE

100 cals; 1g fat (of which 0.1g saturates);
22g carbohydrate; 0.6g salt

1 Put both flours into a large bowl, make a well in the centre and pour in 300ml (11fl oz) tepid water. Crumble the fresh yeast into the water (if using dried yeast, just sprinkle it over). Draw a little of the flour into the water and yeast and mix to form a batter. Sprinkle the salt over the remaining dry flour, so that it doesn't come into contact with the yeast. Cover with a clean teatowel and leave to 'sponge' for 20 minutes.

2 Combine the flour and salt with the batter to make a soft dough and knead for at least 10 minutes or until the dough feels smooth and elastic. Shape into a ball, put into an oiled bowl, cover with the teatowel and leave to rise at warm room temperature until doubled in size, 2–3 hours.

3 Knock back the dough, knead briefly and shape into a round on a lightly floured baking sheet. Slash the top with a sharp knife and dust with flour. Cover and leave to rise for 45 minutes–1½ hours or until doubled in size and spongy.

4 Preheat the oven to 200°C (180°C fan oven) mark 6. Bake the loaf for 45–50 minutes until it sounds hollow when tapped underneath. Transfer to a wire rack and leave to cool.

NOTE
The 'sponging' process in step 1 adds a fermentation stage, which gives a slightly lighter loaf.

GRANARY BREAD

MAKES 1 LOAF – CUTS INTO 16 SLICES

Preparation: 20 minutes, plus rising

Cooking time: 30–35 minutes, plus cooling

125g (4oz) strong plain wholemeal
   flour, plus extra to dust
450g (1lb) malted strong Granary
   flour
2 tsp salt
15g (½ oz) butter, diced
125g (4oz) rolled oats, plus extra
   to dust
2 tsp fast-action dried yeast
   (see note)
150ml (¼ pint) warm milk
1 tbsp malt extract
vegetable oil to grease

PER SLICE
160 cals; 2g fat (of which 0.7g saturates);
30g carbohydrate; 0.6g salt

1 Put the flours into a bowl and stir in the salt. Rub in the butter, then stir in the rolled oats and yeast. Make a well in the centre and add the warm milk, malt extract and 300ml (½ pint) warm water. Work to a smooth soft dough, adding a little extra water if necessary.

2 Knead for 10 minutes or until smooth, then shape the dough into a ball and put into an oiled bowl. Cover and leave to rise in a warm place for 1–2 hours until doubled in size.

3 Knock back the dough on a lightly floured surface and shape into a large round. Put on a baking sheet, cover and leave to rise for a further 30 minutes.

4 Preheat the oven to 230°C (210°C fan oven) mark 8. Using a sharp knife, cut a cross on the top of the loaf and sprinkle a few more oats over. Bake for 15 minutes. Lower the oven setting to 200°C (180°C fan oven) mark 6 and bake for a further 15–20 minutes until the bread is risen and sounds hollow when tapped underneath. Transfer to a wire rack and leave to cool.

NOTE
If available, use 40g (1½oz) fresh yeast instead of dried. Proceed as for White Farmhouse Loaf (see note, page 194).

WHOLEMEAL BREAD

Preparation: 15 minutes, plus rising

Cooking time: 30–35 minutes, plus cooling

225g (8oz) strong plain white flour, plus extra to dust

450g (1lb) strong plain wholemeal flour

2 tsp salt

1 tsp golden caster sugar

2 tsp fast-action dried yeast (see note)

vegetable oil to grease

PER SLICE

140 cals; 1g fat (of which 0.1g saturates); 29g carbohydrate; 0.6g salt

1 Sift the white flour into a large bowl and stir in the wholemeal flour, salt, sugar and yeast. Make a well in the centre and add about 450ml (¾ pint) warm water. Work to a smooth, soft dough, adding a little extra water if necessary.

2 Knead for 10 minutes or until smooth, then shape the dough into a ball and put into an oiled bowl. Cover and leave to rise in a warm place for about 2 hours until doubled in size.

3 Knock back the dough on a lightly floured surface and shape into an oblong. Press into an oiled 900g (2lb) loaf tin, cover and leave to rise for a further 30 minutes.

4 Preheat the oven to 230°C (210°C fan oven) mark 8. Bake the loaf for 15 minutes. Lower the oven setting to 200°C (180°C fan oven) mark 6 and bake for a further 15–20 minutes until the bread is risen and sounds hollow when tapped underneath. Leave in the tin for 10 minutes, then turn out on to a wire rack and leave to cool.

NOTE
If available, use 40g (1½oz) fresh yeast instead of dried. Proceed as for White Farmhouse Loaf (see note, page 194).

FRENCH COUNTRY BREAD

MAKES 1 LARGE LOAF – CUTS INTO ABOUT 12 SLICES

Preparation: 15 minutes, plus kneading and rising
Cooking time: 30–35 minutes, plus cooling

1½ tsp easy-blend dried yeast
300g (10oz) strong white bread flour,
    plus extra to dust
150g (5oz) spelt flour
50g (2oz) rye flour
1½ tsp salt
1 tbsp clear honey
25g (1oz) butter
350ml (12fl oz) milk
oil to grease

PER SLICE

170 cals; 3g fat (of which 1g saturates);
34g carbohydrate; 0.7g salt

1 Put all the ingredients except the oil into the bread maker bucket, following the order and method specified in the manual.
2 Fit the bucket into the bread maker and set to the dough programme. Press start. Oil a large baking sheet.

FREEZING TIP
To freeze, complete the recipe. Once the bread is cold, slice, if you like, for convenience, then pack, seal and freeze. To use, thaw at cool room temperature.

3 Once the dough is ready, turn it out on to a floured surface and punch it down to deflate. Shape the dough into a ball and place on the baking sheet. Cover loosely with lightly oiled clingfilm and leave to rise in a warm place for about 30 minutes until doubled in size. Preheat the oven to 220°C (fan oven 200°C) mark 7.
4 Sprinkle the top of the dough with flour. Using a very sharp knife, make 4 or 5 deep cuts diagonally across the top of the dough, then similarly in the opposite direction to create a diamond pattern.
5 Bake for 15 minutes, then lower the oven setting to 190°C (fan oven 170°C) mark 5 and bake for a further 15–20 minutes until the loaf sounds hollow when tapped underneath, covering with foil if it starts to brown too quickly. Transfer to a wire rack to cool.

SOFT GRAIN OATMEAL BREAD

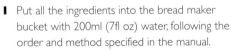
BREAD MACHINE RECIPE

MAKES 1 LARGE LOAF – CUTS INTO ABOUT 12 SLICES

Preparation: 10 minutes, plus kneading

Cooking time: as per your machine, plus cooling

1¼ tsp easy-blend dried yeast

300g (11oz) strong white bread flour

100g (3½oz) medium oatmeal, plus extra to sprinkle

75g (3oz) strong wholemeal or brown bread flour

1 tsp salt

3 tbsp clear or thick honey

150ml (¼ pint) natural yogurt

25g (1oz) butter

PER SLICE

170 cals; 3g fat (of which 1g saturates); 33g carbohydrate; 0.5g salt

1   Put all the ingredients into the bread maker bucket with 200ml (7fl oz) water, following the order and method specified in the manual.
2   Fit the bucket into the bread maker and set to the basic programme with a light crust. Press start.
3   Just before baking, brush the top of the dough with water and sprinkle with oatmeal.
4   After baking, remove the bucket from the machine, then turn out the bread on to a wire rack to cool.

FREEZING TIP
To freeze, complete the recipe. Once the bread is cold, slice, if you like, for convenience, then pack, seal and freeze. To use, thaw at cool room temperature.

OATMEAL SODA BREAD

Preparation: 15 minutes

Cooking time: 25 minutes, plus cooling

25g (1oz) butter, plus extra to grease

275g (10oz) plain wholemeal flour

175g (6oz) coarse oatmeal

2 tsp cream of tartar

1 tsp salt

about 300ml (10fl oz) milk and water, mixed

PER SLICE

183 cals; 4g fat (of which 2g saturates); 31g carbohydrate; 0.6g salt

1 Preheat the oven to 220°C (200°C fan oven) mark 7. Grease and base-line a 900g (2lb) loaf tin.

2 Mix together all the dry ingredients in a bowl. Rub in the butter, then add the milk and water to bind to a soft dough. Spoon into the prepared tin.

3 Bake in the oven for about 25 minutes until golden brown and well risen. Turn out on to a wire rack and leave to cool slightly. It is best eaten on the day it is made.

DARK RYE BREAD

Preparation: 20 minutes, plus rising

Cooking time: about 50 minutes, plus cooling

350g (12oz) rye flour, plus extra to dust

50g (2oz) plain wholemeal flour

zest of 1 lemon

1 tsp salt

25g (1oz) butter

1 tsp caraway seeds, lightly crushed (optional)

125g (4oz) cool mashed potato

15g (½oz) fresh yeast or 1½ tsp traditional dried yeast and 1 tsp sugar

1 tsp sugar

50g (2oz) molasses or black treacle

oil to grease

PER SLICE

112 calories; 2g fat (of which 1g saturates); 22g carbohydrate; 0.4g salt

1 Mix together the flours, lemon zest and salt. Rub in the butter, caraway seeds, if you like, and mashed potato.

2 Blend the fresh yeast with 150ml (¼ pint) tepid water. If using dried yeast, sprinkle it into the water with 1 tsp sugar and leave in a warm place for 15 minutes or until frothy. Heat the other 1 tsp sugar, molasses and 2 tbsp water together. Cool until tepid.

3 Pour the yeast liquid and molasses mixture on to the dry ingredients and beat well to form a firm dough. Knead on a lightly floured surface for 10 minutes or until smooth and no longer sticky. Place in an oiled bowl, cover with oiled clingfilm and leave to rise in a warm place for about 1½ hours until doubled in size.

4 Knead again for 5 minutes, then shape into a large round, about 18cm (7 inch) in diameter. Place on a baking sheet. Cut a criss-cross pattern on the surface of the loaf to a depth of 5mm (¼ inch). Dust with a little more flour. Leave to rise in a warm place for 10–15 minutes. Preheat the oven to 200°C (180°C fan oven) mark 6.

5 Bake the loaf in the oven for about 50 minutes. Turn out on to a wire rack and leave to cool completely.

FREEZING TIP

To freeze, complete the recipe. Once the bread is cold, slice, if you like, for convenience, then pack, seal and freeze. To use, thaw at cool room temperature.

BASIC GLUTEN-FREE WHITE BREAD

BREAD MACHINE RECIPE

Preparation: 5 minutes, plus kneading

Cooking time: as per your machine, plus cooling

1 tsp easy-blend dried yeast

350g (12oz) gluten-free bread flour, for bread machines

½ tsp salt

1 tbsp olive oil

PER SLICE

130 cals; 2g fat (of which 0.2g saturates);
27g carbohydrate; 0.2g salt

FREEZING TIP
To freeze, complete the recipe. Once the bread is cold, slice, if you like, for convenience, then pack, seal and freeze. To use, thaw at cool room temperature.

1 Put all the ingredients into the bread maker bucket with 300ml (½ pint) water, following the order and method specified in the manual.
2 Fit the bucket into the bread maker and set to the programme and crust recommended for gluten-free breads. Press start.
3 After baking, remove the bucket from the machine, then turn out on to a wire rack to cool.

GLUTEN-FREE SEED LOAF

BREAD MACHINE RECIPE

MAKES 1 SMALL LOAF – CUTS INTO ABOUT 10 THICK SLICES

Preparation: 10 minutes, plus kneading

Cooking time: as per your machine, plus cooling

2 tbsp sesame seeds
1 tbsp poppy seeds
1 tbsp pumpkin seeds
1 tbsp linseeds
1 tsp easy-blend dried yeast
350g (12oz) gluten-free fibre mix, for bread
    machines
½ tsp salt
2 tsp light muscovado sugar
15g (½oz) butter

PER SLICE

160 cals; 6g fat (of which 1g saturates);
26g carbohydrate; 0.3g salt

FREEZING TIP

To freeze, complete the recipe. Once the bread is cold, slice, if you like, for convenience, then pack, seal and freeze. To use, thaw at cool room temperature.

1 Mix the seeds together and reserve 1 tbsp to sprinkle. Put all the ingredients into the bread maker bucket with 325ml (11fl oz) water, following the order and method specified in the manual, adding the seeds with the gluten-free fibre mix.

2 Fit the bucket into the bread maker and set to the programme and crust recommended for gluten-free breads. Press start. Fibre mixes are based on the same gluten-free wheat starch as standard gluten-free flour, with added vegetable fibre. Since they usually absorb more water, you need to check the mixture during the kneading cycle, adding a dash more water if necessary.

3 Just before baking starts, scatter the reserved seeds over the surface of the dough.

4 After baking, remove the bucket from the machine, then turn out the bread on to a wire rack to cool.

TOASTED SEED AND NUT BREAD

MAKES 1 MEDIUM LOAF – CUTS INTO ABOUT 10 SLICES

Preparation: 10 minutes, plus kneading

Cooking time: as per your machine, plus cooling

75g (3oz) unblanched hazelnuts, finely chopped
2 tbsp each of poppy, sesame, sunflower and
   pumpkin seeds
1 tsp easy-blend dried yeast
375g (13oz) strong white bread flour
25g (1oz) wheat bran
1 tsp salt
2 tsp light muscovado sugar
2 tbsp hazelnut or sunflower oil

PER SLICE

256 cals; 13g fat (of which 1g saturates); 31g carbohydrate; 0.5g salt

1 Toast the hazelnuts in a dry frying pan over a gentle heat, stirring, until they begin to colour, about 2 minutes. Add the seeds and fry gently for a further 1 minute. Take off the heat.
2 Put all the remaining ingredients in the bread maker bucket with 300ml (½ pint) water, following the order and method specified in the manual. Set aside 2 tbsp of the toasted nut mixture; add the rest to the bucket.
3 Fit the bucket into the bread maker and set to the basic programme with a crust of your choice. Press start.
4 Just before baking starts, brush the top of the dough with 1 tbsp water and sprinkle with the reserved nuts and seeds.
5 After baking, remove the bucket from the machine, then turn out the bread on to a wire rack to cool.

FREEZING TIP

To freeze, complete the recipe. Once the bread is cold, slice, if you like, for convenience, then pack, seal and freeze. To use, thaw at cool room temperature.

CORNBREAD

Preparation: 5 minutes
Cooking time: 25–30 minutes

oil to grease
125g (4oz) plain flour
175g (6oz) polenta (see note) or
    cornmeal
1 tbsp baking powder
1 tbsp caster sugar
½ tsp salt
300ml (½ pint) buttermilk, or equal
    quantities of natural yogurt and
    milk, mixed together
2 medium eggs
4 tbsp extra virgin olive oil

PER SERVING

229 cals; 8g fat (of which 1g saturates);
33g carbohydrate; 1.3g salt

1 Preheat the oven to 200°C (180°C fan oven) mark 6.
   Generously oil a 20.5cm (8 inch) square shallow tin.
2 Put the flour into a large bowl, then add the polenta
   or cornmeal, the baking powder, sugar and salt. Make a
   well in the centre and pour in the buttermilk or yogurt
   and milk mixture. Add the eggs and olive oil and stir
   together until evenly mixed.

3 Pour into the tin and bake for 25–30 minutes until
   firm to the touch. Insert a skewer into the centre –
   if it comes out clean, the cornbread is done.
4 Leave the cornbread to rest in the tin for 5 minutes,
   then turn out and cut into chunky triangles. Serve
   warm with butter.

NOTE
Use dried polenta grains for this recipe.

BLACK OLIVE BREAD

Preparation: 40 minutes, plus rising

Cooking time: 30–35 minutes

2 tsp traditional dried yeast

500g (1lb 2oz) strong white bread
flour, plus extra to dust

2 tsp coarse salt, plus extra to
sprinkle

6 tbsp extra virgin olive oil, plus extra
to grease

100g (3½oz) black olives, pitted and
chopped

PER LOAF

600 cals; 21g fat (of which 3g saturates);
97g carbohydrate; 3.8g salt

1 Put 150ml (¼ pint) hand-hot water into a jug, stir in
the yeast and leave for 10 minutes or until frothy.
Put the flour into a bowl or a food processor, then
add the salt, yeast mix, 200ml (7fl oz) warm water and
2 tbsp olive oil. Using a wooden spoon or the dough
hook, mix for 2–3 minutes to make a soft smooth
dough. Put the dough into a lightly oiled bowl, cover
with oiled clingfilm and leave in a warm place for
45 minutes or until doubled in size.

2 Punch the dough to knock out the air, then knead on a
lightly floured surface for 1 minute. Add the olives and
knead until combined. Divide in half, shape into
rectangles and put into two greased tins, each about
25.5 x 15cm (10 x 6 inch). Cover with clingfilm and
leave in a warm place for 1 hour or until the dough
is puffy.

3 Preheat the oven to 200°C (180°C fan oven) mark 6.
Press your finger into the dough 12 times, drizzle
2 tbsp oil over the surface and sprinkle with salt.
Bake for 30–35 minutes until golden. Drizzle with the
remaining oil. Slice and serve warm.

WALNUT AND GARLIC BREAD

SERVES 8

Preparation: 25 minutes, plus rising

Cooking time: about 1 hour 35 minutes

oil to grease
500g (1lb 2oz) strong white bread
   flour with kibbled grains of rye and
   wheat, plus extra to dust
7g sachet fast-action dried yeast
2 tsp salt
1 tbsp malt extract
50g (2oz) butter, softened
3 garlic cloves, peeled and crushed
100g (3½oz) walnut pieces
1 tbsp milk mixed with 1 tbsp malt
   extract to glaze

PER SERVING

359 cals; 15g fat (of which 4g saturates);
52g carbohydrate; 1.3g salt

1. Lightly oil a 20.5cm (8 inch) springform cake tin. Put the flour, yeast and salt into a freestanding mixer with a dough hook. Add 300ml (½ pint) lukewarm water and the malt extract, then mix to a pliable dough. Increase the speed and machine-knead for 5 minutes.

NOTE
To freeze, follow the recipe and cooking times in step 3, but don't glaze and bake for the final 5 minutes. Leave to cool in the tin. Wrap and freeze for up to two months. To use, thaw, uncovered, at room temperature for 6 hours. Glaze the bread, put it on a hot baking sheet and bake at 220°C (200°C fan oven) mark 7 for 8–10 minutes until hot throughout.

2. Turn out on to a lightly floured surface and roll the dough into a rectangle about 40.5 × 28cm (16 × 11 inch). Mix the butter with the garlic and spread over the dough, then scatter the walnuts over. Starting at one long edge, roll up the dough into a sausage. Cut into eight slices and put in the prepared tin. Cover with lightly oiled clingfilm and leave to rise in a warm place for 45 minutes or until doubled in size.

3. Preheat the oven to 220°C (200°C fan oven) mark 7 and put a baking sheet in to heat. Remove the clingfilm, cover the bread with foil and put on the hot baking sheet. Bake for 20 minutes. Lower the oven setting to 200°C (180°C fan oven) mark 6 and bake for 1 hour 10 minutes. Brush with the glaze and bake, uncovered, for a further 5 minutes or until golden brown. Leave in the tin to cool slightly. Serve warm.

SUN-DRIED TOMATO AND HERB LOAF

BREAD MACHINE RECIPE

MAKES 1 SMALL LOAF – CUTS INTO ABOUT 10 THICK SLICES

Preparation: 10 minutes, plus kneading

Cooking time: as per your machine, plus cooling

small handful of fresh herbs, about 15g (½oz)
    (see variation)
1 tsp easy-blend dried yeast
350g (12oz) gluten-free bread flour, for bread
    machines
½ tsp salt
1 tbsp golden caster sugar
25g (1oz) butter
4 tbsp sun-dried tomato paste

PER SLICE
150 cals; 3g fat (of which 1g saturates); 30g carbohydrate;
0.3g salt

FREEZING TIP
To freeze, complete the recipe. Once the bread
is cold, slice, if you like, for convenience, then
pack, seal and freeze. To use, thaw at cool room
temperature.

1 Reserve several of the herb sprigs to garnish; finely
    chop the rest, discarding any tough stalks. Put all the
    ingredients into the bread maker bucket with 300ml
    (½ pint) water, following the order and method
    specified in the manual, adding the chopped herbs and
    tomato paste with the water.
2 Fit the bucket into the bread maker and set to the
    programme and crust recommended for gluten-free
    breads. Press start.
3 Just before baking, scatter the reserved herb sprigs
    over the surface of the dough.
4 After baking, remove the bucket from the machine,
    then turn out the bread on to a wire rack to cool.

VARIATION
You can use almost any fresh herb in this bread.
Thyme, parsley, fennel and tarragon are all
sufficiently intense, while rosemary and oregano go
particularly well with the sun-dried tomato flavour.

ITALIAN ROSEMARY AND RAISIN LOAF

MAKES 1 MEDIUM LOAF – CUTS INTO ABOUT 10 SLICES

Preparation: 10 minutes, plus kneading

Cooking time: as per your machine, plus cooling

2 medium eggs
1 tsp easy-blend dried yeast
400g (14oz) strong white bread flour
1 tsp salt
3 tbsp freshly chopped rosemary, plus small rosemary sprigs to finish
1 tbsp golden caster sugar
4 tbsp extra virgin olive oil
125g (4oz) raisins

PER SLICE

240 cals; 7g fat (of which 1g saturates); 40g carbohydrate; 0.6g salt

1. Lightly beat the eggs in a measuring jug. Make up the volume to 250ml (9fl oz) with water.
2. Put all the ingredients except the rosemary sprigs and raisins into the bread maker bucket, following the order and method specified in the manual, adding the chopped rosemary after the flour.
3. Fit the bucket into the bread maker and set to the basic programme with raisin setting, if applicable. Select the crust of your choice and press start. Add the raisins when the machine beeps, or halfway through the kneading cycle.
4. Just before baking, press plenty of small rosemary sprigs into the surface of the dough.
5. After baking, remove the bucket from the machine, then turn out the bread on to a wire rack to cool.

FREEZING TIP
To freeze, complete the recipe. Once the bread is cold, slice, if you like, for convenience, then pack, seal and freeze. To use, thaw at cool room temperature.

FENNEL, GREEN PEPPERCORN AND GRUYÈRE BREAD

MAKES 1 MEDIUM LOAF – CUTS INTO ABOUT 10 SLICES

Preparation: 10 minutes, plus kneading

Cooking time: as per your machine, plus cooling

25g (1oz) butter

200g (7oz) fennel bulb, finely chopped

2 tbsp green peppercorns in brine, drained

1 tsp easy-blend dried yeast

400g (14oz) strong white bread flour

1 tsp salt

2 tbsp freshly chopped fennel fronds

50g (2oz) Gruyère cheese, grated

PER SLICE

180 cals; 4g fat (of which 2g saturates); 31g carbohydrate; 0.6g salt

FREEZING TIP

To freeze, complete the recipe. Once the bread is cold, slice, if you like, for convenience, then pack, seal and freeze. To use, thaw at cool room temperature.

1 Melt the butter in a frying pan, add the chopped fennel and fry gently for 5 minutes until very soft. Lightly crush the peppercorns using a pestle and mortar, or a small bowl and the end of a rolling pin.

2 Put the yeast, flour, salt and 250ml (9fl oz) water into the bread maker bucket, following the order and method specified in the manual. Add the fennel fronds and crushed peppercorns.

3 Fit the bucket into the bread maker and set to the basic programme with raisin setting, if applicable. Select the crust of your choice and press start. Add the sautéed fennel and cheese to the bucket when the machine beeps, or halfway through the kneading cycle.

4 After baking, remove the bucket from the machine, then turn out the bread on to a wire rack to cool.

CHICKPEA, CHILLI AND ONION LOAF

BREAD MACHINE RECIPE

**MAKES 1 MEDIUM LOAF –
CUTS INTO ABOUT 10 SLICES**

Preparation: 10 minutes, plus kneading

Cooking time: as per your machine, plus cooling

1 tsp easy-blend dried yeast

400g (14oz) strong white bread flour

1 tsp salt

3 tbsp olive oil

2 tsp golden caster sugar

1 small red onion, peeled and finely chopped

1 green chilli, deseeded and chopped

2 tsp cumin seeds, lightly crushed

100g (3½oz) canned chickpeas, rinsed and drained
   (see note)

PER SLICE

190 cals; 5g fat (of which 1g saturates); 34g carbohydrate; 0.6g salt

FREEZING TIP
To freeze, complete the recipe. Once the bread is cold, slice, if you like, for convenience, then pack, seal and freeze. To use, thaw at cool room temperature.

1 Put all the ingredients except the chickpeas into the bread maker bucket with 200ml (7fl oz) water, following the order and method specified in the manual, adding the onion, chilli and crushed cumin seeds after the flour.

2 Fit the bucket into the bread maker and set to the basic programme with raisin setting, if applicable. Select the crust of your choice and press start. Add the chickpeas when the machine beeps, or halfway through the kneading cycle.

3 After baking, remove the bucket from the machine, then turn out on to a wire rack to cool.

NOTE
Don't be tempted to add the remaining chickpeas from the can to the bread; keep them for a salad or vegetable dish.

SALT AND PEPPER ROLLS

Preparation: 40 minutes, plus rising
Cooking time: 30–35 minutes

700g (1½lb) strong white bread flour,
plus extra to dust
7g sachet fast-action dried yeast
1 tsp sea salt flakes, plus extra to
sprinkle
1 tsp red peppercorns
1 tsp green peppercorns
2 tbsp olive oil, plus extra to grease
1 medium egg, beaten

PER ROLL
157 cals; 2g fat (of which trace saturates);
33g carbohydrate; 0.3g salt

FREEZING TIP
To freeze, complete the
recipe, but only bake the rolls
for 25 minutes, then cool,
wrap and freeze for up to
three months. To use, bake
from frozen in a preheated
oven at 200°C (180°C fan
oven) mark 6 for 12–15
minutes until golden and piping
hot throughout.

1 Sift the flour into a large warmed bowl. Stir in the yeast. Crush the salt and
peppercorns in a pestle and mortar and stir into the flour. Make a well in
the centre of the flour, then pour in the oil and enough lukewarm water
to make a soft dough – about 500ml (almost 1 pint). Knead for 5 minutes
or until smooth. (Alternatively, put the flour, yeast, salt, peppercorns, oil
and water into a freestanding mixer and knead to a soft dough with a
dough hook.)
2 Transfer the dough to a large oiled bowl, cover with oiled clingfilm and
leave in a warm place until doubled in size.
3 Turn the dough out on to a lightly floured surface and knead for about 5
minutes. Return the dough to the oiled bowl, cover with oiled clingfilm and
leave in a warm place until doubled in size.
4 Punch the dough to knock back, then knead for 1 minute. Divide into
16 pieces and shape each one into a roll. Put the rolls on oiled baking
sheets, spaced well apart, cover with oiled clingfilm and leave for about
30 minutes or until spongy. Preheat the oven to 220°C (200°C fan oven)
mark 7.
5 Brush the rolls with beaten egg, sprinkle with a little salt and bake for
30–35 minutes until golden. Serve warm.

FLOURY BAPS

BREAD MACHINE RECIPE

MAKES 8 BAPS

Preparation: 10 minutes, plus kneading
and rising
Cooking time: 18–20 minutes, plus cooling

1 tsp easy-blend dried yeast
450g (1lb) strong white bread flour,
    plus extra to dust
1 tsp salt
1 tsp golden caster sugar
15g (½oz) butter
150ml (¼ pint) milk, plus extra to
    brush
oil to grease

PER BAP

220 cals; 3g fat (of which 1g saturates);
45g carbohydrate; 0.7g salt

1 Put all the ingredients except the oil into the bread maker bucket with 125ml (4fl oz) water, following the order and method specified in the manual.
2 Fit the bucket into the bread maker and set to the dough programme. Press start. Lightly oil a large baking sheet.
3 Once the dough is ready, turn it out on to a lightly floured surface and punch it down to deflate. Divide into 8 even-sized pieces. Shape each piece into a round and flatten with the palm of your hand until about 10cm (4 inch) in diameter.
4 Space slightly apart on the baking sheet and brush lightly with milk. Sprinkle generously with flour, cover loosely with a cloth and leave to rise for 30–40 minutes until doubled in size.
5 Preheat the oven to 200°C (180°C fan oven) mark 6. Using your thumb, make a deep impression in the centre of each bap. Dust with a little more flour and bake for 18–20 minutes until risen and pale golden around the edges. Eat warm or transfer to a wire rack to cool.

NAN

Preparation: 20 minutes, plus rising

Cooking time: 10–12 minutes

15g (½oz) fresh yeast or 1½ tsp
    traditional dried yeast
about 150ml (¼ pint) tepid milk
450g (1lb) plain white flour, plus extra
    to dust
1 tsp baking powder
½ tsp salt
2 tsp caster sugar
1 medium egg, beaten
2 tbsp vegetable oil, plus extra to
    grease
4 tbsp natural yogurt

PER NAN

336 calories; 6g fat (of which 1g saturates);
62g carbohydrate; 0.7g salt

VARIATION

Peshawari nan (nan with sultanas and
almonds): Follow the recipe above to the
beginning of step 4. To make the filling, mix
together 175g (6oz) sultanas, 3 tbsp chopped
fresh coriander, 175g (6oz) ground almonds
and 6 tbsp melted butter. Knead the dough
on a lightly floured surface and divide into 6
equal pieces. Roll each out into a round about
15cm (6 inch) in diameter. Spoon the filling
into the centre of the nan and fold the dough
over to completely enclose the filling. Press
the edges well together to seal. Roll out each
piece on a lightly floured surface and shape
into a large tear-drop about 25cm (10 inch)
long. Cook as in step 5 of the recipe.

1 Blend the fresh yeast with the milk. If using dried yeast,
   sprinkle it into the milk and leave in a warm place for
   15 minutes or until frothy.
2 Sift the flour, baking powder and salt into a large bowl.
   Make a well in the centre and stir in the sugar, egg, oil
   and yogurt. Add the yeast liquid and mix well to a soft
   dough, adding more milk if necessary. Turn the dough
   out on to a lightly floured surface and knead well for
   10 minutes or until smooth and elastic.
3 Place the dough in a bowl, cover with oiled clingfilm
   and leave to rise in a warm place for about 1 hour
   until doubled in size.
4 Preheat the grill. Knead the dough on a lightly floured
   surface for 2–3 minutes, then divide into 6 equal-sized
   pieces. Roll out each piece on a lightly floured surface
   and shape into a large tear-drop about 25.5cm
   (10 inch) long.
5 Place a nan on a baking sheet and put under the hot
   grill. Cook for 1½–2 minutes on each side until golden
   brown and puffy. Cook the remaining nan in the same
   way. Serve warm.

PITTA BREAD

MAKES 16

Preparation: 20 minutes, plus rising

Cooking time: 5–8 minutes per batch, plus cooling

15g (½oz) fresh yeast or 1½ tsp
    traditional dried yeast and
    1 tsp sugar
700g (1½lb) strong white flour, plus
    extra to dust
1 tsp salt
1 tbsp caster sugar
1 tbsp olive oil, plus extra to grease

PER PITTA
159 calories; 1g fat (of which 0.2g saturates);
34g carbohydrate; 0.3g salt

1 Blend the fresh yeast with 450ml (¾ pint) tepid water. If using dried yeast, sprinkle it into the water with the sugar and leave in a warm place for 15 minutes or until frothy.

2 Put the flour, salt and sugar into a bowl, make a well in the centre and pour in the yeast liquid with the olive oil. Mix to a smooth dough, then turn out on to a lightly floured surface and knead for 10 minutes or until smooth and elastic.

3 Place the dough in a large bowl, cover with oiled clingfilm and leave to rise in a warm place until doubled in size.

4 Divide the dough into 16 pieces and roll each into an oval shape about 20.5cm (8 inch) long. Place on floured baking sheets, cover with oiled clingfilm and leave in a warm place for about 30 minutes until slightly risen and

puffy. Preheat the oven to 240°C (220°C) mark 9.

5 Bake the pittas in batches for 5–8 minutes only. They should be just lightly browned on top. Remove from the oven and wrap in a clean teatowel. Repeat with the remaining pittas.

6 When the pittas are warm enough to handle, but not completely cold, transfer them to a plastic bag and leave until cold. This will ensure that they have a soft crust.

7 To serve, warm in the oven, or toast lightly. Split and fill with salads, cheese, cold meats or your favourite sandwich filling. Or, cut into strips and serve with dips.

FAMILY-FAVOURITE PIZZA AND EASY PIZZA SAUCE

SERVES 4

Preparation: 30 minutes, plus rising

Cooking time: 15 minutes

oil to grease
1 pizza base dough (see page 129)
6 tbsp home-made pizza sauce (see right) or good-quality
    ready-made sauce
125g ball buffalo mozzarella, drained and torn into pieces
2 heaped tbsp ready-made pesto
basil and/or oregano leaves and ground black pepper

PER SERVING

368 cals; 16g fat (of which 5g saturates); 44g carbohydrate; 2.4g salt

1 Preheat the oven to 230°C (210°C fan oven) mark 8
   and lightly oil two baking sheets. Knock the air out of
   the pizza dough and divide in half (see step 4, page
   129). Roll each half into a 25.5cm (10 inch) circle.
   Transfer to baking sheets.

2 Spread the bases with the pizza sauce, then top with
   mozzarella and dollops of pesto. Bake for 10–15
   minutes until crisp and golden. Garnish with herbs and
   plenty of ground black pepper.

EASY PIZZA SAUCE

Makes enough sauce to cover 4 pizzas

Preparation: 10 minutes

Cooking time: 1 hour 10 minutes

1 onion, peeled and	1 bay leaf
finely chopped	2 tsp dried oregano
2 tbsp olive oil	1 tsp sugar
3 garlic cloves, peeled	salt and ground black
and crushed	pepper
2 tbsp tomato purée	
2 x 400g tins plum	
tomatoes	

PER SERVING

(3tbsp): 65 cals; 4g fat (of which 0.5g saturates);
6g carbohydrate; 1g salt

1 Fry the onion over a low heat in the oil until
   softened. Add the garlic and cook for 1 minute.
   Add the tomato purée and cook for 1 minute.
   Add the tomatoes, bay leaf, oregano and sugar
   and cook gently for 1 hour, crushing the
   tomatoes with the back of a wooden spoon,
   until the sauce is thick and pulpy.

2 Remove the bay leaf and check the seasoning.
   Use straightaway or cool, freeze in batches and
   use within three months.

NOTES

- Make double the quantity of dough and freeze
  half, wrapped well in clingfilm. After thawing,
  the dough will need to rise for about 1 hour
  before you roll it out.

- If you don't have time to make the dough,
  this recipe works well with good ready-made
  pizza bases.

CHEAT'S GOAT'S CHEESE AND SAUSAGE PIZZA

Preparation: 15 minutes
Cooking time: 30 minutes

1 pizza base dough (see page 129)
4 tsp Dijon mustard
1 large red onion, peeled and thinly
  sliced
225g (8oz) courgettes, trimmed and
  sliced wafer thin
2 spicy pepperoni sausages
2 x 100g (3½oz) packets soft goat's
  cheese
fresh thyme sprigs (optional)
olive oil to drizzle
salt and ground black pepper

PER SERVING

465 cals; 24g fat (of which 11g saturates);
48g carbohydrate; 2.7g salt

1 Preheat the oven to 200°C (180°C fan oven) mark
  6 and put two baking sheets in on separate shelves
  to heat up.

2 Shape the dough into two bases (see step 4, page
  129). When the baking sheets have heated up, take
  them out of the oven (use oven gloves) and put a
  pizza base on each baking sheet. Spread each one
  with half the mustard, then sprinkle the onion and
  courgette slices over the mustard. Season with salt
  and pepper.

3 Remove the sausages from their skins and crumble
  on top of each pizza with the goat's cheese. Sprinkle
  the thyme on top, if you like, and drizzle with the oil.

4 Put the trays back into the oven and cook for
  30 minutes or until the crust and sausage are brown
  and the vegetables are cooked. Swap the pizzas
  around in the oven halfway through cooking so they
  cook evenly.

NOTES

- Pizza should not be a heavy dish, so add
  toppings with a light hand.

- A ceramic baking stone (from good kitchen
  shops) is extremely useful for cooking pizza,
  to help cook the pizza evenly and give
  crunchiness to the base. (Put the stone into
  the oven before preheating.)

POPPY SEED AND HONEY BAGELS

Preparation: 15 minutes, plus rising

Cooking time: 25 minutes, plus cooling

15g (½oz) fresh yeast or 1½ tsp
    traditional dried yeast and
    1 tsp sugar
50g (2oz) butter or margarine
2 tbsp runny honey
275g (10oz) strong plain white flour,
    plus extra to dust
175g (6oz) plain wholemeal flour
1 tsp salt
2 tbsp poppy seeds
oil to grease
milk to glaze

PER BAGEL

164 calories; 5g fat (of which 2g saturates);
29g carbohydrate; 0.5g salt

1 Blend the fresh yeast with 225ml (8fl oz) tepid water. If using dried yeast, sprinkle it into the water with the sugar and leave in a warm place for 15 minutes or until frothy. Heat the butter or margarine with the honey, then leave to cool.

2 Place the flours, salt and 2 tsp poppy seeds in a bowl. Make a well in the centre and pour in the yeast liquid and cooled honey mixture. Mix to a soft dough.

3 Turn the dough out on to a lightly floured surface and knead until smooth and no longer sticky. Place in a lightly oiled bowl, cover loosely with oiled clingfilm and leave in a warm place until doubled in size.

4 Lightly grease several baking sheets. Knead the dough for 5 minutes, then divide the dough into 12 pieces. Knead each piece until smooth, then roll to a sausage shape about 18cm (7 inch) long. Dampen the ends and seal together to form a ring. Place the rings well apart on the baking sheets, cover loosely with oiled clingfilm and leave until doubled in size.

5 Preheat the oven to 200°C (180°C fan oven) mark 6. Half fill a frying pan with water and heat to simmering point, then add the bagels a few at a time. Simmer for 20 seconds only (the bagels will puff up) and drain well, then place on well-oiled baking sheets.

6 Brush each bagel with milk and sprinkle on the remaining poppy seeds. Bake for about 20 minutes until well risen and golden brown.

CRUMPETS

Preparation: 20 minutes, plus rising

Cooking time: about 35 minutes

350g (12oz) strong plain white flour
½ tsp salt
½ tsp bicarbonate of soda
1 ½ tsp fast-action dried yeast
250ml (9fl oz) warm milk
a little vegetable oil to fry
butter to serve

PER CRUMPET

60 cals; 1g fat (of which 0.1g saturates);
12g carbohydrate; 0.2g salt

NOTE
The pan and metal rings
must be well oiled each time,
and heated between frying
each batch.

1 Sift the flour, salt and bicarbonate of soda into a large bowl and stir in the yeast. Make a well in the centre, then pour in 300ml (½ pint) warm water and the milk. Mix to a thick batter.

2 Using a wooden spoon, beat the batter vigorously for about 5 minutes. Cover and leave in a warm place for about 1 hour until sponge-like in texture. Beat the batter for a further 2 minutes, then transfer to a jug.

3 Put a large non-stick frying pan over a high heat and brush a little oil over the surface. Oil the insides of four crumpet rings or 7.5cm (3 inch) plain metal cutters. Put the rings, blunt-edge down, on to the hot pan surface and leave for about 2 minutes until very hot.

4 Pour a little batter into each ring to a depth of 1cm (½ inch). Cook the crumpets for 4–5 minutes until the surface is set and appears honeycombed with holes.

5 Carefully remove each metal ring. Flip the crumpets over and cook the other side for 1 minute only. Transfer to a wire rack. Repeat to use all of the batter.

6 To serve, toast the crumpets on both sides and serve with butter.

CIABATTA

BREAD MACHINE RECIPE

Preparation: 10 minutes, plus kneading and rising

Cooking time: 15–18 minutes, plus cooling

1 tsp easy-blend dried yeast

500g (1lb 2oz) strong white bread flour, plus extra to dust

1½ tsp salt

1 tsp golden caster sugar

2 tbsp olive oil

oil to grease

PER SERVING

250 cals; 4g fat (of which 0.5g saturates); 48g carbohydrate; 0.9g salt

1 Put all the ingredients except the oil into the bread maker bucket with 325ml (11fl oz) water, following the order and method specified in the manual.

2 Fit the bucket into the bread maker and set to the dough programme. Press start. Grease a large baking sheet and sprinkle with flour.

3 Once the dough is ready, turn it out on to a well-floured surface and cut in half, using a floured knife. Shape each piece of dough into a long strip and pass it from one hand to the other until it is stretched to about 28cm (11 inch) long. Lay the 2 dough strips well apart on the baking sheet. Leave to rise in a warm place, uncovered, for 30 minutes until doubled in size.

4 Preheat the oven to 220°C (fan oven 200°C) mark 7. Rub the dough lightly with a little extra flour to dust, then bake for 15–18 minutes until pale golden and crisp on the underside. Transfer to a wire rack to cool. Serve warm or cold.

NOTE
Any leftover ciabatta makes delicious croûtons. Cube and arrange on a baking sheet, then drizzle with a little olive oil. Bake at 180°C (160°C fan oven) gas mark 4 for 10–15 minutes until golden. Keep for up to a week in an airtight container.

FOCACCIA

**MAKES I LARGE FOCACCIA –
CUTS INTO 6 WEDGES**

Preparation: 10 minutes, plus kneading and rising

Cooking time: 20–25 minutes, plus cooling

1 tsp easy-blend dried yeast

475g (1lb 1oz) strong white bread flour, plus extra to dust

1½ tsp salt

3 tbsp olive oil, plus extra to grease

TO FINISH

fresh rosemary sprigs

2 tbsp olive oil

sea salt flakes

PER SERVING

264 cals; 8g fat (of which 1g saturates); 45g carbohydrate; 1.2g salt

NOTES

- The flan ring helps the bread to rise and bake in a perfect round, but don't worry if you haven't got one, just lay the dough, pizza-style, on the baking sheet.

- Other toppings include finely chopped garlic, thinly sliced onions, roughly chopped olives and ground black pepper.

1 Put all the dough ingredients into the bread maker bucket with 300ml (½ pint) water, following the order and method specified in the manual.

2 Fit the bucket into the bread maker and set to the dough programme. Press start. Grease a 28cm (11 inch) metal flan ring (see notes) and place on a greased baking sheet.

3 Once the dough is ready, turn it out on to a floured surface and punch it down to deflate. Roll out to a 25.5cm (10 inch) round and place inside the flan ring, pushing the dough to the edges. (Don't worry if it shrinks back, the dough will expand to fill the ring as it proves.) Cover loosely with oiled clingfilm and leave to rise in a warm place for 30 minutes.

4 Using fingertips dipped in flour, make deep dimples all over the dough. Scatter with small rosemary sprigs, drizzle with the olive oil and sprinkle generously with sea salt flakes. Re-cover with oiled clingfilm and leave for a further 10 minutes, as the dough might have shrunk back when dimpled. Preheat the oven to 200°C (fan oven 180°C) mark 6.

5 Drizzle the dough with water. (This is not essential but helps the crust to stay soft during baking.) Bake for 20–25 minutes until just firm and pale golden. Transfer to a wire rack and leave to cool.

PARMESAN AND OLIVE GRISSINI

MAKES 32

Preparation: 20 minutes, plus kneading
and rising

Cooking time: 18–20 minutes, plus cooling

1 tsp easy-blend dried yeast
500g (1lb 2oz) strong white bread
   flour
1 tsp salt
3 tbsp olive oil
2 tsp golden caster sugar
300ml (½ pint) water
50g (2oz) pitted black olives, finely
   chopped
50g (2oz) Parmesan, freshly grated

TO FINISH
oil to grease
semolina to dust
beaten egg to glaze
coarse salt flakes to sprinkle

PER GRISSINI
872 cals; 2g fat (of which 0.5g saturates);
12g carbohydrate; 0.3g salt

1 Put all the dough ingredients except the olives and Parmesan into the bread maker bucket with 300ml (½ pint) water, following the order and method specified in the manual.

2 Fit the bucket into the bread maker and set to the dough programme with raisin setting, if applicable. Press start. Add the olives and Parmesan when the machine beeps, or halfway through the kneading cycle. Lightly oil 2 large baking sheets and sprinkle with semolina.

3 Once the dough is ready, turn out on to a surface and punch it down to deflate. Cover with a teatowel and leave to rest for 10 minutes.

4 Roll out the dough to a 30.5 x 20.5cm (12 x 8 inch) rectangle, cover loosely with a teatowel and leave for 30 minutes until well risen.

5 Preheat the oven to 220°C (fan oven 200°C) mark 7. Cut the dough across the width into 4 thick bands. From each of these, cut 8 very thin strips and transfer them to the baking sheet, stretching each one until it is about 28cm (11 inch) long, and spacing the strips 1cm (½ inch) apart.

6 Brush very lightly with beaten egg and sprinkle with salt flakes. Bake for 18–20 minutes until crisp and golden. Transfer to a wire rack to cool.

NOTE
For convenience, make them several days in advance and store in an airtight tin. To serve, pop them into a moderate oven for a couple of minutes if they have softened slightly.

PEPPER AND PANCETTA BUNS

BREAD MACHINE RECIPE

1 Heat the oil in a frying pan and fry the peppers for 4–5 minutes until soft. Leave to cool slightly.

2 Put all the remaining dough ingredients except the pancetta into the bread maker bucket with 250ml (9fl oz) water, following the order and method specified in the manual, adding the tomato paste and chopped tarragon with the water.

3 Fit the bucket into the bread maker and set to the dough programme with raisin setting, if applicable. Press start. Add the pancetta and peppers with any cooking juices when the machine beeps, or halfway through the kneading cycle.

4 While the dough is proving, cut out twelve 14cm (5½ inch) squares of baking parchment and have ready a 12-hole muffin or Yorkshire pudding tray.

5 Turn the dough out on to a floured surface and punch it down to deflate. Divide the dough into 12 even-sized pieces. Push a square of parchment into one of the tin sections and drop a piece of dough into the centre. Repeat with the remainder. Cover loosely with a teatowel and leave in a warm place for about 30 minutes until well risen.

6 Preheat the oven to 220°C (fan oven 200°C) mark 7. Bake the buns for 15–18 minutes until risen and golden. Lift the paper cases out of the tin sections and transfer to a wire rack to cool.

ROASTED RED ONION AND GRUYÈRE BREAD

BREAD MACHINE RECIPE

MAKES 1 ROUND BREAD – CUTS INTO 6 LARGE WEDGES

Preparation: 20 minutes, plus kneading and rising
Cooking time: 25–30 minutes

2 tsp fennel seeds
1 tsp easy-blend dried yeast
300g (11oz) strong white bread flour, plus extra to dust
½ tsp celery salt
1 tsp golden caster sugar
2 tbsp olive oil

TOPPING

3 tbsp olive oil, plus extra to grease
450g (1lb) red onions, peeled and thinly sliced
several fresh thyme sprigs, chopped
100g (3½oz) Gruyère cheese, thinly sliced
salt and ground black pepper

PER WEDGE

348 cals; 16g fat (of which 5g saturates); 44g carbohydrate; 0.7g salt

1 Lightly crush the fennel seeds, using a pestle and mortar. Put all the dough ingredients into the bread maker bucket with 200ml (7fl oz) water, following the order and method specified in the manual, adding the crushed fennel seeds with the flour.
2 Fit the bucket into the bread maker and set to the dough programme with pizza setting if available, if not then the dough setting. Press start.
3 While the dough is in the bread maker, prepare the topping. Heat the oil in a frying pan, add the onions and fry gently for about 10 minutes until golden, stirring frequently. Stir in the thyme and seasoning.
4 Place a 28cm (11 inch) round metal flan ring on a baking sheet (see note). Brush the inside of the ring and baking sheet with oil.
5 Once the dough is ready, turn it out on to a floured surface, knead lightly and roll out to a 28cm (11 inch) round. Lift the dough round into the ring on the baking sheet. Arrange the fried onion and cheese slices over the surface to within 1cm (½ inch) of the edges. Cover loosely with oiled clingfilm and leave in a warm place for 20 minutes. Preheat the oven to 220°C (fan oven 200°C) mark 7.
6 Bake for 25–30 minutes until the crust is slightly risen and golden. Serve warm, cut into wedges.

NOTE
If you do not have a suitably sized metal flan ring, simply roll the dough to a large round and place directly on the baking sheet.

SWEET CHERRY BREAD

Preparation: 40 minutes, plus rising

Cooking time: 40 minutes, plus cooling

oil to grease
350g (12oz) strong white bread flour,
  plus extra to dust
½ tsp salt
2 tsp ground mixed spice
1 tsp ground cinnamon
25g (1oz) caster sugar
1 tbsp fast-action dried yeast
75g (3oz) unsalted butter, diced
200ml (7fl oz) warm milk
125g (4oz) white almond paste,
  roughly chopped
125g (4oz) glacé cherries
3 tbsp honey, warmed
75g (3oz) icing sugar, sifted

PER SLICE

310 cals; 4g fat (of which trace saturates);
66g carbohydrate; 0.4g salt

1 Grease a 20.5cm (8 inch) round deep cake tin and base-line with greaseproof paper.
2 Sift the flour, salt, spices and caster sugar into a bowl. Add the yeast, then rub in the butter. Add the milk to make a dough (if the dough is too dry, add a little more milk). Turn out on to a lightly floured surface and knead for 10 minutes. Put the dough into a lightly oiled bowl, cover with oiled clingfilm and leave in a warm place for 2 hours or until doubled in size.
3 Turn out the dough on to a lightly floured surface and knead lightly. Shape into an oval, 60cm (24 inch) long. Scatter the almond paste and cherries over the surface and roll up the dough lengthways, then form it into a tight coil. Put in the cake tin, cover and leave in a warm place for 30 minutes or until doubled in size. Preheat the oven to 180°C (160°C fan oven) mark 4.

4 Bake for 40 minutes or until golden; it should sound hollow when tapped underneath. Turn out on to a wire rack and leave to cool completely. When cool, brush with honey. Mix the icing sugar with a few drops of water and drizzle over the bread.

TO STORE

Store in an airtight container. It will keep for up to two days.

FRUITED MUESLI LOAF

MAKES 1 MEDIUM LOAF – CUTS INTO ABOUT 10 SLICES

Preparation: 10 minutes, plus kneading

Cooking time: as per your machine, plus cooling

1½ tsp easy-blend dried yeast
225g (8oz) strong white bread flour
100g (3½oz) strong brown bread flour
100g (3½oz) natural (no added sugar or salt) muesli
1 tsp salt
1 tbsp clear honey, plus 2 tbsp clear honey to glaze
50g (2oz) raisins
25g (1oz) butter

PER SLICE

200 cals; 3g fat (of which 2g saturates); 39g carbohydrate; 0.6g salt

1 Put all the ingredients except the honey to glaze into the bread maker bucket with 250ml (9fl oz) water, following the order and method specified in the manual.

2 Fit the bucket into the bread maker and set to the programme recommended in the manual, usually multigrain. Select the crust of your choice and press start.

3 After baking, remove the bucket from the machine, then turn out the loaf on to a wire rack to cool. Brush the top of the loaf with honey to glaze.

FREEZING TIP
To freeze, complete the recipe. Once the bread is cold, slice, if you like, for convenience, then pack, seal and freeze. To use, thaw at cool room temperature.

APRICOT AND HAZELNUT BREAD

75g (3oz) hazelnuts

450g (1lb) strong Granary bread flour, plus extra to dust

1 tsp salt

25g (1oz) unsalted butter, diced

75g (3oz) ready-to-eat dried apricots, chopped

2 tsp fast-action dried yeast

2 tbsp molasses

oil to grease

milk to glaze

PER SLICE

118 cals; 4g fat (of which 0.9g saturates); 18g carbohydrate; 0.3g salt

TO STORE

Store in an airtight container. It will keep for up to two days.

VARIATION

Replace the hazelnuts with walnuts or pecan nuts and use sultanas instead of apricots.

1 Spread the hazelnuts on a baking sheet. Toast under a hot grill until golden brown, turning frequently. Put the hazelnuts in a clean teatowel and rub off the skins. Leave to cool. Chop and put to one side.

2 Put the flour into a large bowl. Add the salt, then rub in the butter. Stir in the hazelnuts, apricots and yeast. Make a well in the centre and gradually work in the molasses and about 225ml (8fl oz) hand-hot water to form a soft dough, adding a little more water if the dough feels dry. Knead for 8–10 minutes until smooth, then transfer the dough to an oiled bowl, cover and leave to rise in a warm place for 1–1¼ hours until doubled in size.

3 Punch the dough to knock back, then divide in half. Shape each portion into a small, flattish round and put on a well-floured baking sheet. Cover loosely and leave to rise for a further 30 minutes.

4 Preheat the oven to 220°C (200°C fan oven) mark 7 and put a large baking sheet on the top shelf to heat up.

5 Using a sharp knife, cut several slashes on each round, brush with a little milk and transfer to the heated baking sheet. Bake for 15 minutes, then lower the oven setting to 190°C (170°C fan oven) mark 5 and bake for a further 15–20 minutes until the bread is risen and sounds hollow when tapped underneath. Turn out on to a wire rack and leave to cool completely.

SPICED FRUIT AND NUT LOAF

MAKES I MEDIUM LOAF – CUTS INTO ABOUT 12 SLICES

Preparation: 10 minutes, plus steeping and kneading
Cooking time: as per your machine, plus cooling

100g (3½oz) luxury mixed dried fruit
350ml (12fl oz) hot strong tea
1 tsp easy-blend dried yeast
375g (13oz) gluten-free fibre mix, for bread machines
½ tsp salt
50g (2oz) dark muscovado sugar
2 tsp ground mixed spice
25g (1oz) butter
3 pieces preserved stem ginger, chopped, plus 2 tbsp syrup

PER SLICE

170 cals; 2g fat (of which 1g saturates); 36g carbohydrate; 0.3g salt

1 Put the dried fruit into a bowl, pour the hot tea over it and leave to steep for 1 hour.

2 Tip the fruit and tea into the bread maker bucket. Add all the remaining ingredients except the ginger syrup, following the order and method specified in the manual, adding the chopped ginger with the tea.

3 Fit the bucket into the bread maker and set to the programme and crust recommended for gluten-free breads. Press start.

4 After baking, remove the bucket from the machine, then turn out the bread on to a wire rack to cool. While still warm, brush the top of the loaf with the stem ginger syrup to glaze.

TO STORE

Wrap in greaseproof paper and store in an airtight container. It will keep for up to one week.

CHOCOLATE MACADAMIA LOAF

MAKES I MEDIUM LOAF – CUTS INTO ABOUT 10 SLICES

Preparation: 15 minutes, plus kneading

Cooking time: 15 minutes, plus baking time as per your machine and cooling and setting

100g (3½oz) macadamia nuts, roughly chopped
1 large egg, plus 2 egg yolks
75g (3oz) unsalted butter, melted
2 tsp finely chopped fresh rosemary
1¼ tsp easy-blend dried yeast
400g (14oz) strong white bread flour
¾ tsp salt
50g (2oz) golden caster sugar
75g (3oz) plain chocolate, chopped
175g (6oz) white chocolate, chopped

PER SLICE

450 cals; 25g fat (of which 10g saturates); 52g carbohydrate; 0.6g salt

1   Lightly toast the nuts in a frying pan over a low heat for about 3 minutes, shaking the pan frequently. Tip on to a plate and set aside.

2   Mix together the egg, egg yolks, butter, rosemary and 175ml (6fl oz) water. Put all the ingredients except the nuts and chocolate into the bread maker bucket, following the order and method specified in the manual.

3   Fit the bucket into the bread maker and set to the basic programme with raisin setting, if applicable. Select a light crust and press start. Add the nuts, plain chocolate and 125g (4oz) white chocolate when the machine beeps, or halfway through the kneading programme.

4   After baking, remove the bucket from the machine, then turn out the bread on to a wire rack to cool. Once the bread has cooled, melt the remaining white chocolate carefully in a heatproof bowl set over a pan of hot water, making sure the base of the bowl doesn't touch the water. Stir until smooth, then spread over the top of the loaf. Leave to set.

NOTE

Macadamia nuts are mildly flavoured with an almost buttery taste – not a coincidence as the nut has a high oil content.

PANDOLCE

 BREAD MACHINE RECIPE

MAKES I LARGE LOAF –
CUTS INTO ABOUT 12 SLICES

Preparation: 15 minutes, plus kneading and rising

Cooking time: 30–35 minutes, plus cooling

1 tsp easy-blend dried yeast

500g (1lb 2oz) strong white bread flour, plus extra to dust

½ tsp salt

100g (3½oz) golden caster sugar

50g (2oz) butter, melted, plus extra to grease

1 large egg

finely grated zest of 1 lemon

2 tsp vanilla extract

150g (5oz) candied peel, finely chopped (see notes)

50g (2oz) chopped mixed nuts

icing sugar to dust (optional)

PER SLICE

270 cals; 6g fat (of which 3g saturates); 51g carbohydrate; 0.4g salt

1 Put all the ingredients except the candied peel and nuts into the bread maker bucket with 200ml (7fl oz) water, following the order and method specified in the manual, adding the lemon zest and vanilla extract with the water.

NOTES
- This is similar to Italian panettone, but without all the dried fruit. Candied peel provides the predominant flavour, so it's important to use good-quality peel and chop it yourself, rather than resort to the ready-chopped variety from the supermarkets.

- Like panettone, leftovers freeze well and make a great bread and butter pudding.

2 Fit the bucket into the bread maker and set to the dough programme with raisin setting, if applicable. Press start. Add the candied peel and nuts when the machine beeps, or halfway through the kneading cycle. Grease a 15cm (6 inch) round cake tin, 9cm (3½ inch) deep, and line with a triple thickness strip of baking parchment, to extend 5cm (2 inch) above the rim of the tin.

3 Once the dough is ready, turn out on to a floured surface and punch it down to deflate. Shape into a ball and drop it into the tin. Cover loosely with a teatowel and leave to rise in a warm place for about 45 minutes or until the dough reaches the top of the paper lining. Preheat the oven to 200°C (fan oven 180°C) mark 6.

4 Bake for 30–35 minutes until risen and deep golden, covering with foil if it appears to be browning too quickly. Turn out the bread on to a wire rack and tap the bottom – it should sound hollow. If not, return to the oven for a little longer. Leave on the wire rack to cool and dust with icing sugar before serving, if you like.

PANETTONE

Preparation: 20 minutes, plus standing

Cooking time: 1 hour

450g (1lb) plain white flour
20g (¾oz) fresh yeast or 2¼ tsp traditional dried yeast
225ml (8fl oz) tepid milk
125g (4oz) butter, softened, plus extra to grease
2 medium egg yolks
50g (2oz) caster sugar
75g (3oz) chopped mixed candied peel
50g (2oz) sultanas
pinch of freshly grated nutmeg
egg yolk to glaze

PER SLICE

285 calories; 12g fat (of which 7g saturates); 41g carbohydrate; 0.3g salt

1 Sift the flour into a large bowl and make a well in the centre. Blend the fresh yeast with the milk. If using dried yeast, sprinkle it on to the milk and leave in a warm place for 15 minutes or until frothy. Add the yeast liquid to the flour and mix well together, gradually drawing in the flour from the sides of the bowl. Leave to stand in a warm place for 45 minutes or until doubled in size.

2 Add the softened butter to the dough with the 2 egg yolks, the sugar, candied peel, sultanas and nutmeg. Mix well. Leave to stand again in a warm place for a further 45 minutes or until doubled in size.

3 Meanwhile, line an 18cm (7 inch) circular tin with baking parchment. Place the dough inside the tin and leave in a warm place for about 1 hour until risen to the top. Preheat the oven to 200°C (180°C fan oven) mark 6.

4 Brush the top of the dough with egg yolk to glaze. Bake on the lowest shelf of the oven for 20 minutes, then lower the oven setting to 180°C (160°C fan oven) mark 4 and cook for a further 40 minutes or until a fine warmed skewer inserted into the centre comes out clean. Leave to cool in the tin.

TO STORE

Store in an airtight container. It will keep for up to one week.

CROISSANTS

Preparation: 40 minutes, plus chilling
and standing
Cooking time: 15 minutes

25g (1oz) fresh yeast or 1 tbsp dried
   yeast and 1 tsp sugar
2 medium eggs
450g (1lb) strong white flour, plus
   extra to dust
2 tsp salt
25g (1oz) lard
225g (8oz) unsalted butter, at cool
   room temperature
½ tsp caster sugar

PER CROISSANT

300 calories; 19g fat (of which 11g saturates);
29g carbohydrate; 1.1g salt

1 Blend the fresh yeast with 225ml (8fl oz) tepid water. If using dried yeast, sprinkle it into the water with the sugar and leave in a warm place for 15 minutes or until frothy.

2 Whisk 1 egg into the yeast liquid. Sift the flour and salt into a large bowl and rub in the lard. Make a well in the centre and pour in the yeast liquid. Mix and then beat in the flour until the bowl is left clean. Turn out on to a lightly floured surface and knead well for about 10 minutes until the dough is firm and elastic.

3 Roll out the dough on a lightly floured surface to an oblong about 51 x 20.5cm (20 x 8 inch). Keep the edges as square as possible, gently pulling out the corners to stop them rounding off. Dust the rolling pin with flour to prevent it sticking to the dough.

4 Divide the butter into three. Dot one portion over the top two-thirds of the dough but clear of the edge. Turn up the bottom third of the dough over half the butter, then fold down the remainder. Seal the edges with a rolling pin. Turn the dough so that the fold is on the right.

5 Press the dough lightly at intervals along its length, then roll out to an oblong again. Repeat the rolling and folding with the other two portions of butter. Rest the dough in the fridge for 30 minutes, loosely covered with a clean teatowel. Repeat three more times, cover and chill for 1 hour.

6 Roll out the dough to an oblong about 48 x 33cm (19 x 13 inch), lay a clean teatowel over the top and leave to rest for 10 minutes. Trim off 1cm (½ inch) all around and divide the dough in half lengthways, then into three squares, then across into triangles.

7 Beat the remaining egg, 1 tbsp water and the sugar together for the glaze and brush it over the triangles. Roll each triangle up from the long edge finishing with the tip underneath. Curve into crescents and place well apart on ungreased baking sheets, allowing room to spread. Cover loosely with a clean teatowel. Leave at room temperature for about 30 minutes until well risen and 'puffy'.

8 Preheat the oven to 220°C (200°C fan oven) mark 7. Brush each croissant carefully with more glaze. Bake in the oven for 15 minutes until crisp and well browned.

FIG, LEMON AND CARDAMOM PLAIT

MAKES 1 LARGE LOAF – CUTS INTO ABOUT 12 THICK SLICES

Preparation: 20 minutes, plus kneading and rising

Cooking time: 25 minutes, plus cooling

1½ tsp easy-blend dried yeast
400g (14oz) strong white bread flour, plus extra to dust
100g (3½oz) strong wholemeal bread flour
1 tsp salt
50g (2oz) golden caster sugar
40g (1½oz) unsalted butter, diced
325ml (11fl oz) milk

FILLING

250g (9oz) dried figs
finely grated zest of 2 lemons
1 tbsp lemon juice
100g (3½oz) brazil nuts, coarsely chopped
25g (1oz) golden caster sugar
50g (2oz) unsalted butter, diced, plus extra to grease

ICING

2 tsp cardamom pods
125g (4oz) icing sugar
2 tbsp lemon juice

PER SLICE

380 cals; 13g fat (of which 5g saturates); 61g carbohydrate; 0.6g salt

1 Put all the dough ingredients into the bread maker bucket, following the order and method specified in the manual.
2 Fit the bucket into the bread maker and set to the dough programme. Press start.
3 While the dough is in the bread maker, prepare the filling. Chop the figs into small pieces and mix with the lemon zest and juice, nuts, caster sugar and butter. Grease a large baking sheet.
4 Once the dough is ready, turn out on to a floured surface and punch it down to deflate. Divide into 3 equal pieces. Roll out each piece to a 35.5 x 12.5cm (14 x 5 inch) strip. Don't worry about squaring up the corners.

5 Spoon the filling down each strip to within 1cm (½ inch) of the edges, level out evenly, then press down lightly into the dough. Roll up the dough pieces to make three long, thick sausages, enclosing the filling.
6 Lay the strips in parallel lines with the joins on the underside. Pinch the pieces together at one end, then plait the strips and tuck the ends underneath. Transfer to the baking sheet, cover loosely with oiled clingfilm and leave to rise in a warm place for about 30 minutes or until doubled in size. Preheat the oven to 200°C (fan oven 180°C) mark 6.
7 Bake the plait for 25 minutes until it is risen and golden, and sounds hollow when tapped underneath.
8 To make the glaze, crack the cardamom pods using a pestle and mortar to release the seeds, pick out the shells, then crush the seeds very finely. Put into a bowl with the icing sugar and 4–5 tsp lemon juice. Mix to the consistency of thick pouring cream, adding another 1 tsp lemon juice if necessary. Transfer the plait to a wire rack and spoon the icing over. Leave to cool.

VARIATION

Figs and lemon are a perfect partnership, but you might prefer to substitute another dried fruit, such as raisins, apricots or dates.

CINNAMON AND GINGER SWIRL LOAF

MAKES 1 MEDIUM LOAF – CUTS INTO ABOUT 10 SLICES

Preparation: 15 minutes, plus kneading and rising
Cooking time: 30 minutes, plus cooling

50g (2oz) unsalted butter, melted, plus extra to grease
1 large egg
150ml (¼ pint) milk
1 tsp easy-blend dried yeast
375g (13oz) strong white bread flour, plus extra to dust
½ tsp salt
65g (2½oz) light muscovado sugar
oil to grease

TO FINISH

2 tsp ground cinnamon
½ tsp ground allspice
25g (1oz) demerara sugar, plus extra to sprinkle
25g (1oz) unsalted butter, melted
50g (2oz) fresh root ginger, peeled
milk to brush

PER SLICE

240 cals; 8g fat (of which 4g saturates); 38g carbohydrate; 0.4g salt

1. In a bowl, beat the butter with the egg and milk until evenly combined. Put all the dough ingredients into the bread maker bucket, following the order and method specified in the manual.
2. Fit the bucket into the bread maker and set to the dough programme. Press start.
3. Grease a 900g (2lb) loaf tin. For the filling, mix together the cinnamon, allspice and demerara sugar.
4. Once the dough is ready, turn out on to a floured surface and punch it down to deflate. Roll out to a rectangle 33cm (13 inch) long and make the width of the dough the same as the length of the prepared loaf tin.
5. Brush right up to the edges of the dough with the melted butter and sprinkle with the spice mix. Grate the ginger directly over the spices, distributing it as evenly as possible. Starting from a short end, roll up the dough and fit into the tin with the join underneath.
6. Cover loosely with oiled clingfilm and leave to rise in a warm place for about 1 hour until risen above the top of the tin. Preheat the oven to 200°C (fan oven 180°C) mark 6.
7. Brush the top of the dough with a little milk and sprinkle with extra demerara sugar. Bake for about 30 minutes until risen and deep golden, covering with foil if the crust appears to be browning too quickly. Remove from the tin and transfer to a wire rack to cool. This loaf is best eaten on the day it is made.

PISTACHIO AND ROSEWATER STOLLEN

BREAD MACHINE RECIPE

MAKES I STOLLEN – CUTS INTO ABOUT 10 THICK SLICES

Preparation: 15 minutes, plus kneading and rising

Cooking time: 20–25 minutes, plus cooling

1¼ tsp easy-blend dried yeast
350g (12oz) strong white bread flour, plus extra to dust
½ tsp salt
1 tsp ground mixed spice
25g (1oz) golden caster sugar
50g (2oz) butter, melted
150ml (¼ pint) milk
3 tbsp rosewater
75g (3oz) sultanas
50g (2oz) pistachio nuts
50g (2oz) candied peel, chopped
icing sugar to dust

MARZIPAN

150g (5oz) pistachio nuts, skinned (see note)
40g (1½oz) golden caster sugar
40g (1½oz) golden icing sugar
2 egg yolks
oil to grease

PER SLICE

380 cals; 17g fat (of which 5g saturates); 51g carbohydrate; 0.7g salt

1 Put all the dough ingredients except the sultanas, pistachio nuts, candied peel and icing sugar into the bread maker bucket, following the order and method specified in the manual.
2 Fit the bucket into the bread maker and set to the dough programme with raisin setting, if applicable. Press start. Add the sultanas, pistachio nuts and candied peel when the machine beeps, or halfway through the kneading cycle.
3 Meanwhile, make the marzipan. Put the pistachio nuts in a food processor and blend until finely ground. Add the sugars and egg yolks and blend to a paste. Turn out on to the worksurface and shape into a log, 24cm (9½ inch) long. Grease a large baking sheet.

4 Once the dough is ready, turn out on to a floured surface and punch it down to deflate. Roll out to an oblong, 28cm (11 inch) long and 15cm (6 inch) wide. Lay the marzipan on the dough, slightly to one side of the centre. Brush the long edges of the dough with water, then fold the wider piece of dough over the paste, sealing well.
5 Transfer to the baking sheet, cover loosely with oiled clingfilm and leave in a warm place for about 40 minutes until doubled in size. Preheat the oven to 200°C (fan oven 180°C) mark 6.
6 Bake for 20–25 minutes until risen and golden. Transfer to a wire rack to cool. Serve lavishly dusted with icing sugar.

NOTE

For a vibrantly coloured marzipan it's best to skin the pistachios first – soak them in boiling water for a couple of minutes, then rub between pieces of kitchen paper to remove the skins.

TEAR AND SHARE STOLLEN RING

Preparation: 30 minutes, plus rising

Cooking time: about 25 minutes, plus cooling

450g (1lb) strong white bread flour,
  plus extra to dust
1 tbsp caster sugar
½ × 7g sachet fast-action dried yeast
¼ tsp salt
¼ tsp freshly grated nutmeg
2 large pinches of ground cloves
1 tsp mixed spice
225ml (8fl oz) milk
40g (1½oz) butter, melted, plus a
  little extra to grease
2 medium eggs
50g (2oz) sultanas
100–150g (3½–5oz) marzipan
icing sugar to dust
butter to serve

PER SLICE

268 cals; 7g fat (of which 3g saturates); 48g
carbohydrate; 0.2g salt

1 Put the flour, sugar, yeast, salt and the three spices into a large bowl and mix together. Make a well in the centre. Pour the milk into a pan and heat until lukewarm, then stir in the melted butter. Crack one egg into the well of dry ingredients and pour in half the milk mixture. Working quickly with your hands, mix thoroughly to form a soft but not sticky dough, adding extra milk as necessary.

2 Tip out the dough on to a lightly floured surface, then knead for 5 minutes or until soft and elastic. Transfer to a lightly greased bowl, cover with a clean teatowel and leave to rise somewhere warm, but not hot, for 45 minutes.

3 Knead in the sultanas. Weigh the dough and divide into ten equal pieces. Line a large baking sheet with baking parchment and preheat the oven to 200°C (180°C fan oven) mark 6.

4 Knead the marzipan until soft, then cut into ten pieces. Using your fingers, flatten out one of the pieces of dough slightly, then put a marzipan chunk in the middle. Fold the dough around it, then squeeze together to make a neat ball. Repeat with the remaining pieces of dough.

5 Position the balls in a circle, just touching, on the baking sheet. Use the remaining egg to glaze the ring, then bake for 20–25 minutes until golden. Leave to cool on the baking tray – the stollen ring is quite fragile at this stage. Once cold, carefully transfer to a serving platter or wooden board, dust with icing sugar and serve with butter.

FREEZING TIP

To freeze, complete the recipe to the end of step 4. Leave the stollen on the baking sheet, wrap the whole sheet in clingfilm and freeze for up to one month. To use, thaw at room temperature, then complete the recipe.

STRAWBERRY DOUGHNUTS

MAKES 12

Preparation: 25 minutes, plus rising

Cooking time: about 20 minutes

250g (9oz) plain flour, plus extra
   to dust
1 x 7g sachet fast-action yeast
100g (3½oz) caster sugar
100ml (3½fl oz) milk
25g (1oz) butter
1 medium egg
sunflower oil to deep-fry
175g (6oz) 'no bits' strawberry jam
½ tsp ground cinnamon

PER DOUGHNUT

261 cals; 13g fat (of which 3g saturates); 35g
carbohydrate; 0.1g salt

1 Put the flour, yeast and half the sugar into a large bowl.
   Heat the milk and butter in a small pan until just warm.
   Tip into a jug and beat in the egg. Working quickly,
   pour the liquid into the flour mixture and stir to make
   a soft dough. Tip on to a lightly floured surface and
   knead for 5 minutes or until smooth and elastic.
   Return the dough to the bowl, cover with clingfilm and
   leave to rise in a warm place for 30–40 minutes.

2 Line a baking sheet with parchment paper. When the
   dough is ready, tip on to a lightly floured surface.
   Gently pat out into a rough rectangle 1cm (½ inch)
   thick and, using a 5.5cm (2¼ inch) round pastry cutter,
   stamp out 12 rounds. Transfer to the baking sheet,
   cover loosely with clingfilm and leave to rise in a warm
   place for 20 minutes.

3 Fill a large saucepan one-third full with oil and heat to
   150°C, using a thermometer. Fry the doughnuts in
   batches of four until deep golden brown, about 7
   minutes, turning over halfway through the cooking
   time. Using a slotted spoon, lift the doughnuts on to
   kitchen paper to drain and leave to cool for 5 minutes.
   Cook the remaining doughnuts in the same way.

4 Fit a piping bag with a 5mm (¼ inch) plain nozzle and
   fill with the jam. Use a skewer to poke a hole into the
   centre of each doughnut through the side, then push
   the piping nozzle in and squirt in some jam. Mix the
   remaining caster sugar with the cinnamon and tip on
   to a plate. Roll the filled doughnuts in the sugar
   mixture and serve warm.

NOTE

To oven-bake your doughnuts, complete the
recipe to the end of step 2. Next, preheat the
oven to 200°C (180°C fan oven) mark 6 and
bake the doughnuts for 15 minutes or until
puffed and golden. Complete the recipe from
step 4, brushing the doughnuts with oil before
coating in the sugar mixture.

DANISH PASTRIES

Preparation: 20 minutes, plus resting
and rising

Cooking time: 15 minutes

25g (1oz) fresh yeast or 1 tbsp
    traditional dried yeast and 1 tsp
    sugar
450g (1lb) plain white flour, plus extra
    to dust
1 tsp salt
50g (2oz) lard
2 tbsp caster sugar
2 medium eggs, beaten
300g (10oz) butter or margarine,
    softened
beaten egg to glaze
glacé icing (see page 319) and flaked
    almonds to decorate

ALMOND PASTE

15g (½oz) butter or margarine
75g (3oz) caster sugar
75g (3oz) ground almonds
1 medium egg, beaten

CINNAMON BUTTER

50g (2oz) butter
50g (2oz) caster sugar
2 tsp ground cinnamon

PER DANISH

376 calories; 25g fat (of which 14g saturates);
35g carbohydrate; 0.7g salt

1 Blend the fresh yeast with 150ml (¼ pint) tepid water. If using dried yeast, sprinkle it into the water with the 1 tsp sugar and leave in a warm place for 15 minutes or until frothy.

2 Mix the flour and salt, rub in the lard and stir in the 2 tbsp sugar. Add the yeast liquid and beaten eggs and mix to an elastic dough, adding a little more water if necessary. Knead well for 5 minutes on a lightly floured surface until smooth. Return the dough to the rinsed-out bowl, cover with a clean teatowel and leave the dough to rest in the fridge for 10 minutes.

3 Shape the butter or margarine into an oblong. Roll out the dough on a lightly floured surface to an oblong about three times as wide as the butter. Put the butter in the centre of the dough and fold the sides of the dough over the butter. Press the edges to seal.

4 With the folds at the sides, roll the dough into a strip three times as long as it is wide; fold the bottom third up and the top third down, cover and rest for 10 minutes. Turn, repeat, rolling, folding and resting twice more.

5 To make the almond paste, cream the butter or margarine and sugar, stir in the almonds and add enough egg to make a soft and pliable consistency.

6 Make the cinnamon butter by creaming the butter and sugar and beating in the cinnamon.

7 Roll out the dough into the required shapes (see below) and fill with almond paste or cinnamon butter.

8 After shaping, cover the pastries with a clean teatowel and leave to prove in a warm place for 20–30 minutes. Preheat the oven to 220°C (200°C fan oven) mark 7. Brush the pastries with beaten egg and bake for 15 minutes. While hot, brush with thin glacé icing and sprinkle with flaked almonds.

SHAPING DANISH PASTRIES

Imperial stars: Cut into 7.5cm (3 inch) squares and make diagonal cuts from each corner to within 1cm (½ inch) of the centre. Put a piece of almond paste in the centre of the square and fold one corner of each cut section down to the centre, securing the tips with beaten egg.

Foldovers and cushions: Cut into 7.5cm (3 inch) squares and put a little almond paste in the centre. Fold over two opposite corners to the centre. Make a cushion by folding over all four corners. Secure the tips with a little beaten egg.

Twists: Cut into 25.5 x 10cm (10 x 4 inch) rectangles. Cut each rectangle lengthways to give four pieces. Spread with cinnamon butter and fold the bottom third of each up and the top third down, seal and cut each across into thin slices. Twist these slices and put on a baking sheet.

STICKY CURRANT BUNS

BREAD MACHINE RECIPE

MAKES 8

Preparation: 10 minutes, plus kneading
and rising
Cooking time: 10–15 minutes, plus cooling

1 tsp easy-blend dried yeast

350g (12oz) strong white bread flour,
  plus extra to dust

½ tsp salt

1 tsp ground mixed spice

15g (½oz) butter, plus extra to
  grease

finely grated zest of 1 orange

25g (1oz) light muscovado sugar

200ml (7fl oz) milk

75g (3oz) currants

oil to grease

TO FINISH

25g (1oz) light muscovado sugar

50g (2oz) rough sugar pieces, lightly
  crushed

PER BUN

250 cals; 3g fat (of which 1g saturates);
53g carbohydrate; 0.4g salt

1 Put all the dough ingredients except the currants and oil into the bread maker bucket, following the order and method specified in the manual.

2 Fit the bucket into the bread maker and set to the dough programme with raisin setting, if applicable. Add the currants when the machine beeps, or halfway through the kneading cycle. Lightly grease a large baking sheet.

3 Once the dough is ready, turn out on to a floured surface and punch it down to deflate. Divide into 8 evenly sized pieces, scrunch into rounds and space slightly apart on the baking sheet. Cover with oiled clingfilm and leave to rise in a warm place for 30 minutes until doubled in size. Preheat the oven to 220°C (fan oven 200°C) mark 7.

4 Bake the buns for 10–15 minutes until golden. Meanwhile, put the muscovado sugar in a small pan with 2 tbsp water and heat gently until the sugar dissolves.

5 Transfer the buns to a wire rack and brush with the glaze, sprinkling them with the crushed sugar as you work. Leave to cool.

NOTE
It's the rough, craggy appearance of these buns that makes them so inviting, so don't waste time rolling and shaping them carefully.

LEMON-GLAZED CHELSEA BUNS

BREAD MACHINE RECIPE

MAKES 12

Preparation: 15 minutes, plus kneading
and rising
Cooking time: 25–30 minutes, plus cooling

1 large egg
50g (2oz) unsalted butter, melted,
    plus extra to grease
225ml (7½fl oz) milk
1½ tsp easy-blend dried yeast
400g (14oz) strong white bread flour,
    plus extra to dust
100g (3½oz) strong soft grain or
    Granary flour
1 tsp salt
75g (3oz) light muscovado sugar

FILLING AND TOPPING
2 pieces preserved stem ginger, plus
    3 tbsp syrup
100g (3½oz) raisins
100g (3½oz) sultanas
50g (2oz) light muscovado sugar
2 tsp ground mixed spice
finely grated zest and juice of
    1 lemon
40g (1½oz) unsalted butter, cut into
    pieces

PER BUN
310 cals; 8g fat (of which 4g saturates);
56g carbohydrate; 0.6g salt

NOTE
Like most fruity breads, these
are best eaten warm, so if you
make them ahead, pop them in
the oven for a few minutes
before serving.

1 In a bowl, whisk the egg, butter and milk together with a fork. Put all the dough ingredients into the bread maker bucket, following the order and method specified in the manual.

2 Fit the bucket into the bread maker and set to the dough programme. Press start.

3 Grease a 23cm (9 inch) square cake tin, 7.5cm (3 inch) deep. For the filling, finely chop the stem ginger and mix in a bowl with the raisins, sultanas, 25g (1oz) sugar, the spice and lemon zest.

4 Once the dough is ready, turn out on to a floured surface and punch it down to deflate. Roll out to a 30.5cm (12 inch) square and spread with the filling to within 1cm (½ inch) of the edges. Dot with the butter. Roll up the dough to enclose the filling, then cut into 2.5cm (1 inch) thick slices.

5 Pack the slices, cut-sides uppermost, into the prepared tin, spacing them evenly apart. Cover with oiled clingfilm and leave to rise in a warm place for about 45 minutes until doubled in size and rising up towards the top of the tin. Preheat the oven to 200°C (fan oven 180°C) mark 6.

6 Bake the buns for 20 minutes, then lower the oven setting to 180°C (fan oven 160°C) mark 4 and bake for a further 5–10 minutes until risen and deep golden. In the meantime, mix together the remaining sugar, lemon juice and stem ginger syrup to make a glaze. Transfer the buns to a wire rack and brush with the glaze. Leave to cool until warm.

BRIOCHE

Preparation: 20 minutes, plus rising

Cooking time: 15–20 minutes, plus cooling

15g (½oz) fresh yeast or 1½ tsp fast-
   action dried yeast

225g (8oz) strong plain white flour,
   plus extra to dust

pinch of salt

1 tbsp golden caster sugar

2 extra large eggs, beaten

50g (2oz) butter, melted and cooled
   until tepid

vegetable oil to grease

beaten egg to glaze

PER SERVING

140 cals; 6g fat (of which 3g saturates);

19g carbohydrate; 0.2g salt

1 If using fresh yeast, blend with 2 tbsp tepid water. Mix the flour, salt and sugar together in a large bowl. (Stir in fast-action dried yeast if using.)

2 Make a well in the centre and pour in the yeast liquid (or 2 tbsp tepid water if using fast-action dried yeast) plus the eggs and melted butter. Work the ingredients together to a soft dough.

3 Turn out on to a lightly floured surface and knead for about 5 minutes until smooth and elastic. Put the dough into a large oiled bowl, cover and leave in a warm place for about 1 hour until doubled in size.

4 Knock back the dough on a lightly floured surface. Shape three-quarters of it into a ball and put into an oiled 1.2 litre (2 pint) brioche mould. Press a hole through the centre. Shape the remaining dough into a round, put on top of the brioche and press down lightly. Cover and leave in a warm place until the dough is puffy and nearly risen to the top of the mould.

5 Preheat the oven to 230°C (210°C fan oven) mark 8. Brush the brioche dough lightly with beaten egg and bake for 15–20 minutes until golden.

6 Turn out on to a wire rack and leave to cool. Serve warm or cold.

NOTE
For individual brioches, divide the dough into 10 pieces. Shape as above. Bake in individual tins, for 10 minutes.

HOT CROSS BUNS

Preparation: 30 minutes, plus sponging
and rising

Cooking time: 15–18 minutes, plus cooling

100ml (3½fl oz) warm milk, plus
   extra to glaze
15g (½oz) fresh yeast or 7g sachet
   (2 tsp) traditional dried yeast
50g (2oz) golden caster sugar, plus
   extra to glaze
350g (12oz) strong plain white flour,
   sifted, plus extra to dust
pinch of salt
pinch of ground cinnamon
pinch of freshly grated nutmeg
25g (1oz) chopped mixed candied
   peel
125g (4oz) mixed raisins, sultanas and
   currants
25g (1oz) butter, melted and cooled
   until tepid
1 medium egg, beaten
vegetable oil to grease

PER BUN

140 cals; 2g fat (of which 1g saturates);
28g carbohydrate; 0.2g salt

VARIATION

Rather than mark crosses on
the buns, brush with beaten
egg to glaze, then top each
with a pastry cross and glaze
again. Bake as above.

1 Mix the warm milk with an equal quantity of warm water. Put the yeast
into a small bowl with 1 tbsp of the warm liquid and 1 tsp sugar and set
aside for 5 minutes.

2 Put 225g (8oz) flour and the salt into a large bowl, make a well in the
centre and pour in the yeast mixture. Cover with a clean teatowel and
leave in a warm place for 20 minutes to 'sponge'.

3 Mix the remaining flour and sugar together with the spices, peel and dried
fruit. Add to the yeast mixture with the melted butter and egg. Mix
thoroughly to form a soft dough, adding a little more liquid if needed. Put
the dough into a lightly oiled bowl, cover and leave to rise in a warm place
for 1–1½ hours or until doubled in size.

4 Knock back the dough and knead lightly on a lightly floured surface for
1–2 minutes. Divide the dough into 15 equal-sized pieces and shape into
buns. Put well apart on a large oiled baking sheet. Make a deep cross on
the top of each one with a sharp knife, then cover with a teatowel and
leave in a warm place for about 30 minutes until doubled in size.

5 Preheat the oven to 220°C (200°C fan oven) mark 7. Brush the buns with
milk and sprinkle with sugar, then bake for 15–18 minutes until they sound
hollow when tapped underneath. Transfer to a wire rack and leave to cool.
Serve warm.

STRAWBERRY SAVARIN

Preparation: 15 minutes, plus standing

Cooking time: 40–45 minutes, plus cooling

oil to grease

15g (½oz) fresh yeast or 1½ tsp dried yeast

3 tbsp tepid milk

2 medium eggs, lightly beaten

50g (2oz) butter, melted and cooled

200g (7oz) plain white flour

1 tbsp caster sugar

25g (1oz) desiccated coconut

6 tbsp redcurrant jelly or sieved strawberry jam

5 tbsp lemon juice

450g (1lb) strawberries, hulled and quartered

sour cream to serve

PER SLICE

275 calories; 12g fat (of which 7g saturates);

39g carbohydrate; 0.2g salt

1 Lightly oil a 1.3 litre (2¼ pint) savarin tin or ring mould and turn it upside down on kitchen paper to drain off the excess oil.

2 Blend the fresh yeast with the milk. If using dried yeast, sprinkle it on to the milk and leave in a warm place for 30 minutes or until frothy. Gradually beat the eggs and butter into the yeast liquid.

3 Mix the flour in a bowl with the sugar and coconut. With a wooden spoon, gradually stir in the yeast mixture to form a thick smooth batter. Beat together thoroughly.

4 Turn into the prepared tin, cover with oiled clingfilm and leave in a warm place for about 1 hour until the savarin is nearly doubled in size. Preheat the oven to 190°C (170°C fan oven) mark 5.

5 Bake the savarin for 35–40 minutes until golden. Turn out on to a wire rack placed over a large plate. Put the jelly or jam and lemon juice into a small pan over a low heat.

6 When the jelly or jam is melted, spoon it over the warm savarin until well glazed, allowing any excess to collect on the plate under the wire rack. Transfer the savarin to a serving plate.

7 Return the excess jelly mixture to the pan, add the strawberries and stir to coat. Remove from the heat and cool for 15–20 minutes until almost set, then spoon into the middle of the savarin. Serve warm or cold with sour cream.

VARIATIONS

Strawberry babas: Divide the yeast batter among six 9cm (3½ inch) ring tins. Leave to rise until the moulds are nearly two-thirds full, then bake for 15–20 minutes. Replace the lemon juice with brandy, soak each baba well and place on individual plates. Finish with strawberries and sour cream as above.

Rum babas: Make as strawberry babas but soak the warm babas in a rum syrup made with 8 tbsp clear honey, 8 tbsp water and rum or rum essence to taste. Serve filled with whipped cream.

KUGELHOPF

OVERNIGHT CHILLING REQUIRED

CUTS INTO 12 SLICES

Preparation: 45 minutes, plus soaking, chilling and rising
Cooking time: 50–55 minutes, plus cooling

200g (7oz) raisins, black seedless if possible
3 tbsp light rum
2 tsp fast-action dried yeast
300g (11oz) plain white flour, plus extra to dust
4 large eggs
100ml (3½fl oz) milk
225g (8oz) unsalted butter, softened, plus extra to grease
75g (3oz) caster sugar
pinch of salt
zest of 1 lemon
100g (3½oz) split blanched almonds, lightly toasted
whole glacé fruits and nuts to decorate
icing sugar to dust

PER SLICE
382 cals; 22g fat (of which 11g saturates); 39g carbohydrate; 0.4g salt

1 Combine the raisins and rum, cover and soak overnight. Put the yeast and flour into a food mixer. Lightly whisk the eggs and milk and then, with the machine running on a slow speed, pour in the egg mixture and mix for 10 minutes or until the dough is very smooth, shiny and elastic. In another bowl, beat the butter, caster sugar, salt and lemon zest and then, with the mixer running, add to the dough, a spoonful at a time, until evenly incorporated. Turn the mixture into a large, lightly floured bowl. Cover with clingfilm and chill overnight.

NOTES

- If you don't have a mixer with a beater attachment, use a food processor with a flat plastic blade.

- This cake is made with yeast, so it's best eaten within two days or it will go stale. If you have any left over, wrap and freeze in slices – toast or use for making bread and butter pudding.

2 Generously butter a 2 litre (3½ pint) kugelhopf ring mould. Press one-third of the almonds on to the sides of the mould. Chill. Roughly chop the remaining almonds. Mix by hand into the dough with the raisins and rum, then put into the mould, cover and leave for 3 hours in a warm place until it feels spongy and has risen to within 2cm (¾ inch) of the top of the mould.

3 Preheat the oven to 200°C (180°C fan oven) mark 6. Bake the kugelhopf on a shelf below the centre of the oven for 10 minutes. Cover with greaseproof paper, lower the oven setting to 190°C (170°C fan oven) mark 5 and bake for 40–45 minutes until the kugelhopf sounds hollow when you tap the mould. Cool in the tin for 15 minutes, then turn out on to a wire rack and leave to cool completely. Decorate with glacé fruits and nuts and serve dusted with icing sugar.

ROASTED FRUIT

SERVES 4

Preparation: 10 minutes
Cooking time: about 30 minutes

4 ripe peaches
150ml (¼ pint) orange juice
100ml (3½fl oz) dessert wine, such
    as Muscat de Beaumes de Venise
    (optional)
4 figs, trimmed
2 tbsp clear honey
150g (5oz) blueberries
crème fraîche or vanilla ice cream to
    serve

PER SERVING
140 cals; 0.5g fat (of which 0g saturates); 30g
carbohydrate; 0.2g salt

1 Preheat the oven to 200°C (180°C fan oven) mark 6. Halve the peaches and remove and discard the stones. Arrange cut-side up in a medium roasting tin or heatproof serving dish. Pour the orange juice and Muscat, if using, over them and roast for 15 minutes.

2 Meanwhile, put the figs on a board and cut each into quarters, leaving them attached at the base. Nestle in among the peach halves and drizzle the honey over. Return to the oven for 10 minutes or until all the fruit is tender.

3 Preheat the grill to medium. Scatter the blueberries over the roasted fruit and grill for 1–2 minutes until the berries have burst and released some of their juice. Serve immediately with crème fraîche or vanilla ice cream.

BAKED APRICOTS WITH CARAMELISED NUTS

Preparation: 20 minutes

Cooking time: 45–50 minutes, plus cooling

700g (1½lb) firm apricots
50g (2oz) butter
125g (4oz) caster sugar
100ml (3½fl oz) orange juice
vanilla ice cream to serve (optional)

CARAMELISED NUTS
75g (3oz) whole almonds, skinned
125g (4oz) caster sugar

PER SERVING
419 cals; 21g fat (of which 7g saturates); 55g carbohydrate; 0.2g salt

NOTES
- If the caramelised almond mixture sets, put back on the heat to warm slightly before spooning over the apricots.

- For convenience, prepare ahead. Complete the recipe to the end of step 2, then caramelise the nuts as in step 3. Spoon the almonds over the apricots, then cool, cover and chill for up to three days. To use, warm the apricots and almonds in a shallow pan until the syrup melts. Complete the recipe.

1 Preheat the oven to 200°C (180°C fan oven) mark 6. Slit the apricots down one side (so they still look whole) and remove the stones. Put the apricots into an ovenproof dish. Gently melt the butter and sugar in a pan, stirring occasionally, until golden; remove from the heat. Carefully stir in the orange juice (it may splutter as the sugar hardens into lumps). Return the mixture to a low heat and stir until the sugar has dissolved, then pour over the apricots.

2 Bake in the oven for 45 minutes or until the apricots are just soft, spooning the liquid over the fruit from time to time. Set aside and leave to cool. (Remove the skins at this stage, if you like.)
3 To make the caramelised nuts, put the almonds into a pan of cold water, bring to the boil and simmer for 2 minutes. Drain and cut the almonds into thick shreds (they will now be soft enough to chop without splintering). Put under a hot grill and toast until golden.
4 Put the sugar and 150ml (¼ pint) water into a pan, bring to the boil and bubble until the syrup turns a deep golden caramel. Take the pan off the heat and add 4 tbsp warm water. Return the pan to the heat and cook gently until the sugar has dissolved. Allow the mixture to cool, then stir in the almonds. Serve the apricots with scoops of vanilla ice cream, if you like, with the caramelised nuts spooned over the top.

FREEZING TIP
To freeze, complete the recipe to the end of step 1, then cool, wrap and freeze. To use, thaw the apricots for 4 hours or overnight at cool room temperature. Complete the recipe.

PEACH BRÛLÉE

SERVES 4

Preparation: 10 minutes

Cooking time: about 10 minutes

4 ripe peaches, halved and stoned

8 tsp soft cream cheese

8 tsp golden caster sugar

PER SERVING

137 cals; 6g fat (of which 4g saturates);

21g carbohydrate; 0.1g salt

1 Preheat the grill until very hot. Fill each stone cavity in the fruit with 2 tsp cream cheese, then sprinkle each one with 2 tsp caster sugar.

2 Put the fruit halves on a grill pan and cook under the very hot grill until the sugar has browned and caramelised to create a brûlée crust. Serve warm.

VARIATION
Use nectarines instead of peaches.

BAKED APPLES WITH OATS AND BLUEBERRIES

SERVES 4

Preparation: 15 minutes
Cooking time: 30–40 minutes

4 Bramley apples
25g (1oz) pecan nuts, chopped
25g (1oz) rolled oats
50g (2oz) blueberries
2 tbsp light muscovado sugar
4 tbsp orange juice

PER SERVING
164 cals; 5g fat (of which trace saturates);
29g carbohydrate; 0g salt

1 Preheat the oven to 200°C (180°C fan oven) mark 6. Core the apples, then use a sharp knife to score around the middle of each (this will stop the apple from collapsing). Put the apples into a roasting tin.

2 Put the pecan nuts into a bowl together with the oats, blueberries and sugar. Mix together, then spoon into the apples, pour 1 tbsp orange juice over each apple and bake in the oven for 30–40 minutes until the apples are soft.

PEAR AND BLACKBERRY CRUMBLE

SERVES 6

Preparation: 20 minutes
Cooking time: 35–45 minutes

450g (1lb) pears, peeled, cored and
   chopped, tossed with the juice of
   1 lemon
225g (8oz) golden caster sugar
1 tsp mixed spice
450g (1lb) blackberries
100g (3½oz) butter, chopped, plus
   extra to grease
225g (8oz) plain flour
75g (3oz) ground almonds
cream, custard or ice cream to serve

PER SERVING
525 cals; 21g fat (of which 9g saturates);
81g carbohydrate; 0.3g salt

VARIATION
Use apples instead of pears.

1 Put the pears and lemon juice into a bowl, add 100g (3½oz) sugar and the
   mixed spice, then add the blackberries and toss thoroughly to coat.
2 Preheat the oven to 200°C (180°C fan oven) mark 6. Lightly grease a
   1.8 litre (3¼ pint) shallow dish, then carefully tip the fruit into the dish in
   an even layer.
3 Put the butter, flour, ground almonds and the remaining sugar into a food
   processor and pulse until the mixture begins to resemble breadcrumbs.
   Tip into a bowl and bring parts of it together with your hands to make
   lumps. Spoon the crumble topping evenly over the fruit, then bake for
   35–45 minutes until the fruit is tender and the crumble is golden and
   bubbling. Serve with cream, custard or ice cream.

APPLE CRUMBLE

SERVES 4

Preparation: 15 minutes

Cooking time: 45 minutes

125g (4oz) plain flour
50g (2oz) unsalted butter, cubed
50g (2oz) golden caster sugar
450g (1lb) apples, peeled, cored and
    sliced
custard or double cream to serve

PER SERVING

425 cals; 18g fat (of which 7g saturates);
74g carbohydrate; 0.3g salt

1 Preheat the oven to 180°C (160°C fan oven) mark 4. Put the flour into a
   bowl, add the butter and rub in with your fingertips until the mixture
   resembles fine breadcrumbs. Stir in half the sugar. Put to one side.
2 Arrange half the apples in a 1.1 litre (2 pint) pie dish and sprinkle with the
   rest of the sugar. Add the remaining apple slices to the dish. Spoon the
   crumble mixture over the fruit.
3 Bake in the oven for about 45 minutes until the fruit is soft. Serve hot with
   custard or a drizzle of double cream.

AMERICAN-STYLE PLUM COBBLER

SERVES 6

Preparation: 25 minutes

Cooking time: 40 minutes

900g (2lb) plums, halved and stoned

150g (5oz) golden caster sugar, plus
   3 tbsp

1 tbsp cornflour

250g (9oz) self-raising flour

100g (3½oz) chilled unsalted butter,
   diced

175ml (6fl oz) buttermilk or whole
   natural yogurt

PER SERVING

451 cals; 15g fat (of which 9g saturates);
76g carbohydrate; 0.3g salt

1 Preheat the oven to 200°C (180°C fan oven) mark 6. Cut the plums into chunky wedges. Tip into an ovenproof dish measuring 25.5 x 18 x 7.5cm (10 x 7 x 3 inch) and toss together with 3 tbsp sugar and the cornflour.

2 Whiz the flour, butter and 100g (3½oz) sugar in a food processor until the mixture forms fine crumbs. (Alternatively, rub the fat into the flour by hand or using a pastry cutter, then stir in the sugar.) Add the buttermilk or yogurt and blend for a few seconds until just combined.

3 Scatter clumps of the dough over the plums, leaving some of the fruit exposed. Sprinkle the cobbler with the remaining sugar and bake for 40 minutes or until the fruit is tender and the topping is pale golden.

VARIATION
Toss the plums with the grated zest of ½ orange before baking, and add the grated zest of the remaining ½ orange to the cobbler mixture along with the buttermilk.

CHERRY CLAFOUTIS

SERVES 6

Preparation: 20 minutes, plus soaking
Cooking time: about 1 hour

350g (12oz) cherries, pitted
3 tbsp Kirsch
125g (4oz) golden caster sugar
4 large eggs
25g (1oz) plain flour, sifted
150ml (¼ pint) milk
150ml (¼ pint) double cream
1 tsp vanilla extract
a little butter to grease

PER SERVING

326 cals; 18g fat (of which 10g saturates);
33g carbohydrate; 0.2g salt

VARIATION

For an autumnal clafoutis,
replace the cherries with
blackberries, the Kirsch with
blackberry or blackcurrant
liqueur and the vanilla with
¼ tsp ground cinnamon.

1 Put the cherries into a bowl with the Kirsch and 1 tbsp sugar. Mix together, cover and set aside for 1 hour.

2 Meanwhile, whisk together the eggs, 100g (3½oz) of the sugar and the flour in a bowl. Put the milk and cream into a small pan and bring to the boil. Pour on to the egg mixture and whisk until combined. Stir in the vanilla extract, then strain into a bowl. Cover and set aside for 30 minutes. Preheat the oven to 180°C (160°C fan oven) mark 4.

3 Lightly grease a 1.7 litre (3 pint) shallow ovenproof dish and sprinkle with the remaining caster sugar. Spoon the Kirsch-soaked cherries into the dish. Whisk the batter again, then pour it over the cherries. Bake for 50 minutes–1 hour until golden and just set. Serve warm.

STEAMED SYRUP SPONGE PUDDINGS

SERVES 4

Preparation: 20 minutes

Cooking time: 35 minutes or 1½ hours

125g (4oz) butter, softened, plus
   extra to grease
3 tbsp golden syrup
125g (4oz) golden caster sugar
few drops of vanilla extract
2 medium eggs, beaten
175g (6oz) self-raising flour, sifted
about 3 tbsp milk
custard or cream to serve

PER SERVING
580 cals; 29g fat (of which 17g saturates);
76g carbohydrate; 0.7g salt

VARIATIONS

Steamed jam sponge puddings: Put 4 tbsp
raspberry or blackberry jam into the bottom of the
basins instead of the syrup.

Steamed chocolate sponge puddings: Omit
the golden syrup. Blend 4 tbsp cocoa powder with
2 tbsp hot water, then gradually beat into the
creamed mixture before adding the eggs.

1 Half-fill a steamer or large pan with water and put it on
   to boil. Grease four 300ml (½ pint) basins or a 900ml
   (1½ pint) pudding basin and spoon the golden syrup
   into the bottom.

2 In a bowl, cream the butter and sugar together until
   pale and fluffy. Stir in the vanilla extract. Add the eggs, a
   little at a time, beating well after each addition.

3 Using a metal spoon, fold in half the flour, then fold in
   the rest with enough milk to give a dropping
   consistency. Spoon the mixture into the prepared
   pudding basin(s).

4 Cover with greased and pleated greaseproof paper and
   foil and secure with string. Steam for 35 minutes for
   individual puddings or 1½ hours for one large pudding,
   checking the water level from time to time and topping
   up with boiling water as necessary. Turn out on to
   warmed plates and serve with custard or cream.

PEAR AND GINGER STEAMED PUDDING

Preparation: 20 minutes

Cooking time: 1 hour 35 minutes, plus cooling

125g (4oz) butter, softened, plus
    extra for greasing
1 large pear, peeled, cored and diced
2 tbsp golden caster sugar
2 balls preserved stem ginger, finely
    chopped, plus 2 tbsp ginger syrup
4 tbsp golden syrup
125g (4oz) light muscovado sugar
finely grated zest of 1 lemon
2 medium eggs, beaten
175g (6oz) self-raising flour
2 tsp ground ginger
3 tbsp perry or pear juice

PER SERVING

314 cals; 14g fat (of which 9g saturates);
45g carbohydrate; 0.6g salt

1 Grease a 900ml (1½ pint) pudding basin. Put the pear into a pan with 2 tbsp water and the caster sugar and simmer for 5 minutes. Stir in the stem ginger, ginger syrup and golden syrup and leave to cool. Tip into the basin.

2 Using a hand-held electric whisk, beat the butter, muscovado sugar and lemon zest in a bowl until light and fluffy. Beat in the eggs a little at a time.

3 Fold in the flour and ground ginger, then fold in the perry or pear juice. Pour the mixture into the basin on top of the pear compote. Cut out a piece each of greaseproof and foil, each measuring 30.5 x 30.5cm (12 x 12 inch). Fold a pleat in the middle and put on top of pudding. Tie under the rim with string, using extra to make a knotted handle over the top. Trim excess paper and foil.

4 Sit the basin on an upturned saucer in a large pan. Pour in enough boiling water to come halfway up the basin. Cover and steam for 1¼–1½ hours, topping up with extra boiling water when necessary. Turn out on to a plate and serve.

STICKY TOFFEE PUDDINGS

SERVES 4

Preparation: 20 minutes
Cooking time: 25–30 minutes, plus resting

1 tbsp golden syrup
1 tbsp black treacle
150g (5oz) butter, softened
25g (1oz) pecan nuts or walnuts,
    finely ground
75g (3oz) self-raising flour
125g (4oz) caster sugar
2 large eggs, beaten
cream or custard to serve

PER SERVING

565 cals; 38g fat (of which 21g saturates);
53g carbohydrate; 0.9g salt

1 Preheat the oven to 180°C (160°C fan oven) mark 4. Put the syrup, treacle and 25g (1oz) butter into a bowl and beat until smooth. Divide the mixture among four 150ml (¼ pint) timbales or ramekins and set aside.

2 Put the nuts into a bowl, sift in the flour and mix together well.

3 Put the remaining butter and the sugar into a food processor and blend briefly. (Alternatively, use a hand-held electric whisk.) Add the eggs and the flour mixture and blend or mix again for 30 seconds. Spoon the mixture into the timbales or ramekins, covering the syrup mixture on the bottom. Bake for 25–30 minutes until risen and golden.

4 Remove the puddings from the oven and leave to rest for 5 minutes, then unmould on to warmed plates. Serve immediately with cream or custard.

STEAMED LEMON PUDDINGS

Preparation: 20 minutes

Cooking time: 40 minutes, plus standing

175g (6oz) unsalted butter, softened,
  plus extra to grease
6 tbsp lemon curd
175g (6oz) golden caster sugar
3 medium eggs
finely grated zest and juice of ½ large
  lemon
175g (6oz) self-raising flour
2 tsp baking powder
icing sugar to dust
Vanilla Custard to serve (see
  page 316)

**PER SERVING (WITHOUT
CUSTARD)**

532 cals; 29g fat (of which 16g saturates);
66g carbohydrate; 0.6g salt

FREEZING TIP
To freeze, complete the recipe to
the end of step 4 up to three
months ahead, then turn out the
puddings into a freezerproof
container, cool and freeze. To
use, thaw the puddings at cool
room temperature for 45
minutes. Preheat the oven to
200°C (180°C fan oven) mark 6.
Grease an ovenproof dish. Put
the puddings in the dish, lemon
curd-side up, drizzle 5 tbsp water
over all and cover loosely with
foil. Reheat for 30–35 minutes,
turn out on to plates and serve
as in step 5.

1 Preheat the oven to 180°C (160°C fan oven) mark 4. Grease six 200ml
  (7fl oz) dariole moulds and put 1 tbsp lemon curd in each.
2 Put the butter and caster sugar into a bowl and, using a hand-held electric
  whisk, beat until fluffy. Beat in the eggs, lemon zest and juice. Using a metal
  spoon, fold in the flour and baking powder.
3 Spoon the mixture into the prepared moulds, level the tops and cover
  each with a disc of greaseproof paper, then wrap in foil. Put the puddings
  into a roasting tin and pour in enough hot water to come halfway up the
  sides of the moulds. Cook for 40 minutes or until risen and cooked in
  the centre.
4 Lift the puddings out of the tin and leave to stand for 10 minutes. Run a
  palette knife around the edge of each dariole mould and turn out on to
  individual plates.
5 Dust with icing sugar and serve with vanilla custard.

SPOTTED DICK

Preparation: 15 minutes

Cooking time: 2 hours

125g (4oz) fresh breadcrumbs

75g (3oz) self-raising flour, plus extra
   to dust

75g (3oz) shredded suet

50g (2oz) caster sugar

175g (6oz) currants

finely grated zest of 1 lemon

5 tbsp milk

butter to grease

custard to serve

PER SERVING

502 calories; 18g fat (of which 10g saturates);
84g carbohydrate; 0.8g salt

1. Half-fill a preserving pan or large saucepan with water and put on to boil.
2. Place the breadcrumbs, flour, suet, sugar, currants and lemon zest in a bowl and stir well until thoroughly mixed. Pour in the milk and stir until well blended. Using one hand, bring the ingredients together to form a soft, slightly sticky dough.
3. Turn the dough out on to a lightly floured surface and knead gently until just smooth. Shape into a neat roll about 15cm (6 inch) in length.
4. Make a 5cm (2 inch) pleat across a clean teatowel or pudding cloth (or pleat together sheets of greased greaseproof paper and strong foil). Encase the roll in the cloth or foil, pleating the open edges tightly together. Tie the ends securely with string to form a cracker shape. Make a string handle across the top. Lower the suet roll into the pan of boiling water and boil for 2 hours, topping up with water as necessary.
5. Using the string handle, lift the spotted dick out of the water. Place on a wire rack standing over a plate and allow excess moisture to drain off.
6. Snip the string and gently roll the pudding out of the cloth or foil on to a warmed serving plate. Serve sliced, with custard.

FIG, ORANGE AND CRANBERRY CHRISTMAS PUDDING

LONG SOAKING REQUIRED

SERVES 8

Preparation: 20 minutes, plus overnight soaking

Cooking time: 4½–5 hours

125g (4oz) each sultanas, currants and raisins

75g (3oz) dried cranberries

75g (3oz) dried figs, finely chopped

75ml (3fl oz) orange liqueur, such as Cointreau

zest and juice of 1 orange

butter to grease

1 pear

2 medium eggs

50g (2oz) each shredded vegetarian suet and self-raising
 flour

75g (3oz) fresh white breadcrumbs

½ tsp each mixed spice and ground cinnamon

pinch of freshly grated nutmeg

100g (3½oz) soft dark brown sugar

25g (1oz) brazil nuts, roughly chopped (optional)

PER SERVING

435 cals; 12g fat (of which 5g saturates); 75g carbohydrate; 0.8g salt

1 Put the dried fruit into a large non-metallic bowl and stir in the liqueur, orange zest and juice. Cover and leave to soak overnight at room temperature.

2 Lightly grease a 1 litre (1¾ pint) pudding basin and line the bottom with a circle of baking parchment. Lay a 35.5cm (14 inch) square of foil on top of a square of baking parchment the same size. Fold a 4cm (1½ inch) pleat down the centre of both and set aside.

3 Core the pear, then grate into the soaked fruit mixture. Beat the eggs and add to the bowl, then add all the remaining ingredients and stir well. Spoon into the prepared basin, pressing down firmly, and level the top. Put the pleated foil square (foil-side up) on top of the pudding and smooth down to cover. Using a long length of string, securely tie down the square just under the lip of the basin and knot it. Bring the excess string over the top of the bowl and tie it to the string under the lip on the other side to make a handle. Scrunch the edge of the parchment up underneath the foil.

4 Put an upturned heatproof saucer into a deep pan and balance the pudding on top. Pour in enough water to come halfway up the sides of the basin, cover the pan with a tight-fitting lid and bring to a simmer. Cook for 4½–5 hours, checking the water level regularly and topping up as necessary with boiling water. Remove the pudding from the pan and cool. Once it is cold, wrap the entire basin tightly in clingfilm and a layer of foil. Store in a cool, dark place for up to two months.

TO REHEAT

Remove the foil and clingfilm wrapping. Re-cover the top of the basin with baking parchment and foil. Cook the pudding as in step 4 for 2 hours. Discard the foil and parchment. Slide a knife around the edge of the pudding, then turn out on to a plate and leave to stand for 15 minutes before serving.

BREAD AND BUTTER PUDDING

Preparation: 10 minutes, plus soaking

Cooking time: 30–40 minutes

50g (2oz) butter, softened, plus extra
   to grease
275g (10oz) white farmhouse bread,
   cut into 1cm (½ inch) slices, crusts
   removed
50g (2oz) raisins or sultanas
3 medium eggs
450ml (¾ pint) milk
3 tbsp golden icing sugar, plus extra
   to dust

PER SERVING

450 cals; 13g fat (of which 5g saturates);
70g carbohydrate; 1.1g salt

1 Lightly grease four 300ml (½ pint) gratin dishes or one 1.1 litre (2 pint)
   ovenproof dish. Butter the bread, then cut into quarters to make triangles.
   Arrange the bread in the dish(es) and sprinkle with the raisins or sultanas.
2 Beat the eggs, milk and sugar in a bowl. Pour the mixture over the bread
   and leave to soak for 10 minutes. Preheat the oven to 180°C (160°C fan
   oven) mark 4.
3 Put the pudding(s) in the oven and bake for 30–40 minutes. Dust with
   icing sugar to serve.

PANETTONE PUDDING

Preparation: 20 minutes, plus soaking

Cooking time: 35–45 minutes

50g (2oz) butter, at room
   temperature, plus extra to grease
500g (1lb 2oz) Panettone (see page
   231, and note), cut into slices
   about 5mm (¼ inch) thick
3 large eggs, beaten
150g (5oz) golden caster sugar
300ml (½ pint) milk
150ml (¼ pint) double cream
grated zest of 1 orange

PER SERVING

581 cals; 29g fat (of which 16g saturates);
73g carbohydrate; 0.9g salt

1   Grease a 2 litre (3½ pint) ovenproof dish. Lightly butter the panettone slices, then tear them into pieces and arrange in the dish.

2   Mix the eggs with the sugar in a large bowl, then whisk in the milk, cream and orange zest. Pour the mixture over the buttered panettone and leave to soak for 20 minutes. Preheat the oven to 170°C (150°C fan oven) mark 3.

3   Put the dish into a roasting tin and pour in enough hot water to come halfway up the sides. Bake for 35–45 minutes until the pudding is just set in the middle and golden.

NOTE
Panettone is a yeasted fruit cake that is a traditional Christmas treat in Italy and is most widely available around Christmas time. You can use brioche or cinnamon and raisin bread as an alternative.

CHOCOLATE BREAD PUDDING

Preparation: 20 minutes, plus chilling

Cooking time: 55 minutes–1¼ hours

200g (7oz) baguette

100g (3½oz) milk chocolate, roughly
  chopped

500g carton fresh custard

150ml (¼ pint) semi-skimmed milk

1 large egg, beaten

butter to grease

1 tbsp demerara sugar

50g (2oz) walnuts, finely chopped

50g (2oz) plain or milk chocolate, in
  chunks

single cream to serve (optional)

PER SERVING

390 cals; 17g fat (of which 6g saturates);
51g carbohydrate; 0.7g salt

1 Roughly chop the baguette and put it into a large bowl. Put the chopped milk chocolate into a pan with the custard and milk over a low heat. Stir gently until the chocolate has melted. Beat in the egg.

2 Pour the chocolate mixture over the bread, stir well to coat, then cover and chill for at least 4 hours.

3 Preheat the oven to 180°C (160°C fan oven) mark 4. Grease a 1.4 litre (2½ pint), 7.5cm (3 inch) deep ovenproof dish. Spoon the soaked bread into the dish and bake for 30–40 minutes.

4 Sprinkle with the sugar, walnuts and chocolate chunks. Put the dish back in the oven for 20–30 minutes until lightly set. Serve the pudding warm, with single cream, if you like.

VARIATION
Instead of baguette, use croissants or brioche for a richer pudding.

QUICK CHOCOLATE PUDDINGS

Preparation: 15 minutes
Cooking time: 12–15 minutes

100g (3½oz) butter, plus extra to
    grease
100g (3½oz) golden caster sugar,
    plus extra to dust
100g (3½oz) plain chocolate (at least
    70% cocoa solids), broken into
    pieces
2 large eggs
20g (¾oz) plain flour
icing sugar to dust

PER SERVING

468 cals; 31g fat (of which 19g saturates);
46g carbohydrate; 0.6g salt

1 Preheat the oven to 200°C (180°C fan oven) mark 6. Grease four 200ml
   (7fl oz) ramekins and dust with sugar. Melt the chocolate and butter in a
   heatproof bowl set over a pan of gently simmering water, making sure the
   base of the bowl doesn't touch the water. Take the bowl off the pan and
   leave to cool for 5 minutes.
2 Whisk the eggs, caster sugar and flour together in a bowl until smooth.
   Fold in the chocolate mixture and pour into the ramekins.
3 Stand the dishes on a baking tray and bake for 12–15 minutes until the
   puddings are puffed and set on the outside, but still runny inside. Turn out,
   dust with icing sugar and serve immediately.

BAKED ALASKA

LONG FREEZING REQUIRED

SERVES 8

Preparation: 30 minutes, plus freezing

Cooking time: 3–4 minutes

1 large sponge flan case, 25.5cm (10 inch) diameter

5 tbsp orange juice

7 tbsp jam – any kind

1.5 litre tub vanilla ice cream

6 large egg whites

pinch of cream of tartar

pinch of salt

275g (10oz) golden caster sugar

PER SERVING

659 cals; 30g fat (of which 17g saturates);

91g carbohydrate; 0.5g salt

1 Put the flan case on an ovenproof plate. Spoon the orange juice over the sponge, then spread with the jam. Scoop the ice cream on top of the jam, then put in the freezer for at least 30 minutes.

2 Put the egg whites into a large, clean, grease-free bowl and whisk until stiff. Beat in the cream of tartar and salt. Using a large spoon, fold in the sugar, 1 tbsp at a time, then whisk until very thick and shiny.

3 Spoon the meringue over the ice cream to cover, making sure that the meringue is sealed to the flan case edge all the way round. Freeze for at least 1 hour or overnight.

4 Preheat the oven to 230°C (210°C fan oven) mark 8. Bake for 3–4 minutes until the meringue is tinged golden brown. Serve immediately. If the Baked Alaska has been in the freezer overnight, bake and leave to stand for about 15 minutes before serving.

RICE PUDDING

Preparation: 5 minutes

Cooking time: 1½ hours

butter to grease

125g (4oz) short-grain pudding rice

1.1 litres (2 pints) milk

50g (2oz) golden caster sugar

1 tsp vanilla extract

grated zest of 1 orange (optional)

freshly grated nutmeg to taste

PER SERVING

239 cals; 8g fat (of which 5g saturates);

34g carbohydrate; 0.2g salt

1 Preheat the oven to 170°C (150°C fan oven) mark 3. Lightly grease a
   1.7 litre (3 pint) ovenproof dish.

2 Put the rice, milk, sugar, vanilla extract and orange zest, if using, into the
   dish and stir everything together. Grate the nutmeg over the top of
   the mixture.

3 Bake the pudding in the middle of the oven for 1½ hours or until the top
   is golden brown.

STRAWBERRY PAVLOVA WITH ROSEWATER SYRUP

Preparation: 20 minutes

Cooking time: about 50 minutes, plus cooling

10 medium egg whites

600g (1lb 5oz) caster sugar

1¾ tbsp cornflour

1kg (2¼lb) strawberries, hulled

150ml (5fl oz) dessert wine, such as
  Muscat de Beaumes de Venise

1 tsp rosewater

600ml (1 pint) double cream

3 tbsp icing sugar, sifted

PER SERVING

614 cals; 32g fat (of which 20g saturates);

78g carbohydrate; 0.3g salt

1 Preheat the oven to 150°C (130°C fan oven) mark 2. Line a large baking sheet with baking parchment. Use a pencil to draw a 28cm (11 inch) diameter circle on the parchment, then flip it over so the pencil mark is underneath.

2 Using electric beaters, whisk the egg whites in a large, grease-free bowl until stiff but not dry. Gradually add 550g (1¼lb) caster sugar, whisking all the time, until the mixture is stiff and glossy. Quickly beat in 1 tbsp cornflour.

3 Spoon the mixture on to the prepared baking tray within the marked circle, pushing it into peaks at the edges of the circle. Bake for 40 minutes or until the meringue is firm to the touch and peels away from the parchment. Transfer to a rack and leave to cool.

4 Meanwhile, put 200g (7oz) strawberries with the wine, remaining caster sugar and the rosewater into a pan. Heat and simmer gently for 5 minutes. Blend until smooth, then push through a fine sieve, discarding the pips. Return the mixture to the pan and whisk in the remaining cornflour. Heat gently for 3–4 minutes until the syrup thickens, whisking constantly to remove any lumps. Take off the heat and leave to cool.

5 Transfer the cooled meringue to a serving plate. Gently whip the cream with the icing sugar until it just holds its shape. Dollop on top of the meringue, then pile on the remaining strawberries. Drizzle the cooled syrup over and serve.

NOTE
For convenience, prepare ahead. Cook the meringue, make the strawberry syrup and hull the strawberries up to one day ahead. Cool the meringue on the baking sheet, then cover with clingfilm and store at room temperature. Cool the syrup, then cover and chill. Keep the hulled strawberries covered in the fridge. Whip the cream mixture up to 2 hours ahead, then chill. To serve, bring the syrup, strawberries and cream up to room temperature, then complete the recipe.

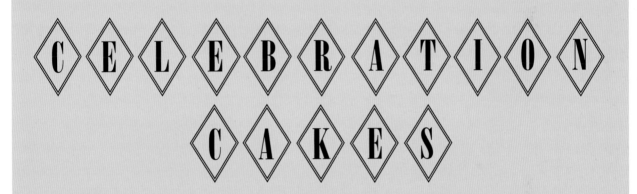

CELEBRATION CAKES

WHITE CHOCOLATE AND ORANGE CAKE

SERVES 14

Preparation: 35 minutes

Cooking time: 45–50 minutes, plus cooling and chilling

butter to grease
6 large eggs, separated
250g (9oz) golden caster sugar
150g (5oz) self-raising flour
150g (5oz) ground almonds
grated zest of 2 oranges
350g (12oz) strawberries, hulled and thinly sliced

SYRUP

100g (3½oz) golden granulated sugar
250ml (9fl oz) sweet white wine
juice of 3 large oranges

WHITE CHOCOLATE GANACHE

225g (8oz) white chocolate, chopped
568ml carton double cream

PER SERVING

530 cals; 34g fat (of which 17g saturates); 49g carbohydrate; 0.3g salt

NOTE

**Three-tier Celebration Cake: To make two smaller
tiers,** make another quantity of syrup, to drizzle over the
extra cakes. Using the quantities below, follow the above
method. Assemble up to 4 hours ahead, wrap loosely
and keep chilled in the fridge.

Ingredients	12-portion middle tier	4-portion top tier
	15cm (6 inch) cake tin	200g clean baked bean tin
eggs	3	1
golden caster sugar	125g (4oz)	40g (1½oz)
self-raising flour	75g (3oz)	25g (1oz)
ground almonds	75g (3oz)	25g (1oz)
orange zest	from 1 orange	1 tsp
GANACHE		
white chocolate	125g (4oz)	50g (2oz)
double cream	284ml carton	142ml carton
strawberries	175g (6oz)	50g (2oz)
Cooking time	30–35 minutes	25–30 minutes

1 Preheat the oven to 180°C (160°C fan oven) mark 4.
Grease a deep 23cm (9 inch) round cake tin and base-
line with greaseproof paper.

2 Put the egg whites into a clean, grease-free bowl and
whisk until soft peaks form. Gradually beat in 50g (2oz)
sugar. Whisk until the mixture stands in stiff peaks and
looks glossy.

3 Put the egg yolks and remaining sugar in another bowl
and whisk until soft and moussey. Carefully stir in the
flour to make a paste.

4 Using a clean metal spoon, add a third of the egg white
to the paste and fold in carefully. Put the remaining egg
white, the ground almonds and orange zest into the
bowl and fold in, taking care not to knock too much
volume out of the egg white. You should end up with a
smooth batter.

5 Spoon into the prepared tin and bake in the oven for
35 minutes or until a skewer inserted into the centre
comes out clean. Cool in the tin for 10 minutes, then
turn out on to a wire rack and leave to cool completely.

6 Put the syrup ingredients into a small pan and stir over a
gentle heat until the sugar has dissolved. Bring to the boil
and bubble for 5 minutes or until syrupy. Leave to cool
and set aside.

7 To make the ganache, put the chocolate into a
heatproof bowl with half the cream. Set over a pan of
simmering water, making sure that the base of the bowl
doesn't touch the water, and leave until the chocolate
has melted, then stir. Don't stir the chocolate until it has
completely melted. Leave to cool until beginning to
thicken, then beat with a wooden spoon until cold and
thick. Put the remaining double cream into a bowl and
whip lightly. Beat a large spoonful of the whipped cream
into the chocolate cream to loosen it, then fold in the
remainder. Cover and leave to chill for 2 hours.

8 Cut the cake in half horizontally, pierce all over with a
skewer and put it, cut-sides up, on an edged tray or
baking sheet. Spoon the syrup over and leave to soak in.

9 Spread a quarter of the ganache over the base cake and
scatter with 225g (8oz) strawberries. Cover with the top
half of the cake and press down lightly. Using a palette
knife, smooth the remaining ganache over the top and
sides of the cake. Cover loosely and leave to chill for up
to 4 hours. Decorate with the remaining strawberries
and serve. To turn this into a tiered cake, see note (left).

ROSEBUD WEDDING CAKE

OVERNIGHT PREPARATION NEEDED

CUTS INTO
180–200 SLICES

Preparation: at least 1 day, plus drying

250g (9oz) sugar flower paste (available from cake
   decorating suppliers)
pink food colouring
5kg (11lb) white ready-to-roll icing
white royal icing (see page 320) made with 225g (8oz) icing
   sugar
one 30.5cm (12 inch) round Rich Fruit Celebration Cake,
   covered in almond paste set on a 40.5cm (16 inch) cake
   board (drum)
one 23cm (9 inch) round Rich Fruit Celebration Cake,
   covered in almond paste set on a 23cm (9 inch) cake
   board (double thick)
one 15cm (6 inch) round Rich Fruit Celebration Cake,
   covered in almond paste set on a 15cm (6 inch) cake
   board (double thick)
no. 2 and no. 3 piping nozzles
6 plastic cake dowels
pink ribbon
fresh pink roses (optional)

PER SLICE
555 cals; 16g fat (of which 5g saturates); 92g carbohydrate; 0.2g salt

1   To make sugar roses, colour the flower paste different
    shades of pale pink. Make a cone shape a bit smaller
    than the size of the petal. Roll the flower paste out
    thinly, using only small amounts at a time, and cut out
    a 5-petal rose shape with a cutter. Thin the edges of
    the petals slightly with a bone tool, or roll them over
    a cocktail stick.
2   Dampen the lower part of each petal with a little
    water and wrap the petals around the cone one at
    a time, slightly overlapping each petal as you go.
    Repeat with a second set of 5 petals. Using your
    fingers, curl the outer edges of the petals to give a
    natural rose shape. Repeat to make at least 12 roses.
    Use a smaller cutter to make at least 24 roses for the
    sides of the cakes. Leave overnight to harden.

3   Take the largest cake on its cake board. Roll out some
    of the ready-to-roll icing so that it is 4–5 mm (¼ inch)
    thick and large enough to cover the cake. Dampen
    the cake with a little boiled water. Lift the icing on to
    the cake and smooth over the top and sides, trimming
    the excess icing away around the base. Dampen the
    surrounding cake board. Roll out a long thin strip of
    icing to cover the board and trim away the excess.
    Ice the two smaller tiers in the same way.
4   Cut a circle of greaseproof paper to the size of
    the top of each cake. Fold the largest two into
    8 segments, the smallest into 6 segments. Using a
    compass or the bottom of a glass with the right
    diameter, pencil a scallop on the rounded edge
    between the folds about 5cm (2 inch) deep for the
    larger cakes and 2.5cm (1 inch) deep for the top tier.
    Cut out the scallops.
5   Open out the paper and place the smallest piece in
    the centre of the smallest cake and the two larger
    pieces in the centre of the two larger cakes. Hold the
    paper with one hand while pricking the scalloped
    outline on to the icing.
6   For the side scallops, cut a strip of greaseproof paper
    the circumference of the cake. As before, fold into
    8 segments and mark the scallops in the same way.
    Remove the paper and, using an icing bag fitted with
    the plain no. 3 icing nozzle and filled with white royal
    icing, pipe a line of icing along the line of the scallops.
    Leave to dry for about 1 hour before piping a second,
    thinner line on top of the first using the no. 2 nozzle.
7   Push three dowels into each of the two larger cakes
    (see page 297). Using a pencil, mark the dowels
    where they are level with the top of the cake.
    Remove the dowels and cut each one where marked.
    However, if the top of the cake is not completely flat,
    make sure the three dowels are cut to equal length
    otherwise the cake above may slope. Push the dowels
    back into the holes. Carefully stack the middle and
    top cakes.
8   Secure a piece of ribbon around each cake with a
    small dot of royal icing.
9   Complete the decoration by piling up the large icing
    roses on the centre of the top cake and placing a
    smaller rose at each of the points where the scallops
    meet. Surround with fresh roses and petals, if you like.

BEST EVER CHRISTMAS CAKE

OVERNIGHT PREPARATION NEEDED

CUTS INTO 24 SLICES

Preparation: 30 minutes, plus soaking
Cooking time: about 4 hours, plus cooling

500g (1lb 2oz) sultanas
400g (14oz) raisins
150g (5oz) each Agen prunes and dried figs, roughly
    chopped
200g (7oz) dried apricots, roughly chopped
zest and juice of 2 oranges
200ml (7fl oz) hazelnut liqueur, such as Frangelico Hazelnut
    Liqueur, plus extra to drizzle
250g (9oz) unsalted butter, softened, plus extra to grease
150g (5oz) each dark muscovado and light brown soft sugar
200g (7oz) plain flour, sifted
1 tsp ground cinnamon
1 tsp mixed spice
¼ tsp ground cloves
¼ tsp freshly grated nutmeg
pinch of salt
4 large eggs, beaten
100g (3½oz) toasted, blanched hazelnuts, roughly chopped
40g (1½oz) toasted pinenuts
1 tbsp brandy (optional)

PER SLICE

375 cals; 14g fat (of which 6g saturates); 56g carbohydrate; 0.4g salt

NOTE
For convenience, prepare ahead. Complete the
recipe up to three months ahead and store as in
step 6. It can be doused in alcohol every week if
you like a stronger taste.

1 Put the fruit into a non-metallic bowl and stir in the
orange zest and juice and the hazelnut liqueur. Cover
and leave to soak overnight or, preferably, up to 3 days.

2 Preheat the oven to 140°C (120°C fan oven) mark 1.
Grease a 23cm (9 inch) cake tin and double-line with
greaseproof paper, making sure the paper comes at
least 5cm (2 inch) above the top of the tin. Then wrap
a double layer of greaseproof paper around the
outside of the tin, securing with string – this will stop
the cake burning.

3 Using a hand-held electric mixer, beat together the
butter and sugars in a large bowl until light and fluffy –
this should take about 5 minutes.

4 In a separate bowl, sift together the flour, spices and
salt. Beat 2 tbsp of the flour mixture into the butter
and sugar, then gradually add the eggs, making sure the
mixture doesn't curdle. If it looks as if it might be
about to, add a little more flour.

5 Using a large metal spoon, fold the remaining flour into
the mixture, followed by the soaked fruit and the nuts.
Tip into the prepared tin and level the surface. Using
the end of the spoon, make a hole in the centre of the
mix, going right down to the base of the tin – this will
stop the top of the cake rising into a dome shape as it
cooks. Bake for 4 hours or until a skewer inserted into
the centre comes out clean. Cover with foil if it is
browning too quickly. Leave to cool in the tin for 10
minutes, then turn out on to a wire rack, keeping the
greaseproof paper wrapped around the outside of the
cake, and leave to cool completely.

6 To store, leave the cold cake in its greaseproof paper.
Wrap a few layers of clingfilm around it, then cover
with foil. Store in a cool place in an airtight container.
After two weeks, unwrap the cake, prick all over and
pour over 1 tbsp of hazelnut liqueur, or brandy if you
prefer. Rewrap and store as before. Ice up to three
days before serving (see opposite).

ICING THE CAKE

MAKES ENOUGH TO COVER
A 23CM (9 INCH) CAKE

Preparation: 30 minutes, plus drying
Cooking time: 3–4 minutes, plus cooling

4 tbsp apricot jam
1 fruit cake (see opposite)
sifted icing sugar to dust
450g packet ready-to-roll marzipan
vegetable oil to grease
150g (5oz) glacier mint sweets
500g packet royal icing sugar

75 x 2cm (30 x ¾ inch) silver ribbon
silver candles

PER SERVING (INCLUDING CAKE)
569 cals; 17g fat (of which 6g saturates); 100g carbohydrate; 0.2g salt

1 Gently heat the jam in a pan with 1 tbsp water until softened, then press through a sieve into a bowl to make a smooth glaze. Put the cake on a board and brush over the top and sides with the glaze.

2 Dust a rolling pin and worksurface with a little icing sugar and roll out the marzipan to a round about 15cm (6 inch) larger than the cake. Position over the cake and ease to fit around the sides, pressing out any creases. Trim off the excess around the base. Leave to dry for 24 hours.

3 Preheat the oven to 180°C (160°C fan oven) mark 4. Line a baking sheet with foil and brush lightly with oil. Unwrap the mints and put pairs of sweets on the baking sheet about 1cm (½ inch) apart, leaving 5cm (2 inch) of space between each pair, to allow room for them to spread as they melt. Cook for 3–4 minutes until the sweets have melted and are just starting to bubble around the edges. Leave to cool on the foil for 3–4 minutes until firm enough to be lifted off. Use kitchen scissors to snip the pieces into large slivers and shards.

4 Wrap the ribbon around the edge of the cake. Put the icing sugar in a bowl and make up according to packet instructions. Using a small palette knife, spread the icing over the top of the cake, flicking it into small peaks as you go. Then tease the edges of the icing down the sides of the cake to form icicles.

5 While the icing is still soft, push the mint shards into the top of the cake and insert the silver candles. Leave the cake to dry. Light the candles and serve.

TO STORE
Once cut into, store the cake in a container in a cool, dry place. It will keep for up to two weeks.

SNOWY YULE LOG

Preparation: 25 minutes

Cooking time: 15 minutes, plus cooling

a little butter to grease
75g (3oz) plain flour
1 tsp baking powder
¼ tsp salt
4 medium eggs
150g (5oz) caster sugar
1 tsp vanilla extract
75g (3oz) ground almonds
284ml carton double cream
2 tbsp golden icing sugar, sifted, plus extra to dust
50g (2oz) flaked almonds, toasted

PER SLICE

412 cals; 31g fat (of which 12g saturates); 33g carbohydrate;
0.1g salt

1 Preheat the oven to 180°C (160°C fan oven) mark 4. Grease a 33 x 23cm (13 x 9 inch) Swiss roll tin and line with greaseproof paper. Sift the flour, baking powder and salt together.

2 Using a hand-held electric whisk, beat the eggs, caster sugar and vanilla extract in a bowl for 5–10 minutes until pale and fluffy. The mixture is ready when it leaves a ribbon-like trail as you lift the beaters.

3 Using a large metal spoon, carefully fold in the ground almonds and the flour mixture, taking care not to beat too much air out of the mixture. Pour into the prepared tin and spread the mixture in a thin layer right to the edges.

4 Bake for 12–15 minutes until the edges begin to pull away from the sides of the tin and the cake springs back when you press it gently with a finger. Leave to cool in the tin.

5 Lightly whip the cream and icing sugar in a bowl until soft peaks form. Put a sheet of greaseproof paper, larger than the cake, on the worksurface and dust heavily with icing sugar. Flip the cake on to the paper. Remove the tin and carefully peel away the attached paper.

6 Spread the cream over the cake and sprinkle with the flaked almonds. Using the greaseproof paper to help, roll up lengthways. Don't worry if cracks appear – they'll add to the log effect.

7 Carefully transfer to a serving plate. Dust with icing sugar and serve in slices.

VARIATION

To decorate the Yule Log: Melt 50g (2oz) dark chocolate in a heatproof bowl set over a pan of simmering water, making sure the base of the bowl doesn't touch the water. Wash 4 holly leaves and dry, then paint chocolate thickly on the shiny side of each. Put on a baking sheet lined with greaseproof paper and chill until the chocolate has set. For the white holly leaves, repeat the process with 25g (1oz) good-quality white chocolate. Fill a disposable piping bag with the remaining dark chocolate and cut off the tip. Write 'Noel' on a piece of greaseproof, then chill to set. Carefully peel away the holly leaves from the chocolate and the greaseproof paper from the word 'Noel' and lay them on top of the log.

GINGERBREAD HOUSE

MAKES 4 HOUSES

Preparation: 4 hours, plus 30 minutes chilling and 5 hours drying
Cooking time: 10 minutes

150g (5oz) butter, plus extra to grease
350g (12oz) plain white flour, sifted
1 tsp bicarbonate of soda
2 tbsp ground ginger
200g (7oz) light muscovado sugar
2 tbsp golden syrup
1 medium egg, beaten

FOR THE DECORATION
200g (7oz) icing sugar, sifted
1 medium egg white
75g (3oz) assorted sweets

MATERIALS
Card to make the three templates:
roof: 10 x 6.5cm (4 x 2½in)
end wall: 10 x 6cm (4 x 2¼in)
side wall: 6 x 8cm (2¼ x 3¼in)
four 15cm (6in) cake boards covered in paper ribbon and
    cellophane

PER HOUSE
1000 calories; 34g fat (of which 20g saturates); 172g carbohydrate;
0.7g salt

1   Grease two baking sheets. Cut the card into templates
    for the roof and walls. Put the flour, bicarbonate of
    soda and ginger into a bowl. Rub in the butter until the
    mixture resembles breadcrumbs. Stir in the sugar.
    Warm the golden syrup in a pan, pour on to the flour
    with the beaten egg and stir. Bring together into a soft
    dough and knead until smooth. Divide into four pieces,
    wrap in clingfilm and chill for 15 minutes.

NOTE
Pipe names on the heart-shaped gift tags and leave the
house and tags to set for at least 2 hours. Wrap each
gingerbread house in cellophane and tie with ribbon.
Attach the gift tags with ribbon.

2   Roll out one piece of dough to 3mm (⅛in) thick. Cut
    out two of each template. Put on to the baking sheets.
    Repeat with the remaining dough. Stamp out four
    hearts from the trimmings and skewer a hole in the
    top of each. Put on to the baking sheets. Chill for 15
    minutes. Preheat the oven to 190°C (170°C fan oven)
    mark 5. Bake for 8–10 minutes until golden. While still
    warm, push a skewer through the holes. Leave on the
    baking sheets for 5 minutes, then transfer to a wire
    rack to cool completely.

3   To decorate, beat the icing sugar into the egg white
    until the mixture stands in peaks. Spoon into a piping
    bag and pipe windows and doors on the walls and
    squiggly lines on the roof. Leave to dry for 2 hours.
    Pipe icing along the edge of the side walls and stick to
    the end walls. Leave to dry for 1 hour, then place on a
    board and fill with sweets. Pipe icing along the top of
    each house and the roof pieces and press gently in
    position; hold for 1–2 minutes until secure.

SIMNEL CAKE

CUTS INTO 12–16 SLICES

Preparation: 1½ hours

Cooking time: 2¾ hours, plus cooling and setting

250g (9oz) unsalted butter, softened, plus extra to grease

grated zest of 2 unwaxed lemons

250g (9oz) golden caster sugar

4 large eggs, beaten

250g (9oz) plain flour

½ tsp ground mixed spice

75g (3oz) ground almonds

50g (2oz) mixed candied peel, finely chopped

150g (5oz) currants

300g (11oz) sultanas

75g (3oz) natural glacé cherries, halved

100g (3½oz) icing sugar, plus extra to dust

600g (1lb 5oz) almond paste (see page 320) or ready-made
   white marzipan

2 tbsp thin honey, warmed

1 medium egg, beaten, to glaze

PER SLICE

750–565 cals; 36–27g fat (of which 12–9g saturates);
104–78g carbohydrate; 0.5–0.4g salt

1 Preheat the oven to 170°C (150°C fan oven) mark 3.
Grease a 20.5cm (8 inch) round, 7.5cm (3 inch) deep
cake tin and line with greaseproof paper.

2 Using a freestanding mixer or hand-held electric whisk,
beat the butter and lemon zest together until very
soft. Gradually add the sugar and continue beating until
light and fluffy. Slowly beat in the eggs until evenly
incorporated.

NOTE

Simnel cake is the classic Easter celebration cake,
its marzipan balls representing the disciples – either
11 or 12 – depending on whether you think Judas
should be included.

3 Sift in the flour with the mixed spice, then add the
ground almonds, candied peel, currants, sultanas and
glacé cherries. Using a large metal spoon, fold the
ingredients together, until evenly combined. Set aside.

4 Spoon just over half of the cake mixture into the
prepared tin and level the surface. Roll out 200g (7oz)
almond paste on a surface lightly dusted with icing
sugar to an 18cm (7 inch) round.

5 Put the almond paste round on top of the mixture in
the tin, then cover with the remaining cake mixture.
Smooth the surface and make a slight hollow in the
centre, then brush lightly with cold water. Wrap a
double layer of brown paper around the outside of
the tin (see step 2, page 276) and secure with string.
Bake for 1¼ hours. Cover with greaseproof paper,
lower the oven setting to 150°C (130°C fan oven)
mark 2 and bake for a further 1½ hours or until
cooked to the centre.

6 Cool in the tin for 1 hour, then turn out on to a wire
rack and leave to cool completely. Wrap in
greaseproof paper and foil and store in an airtight
container for up to two weeks.

7 When ready to decorate, roll out 200g (7oz) almond
paste to a 20.5cm (8 inch) round. Cut a 7.5cm (3
inch) round from the centre and add this piece to the
remaining almond paste. Brush the top of the cake
with honey, cover with the almond paste ring and
press down. Crimp the edge with your fingers.

8 Divide the rest of the almond paste into 11 or 12
pieces (see note) and shape into oval balls. Brush the
ring with the beaten egg, position the balls on top and
brush them with egg. Put a disc of foil over the
exposed centre of the cake, then put under a hot grill
for 1–2 minutes to brown the almond paste.

9 Mix the icing sugar with 2–3 tbsp warm water to
make a smooth icing. Remove the foil disc, then pour
the icing on to the exposed centre and smooth it with
a palette knife. Leave the icing to set. To finish, secure a
yellow ribbon around the side of the cake.

SLEEPING BEAUTY'S CASTLE

Preparation: 1 hour

1 x white ready-iced square 23cm (9 inch) sponge cake (see
    page 16)
5 raspberry or strawberry Swiss rolls, about 9cm (3½ inch)
    long
450g (1lb) white ready-to-roll icing (sugar paste)
icing sugar to dust
apricot glaze (see page 320)
1 x white ready-iced round 15cm (6 inch) sponge cake (see
    page 16)
2 x quantity of pink buttercream icing (see page 321)
5 ice cream sugar cones

DECORATION
multicoloured sprinkles
red, pink, yellow, green and white writing icing
sugar flowers
small round pink sweets or pink edible balls
paper flag

PER SERVING
425 cals; 8g fat (of which 3g saturates); 86g carbohydrate; 0.2g salt

1 Put the square cake on a 30.5cm (12 inch) square cake
   board. Measure the circumference of a Swiss roll with
   a piece of string. Divide the ready-to-roll icing into five
   pieces. Lightly dust a worksurface with icing sugar, then
   roll out each piece of icing thinly into a rectangle the
   length of the Swiss roll by the length of the piece of
   string. Neaten the edges with a sharp knife. Brush each
   piece of icing with apricot glaze and roll around a
   Swiss roll, gently working the edges together to seal.

2 Put the round cake in the centre of the square cake.
   Put a dollop of buttercream at each corner of the
   square cake and position four of the Swiss rolls, with
   the sealed edge facing inwards, to make towers.
   Smooth pink buttercream over four of the cones and
   spread a little on top of each tower. Dip the tips of the
   cones in sprinkles, then fix on top of the towers. Using
   red writing icing, draw a simple window, divided by
   four panes, at the top of each tower.

3 At the front of the castle, use red writing icing to draw
   a door with a doorknob. Use pink and yellow writing
   icing to draw small flowers around the castle and
   below the windows. Fix a few sugar flowers to the
   walls with writing icing. Connect the flowers with
   green writing icing to represent stems. Use the green
   writing icing to draw clumps of grass around the base
   of the wall. Stick a sugar flower to the paper flag with
   writing icing.

4 Position the remaining Swiss roll in the centre of the
   round cake. Cover the remaining cone with
   buttercream, dip in sprinkles and position on top of
   the round cake, fixing with a little buttercream. Draw
   on windows and decorate with sugar flowers as
   before. Make blobs of white writing icing, just touching
   each other, around the edges of the cones and
   decorate with pink sweets or edible balls. Stick the
   paper flag into the central tower.

NOTE
For convenience, complete the recipe up to one day
in advance.

CREEPY-CRAWLY CAKE

OVERNIGHT PREPARATION NEEDED

SERVES 12

Preparation: 1½ hours
Cooking time: 25–30 minutes, plus cooling and drying

butter to grease
1 x 4-egg quantity of chocolate Victoria sponge mixture
  (see page 11)
½ x quantity of chocolate buttercream icing (see page 321)

DECORATION
225g (8oz) white ready-to-roll icing (sugar paste)
assorted food colourings, including brown and black
red and black liquorice bootlaces and jelly creepy-crawly
  sweets, such as snakes and frogs
a little glacé icing (see page 320)
a chocolate matchstick (optional)

ICING
450g (1lb) icing sugar, sifted
225g (8oz) butter, softened
few drops of vanilla extract
green food colouring

PER SERVING
534 cals; 26 fat (of which 17g saturates); 76g carbohydrate; 0.6g salt

1 To make a trap door, use 125g (4oz) ready-to-roll icing. Knead in a few drops of brown food colouring and roll out to a thickness of 5mm (¼ inch), then use a small tumbler to cut out a circle. Place on a baking tray lined with baking parchment and leave in a cool place overnight to dry.

2 Use the remaining white and brown icing to make a selection of spiders and beetles, colouring the icing accordingly. Use the liquorice to make spiders' legs. Pipe eyes on the creatures with white glacé icing. Allow to dry overnight.

3 The next day, grease two 20.5cm (8 inch) round sandwich tins and line with greaseproof paper. Make and bake the sponge mixture according to the instructions on page 11. Cool in the tins for 5 minutes, then turn out on to a wire rack, remove the lining paper and leave to cool completely.

4 Sandwich the cold cakes together with chocolate buttercream. Cut out a hole 1cm (½ inch) deep and 6.5cm (2½ inch) wide in the centre of the cake. Discard (or eat) the trimmings.

5 For the icing, beat the icing sugar into the butter with the vanilla. Beat in the food colouring. Put the cake on a board or plate and cover with the icing. Secure the trap door over the hole in the middle of the cake. Prop open with a cocktail stick painted with brown food colouring, or a chocolate matchstick. Arrange the creatures over the cake, with some creepy-crawlies crawling out of the trap door. Leave to dry.

NOTE
For convenience, complete the recipe up to one day in advance.

CLOWN CAKE

SERVES 15

Preparation: 45 minutes

25g (1oz) each of white, green, black
and blue ready-to-roll icing (sugar
paste)
50g (2oz) red ready-to-roll icing
(sugar paste)
black and yellow writing icing
1 x white ready-iced 20.5cm (8 inch)
sponge cake (see page 16)

PER SERVING
300 cals; 8g fat (of which 2g saturates);
55g carbohydrate; 0.1g salt

1 First make the shapes for the clown's face. Roll out the white ready-to-roll icing and cut out two ovals for eyes. Roll out half the red icing and cut out a crescent shape for the mouth. Mark a smiley line along the centre of the mouth with black writing icing. Knead the trimmings and the other piece of red icing together and roll into a ball for his nose. Roll out a small piece of green icing and, using a star-shaped cutter, stamp out two stars for his cheeks.

2 Brush the backs of the shapes with water and position on the cake. Roll out the black icing and cut out two small circles to make pupils for the eyes, then stick on to the white ovals. Use the black and yellow writing icing to give him eyebrows and a swirl of hair.

3 Roll out the blue icing and cut out two sides of a bow tie. Roll the trimmings into a ball and flatten slightly to make the centre knot. Fix the two bow-tie pieces to the bottom edge of the cake with writing icing. Position the knot on top. Use the yellow writing icing to pipe polka dots on the tie.

NOTE
For convenience, complete the recipe up to one day in advance.

TOADSTOOL

Preparation: 1½ hours
Cooking time: 40 minutes, plus cooling

butter to grease
1 x 3-egg quantity of Victoria sponge mixture (see page 10)
700g (1½lb) white ready-to-roll icing (sugar paste)
brown, red, green and yellow food colourings
½ x quantity of buttercream icing (see page xxx)
cornflour to dust
sugar flowers, dolly mixtures and butterfly decorations

PER SERVING
433 cals; 10g fat (of which 6g saturates); 87g carbohydrate; 0.3g salt

1 Preheat the oven to 190°C (170°C fan oven) mark 5. Grease a 900g (2lb) food can and a 1.1 litre (2 pint) pudding basin and base-line with baking parchment. It doesn't matter how big the basin is, as long as it holds at least 1.1 litres (2 pints). A wide, shallow cake makes a better-looking toadstool.

2 Make the cake mixture according to the instructions on page 10. Half-fill the food can and put the remaining mixture into the pudding basin. Bake for about 30 minutes for the 'stalk' in the food can and 40 minutes for the 'mushroom cap' in the pudding basin. Transfer both to a wire rack and leave to cool.

3 Take 350g (12oz) ready-to-roll icing. Colour a walnut-sized piece with brown food colouring and the rest red. Colour 125g (4oz) green and leave the remaining 225g (8oz) white. Roll out the green icing and cut into a kidney shape as a 'grass' base. Fix to a cake board with a little water. Unmould the cakes. Using the food can that the stalk was baked in as a template, cut a semi-circle from one side of the grass.

4 Reserve 50g (2oz) white icing. Colour the rest yellow and roll out into a long oblong to fit the stalk. Trim the edges. Spread buttercream thinly around the stalk cake then, holding the cake by the ends, set it at one end of the icing. Roll up the icing around the stalk and press the seam together. With a dab of buttercream, fix the stalk upright in the cut-out semi-circle in the green icing. Spread the top with buttercream.

5 Roll out the red icing to fit the mushroom cap. Set the cake flat on the worksurface. Cover the upper surface thinly with buttercream. Lay the red icing over the cake. Smooth in place and trim around the base. Dust the worksurface lightly with cornflour and carefully turn the cake upside down.

6 Colour the remaining buttercream dark brown. Insert a small, fluted nozzle into a piping bag. Fill the bag with the buttercream. Mark a circle in the centre of the base of the mushroom cap, where the stalk will fit. Pipe lines of buttercream radiating from this, to look like the 'gills' of a toadstool. Cover the sponge and red icing join. Turn the cake the right way up and set on top of the stalk. Roll out the reserved white icing and the brown icing. Cut the white icing into dots. Arrange on top of the toadstool, using a little buttercream to fix them. Cut the brown icing into windows and a door and fix to the stalk in the same way. Decorate the 'grass' with sugar flowers, sweets and butterflies.

NOTE
For convenience, complete the recipe up to one day in advance.

GINGERBREAD FOOTBALLERS

MAKES 20

Preparation: 5 minutes, plus chilling

Cooking time: 12–15 minutes, plus cooling and setting

125g (4oz) cold butter, diced, plus extra to grease

350g (12oz) plain flour, plus extra to dust

1 tsp bicarbonate of soda

2 tsp ground ginger

175g (6oz) light soft brown sugar

4 tbsp golden syrup

1 medium egg, beaten

assorted writing icings

star and football decorations (optional)

PER BISCUIT

157 cals; 6g fat (of which 4g saturates); 26g carbohydrate; 0.2g salt

1 Lightly grease three baking sheets with butter. Sift the flour, bicarbonate of soda and ginger into a mixing bowl. Rub in the butter until the mixture resembles fine breadcrumbs, then stir in the sugar. (Alternatively, use a food processor.) Beat the syrup with the egg, then stir into the flour mixture and mix to make a dough. Knead until smooth, then divide in half and wrap in clingfilm. Chill for 30 minutes.

2 Preheat the oven to 190°C (170°C fan oven) mark 5. Turn out the dough on to a lightly floured surface and cut in half. Roll out each half until about 5mm (¼ inch) thick. Using a gingerbread man cutter, cut out shapes. Repeat with the second half of the dough. Re-roll the trimmings until all of the dough has been used. Put the gingerbread men on the prepared baking sheets.

3 Bake for 12–15 minutes until golden brown. Leave on the baking sheets to cool slightly, then transfer to wire racks and leave to cool completely.

4 When the gingerbread has cooled completely, decorate the footballers. Using black writing icing, give each man a pair of eyes and a dot for a nose. Use red icing for a mouth and black or yellow icing for hair. Choosing the colour(s) of your child's favourite football strip, draw an outline around the edge of the gingerbread to represent a shirt and shorts, then fill in the shirt with stripes if you like. Use contrasting icing to write a number on the front of each shirt. Decorate the shorts with stars, if you like, and attach footballs with a dot of writing icing. Leave to set for about 30 minutes. Remember to remove non-edible decorations before eating.

TO STORE

Store in an airtight container. They will keep for up to one week.

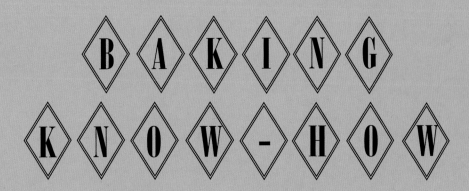

BAKING EQUIPMENT

Not much in the way of specialist equipment is needed for baking, although one or two items in particular, such as a food processor and electric whisk, will make life much easier. Remember that kitchen equipment is subject to a great deal of wear and tear, so look for good-quality items. Below are the essentials when baking.

Scales Accurate measurement is essential when following most baking recipes. The electronic scale is the most accurate and can weigh up to 2kg (4½lb) or 5kg (11lb) in increments of 1–5g. Buy one with a flat platform on which you can put your bowl or measuring jug. Always set the scale to zero before adding the ingredients.

Measuring jugs, cups and spoons Jugs can be plastic or glass, and are available, marked with both metric and imperial, in sizes ranging from 500ml (18fl oz) to 2 litres (3½ pints), or even 3 litres (5¼ pints). Measuring cups are bought in sets of ¼, ⅓, ½ and 1 cups. A standard 1 cup measure is equivalent to about 250ml (9fl oz). Measuring spoons are useful for the smallest units and accurate spoon measurements go up to 15ml (1 tbsp). These may be in plastic or metal and often come in sets attached together on a ring.

Mixing bowls Stainless steel bowls work best when you are using a hand whisk, or when you need to place the bowl into a larger bowl filled with iced water for chilling down or to place it over simmering water (when melting chocolate, for example).

Plastic or glass bowls are best if you need to use them in the microwave. Bowls with gently tapered sides – much wider at the rim than at the base – will be useful for mixing dough.

Mixing spoons For general mixing, the cheap and sturdy wooden spoon still can't be beaten. The spoon should be stiff, so that it can cope with thick mixtures such as dough. A large metal spoon for folding ingredients together is also an invaluable item to have.

Other useful items These include spatulas, fine sieve, wire whisks, pastry brush, rolling pin, graters (fine and coarse), tape measure and paint brushes (for cake decorating).

BAKEWARE

As well as being thin enough to conduct heat quickly and efficiently, bakeware should be sturdy enough not to warp. Most bakeware is made from aluminium, and it may have enamel or non-stick coatings. A newer material for some bakeware is flexible, oven-safe silicone. It is safe to touch straight from the oven, is inherently non-stick and is also flexible – making it a lot easier to remove muffins and other bakes from their pans than it used to be.

Baking trays/Baking sheets Shallower than a roasting tin, these have many uses in baking. Choose ones that are large (but which fit comfortably in your oven) to avoid having to bake in batches. Buy the best you can afford.

Baking dishes Usually ceramic or Pyrex, you should have them in several sizes, ranging from 15–23cm (6–9 inch) to 25.5–35.5cm (10–14 inch).

Cake tins Available in many shapes and sizes, tins may be single-piece, loose-based or springform.

Loaf tins Available in various sizes, but one of the most useful is a 900g (2lb) tin.

Pie tins You should have both single-piece tins and loose-based tins for flans and pies.

Muffin tins These come in various sizes and depths and are available in both aluminium and silicone. If you make a lot of muffins and cupcakes it's worth investing in different types.

ELECTRICAL EQUIPMENT

Food processor Perfect for making breadcrumbs or pastry or for chopping large quantities of nuts. Most come with a number of attachments – dough hooks, graters, slicers.

Blenders Less versatile than food processors, but perfect for certain tasks, such as puréeing fruit. The traditional jug blender is great but some cooks prefer a 'stick' blender, which can be used directly in a pan, bowl or jug.

Freestanding mixers These powerful machines are particularly useful for bread-making and lengthy whisking, but they take up quite a lot of space on the worksurface.

Hand-held electric mixers and whisks Useful for creaming together butter and sugar in baking and for making meringues. They don't take up a lot of space and can be packed away easily.

Bread machines Kneading bread by hand doesn't take much time and effort, but bread machines are useful for making and baking bread if you have limited time and want to get on with something else. Doughs can also be prepared by the machine and then shaped and baked in the oven.

Ice-cream makers Even if you make ice cream only a few times a year, investing in a good machine will save lots of time and produce better results than an inferior model. The type with two freezing tubs enables you to make two flavours at once, or a larger quantity of a single flavour. A multi-speed ice-cream maker will make ice cream quickly and allow you to make other frozen desserts such as frozen yogurts and smoothies.

Successful cake-making

The key to successful baking lies in using good-quality ingredients at the right temperature, measuring them accurately (using scales and measuring spoons) and following recipes very carefully. Weigh out all the ingredients before you start, using either metric or imperial measures, never a combination of the two. Check that all storecupboard ingredients to be used are well within their 'use-by' date. See also pages 299–303.

INGREDIENTS

FAT Unsalted butter gives the best results in most recipes. **Margarine** can be substituted in many recipes, although it doesn't lend such a good flavour, but **low-fat** 'spreads', with their high water content, are not suitable. For most cake recipes, you need to use the fat at room temperature. If necessary you can soften it, cautiously, in the microwave.

EGGS Eggs should also be used at room temperature; if taken straight from the fridge they are more likely to curdle a cake mixture. Make sure you use the correct size – unless otherwise stated, medium eggs should be used in all the recipes. A fresh egg should feel heavy in your hand and will sink to the bottom of the bowl or float on its side when put into water. Older eggs, over two weeks old, will float vertically.

SUGAR Golden caster sugar is generally used for cakes, but for a richer colour and flavour, **light or dark muscovado sugars** can be substituted. **Icing sugar** is ideal for icings, frostings and buttercreams.

FLOUR Self-raising white flour is used in most cake recipes, as it provides a raising agent, whereas **plain white flour** is generally used for biscuits and cookies. **Plain or self-raising wholemeal** flour can be substituted, although the results will be darker and denser and nuttier in flavour. **Half white and half wholemeal** makes a good compromise if you want to incorporate extra fibre. If you sieve it before use, tip the bran left in the sieve into the bowl.

NUTS Some nuts can be bought ready-prepared, others need preparation. After nuts have been shelled, they are still coated with a skin, which, although edible, tastes bitter. This is easier to remove if the nuts are blanched or toasted. **To blanch**, put the shelled nuts in a bowl and cover with boiling water. Leave for 2 minutes, then drain. Remove the skins by rubbing the nuts in a teatowel or squeezing between your thumb and index finger. **Toasting** also improves the flavour. Preheat the oven to 200°C (180°C fan oven) mark 6. Put the shelled nuts on a baking sheet in a single layer and bake for 8–15 minutes until the skins are lightly coloured. Remove the skins by rubbing the nuts in a teatowel. Unless you want very large pieces, the easiest way **to chop** nuts is to put the cold, skinned nuts in a food processor and pulse at 10-second intervals. Or, place a chopping board on a folded teatowel on the worksurface and use a cook's knife to chop to the size of coarse breadcrumbs. Only chop about 75g (3oz) of nuts at a time. Store in an airtight container for up to two weeks. **To slice** nuts, put them on a board and, using a cook's knife, carefully slice the nuts as thinly as required. **To make slivers**, carefully cut the slices to make narrow matchsticks.

Nuts: blanching, toasting and cutting

Cake-making methods

METHODS

A wide variety of cakes can be prepared using just three basic techniques: creaming (Victoria Sponge, page 10), all-in-one (Sticky Lemon Polenta Cake, page 23) and whisking (Whisked Sponge, page 12). These straightforward basic recipes can be adapted in several ways.

CAKE TINS

To ensure successsful home baking, make sure that you have the correct cake tin – the cake tin sizes quoted in the recipes refer to the base measurement – and take care to line the tin properly where necessary. Allow at least 15 minutes to heat the oven to the correct oven temperature.

LINING TINS

Always line your cake tin with greaseproof paper – this will help to stop the cake sticking to the sides of the tin or burning (use baking parchment for roulades and meringues). Lightly grease the tin first to help keep the paper in place. Apply the butter with a small piece of greaseproof paper. Don't thickly grease the tin, as this will 'fry' the edges of the cake.

SQUARE TIN

1 Cut out a square of greaseproof paper slightly smaller than the base of the cake tin. Cut four strips each about 2cm (¾ inch) wider than the depth of the tin and fold up one of the longest edges of each strip by 1cm (½ inch).

2 Lightly grease the tin with butter, making sure it is coated on all sides and in the corners.

3 Cut one strip to the length of the side of the tin and press into place in one corner and then along the length of the strip, with the narrow folded section sitting on the base. Continue, cutting to fit into the corners, to cover all four sides.

4 Lay the square on the base of the tin, then grease the paper, taking care not to move the side strips.

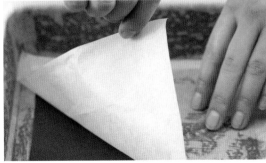

Lining a square tin

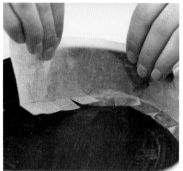

Lining a round tin

ROUND TIN

1 Put the tin on a sheet of greaseproof paper and draw a circle around its circumference. Cut out the circle just inside the drawn line.

2 Cut a strip or strips about 2cm (¾ inch) wider than the depth of the tin and fold up one long edge of each strip by 1cm (½ inch). Make cuts, about 2.5cm (1 inch) apart, through the folded edge of the strip(s) up to the fold line.

3 Lightly grease the tin with butter, making sure it is completely coated.

4 Press the strip(s) on to the sides of the tin so that the snipped edge sits on the base.

5 Lay the circle in the bottom of the tin and grease the paper.

SHAPED TINS

- Round and square are the traditional shapes for cake tins, but tins come in many different shapes, including numerals, and can be either purchased or hired from cake decorating shops. The advantage of these tins is that they give more scope for matching the cake to the occasion.

- To line a shaped tin, follow the instructions for a round tin, above.

SWISS ROLL TIN

Use this method for a Swiss roll or any other shallow baking tin.

1 Lightly grease the tin with butter, making sure it is completely coated.

2 Cut a piece of baking parchment into a rectangle 7.5cm (3 inch) wider and longer than the tin. Press it into the tin and cut at the corners, then fold to fit neatly. Grease all over.

LOAF TIN

1 Lightly grease the tin with butter, making sure it is completely coated.

2 Cut out a sheet of greaseproof paper to the same length as the base and wide enough to cover both the base and the long sides. Press it into position, making sure that it sits snugly in the corners.

3 Now cut another sheet to the same width as the base and long enough to cover both the base and the ends of the tin. Press into place. Grease the paper all over.

Lining a loaf tin

Making roulades

LINERS

Reusable, non-stick, silicone baking mats and liners are widely available and, as there is no need to grease them, they reduce the fat in your baking. Look out also for silicone muffin trays and cupcake moulds.

MAKING ROULADES

A roulade is made from a very light cake mixture and does not contain flour. It remains very soft when baked, and can therefore be easily rolled around a layer of filling such as jam and cream (see Black Forest Roulade, page 37).

MAKING CUPCAKES AND MUFFINS

Cupcakes and muffins are two members of the same family: individual cakes, usually based on a mixture made with self-raising flour, baked in bun tins or muffin pans, so that it rises and sets to an airy texture (see pages 54–73). The secret to really light, fluffy muffins is a light hand. Be sure to sift the flour and stir the mixture as little as possible; it's ok if it looks a little lumpy. Over-mixing will give tough, chewy results.

MAKING CHEESECAKES

A cheesecake is more of a deep tart than a cake. It is essentially a rich flavoured mixture of eggs, cream and full- or low-fat soft cheese, curd cheese or cottage cheese – set on a buttery biscuit, sponge or pastry base. Cheesecakes are either baked to cook and set the filling, or uncooked and set with gelatine. Use a spring-release cake tin to make the cake easier to unmould.

When baking cheeesecakes, watch the temperature – too high a heat can cause the top to crack (see page 300).

The mixture for an uncooked cheesecake is poured on to a biscuit crumb base that has been pressed into a flan tin, then chilled until firm. The whole cheesecake is then chilled to set.

Making cupcakes and muffins

Making cheesecakes

BAKING THE CAKE

Bake the cake mixture as soon as you have made it, as the raising agents will start to react straightaway. Once the cake is in the oven, resist the temptation to open the door – a sudden gush of cold air will make a part-baked cake sink. Instead, wait until the cooking time is almost up before testing. If your cake appears to be browning too quickly, cover the top loosely with greaseproof paper towards the end of cooking.

Apart from very light sponges, all cakes are best left to stand in their tin for 5–10 minutes after baking to firm up slightly.

TESTING CAKES

Ovens vary and the time given in the recipe might be too short or too long to correctly cook what you are baking. So always test to ensure a successful result.

TESTING SPONGES

1 Gently press the centre of the sponge. It should feel springy. If it's a whisked cake, it should be just shrinking away from the sides of the tin.
2 If you have to put it back into the oven, close the door gently so that the vibrations don't cause the cake to sink in the centre.

TESTING FRUIT CAKES

1 To test if a fruit cake is cooked, insert a skewer into the centre of the cake, leave for a few moments, then pull it out. If it comes away clean, the cake is ready.
2 If any mixture sticks to the skewer, the cake is not quite done, so put the cake back in the oven for a few more minutes, then test again with a clean skewer.

COOLING CAKES

- Sponge cakes should be taken out of their tins soon after baking. Invert on to a wire rack lined with sugar-dusted baking parchment.

- Leave fruit cakes to cool in the tin for 15 minutes before turning out.

- Allow rich fruit cakes to cool completely before turning out; there is a risk of breaking otherwise.

STORING CAKES

With the exception of rich fruit cakes and gingerbread, most cakes are best enjoyed freshly baked. If storing is necessary, use a cake tin or large plastic container. Make sure that the cake is completely cold before you put it into the container. If you haven't a large enough container, wrap the cake in a double layer of greaseproof paper and overwrap with foil. Avoid putting rich fruit cakes in direct contact with foil – the fruit may react with it. Never store a cake in the same tin as biscuits, as the biscuits will quickly soften.

Most cakes, particularly sponges, freeze well, but they are generally best frozen before filling and decorating. If freezing a finished gâteau, open-freeze first, then pack in a rigid container.

Testing sponges *Testing fruit cakes*

Tiered Cakes

If you are making a tiered cake, it is most important for the final overall result to choose the sizes of the tiers carefully, avoiding a combination that would look too heavy. Good proportions for a three-tier cake are 30.5, 23 and 15cm (12, 9 and 6 inch).

USING PILLARS TO SEPARATE TIERS

Pillars are the traditional method of separating tiers of cakes. They are available in a variety of heights, colours and patterns and some can be fitted with dowels inside, which will support the weight of very heavy cakes.

For round and square cakes up to 25.5cm (10 inch) use four pillars; use eight pillars for larger cakes.

If the cake needs to be transported, assemble at the venue instead of in the kitchen, marking the position of the pillars with pin marks before decorating.

1 Carefully position four pillars on top of the bottom (largest) cake layer, ensuring they are in the correct position to support the next layer. Secure them with royal icing.
2 Place the second cake layer on top, then the remaining pillars. Secure the pillars with icing and place the remaining cake layer on top.
3 Make sure that the tiers are level and stable and that any joins all face towards the back.

STACKING A CAKE

Tiers of cakes are stacked centrally on top of each other but are actually supported by hidden boards that are the same diameter as the cake and dowelling rods.

1 Using a pin, mark the diameter of the middle cake on top of the first (largest) cake. Measure a square within the diameter and push a dowel into each corner until it reaches the bottom of the cake.
2 Using a pencil, mark on each dowel where it emerges from the surface of the cake. Remove.
3 Cut the dowels at the pencil mark with a craft knife or hacksaw, making sure they are all the same length. Push back into the holes. Spread a little royal icing over the centre.
4 Put the next cake layer on top, then repeat the previous steps.
5 Top with the last layer and decorate as desired.

Stacking a tiered cake

Successful biscuit-making

As with cake-making, the key to successful biscuit-making is to accurately weigh the ingredients and follow the recipe carefully. See also page 303.

METHODS

The main techniques in biscuit making are: creaming (Chocolate Chip Oat Cookies, page 91), the all-in-one method (Peanut and Raisin Cookies, page 92), rolled (Christmas Cookies, page 97), refrigerator biscuits (Refrigerator Cake, page 121 – form the mixture into a roll, chill until firm, then cut into slices), whisked (Almond Macaroons, page 94), melted (Ginger Biscuits, page 98), moulded (The Ultimate Chocolate Chip Cookie, page 090), and piped (Amaretti Biscuits, page 105).

BAKING SHEETS

Use a shiny-based baking sheet; a darker-coloured sheet will absorb a greater amount of heat and can therefore burn the undersides of the biscuits.

BAKING BISCUITS

For hints on baking the perfect biscuits and cookies, see page 303. Once baked, biscuits, with their high sugar content, will seem very soft. They should be left on the baking sheet for a few minutes before transferring to a wire rack.

STORING BISCUITS

Most biscuits are best enjoyed freshly baked. However, if storing, never put in the same tin as a cake, and preferably not with other types of biscuits, as they quickly soften and absorb other flavours.

CRUSHING BISCUITS FOR CHEESECAKE BASES

Crush the biscuits to a fine powder in a food processor. (Alternatively, put them into a plastic bag and crush with a rolling pin.)

FILLING BISCUITS

Cream filling: To sandwich about 18 biscuits, cream 50g (2oz) butter until soft, then beat in 75g (3oz) sifted icing sugar. Mix well and soften by adding a few drops of orange juice or vanilla extract until the mixture is of a firm, spreadable consistency. Spread the mixture on to the flat side of a biscuit and gently press a second biscuit on top to make a sandwich.

Chocolate filling: To fill about 18 biscuits, cream 50g (2oz) butter until soft, then add 75g (3oz) icing sugar and 2 tsp cocoa powder. Mix well and add a few drops of milk to soften if necessary.

Toffee filling: Spread dulce de leche (see page 330) over one biscuit and top with another. Roll the edges in desiccated coconut, if you like.

See also Decorating biscuits, page 323.

Filling biscuits

DOS AND DON'TS OF CAKE- AND BISCUIT-MAKING

How to make perfect cakes

- Weigh out all the ingredients carefully before starting the recipe, so that you have everything to hand when you begin to make the cake.

- Always work in metric or imperial – never mix the two measurements.

- Check that you have the correct cake tin for the job. The tin sizes quoted in this book refer to the base measurement of the tin.

- Always line the tin properly where necessary.

- Allow the oven to preheat to the correct temperature.

- Try not to be heavy-handed – when folding in flour, use light strokes so the air doesn't get knocked out.

- Don't let a cake mixture sit around once you've made it: pop it straight into the cake tin and into the oven, otherwise the raising agents will start to react.

- After it has come out of the oven, leave the cake in the tin to cool for 10 minutes and then turn out on to a wire rack to cool completely.

- Let the tins cool completely before washing them in warm, soapy water with a non-abrasive sponge.

What went wrong?

THE CAKE SINKS IN THE MIDDLE
- The oven door was opened too soon.

- The cake was under-baked.

- The ingredients haven't been measured accurately.

- The wrong size cake tin may have been used.

THE CAKE HAS A CRACKED, DOMED TOP
- The oven temperature was too hot.

- The cake was too near the top of the oven.

- Insufficient liquid was used.

- The baking tin was too small.

- Too much raising agent was used.

THE CAKE HAS A DENSE TEXTURE
- The mixture curdled when adding the eggs.

- Too much liquid was used.

- The mixture was over-folded.

- Too little raising agent was used or an ineffective raising agent that is past its 'use-by date' was used.

THE FRUIT HAS SUNK TO THE BOTTOM
- The mixture was too soft to support the weight of the fruit. This is liable to happen if the fruit was too sticky or wet.

THE CAKE EDGES ARE CRUNCHY
- The baking tin was over-greased.

How to make perfect cheesecakes

- When making cheesecakes, bring eggs and cream cheese to room temperature before using.

- Use good-quality cream cheese for the best results.

- Cream cheese will give richer-tasting cheesecakes.

What went wrong?

THE CHEESECAKE IS DRY
- The cheesecake was over-baked.

CRACK IN THE SURFACE OF THE CHEESECAKE
- The cheesecake was over-baked.

- The cheesecake was cooled too quickly – leave to cool in a switched-off oven with the door ajar.

THE CHEESECAKE CENTRE IS STILL RUNNY
- The cheesecake was under-cooked.

- The oven temperature was too low.

THE CHEESECAKE IS GRAINY IN TEXTURE
- The cheesecake was over-baked.

- The oven temperature was too high.

How to make perfect tortes

A torte is usually made with eggs, sugar, nuts and/or chocolate and little or no flour. Most tortes have icing of one type or another and some are multilayered.

- Flour or ground nuts should be folded into the whisked egg mixture very gently to ensure minimum loss of air.

- Make sure the torte is completely cold before cutting into layers to assemble.

- Before cutting into layers, insert two or three cocktail sticks into the side of the cake – when you reassemble, line up the sticks to ensure that the torte is level.

- For maximum flavour and moistness, brush the surface of torte layers with a flavoured sugar syrup or liqueur before assembling. Leave to soak in well before spreading over any filling.

- Allow buttercream to come to room temperature before decorating the torte – it will be easier to spread on the delicate surface.

- Lavishly filled, layered tortes taste better if left to mature for a day or two before serving.

- Use a long, sharp, pointed knife for cutting delicate layered tortes.

- To cut cleanly, warm the knife blade under hot running water, then dry it and slice the torte.

- Once the torte is filled, keep it chilled in a large, airtight container.

What went wrong?

THE TORTE HAS NOT RISEN SUFFICIENTLY OR HAS COLLAPSED
- The eggs were too cold – warm eggs create more volume when whisked.

- The eggs weren't whisked enough.

- The eggs were overwhisked.

- The melted butter or dry ingredients were overfolded, causing the loss of volume.

- The oven door was opened before the cake had set.

THE TORTE HAS A HARD CRUST
- The whisked egg was too hot when the flour was folded in.

THE TORTE IS DRY OR CRUMBLES WHEN CUT
- Insufficient butter in the mixture – if this happens, brush the cake layers with sugar, syrup or alcohol to moisten.

- The filled cake hasn't been given sufficient standing time once layered and filled – leave for at least 4 hours before eating,

THE BUTTERCREAM FILLING HAS SPLIT
- The butter was too cold.

- The flavouring was added too quickly.

How to make perfect traybakes

Most traybakes keep well for several days, or longer, if stored in an airtight tin.

- If you don't have the size traybake tin specified in a recipe, find a similar one that has sides that add up to the same amount.

- Be careful not to overcook traybakes. They are ready when they are golden brown, but will not be set firm when they come out of the oven.

- Brownies should always be slightly under-cooked to ensure their distinctive soft and squidgy texture – a skewer inserted into the centre should still have a little mixture clinging to it.

- Some traybakes (such as flapjacks) are soft mixtures when hot and firm up when cold (especially when made with golden syrup or honey), so it is essential to mark the cooked bake into squares or bars while it is hot. Leave to cool completely in the baking tray before turning out of the tin.

- Remove carefully, using a spatula or palette knife, as some bakes can be a little crumbly.

- Some traybakes have a more 'cakey' mixture (they contain a larger amount of flour and some eggs) and can be made with two different layers of mixture or an iced topping. Leave to cool before cutting.

What went wrong?

THE BROWNIES ARE DRY AND CRUMBLY
- The brownie was cooked for too long. Test with a skewer – a little of the mixture should cling to it.

- The oven temperature was too high.

THE BROWNIES HAVE A THICK CRUST
- There is too much sugar in proportion to the other ingredients.

THE FLAPJACKS ARE GREASY
- Too much butter in proportion to other ingredients.

How to make perfect cookies and biscuits

- Don't over-flour the worksurface when rolling out – it can make biscuits too dry.

- Be aware that re-rolled dough can result in tougher cookies.

- Use a shiny-based baking sheet.

- Don't overcrowd the biscuits on the baking sheet or in the oven – air needs to circulate all around them. If you are baking more than one sheet, make sure they are on shelves at least 20.5cm (8 inch) apart and be prepared to have them bake at different speeds. Watch them closely for uneven cooking.

- Turn the baking sheet(s) around once or twice during baking. Most ovens get hotter in some places than in others, and this can cause uneven cooking.

- Leave biscuits to set for 1 minute on the baking sheet once out of the oven, then transfer immediately to a wire rack (but see below). If left on the sheet the hot baking sheet will continue to cook them, and steam will build up underneath, which can make the bases soggy. Some biscuits, however (particularly those made with syrup), need to be left on the baking sheet to firm up a little before they are transferred to a rack. Put the biscuits on a fairly fine-meshed rack if at all possible. If possible, raise the rack by putting it on supports so that it is at least a few centimetres higher than the worksurface it's resting on: the more air circulating underneath, the crisper the bases will be.

- Start testing biscuits slightly before you expect them to be cooked. And watch them very closely during the final minutes, as they can go from perfect to overcooked in a matter of only a few seconds.

- Cool biscuits completely before storing.

What went wrong?

THE BISCUITS ARE TOUGH
- They have been over-baked.

- The dough was over-worked when the flour was added.

THE BISCUIT MIXTURE SPREADS WHEN BAKING
- Too much sugar or fat in the recipe.

- Too much air was beaten into the butter.

- The dough was under-chilled before baking.

THE BISCUITS HAVE A CAKE-LIKE TEXTURE
- There is too much flour in proportion to the other ingredients.

- The oven temperature was too high.

BREAD-MAKING TECHNIQUES

Baking bread is one of the greatest pleasures of the kitchen, and one of the simplest. Simple loaves provide the foundation for further experimentation, so they are the best place to start with bread-making (see White Farmhouse Loaf, page 194). See also pages 308–9.

INGREDIENTS

The basic ingredients for bread-making are very simple, but you can also experiment with flavourings. Savoury doughs can be enhanced with cheese, fresh herbs, olives or sun-dried tomatoes, for example; while sweet doughs are enriched with dried fruits, nuts, vanilla sugar, or scented spices like cinnamon and nutmeg.

YEAST Yeast is available in a number of different forms, which are interchangeable in recipes providing that the method is adjusted accordingly. As a rough guide, 15g (½oz) fresh yeast, a 7g sachet (2 tsp) fast-action (easy-blend) dried yeast, or 1 tbsp ordinary dried yeast is enough to rise 700g (1½lb) flour. In general, if you add more than this, the dough will not rise any higher and the bread is likely to have an unpleasant yeasty taste. However, if the dough is enriched with fruit, sugar, butter or nuts, the rise is more difficult and you will usually need more yeast – be guided by the recipes. **Fast-action dried yeast**, also called easy-blend dried yeast, is now the most readily available dried form. It is sprinkled directly into the flour and the liquid is mixed in afterwards. After kneading, the dough can be shaped straightaway and only requires one rising. However, for enriched doughs – particularly heavily fruited ones – better results are obtained if the dough is given the traditional two rises. Always make sure you adhere to the 'use-by' date on the pack; fast-action dried yeast won't work if it is stale. **Traditional dried yeast** needs sugar to activate it. If using milk as the liquid, the natural sugars present in the milk will be enough; if using water, you will need to add a pinch of sugar. To use traditional dried yeast, blend it with the warm liquid (see opposite), adding a pinch of sugar if needed, and leave it in a warm place for about 15 minutes or until a frothy head develops. This shows that the yeast is active. If it refuses to froth, then it is probably past its 'use-by date'; discard and begin again with a fresh pack of yeast. **Fresh yeast** is a living organism and must be handled in the right way in order to work effectively. It is available from some

Leaving the dough to rise

healthfood shops, bakers and supermarkets. It should be firm, moist and creamy coloured with a good 'yeasty' smell. If it is dry and crumbly with brown patches, it is probably stale and won't work effectively. When you buy fresh yeast it is alive, but inactive. Only when it is mixed with a warm liquid does it become active and release the gases that make the dough rise. Fresh yeast is easy to use: simply blend with a little of the liquid specified in the recipe, add the remaining liquid, then mix into the flour. Fresh yeast will stay fresh for about three days if stored in the fridge, or it can be frozen for up to three months. **Sourdough starter** is a traditional method that has regained popularity. A mixture of yeast, flour and water is left to ferment for several days and then added to the dough. A sourdough starter produces a close-textured loaf with a distinctive flavour. If you make bread regularly, a sourdough starter is a convenient way of leavening. Simply blend 15g (½oz) fresh yeast (or 1 tsp dried yeast) with 450ml (¾ pint) warm water and about 225g (8oz) strong plain white flour or enough to make a thick pourable batter. Cover the bowl with a damp cloth and leave at room temperature for 3–5 days to ferment and develop the sourdough flavour. Use 125ml (4fl oz) starter to replace each 15g (½oz) fresh yeast called for in a recipe, then make the bread in the usual way. To store, keep it in the fridge and use within 1 week. Sourdough starter keeps well but must be 'refreshed'. Keep the starter covered in the fridge and whisk in a handful of flour and a small cup of water every day – this provides fresh nutrients for the yeast and aids its leavening properties.

LIQUID No matter which variety of yeast you are using, the liquid should be just warm or tepid, that is at a temperature of 43°C, which will feel slightly warm to the fingertips. If it is too hot it could kill the yeast; if too cold the yeast will not begin to work. **Milk** gives bread a slightly softer texture than water. You should always regard any quantity of liquid specified in a recipe as a guide because flour absorbency varies according to the type of flour, and from brand to brand.

FLOUR Various flours are used for bread-making. **Strong flours** give better results because they have a higher proportion of protein, which helps the formation of gluten – the substance that stretches the dough and traps in air as it cooks, to give bread its characteristic airy texture. **Ordinary plain flour** produces a close-textured crumbly loaf. **Strong white bread flour** is ideal. If possible, use unbleached white flour, which has not been chemically treated to whiten it. **Strong wholemeal bread flour** is ground from the whole wheat kernel and has a coarser texture than white flour, with a fuller flavour and more nutrients; it is also an excellent source of fibre. This flour lends a distinctive flavour, but it is best used with some strong white flour to obtain a good textured loaf. Bread made with 100% wholemeal flour has a heavy, dense texture. **Strong brown bread flour** has a percentage of the bran removed and therefore has a finer texture than wholemeal flour. **Stoneground flour** takes its name from the specific grinding process – between stones – which heats the flour and gives it a slightly roasted, nutty flavour. Both stoneground wholemeal and brown flours are available. **Granary flour** is a strong brown flour, with added malted wheat flakes, which give it

a distinctive flavour. **Rye flour** makes a dark, close-textured bread with plenty of flavour. As it is low in gluten, it must be mixed with a strong white flour for best results.

SALT An important ingredient in breads because it controls fermentation, strengthens gluten and improves the flavour. However, it also slows down the action of yeast, so don't add too much. Be guided by the amount specified in the recipe.

FAT Some recipes call for a little fat to be rubbed into the flour before the yeast is added. This improves the keeping quality of the bread and imparts extra flavour, but too much fat will slow down the action of the yeast.

MIXING AND KNEADING THE DOUGH

Some recipes recommend warming the flour and mixing bowl in advance. If using fresh or 'ordinary' dried yeast, or if you are working in a cold room, this helps to speed things up a little, but otherwise it isn't necessary.

After mixing the yeast and liquid into the dry ingredients, vigorous kneading is required to strengthen the gluten in the flour, make the dough elastic and ultimately to achieve a good rise. If you omit this stage, the dough will not rise. There is nothing difficult about kneading and, contrary to popular belief, it doesn't take long – 10 minutes should be enough. Turn the dough on to a floured surface, fold it firmly towards you, then quickly and firmly push it down and away from you with the heel of your hand. Give it a quarter turn and continue kneading until the dough feels elastic and smooth: it shouldn't be sticky. As an alternative to kneading by hand, you can use a large mixer with a dough hook attachment.

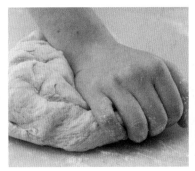
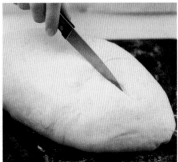

Mixing and kneading the dough

Baking in a bread machine

BREAD MACHINES

Bread machines can make doughs for all kinds of shaped breads. They knead, prove and bake, but models vary. Most will bake different sizes of loaf as well as different breads; some have a 'beep' function to tell you when to add other ingredients during the dough cycle. Most allow you to select the crust colour, and some have a timer so that you can set the machine to bake bread ready for a selected time, such as first thing in the morning. See also page 309.

RISING

Put the kneaded dough into a clean bowl and cover with a clean teatowel, an oiled plastic bag or oiled clingfilm to prevent a skin forming. Leave in a warm place until the dough has doubled in size and springs back when pressed. The time it takes for the dough to rise will depend on the ambient temperature. If the bowl is near a warm oven or in an airing cupboard, rising can take just 30 minutes; at cooler temperatures it may take well over an hour. Don't be tempted to put it somewhere hot to speed things up; you will end up with a badly shaped, uneven-textured loaf, or you could even kill the yeast. For a slower rise, leave the dough in the fridge overnight, then bring it to room temperature in the morning before shaping.

KNOCKING BACK AND PROVING

The risen dough is 'knocked back' (kneaded) to smooth out any air pockets. Just 2–3 minutes kneading is sufficient before shaping. Leave the shaped dough once again in a warm place until it has doubled in size and springs back when pressed. This proving stage is quicker than the first rising.

SHAPING BREAD

The shape and size of bread can be varied almost endlessly after the first rise. After the second rising, the dough is ready to bake. Understanding the basics will ensure success. The simplest way to shape a loaf is to roll the dough into a ball, flatten it slightly and put on a baking sheet. Alternatively, shape the dough as follows:

Long loaves After knocking back, cut the dough into pieces, each weighing about 200g (7oz). Roll one piece until it is about 40.5cm (16 inch) long. Transfer to a baking sheet, seam-side down. Repeat with the remaining pieces. Cover with oiled clingfilm and leave to prove (rise) for 30 minutes. Slash 3–4 times before baking.

Traditional tin loaf Flatten the dough to an oblong, the length of the dough, but three times as wide. Fold this in three, then put into the tin, to two-thirds fill it.

Shaping bread

Cottage loaf Cut off one-third of the dough. Shape both pieces into rounds and put the smaller one on top of the larger round. Push the handle of a wooden spoon down through the middle.

Plait Divide the dough into three equal-sized pieces. Roll each piece into a long sausage, then pinch these together at one end and plait loosely. Pinch the other ends together firmly.

Twist Divide the dough into two equal-sized pieces. Roll each piece of dough into a long sausage. Hold one end of the two pieces of dough together and twist. Dampen the ends and tuck under.

Baton Shape the dough into a long sausage with tapering ends about 20.5cm (8 inch) long.

Rings Take a piece of dough and form into a long sausage. Bend it round to form a ring, then dampen the ends and mould them together.

Simple rolls After knocking back, cut the dough into even pieces, each about 40g (1½oz). Roll each piece with the palm of hand on lightly floured surface to make a ball. Place on a greased baking sheet, seam-side down, and press down slightly. Cover with clingfilm and leave to prove for 30 minutes before baking.

Knots Shape each piece of dough into a long sausage, then tie into a knot.

GLAZING

Glazing bread before baking gives an attractive finish.

- For a golden, shiny effect, brush with beaten egg or egg beaten with a little water or milk.

- For a crusty finish, brush with salted water, made by dissolving 2 tsp salt in 2 tbsp water.

- For a soft golden crust, brush with milk. Some breads and yeast buns are glazed after baking with warm honey or syrup.

FINISHES

As well as glazing the dough before baking (see below left), other finishes can add interest, variety and extra fibre. Lightly sprinkle the surface of the dough with seeds, such as poppy, caraway, fennel or sesame, or try barley or wheat flakes on wholemeal bread.

BAKING THE BREAD

Bread is baked in a hot oven to kill the yeast and halt its action. If the bread shows signs of browning too quickly, cover with foil. When cooked, the bread should be well risen, firm to the touch and golden brown; if you turn it over and tap it on the bottom the loaf should sound hollow. To crisp the crust of large loaves all over, return them to the oven upside down for about 10 minutes. Always remove bread from the tins before transferring to wire racks to cool.

Tapping bread   *Cooling bread on a wire rack*

STORING BREAD

Bread with a high fat or sugar content should keep well for 3–4 days, but other home-made bread stales quite quickly. It is best stored in a dry, well-ventilated bread bin, not the fridge, and eaten the day it is made.

Bread freezes well for a relatively short time, up to 1 month, after which the crust begins to deteriorate and lift off. Frozen or slightly stale bread can be freshened in a warm oven.

Quick yeastless breads, leavened with baking powder or bicarbonate of soda rather than yeast, tend to stale quickly. They are invariably at their best eaten fresh and warm from the oven.

DOS AND DON'TS OF BREAD-MAKING

How to make perfect bread

- Make sure shaped dough has risen sufficiently – usually to double.

- Always oil or flour the loaf tin, or baking sheet, to prevent sticking.

- Make sure the oven is at the correct temperature before baking.

- Bake on a preheated ceramic baking stone (from good kitchen shops) if possible, even if the bread is in a loaf tin. The heat of the stone will give the bread a crisp base.

- If baked bread is left for too long either in the loaf tin or on the baking sheet, steam will gather and, as a result, the underneath will start to become soggy. To prevent this, always remove the loaf immediately and put it on a wire rack. Then leave it to cool completely before slicing, as you like.

What went wrong?

THE LOAF HASN'T RISEN PROPERLY
- Not enough liquid was added during mixing.

- Too much salt or sugar was added during mixing.

- The yeast was stale.

- The liquid was too hot and killed the yeast.

- The second proving wasn't long enough.

- The second proving was too long causing it to collapse during baking.

THE BREAD IS CAKE-LIKE OR OVER-DENSE
- The dough wasn't kneaded for long enough.

- The dough was under-proved.

- Too much salt was added.

- Too much fat was added.

- Not enough, or too little, liquid was added.

THE BREAD HAS HOLES IN IT
- The dough wasn't knocked back sufficiently.

- The dough was over-proved.

THE BREAD HAS A CRACKED CRUST
- The oven was too hot.

- The dough was under-proved.

Dos and don'ts of machine-baked bread

- Use recipes that have been designed for bread machine use only, as conventional bread recipes use different quantities of ingredients and are not converted easily.

- Measure out all the ingredients carefully, as exact quantities are essential for a perfect loaf.

- Always follow the bread machine instructions carefully; it is essential that the ingredients go into the machine in the order stated, as the yeast must not come into contact with the liquid until the machine begins to mix.

- Avoid lifting the lid during the rising and baking cycles, as this may cause the loaf to sink.

- The loaf is best removed from the machine as soon as it is baked, otherwise it will become soggy.

PASTRY-MAKING TECHNIQUES

The art of making good pastry lies in paying careful attention to the recipe and using the correct proportion of fat to flour. It is important to 'rest' pastry before baking, as it gets stretched during shaping and if not allowed to 'rest' and firm up, it may shrink away from the sides of the tin during baking.

INGREDIENTS

FLOUR For most pastries, **plain flour** works best, as it gives a light, crisp result. Self-raising flour would produce a soft spongy pastry. Wholemeal flour gives a heavier dough, which is more difficult to roll. For wholemeal pastry, it is therefore preferable to use half wholemeal and half white flour. Puff pastry is usually made with strong plain (bread) flour as this contains extra gluten to strengthen the dough, enabling it to withstand intensive rolling and folding. A little lemon juice is usually added to puff pastry to soften the gluten and make the dough more elastic.

FAT Traditionally, shortcrust pastry is made with a mixture of **lard** (for shortness) and **either butter or margarine** (for flavour). However, it is now more often made with a mixture of **white vegetable fat** and butter or margarine, or all butter for a rich flavour. If margarine is preferred, it should be the hard, block type rather than soft-tub margarine.

LIQUID Care must be taken when adding the liquid to a pastry dough: too much will result in a tough end result; too little will produce a crumbly pastry, which is difficult to handle. Use **chilled water** and add just enough to bind the dough. **Egg yolks** are often used to enrich pastry.

QUANTITIES

Tart tins vary in depth, which affects the quantity of pastry needed. The following quantities are approximate.

TART TIN SIZE	PASTRY
18cm (7 inch)	125g (4oz)
20.5cm (8 inch)	175g (6oz)
23cm (9 inch)	200g (7oz)
25.5cm (10 inch)	225g (8oz)

USING PASTRY

A light touch and a little care with rolling and lifting your prepared dough will ensure your pastry case or pie crust is crisp and perfect. Take your time for the best results.

LINING TART AND PIE TINS

1 Working carefully, roll out chilled dough on a floured surface to make a sheet at least 5cm (2 inch) larger than the tart tin or pie dish. Roll the dough on to the rolling pin, then unroll it on to the tin, covering it completely with an even overhang all round. Don't stretch the dough.

2 Lift the hanging dough with one hand while you press it gently but firmly into the base and sides of the tin. Don't stretch the dough while you're pressing it down.

3 For a tart case, roll the rolling pin over the tin and remove the excess dough for later use. For a pie dish, ensure the pastry covers the lip of the dish.

4 Push the dough into and up the sides of the tin or dish, so that the dough rises a little over the edge.

Lining tart tins and pie dishes

BAKING BLIND

Cooking the pastry before filling gives a crisp result.

1 Preheat the oven according to the recipe. Prick the pastry base with a fork. Cover with foil or greaseproof paper 8cm (3¼ inch) larger than the tin.

2 Spread baking beans on top. Bake for 15 minutes. Remove the foil or paper and beans and bake for 5–10 minutes until light golden.

Baking blind

TOPPING

Covered pies need a lid of equal thickness to the base.

1 Roll out the pastry on a floured surface to about 2.5cm (1 inch) larger than the baking tin or dish. Roll on to the rolling pin, then unroll over the pie with an even overhang.

2 Using a small knife, cut off the overhang just outside the rim.

Topping

SEALING

1 Using your thumb and index finger, pinch the base and top of the pastry dough all the way round the rim. You don't need to squeeze hard, just firmly enough to stick them together. If the pie has no base, just press the top down on the rim of the tin or dish.

2 Use a fork to make decorative fluting marks on the rim – simply press all around the edge of the pie with the back of a floured fork. (See also below.)

Sealing

FINISHING

1 If you want to make decorations for the pie using leftover pastry, cut them out using pastry cutters and put them in place, using a little water to stick them to the pastry. For pastry leaves, cut neat strips from the pastry trimmings, then cut these on the diagonal into diamonds, to shape leaves. Use the back of the knife to mark veins and pinch one end to form a stem.

2 Brush the top of the pastry with beaten egg if you wish. Cut two slits in the top of the pie using a small, sharp knife to let the steam escape during baking.

Finishing

DOS AND DON'TS OF PASTRY-MAKING

How to make perfect shortcrust, pâte sucrée and puff pastry

- Work in a cool kitchen.

- Always use chilled water and butter whenever specified.

- It helps to chill the bowl too, if your hands are very warm.

- Use good-quality butter for tastier pastry.

- Use your fingertips when rubbing in.

- Avoid over-handling the pastry or it will become heavy.

- Don't over-flour the worksurface, as it will make your pastry too dry.

- Allow pastry to relax for easier rolling out.

- To stop it collapsing, chill the pastry well before putting in the oven.

Shortcrust pastry – what went wrong?

THE TART EDGES ARE UNEVEN/
SHRUNKEN
- It wasn't chilled thoroughly before baking.

- Too much water was added at the mixing stage.

- The oven temperature wasn't hot enough.

- The pastry was over-stretched when rolling and lining.

THE PASTRY IS TOUGH
- The fat wasn't rubbed in properly.

- Too little fat.

- Too much water was added during mixing.

- The pastry was kneaded too much, which over-developed the gluten.

THE PASTRY IS SOFT AND CRUMBLY
- Too much fat was added.

- Too little water was added.

THE PASTRY HAS BLISTERED
- The fat wasn't rubbed in properly.

- Too much water was added.

THE PASTRY IS GREASY
- It was overcooked.

- It was overworked.

Pâte sucrée – what went wrong?

THE PASTRY IS TOUGH
- The pastry was overworked when the dough was brought together.

- The pastry was overcooked.

THE PASTRY IS OILY
- The butter was too warm.

Puff pastry – what went wrong?

THE PASTRY HASN'T RISEN
- The butter broke through the pastry when rolled.

- The pastry was rolled and folded too many times.

THE PASTRY ISN'T FLAKY
- Butter not cool enough when used.

- Insufficient resting and chilling.

- Over-heavy rolling.

FAT HAS RUN OUT DURING BAKING
- The oven was too cool.

- The ends of the pastry were not sealed.

THE PASTRY IS OILY
- The pastry was over-baked.

- The pastry was not properly chilled.

THE PASTRY IS TOUGH
- Too much water was added at the first stage.

How to make perfect choux pastry

This soft pastry is usually spooned or piped and is excellent for making cream-filled buns, profiteroles and savouries. It contains a lot of water and so it puffs up beautifully and is wonderfully light and airy.

- Before you start, have all the ingredients carefully measured and in place.

- Tip in all the flour at once, then leave the mixture to cool before beating in the eggs gradually.

- Use a dampened baking sheet (the steam will help the pastry to rise), and don't open the oven door for the first 20 minutes of baking, as the cold air will make the pastry sink.

Choux pastry – what went wrong?

THE MIXTURE IS TOO SOFT
- Insufficient cooking of flour before adding the egg.

- Insufficient beating after addition of egg.

THE PASTRY HASN'T RISE ENOUGH DURING BAKING
- Not enough egg was beaten into the mixture.

- The mixture was too warm when the egg was added.

- The oven was too cool.

- The mixture was under-cooked.

- The mixture wasn't beaten enough.

- The oven door was opened before the pastry had set.

THE PASTRY HAS SUNK
- Insufficient baking, which can sometimes be remedied by returning the pastry to the oven.

How to work with filo pastry

Making filo pastry is time-consuming, but ready-made filo is an excellent alternative. The delicate sheets of pastry are usually brushed with butter, then layered and filled to create crisp, golden treats.

- Filo pastry is often sold frozen; if you plan to put it into the freezer at home, get it home quickly so that it doesn't thaw.

- Thaw it completely before you start to work with it, otherwise it can crack or crumble. The best way to do this is to leave it to thaw overnight in the fridge.

- As you work, cover the unused sheets with a clean damp teatowel, to prevent them from drying out.

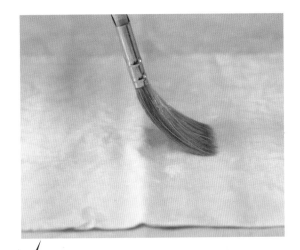

Filo pastry – what went wrong?

THE PASTRY CRACKS WHEN ROLLED
- The pastry became too dry. Brush with oil or melted butter. Keep the rest of the pastry covered with a damp teatowel while assembling.

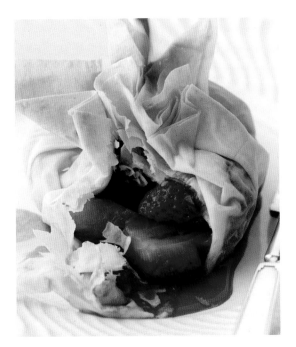

Vanilla Ice Cream

To serve four to six, you will need:
300ml (½ pint) full-fat milk, I vanilla pod, split lengthways, 3 medium egg yolks, 75g (3oz) golden caster sugar, 300ml (½ pint) double cream.

I Put the milk and vanilla pod into a pan. Heat slowly until almost boiling. Cool for 20 minutes, then remove the vanilla pod. Whisk the egg yolks and sugar together in a large bowl until thick and creamy. Gradually whisk in the milk, then strain back into the pan.
2 Cook over a low heat, stirring with a wooden spoon, until thick enough to coat the back of the spoon – do not boil. Pour into a chilled bowl and leave to cool.
3 Whisk the cream into the custard. Pour into an ice-cream maker and freeze or churn according to the manufacturer's instructions or make by hand (see below). Store in a covered freezerproof container for up to two months. Put the ice cream in the fridge for 15–20 minutes before serving to soften slightly.

VARIATIONS

Fruit Ice Cream: Sweeten 300ml (½ pint) fruit purée (such as rhubarb, gooseberry, raspberry or strawberry) to taste, then stir into the cooked custard and churn.
Chocolate Ice Cream: Omit the vanilla and add 125g (4oz) plain chocolate to the milk. Heat gently until melted, then bring almost to the boil and proceed as above.
Coffee Ice Cream: Omit the vanilla and add 150ml (¼ pint) cooled strong coffee to the cooked custard.

MAKING ICE CREAM BY HAND

I If possible, set the freezer to fast freeze I hour ahead. Pour the ice cream mixture into a shallow freezerproof container, cover and freeze until partially frozen.
2 Spoon into a bowl and mash with a fork to break up the ice crystals. Return to the container and freeze for a further 2 hours. Repeat and freeze for another 3 hours.

Vanilla Custard

To serve eight, you will need: 600ml (I pint) full-fat milk, I vanilla pod or I tbsp vanilla extract, 6 large egg yolks, 2 tbsp golden caster sugar, 2 tbsp cornflour.

I Put the milk into a pan. Split the vanilla pod and scrape the seeds into the pan, then drop in the pod. If using vanilla extract, pour it in. Bring to the boil, then turn off the heat and leave to cool for 5 minutes.
2 Put the egg yolks, sugar and cornflour into a bowl and whisk to blend. Remove the vanilla pod from the milk and gradually whisk the warm milk into the egg mixture.
3 Rinse out the pan. Pour the custard back in and heat gently, stirring constantly, for 2–3 minutes. The mixture should thicken enough to coat the back of a wooden spoon in a thin layer. Remove the pan from the heat.

NOTE

For convenience, make the custard up to 4 hours in advance. If you are not serving the custard immediately, pour it into a jug. Cover the surface with a circle of wet greaseproof paper to prevent a skin from forming, then cover with clingfilm and chill. To serve hot, reheat very gently.

Vanilla custard

Raspberry Coulis

Brandy Butter

Raspberry Coulis

To serve four to six, you will need: 225g (8oz) raspberries, 2 tbsp Kirsch or framboise eau de vie (optional), icing sugar to taste.

1 Put the raspberries into a blender or food processor with the Kirsch or eau de vie, if using. Whiz until they are completely puréed.
2 Transfer the purée to a fine sieve, then using a spoon, press and scrape it through the sieve until nothing is left but the pips.
3 Sweeten with icing sugar to taste and chill in the fridge until needed.

VARIATION
Use different soft fruits and liqueurs. For example, try crème de cassis with blackcurrants or Amaretto with apricots.

Chantilly Cream

To serve eight, you will need: 284ml carton double cream, 1 tbsp golden caster sugar, finely grated zest of 1 orange (optional).

1 Whip the cream with the sugar until it forms soft peaks. Fold in half the grated orange zest, if you like. Cover and chill until needed.
2 Serve the Chantilly cream sprinkled with the remaining orange zest, if you like.

NOTE
Flavour the Chantilly cream with 2 tbsp Grand Marnier to serve with fruity puddings.

Brandy Butter

To serve eight, you will need: 150g (5oz) unsalted butter, at room temperature, 150g (5oz) golden icing sugar, sifted, 3 tbsp brandy.

1 Put the butter into a bowl and whisk to soften. Gradually whisk in the icing sugar, pouring in the brandy just before the final addition. Continue whisking until the mixture is pale and fluffy, then spoon into a serving dish.
2 Cover and chill until needed. Remove from the fridge 30 minutes before serving.

NOTE
For a light, fluffy texture, whisk the brandy butter using an electric mixer just before serving.

Crème Pâtissière

To make 450ml (¾ pint) you will need: 300ml (½ pint) full-fat milk, 1 vanilla pod, split, or 1 tsp vanilla extract, 3 medium egg yolks, beaten, 50g (2oz) golden caster sugar, 2 tbsp plain flour, 2 tbsp cornflour.

1 Pour the milk into a heavy-based pan. Scrape the vanilla seeds into the milk and add the pod, or add the vanilla extract. Slowly bring to the boil, take off the heat and leave to infuse for 10 minutes. Discard the pod.
2 Whisk the egg yolks and sugar together in a bowl until thick and creamy, then whisk in the flour and cornflour until smooth. Gradually whisk in the hot milk, then strain back into the pan. Slowly bring to the boil, whisking constantly. Cook, stirring, for 2–3 minutes until thickened and smooth. Pour into a bowl, cover the surface with a circle of wet greaseproof paper and leave to cool. Use as a filling for fruit flans and other pastries.

CREATIVE DECORATING

Each icing or frosting has its own characteristics in texture, flavour, colour and consistency, and may be used to fill, cover and decorate cakes. Some icings are satin smooth and may be poured over the cake to give a smooth, glossy finish, whereas other varieties may need spreading or swirling to give a textured appearance.

ICING AND FROSTING

Icings and frostings are used to fill, cover and decorate cakes. Some icings are poured over the cake to give a smooth glossy finish, others need to be spread or swirled to give a textured finish. Fresh whipped cream and buttercream may be smoothed flat, textured with a palette knife, or piped. Sometimes the same mixture is used to fill and cover the cake, or it may be different – a jam-filled sponge, for example, can be topped with buttercream or glacé icing.

The filling must have the right consistency for spreading: if too firm it will pull the crumbs from the cake, making an untidy layer; if too soft it will cause the cake layers to slip and move around, and ooze out of the side of the cake. Use a palette knife dipped in hot water for spreading the filling. Jam should be warmed gently until thinned to a spreading consistency.

EQUIPMENT FOR ICING

The basic skills of icing and decorating a cake can be mastered with just a few tools. Some useful pieces of equipment are:

- A metal palette knife for applying and spreading royal icing, and a metal or plastic cake scraper for smoothing it out.
- An icing ruler, piping bags and a selection of nozzles for piping decorations.

Piping bags and a selection of nozzles

Knife, plastic scraper and palette knife

A selection of brushes

When applying marzipan or fondant icing, a plastic smoother will take out rolling pin or fingernail marks and ease the paste to the edge of the cake. But the same thing can be achieved by dusting your hands with icing sugar and smoothing them over the surface of the cake. If you are planning to make more intricate or formal cakes, it is worth investing in some specialist equipment from a cake decorating shop or website. A plastic turntable makes it easier when doing elaborate piping, while sets of modelling tools will help you to create fabulous figurines,

bows, ribbons or flowers. Piping nails are used to help create three-dimensional shapes with royal icing. Crimpers come in various patterns to give a decorative edging to fondant-covered cakes. Other useful tools to keep in your cake decorating tool box include a Stanley knife, a selection of fine paintbrushes for applying food colouring directly to icing or dusting on food powders, and a small plastic rolling pin for rolling out tiny amounts of fondant icing when modelling. Cocktail sticks are useful when modelling figurines and flowers and for applying minute amounts of food colouring paste to almond paste or icing.

Splitting and filling a cake

FILLING AND TOPPING CAKES

To make sponge cakes even tastier, they can be split and filled with jam, cream or buttercream. Icings complete a special-occasion cake and are especially good when covering home-made almond paste.

SPLITTING AND FILLING A CAKE

1 Leave the cake to cool completely before splitting. Use a knife with a shallow thin blade, such as a bread knife, a ham knife, or a carving knife. Cut a notch from top to bottom on one side so you will know where to line the pieces up.

2 Cut midway between top and bottom, about 30% of the way through the cake. Turn the cake while cutting, taking care to keep the blade parallel with the base, until you have cut all the way around.

3 Cut through the central core and lift off the top of the cake.

4 Warm the filling slightly to make it easier to spread, then spread on top of the base, stopping 1cm (½ inch) from the edge. Add the top layer of cake.

BASIC ICINGS AND FROSTINGS

There are lots of options for covering cakes, depending on the finish you require. Royal and glacé icings are the classics. Almond paste, followed by a layer of ready-to-roll icing (sugar paste) is popular, as is buttercream or apricot glaze.

Glacé Icing

To make 225g (8oz), enough to cover 18 fairy cakes, you will need: 225g (8oz) icing sugar, a few drops of vanilla or almond flavouring (optional), 2–3 tbsp boiling water, food colouring (optional).

1 Sift the icing sugar into a bowl. Add a few drops of flavouring, if you like.

2 Using a wooden spoon, gradually stir in enough water until the mixture is the consistency of thick cream. Beat until white and smooth and the icing is thick enough to coat the back of the spoon. Add colouring, if you like, and use immediately.

VARIATIONS

Orange or lemon: Replace the water with strained orange or lemon juice.
Chocolate: Sift 2 tsp cocoa powder with the icing sugar.
Colour: Add a few drops of liquid food colouring, or use food colouring paste for a stronger colour.

NOTE

Food colourings are available in liquid, paste or powder form (see page 323). Add minute amounts with the tip of a cocktail stick until the desired colour is achieved.

Royal Icing

Royal icing can also be bought in packs from supermarkets. Simply add water or egg white to use.

To make 450g (1lb), enough to cover the top and sides of a 20.5cm (8 inch) cake, you will need: 2 medium egg whites, ¼ tsp lemon juice, 450g (1lb) icing sugar, sifted, 1 tsp glycerine.

1 Put the egg whites and lemon juice into a clean bowl. Stir to break up the egg whites. Add sufficient icing sugar to mix to the consistency of unwhipped cream. Continue mixing and adding small quantities of icing sugar until the desired consistency is reached, mixing well and gently beating after each addition. The icing should be smooth, glossy and light, almost like a cold meringue in texture, but not aerated. Do not add the icing sugar too quickly or it will produce a dull heavy icing. Stir in the glycerine until well blended. (Alternatively, for large quantities of royal icing, use a food mixer on the lowest speed, following the same instructions as before.)
2 Allow the icing to settle before using it; cover the surface with a piece of damp clingfilm and seal well, excluding all the air.
3 Stir the icing thoroughly before use to disperse any air bubbles, then adjust the consistency if necessary by adding more sifted icing sugar.

Apricot Glaze

To make 450g (1lb), you will need: 450g (1lb) apricot jam, 2 tbsp water.

1 Put the jam and water into a saucepan and heat gently, stirring occasionally, until melted. Boil the jam rapidly for 1 minute, then strain through a sieve.
2 Using a wooden spoon, rub through as much fruit as possible. Discard the skins left in the sieve.
3 Pour the glaze into a clean, hot jar, then seal with a clean lid and cool. Store in the fridge for up to two months. You only need 3–4 tbsp apricot glaze for a 23cm (9 inch) cake, so this quantity will glaze 6–7 cakes.

Almond Paste

To make 450g (1lb) almond paste, enough to cover the top and sides of an 18cm (7 inch) round cake or 15cm (6 inch) square cake, you will need: 225g (8oz) ground almonds, 125g (4oz) golden caster sugar, 125g (4oz) sifted golden icing sugar, 1 large egg, 2 tsp lemon juice, 1 tsp sherry, 1–2 drops vanilla extract.

1 Put the ground almonds and sugars into a bowl and stir to combine. In another bowl, whisk together the remaining ingredients, then add to the dry ingredients.
2 Stir well to mix, pounding gently to release some of the oil from the almonds. Knead with your hands until smooth, then cover until ready to use.

NOTE
If you wish to avoid using raw egg to bind the almond paste, mix the other liquid ingredients with a little water instead.

Fondant Icing

To make 500g (1lb 2oz), enough to cover the top and sides of an 18cm (7 inch) round cake or 15cm (6 inch) square cake, you will need: 500g (1lb 2oz) golden icing sugar, plus extra to dust, 1 medium egg white, 2 tbsp liquid glucose, warmed, 1 tsp vanilla extract.

Whiz the icing sugar in a food processor for 30 seconds, then add the egg white, glucose and vanilla extract and whiz for 2–3 minutes until the mixture forms a ball.

Vanilla Frosting

To make about 175g (6oz), enough to cover the top and sides of an 18cm (7 inch) cake, you will need: 150g (5oz) icing sugar, 5 tsp vegetable oil, 1 tbsp milk, a few drops of vanilla extract.

Sift the icing sugar into a bowl and, using a wooden spoon, beat in the oil, milk and vanilla extract until smooth.

Coffee Fudge Frosting

To make 400g (14oz), enough to cover the top and sides of a 20.5cm (8 inch) cake, you will need: 50g (2oz) unsalted butter, 125g (4oz) light muscovado sugar, 2 tbsp single cream or milk, 1 tbsp coffee granules, 200g (7oz) golden icing sugar, sifted.

1 Put the butter, muscovado sugar and cream or milk into a pan. Dissolve the coffee in 2 tbsp boiling water and add to the pan. Heat gently until the sugar dissolves, then bring to the boil and boil briskly for 3 minutes.
2 Remove from the heat and gradually stir in the icing sugar. Beat well with a wooden spoon for 1 minute until smooth.
3 Use the frosting immediately, spreading it over the cake with a wet palette knife, or dilute with a little water to use as a smooth coating.

VARIATION

Chocolate fudge frosting: Omit the coffee. Add 75g (3oz) plain chocolate, in pieces, to the pan with the butter at the beginning of step 1.

American Frosting

To make 225g (8oz), enough to cover the top and sides of a 20.5cm (8 inch) cake, you will need: 1 large egg white, 225g (8oz) golden caster or granulated sugar, pinch of cream of tartar.

1 Whisk the egg white in a clean bowl until stiff. Put the sugar, 4 tbsp water and the cream of tartar into a heavy-based pan. Heat gently, stirring, until the sugar has dissolved. Bring to the boil, without stirring, and boil until the sugar syrup registers 115°C on a sugar thermometer.
2 Remove from the heat and, as soon as the bubbles subside, pour the syrup on to the egg white in a thin stream, whisking constantly until thick and white. Leave to cool slightly.
3 When the frosting begins to turn dull around the edges and is almost cold, pour quickly over the cake and spread evenly with a palette knife.

Seven-minute Frosting

To make about 175g (6oz), enough to cover the top and sides of an 18cm (7 inch) cake, you will need: 1 medium egg white, 175g (6oz) caster sugar, 2 tbsp water, pinch of salt, pinch of cream of tartar.

1 Put all the ingredients into a heatproof bowl and whisk lightly using an electric or hand whisk.
2 Put the bowl over a pan of hot water, making sure the base of the bowl doesn't touch the water, and heat, whisking continuously, until the mixture thickens sufficiently to stand in peaks. This will take about 7 minutes.
3 Pour the frosting over the top of the cake and spread with a palette knife.

Buttercream

To cover the top of a 20.5cm (8 inch) cake, you will need: 75g (3oz) unsalted butter, 175g (6oz) icing sugar, sifted, a few drops of vanilla extract, 1–2 tbsp milk.

1 Soften the butter in a mixing bowl, then beat until light and fluffy.
2 Gradually stir in the remaining ingredients and beat until smooth.

VARIATIONS

Citrus: Replace the vanilla with a little grated orange, lemon or lime zest, and use some of the fruit's juice in place of the milk.
Chocolate: Blend 1 tbsp cocoa powder with 2 tbsp boiling water. Cool, then add to the mixture in place of the milk.
Colour: For a strong colour, use food colouring paste; liquid colouring gives a paler effect (see page 323).

Easiest Icing

To make 675g (1½lb), enough to cover a 20.5cm (8 inch) almond paste-covered cake, you will need: 3 medium egg whites, 2 tbsp lemon juice, 2 tsp glycerine, 675g (1½lb) icing sugar, sifted.

1 Put the egg whites into a large bowl and whisk until frothy. There should be just a layer of bubbles across the top. Add the lemon juice, glycerine and 2 tbsp icing sugar and whisk until smooth.
2 Whisk in the rest of the sugar, a little at a time, until the mixture is smooth, thick and forming soft peaks.
3 Using a palette knife, smooth half the icing over the top and sides of the cake, then repeat using the remaining icing to cover. Run the knife around the sides to neaten, then use the tip to make peaks all over the top. Leave to dry in a cool place for at least 48 hours.

Chocolate Ganache

To make 225g (8oz), enough to cover an 18cm (7 inch) round cake, you will need: 225g (8oz) good-quality plain dark chocolate (with 60–70 per cent cocoa solids), chopped into small pieces, 250ml (9fl oz) double cream.

1 Put the chocolate into a medium heatproof bowl. Pour the cream into a small heavy-based pan and bring to the boil.
2 Immediately pour the cream on to the chocolate and stir gently in one direction until the chocolate has melted and the mixture is smooth. Set aside to cool for 5 minutes.
3 Whisk the ganache until it begins to hold its shape. Used at room temperature, the mixture should be the consistency of softened butter.

NOTE
Use ganache at room temperature as a smooth coating for special cakes, or chill it lightly until thickened and use to fill meringues, choux buns or sandwich cakes.

VARIATIONS
These are all suitable for a sauce made with 225g (8oz) chocolate:
- **Milk or single cream:** Substituted in whole or in part for the water.
- **Coffee:** Stir in 1 tsp instant coffee or a shot of espresso when melting the chocolate.
- **Spices:** Add a pinch of ground cinnamon, crushed cardamom seeds or freshly grated nutmeg to the melting chocolate.
- **Vanilla extract:** Stir in ¼ tsp vanilla when melting the chocolate.
- **Rum, whisky or Cognac:** Stir in about 1 tsp alcohol when melting the chocolate.
- **Butter:** Stir in 25g (1oz) towards the end of heating.

Icing biscuits and decorating with nuts and sweets

Decorating biscuits

The simplest way to decorate a biscuit is to dust it with icing sugar, but there are also several techniques you can try to achieve a more elaborate effect.

DECORATING BISCUITS BEFORE BAKING

Place a glacé cherry or whole nut, such as an almond, or a half-walnut on the raw biscuit dough before it is cooked. Press the decoration gently into the surface. This is suitable for firmer biscuit and moulded and rolled biscuits.

KID'S COOKIES

Small children can have fun decorating cut-out shapes from a rolled cookie mixture. Coloured sweets look pretty, but for a healthier option, try using nuts, seeds and dried fruit, such as raisins.

ICING BISCUITS

Mix 125g (4oz) icing sugar with a little water, or lemon or orange juice, until smooth and runny. To drizzle, spoon thin trails of icing over the cooled biscuits. To spread, make the icing a little thicker. If the biscuits are for children they can be decorated with brightly coloured sweets.

Flavourings and food colourings

An excellent range of flavourings and food colourings are now available in supermarkets, but the dedicated cake decorator may want to visit a specialist cake decorating shop or website, as there are now so many fabulous products to help you create stunning designs for every occasion.

FLAVOURINGS

Choose extracts rather than essence, as they have a more intense flavour. They tend to be more expensive but a little goes a long way. Flavours include vanilla (also available as a paste), almond, peppermint, orange, lemon, chocolate and coffee. Knead a few drops into fondant icing or use to flavour buttercreams and cake mixes. Orange flower water and rosewater also make delicate flavourings for icings.

LIQUID PASTES AND LIQUID COLOURINGS

Liquid colourings tend to be cheaper and more suitable for adding to cake mixes. When working with icing, whether it's buttercream, fondant or royal, use pastes whenever possible as they give a more intense colour and will not effect the consistency. They are also easier to knead into almond paste or fondant icing. Apply with a cocktail stick a dot at a time until you have reached the desired level of colour – don't be tempted to add too much at once because once it's there you can't take it away. The pastes can also be applied neat with a paintbrush to add fine definition to work.

EDIBLE DUSTS AND POLLENS

These give texture and colour, especially when added to the stamens or centres of flowers. Apply sparingly with a small paintbrush. They can also be used to create textured finishes such as moss or soil. You can also buy dusts to add shimmer, or metallic dusts that add a gold, silver, bronze or copper sheen.

EDIBLE GOLD AND SILVER LEAF

These are applied with a small paintbrush to icing or as a finishing touch on chocolates. They usually come in sheets that can be applied over larger surfaces or as flakes that can even be added to champagne!

BASE-ICING TECHNIQUES

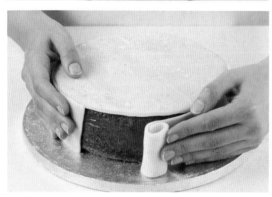

Covering a cake with almond paste

COVERING A CAKE WITH ALMOND PASTE

Once you have covered the cake with almond paste, you need to allow time for it to dry, for at least 12 hours and up to two days, before covering with icing. Home-made almond paste takes a little longer to dry out than the ready-made variety.

1 Trim the top of the cake level if necessary, then turn the cake over to give a flat surface to work on. Place on the cake board, which should be at least 5cm (2 inch) larger than the cake. Brush the cake with warmed apricot glaze (see page 320).

2 Dust the worksurface with sifted icing sugar. Roll out half the almond paste to fit the top of the cake. Lift the almond paste on top of the cake and smooth over, neatening the edges.

3 Cut a piece of string the same height as the cake with the almond paste topping, and another to fit around the diameter of the cake. Roll out the remaining almond paste and, using the string as a guide, trim it to size. Roll up the almond paste strip loosely. Place one end against the side of the cake and unroll the almond paste around the cake to cover it. Use a palette knife to smooth over the sides and joins. Leave the cake in a cool, dry place to dry out for at least 24 hours before covering with ready-to-roll icing. Allow to dry for at least two days before applying royal icing.

COVERING A CAKE WITH READY-TO-ROLL ICING (SUGAR PASTE)

Also known as fondant icing, ready-to-roll icing is pliable and can be used to cover cakes or moulded into shapes for decoration. Blocks of ready-to-roll icing (sugar paste) are available in a variety of colours from supermarkets and specialist cake decorating shops, or you can colour white icing to your desired shade (see page 320).

A 450g (1lb) pack will cover an 18cm (7 inch) cake. Wrap any unused icing in clingfilm to stop it drying out and store in a cool, dry place.

1 Dust the worksurface and rolling pin with sifted icing sugar. Knead the icing until pliable, then roll out into a round or square 5–7.5cm (2–3 inch) larger than the cake all round. Lift the icing on top of the cake and allow it to drape over the edges.
2 Dust your hands with sifted icing sugar and press the icing on to the sides of the cake, easing it down to the board.
3 Using a sharp knife, trim off the excess icing at the base to neaten. Reserve the trimmings to make decorations if required.
4 Using your fingers dusted with a little sifted icing sugar, gently rub the surface in a circular movement to buff the icing and make it smooth.

COVERING A CAKE WITH BUTTERCREAM

1 Stir the buttercream just before applying. Using a small palette knife dipped in hot water, spread the icing smoothly and evenly.
2 For a textured effect, paddle the palette knife backwards and forwards, or swirl the icing decoratively. For a more formal finish, pipe a design directly on to the surface of the cake, such as a piped scroll, shell or swirl edging.

COVERING A CAKE WITH ROYAL ICING

1 When applying royal icing, first cover the cake with apricot glaze (see page 320).
2 Stir the royal icing just before using, to make sure it is easy to spread.
3 Put the cake on a plate or cake board and use a palette knife to spread the icing evenly over the cake.

Covering a cake with ready-to-roll icing

Covering a cake with buttercream

COVERING A CAKE WITH FROSTING

1 Make sure the frosting is the correct consistency – thick enough to coat the back of a spoon. Frostings are often warm at this stage; if too thick, the bowl will need to be placed over hot water, or the frosting may be thinned with a little water. On the other hand, if the frosting is too slack, leave it to cool and thicken slightly.
2 Pour all the frosting over the top of the cake and allow it to fall over the sides, gently tapping the cake to encourage it to flow; don't be tempted to use a knife, which would leave marks. When the frosting has stopped falling, neaten the bottom edge and leave to dry.

Once a cake has been iced or frosted, the sides may be coated with crushed praline, grated chocolate or toasted chopped or flaked nuts; pistachio nuts, in particular, add colour as well as texture. Simple finishing touches are often the most effective – a drizzle of melted chocolate or caramel, fresh or frosted herbs and flowers, fresh fruit, toasted nuts and chocolate curls all work well.

CHOCOLATE AND SUGAR

Working with chocolate

The type of chocolate you choose to work with will have a dramatic effect on the end product. For the best results, buy chocolate that has a high proportion of cocoa solids, preferably at least 70%. Most supermarkets stock a selection of different percentages. Chocolate with a high percentage of cocoa solids has a rich flavour and is perfect for sauces, ganache (see page 322), most sweets, cakes and desserts. At the top end of the scale, couverture chocolate is the one preferred by chefs for confectionery work and gives an intense chocolate flavour that is probably best reserved for special mousses and gâteaux. It is available in milk, plain and white varieties from specialist chocolate shops. For most purposes, a good-quality chocolate with a high proportion of cocoa solids will usually give great results.

MELTING CHOCOLATE

For cooking or making decorations, chocolate is usually melted first. You can do this in two ways:

1 Break the chocolate into pieces and put in a heatproof bowl or in the top of a double boiler. Set over a pan of gently simmering water, making sure the base of the bowl doesn't touch the water. Heat very gently until the chocolate starts to melt, then stir regularly until completely melted.

2 To melt chocolate in the microwave, break the chocolate into pieces and put in a microwave-proof bowl. Microwave at full power for 1 minute. Stir, then cook again for 30 seconds at a time until the chocolate is smooth and melted.

NOTES

- When melting chocolate, use a gentle heat.
- Don't let water or steam touch the chocolate or it will become hard and unworkable. If it has 'seized', try stirring in a few drops of flavourless vegetable oil.

CHOCOLATE MOULDS

You can make almost any hollow container – such as an espresso cup or petit four case – into a mould.

1 Pour the melted chocolate into the mould, turning it to coat it evenly, and then pour out the excess. Chill until set.

2 Repeat the process until you have achieved the required thickness that you want (see notes). Leave to set, and then turn out, remembering to handle very gently.

3 Alternatively, you can use a small paintbrush to layer the chocolate. Simply dip the brush – scrupulously clean, of course – into the melted chocolate and paint the inside of the mould with it. Chill until set, then repeat layering with chocolate until you have achieved the thickness required for your particular purpose.

NOTES

- Your mould should not have any awkward curves or angles, or you will not be able to release the chocolate from the mould. A bowl or straight-sided shape is best.
- The larger the mould, the thicker the chocolate layer should be. For something small like a teacup, the thickness can be just a few coatings of chocolate; while for larger moulds, it should be around 6mm (¼ inch).
- The mould must be spotlessly clean, completely dry and free of lint or fibres.

Melting chocolate

Chocolate moulds

GANACHE

This topping is made from good-quality chocolate mixed with cream and butter. Increasing the ratio of cream to chocolate will make the ganache lighter, and sometimes the butter is left out so that the ganache won't be too rich. The recipe on page 322 is very versatile.

CHOCOLATE DECORATIONS

Chocolate decorations give an elegant, luxurious finish to cakes and biscuits. Avoid over-handling the finished decorations, as chocolate melts and marks easily.

CHOCOLATE WAFERS

1 You can make flat or curved wafers in any shape you like. Cut a piece of greaseproof paper to the required width.
2 Brush the paper evenly with melted chocolate and leave until the chocolate has almost set.
3 Using a knife, cut the chocolate (while still on the paper) into pieces of the desired size and shape (straight or curved, square or triangular, narrow or wide). You can also cut out chocolate shapes using small cutters.
4 Leave to cool and harden completely, either on the worksurface (for flat wafers) or draped over a rolling pin (for curled).
5 Carefully peel the wafers off the paper, handling them as little as possible, and store in the refrigerator for up to 24 hours.

CHOCOLATE CURLS

1 Melt the chocolate (see opposite), then spread it out in a thin layer on a marble slab or clean worksurface. Leave to firm up.
2 Using a sharp, flat-ended blade (such as a pastry scraper or a very stiff spatula), scrape through the chocolate at a 45-degree angle. The size of the curls will be determined by the width of the blade.

Chocolate wafers

Chocolate curls

Chocolate shavings

CHOCOLATE SHAVINGS

This is the easiest decoration of all because it doesn't call for melting the chocolate. Use chilled chocolate.

1 Hold a chocolate bar upright on the worksurface and shave pieces off the edge with a swivel peeler.
2 Alternatively, grate the chocolate, against a coarse or medium-coarse grater, to make very fine shavings.

CHOCOLATE CARAQUE

1 Pour cooled, melted chocolate on to a marble slab or cool worksurface. Using a palette knife, spread out the chocolate as evenly as possible to a thickness of 1–2mm (1/16 inch). Let the chocolate cool to almost setting point.
2 Using a metal scraper or large cook's knife held at a 45-degree angle against the marble or worksurface, push the blade away from you slowly to roll the chocolate into a cylinder. If the chocolate is too warm it will stick, if it is too cold it will only form shavings.

CHOCOLATE LEAVES

1 Wash and dry some unsprayed rose or other non-toxic leaves, such as bay leaves. Using a small paintbrush, coat the shiny sides of the leaves with a layer of cooled, melted chocolate. Spread it right out to the edge, but wipe off any chocolate that drips over the edge.
2 Leave to set in a cool, dry place on a baking sheet lined with baking parchment.
3 When completely set, carefully peel away the leaves and store the chocolate leaves in the fridge in an airtight container between sheets of silicone paper for up to a month.

CHOCOLATE TRIANGLES

1 Cut a length of silicone paper about 5cm (2 inch) deep. Brush with a cooled, melted layer of chocolate 1–2mm (1/16 inch) thick. Let cool to almost setting point.
2 Mark into triangles and leave to set but do not chill. For curved triangles, set the chocolate-coated paper along the length of a rolling pin.
3 When the chocolate is completely set, carefully remove from the paper and store in the fridge in an airtight container between sheets of silicone paper for up to a month.

PIPED CHOCOLATE DECORATIONS

Chocolate can be piped into decorative shapes to adorn cakes and desserts.

1 Draw your chosen designs on to a piece of white paper or card. Tape a large piece of silicone paper over it – work on a flat surface where your decorations can be left to dry completely before moving.
2 Fill paper piping bags, or a piping cone fitted with a fine nozzle, with cooled, melted chocolate – a tablespoon of sugar syrup stirred in to the chocolate will make it easier to work with.
3 Holding the bag vertically and with light pressure, pipe the chocolate on to the outline of your drawing. Leave to set completely.
4 Using a metal palette knife, carefully remove the piped lines. Store in the fridge in an airtight container between sheets of silicone paper for up to a month.

Chocolate leaves

Piping chocolate decorations

Working with sugar

Sugar is a wonderfully versatile ingredient. When heated it can be transformed entirely – into crisp caramel and praline and delicate spun sugar, to name but a few.

DRY CARAMEL

Use to make decorations. They can be made up to 24 hours in advance and stored in airtight container.

1 Line a baking sheet with oiled greaseproof paper. Put 200g (7oz) caster sugar in a heavy-based pan with 4 tbsp water. Heat gently until the sugar dissolves.
2 Bring to the boil, then cook until it turns a medium caramel colour. Dip the base of the pan in cold water. Use immediately before the caramel begins to harden.
3 For caramel flowers, with a fork make abstract shapes 4cm (1½ inch) in diameter on oiled greaseproof paper.
4 For caramel cages, lightly oil the back of a ladle. Drizzle caramel threads in a crisscross pattern, finishing with thread around the rim.

NOTES

- Once the syrup starts to colour, watch it closely – the colour can deepen rapidly, and very dark caramel tastes bitter.
- Have a pan of cold water ready to dip the base of the pan into to stop the caramel cooking further.

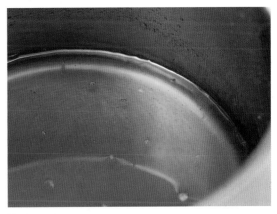

Sugar syrup

SUGAR SYRUP

To serve four, you will need: 275g (10oz) granulated sugar.

1 Put the sugar into a pan with 600ml (1 pint) cold water. Put the pan over a low heat and heat gently until the sugar has completely dissolved.
2 Bring the mixture to the boil and cook for 2–5 minutes, depending on the depth of colour required.
3 Leave the syrup to cool and use immediately or store in a clean jar in the refrigerator for up to one week.

FLAVOURINGS

- Add the thinly pared zest of 1 lemon or ½ orange to the sugar and water in step 1.
- For a boozy sugar syrup, add 1–2 tbsp brandy or rum at the end of step 2.

Dry caramel

Spun sugar

SPUN SUGAR

One of the most attractive sugar decorations, spun sugar is made from a light caramel syrup spun into a nest of hair-thin threads. The only equipment you need is a pair of forks, a rolling pin and sheets of paper to catch any drips of syrup that fall to the floor while you work.

1 Put the sugar and water into a heavy-based pan, using 4 tbsp water per 200g (7oz) sugar. Heat gently until the sugar dissolves.
2 Turn the heat up to high and bring to the boil. Continue to boil the syrup until it turns a light caramel colour. Dip the bottom of the pan in cold water to cool it, then leave to cool for 5 minutes.
3 Meanwhile, spread sheets of paper over the floor or table where you will be working.
4 Dip two or more forks, held in one hand, into the caramel. Flick them back and forth over a rolling pin held over the paper in your other hand, so that wispy threads fall over the pin.
5 When the rolling pin is full, carefully slide the threads off and gently form them into a ball or keep them as straight threads. Use immediately to decorate desserts.

DULCE DE LECHE

A soft toffee sauce – use as a filling or with desserts such as banoffee pie.

1 Pierce two holes in a can of condensed milk. Place in a pan. Pour water three-quarters up the can.
2 Simmer for 2 hours (for a runny sauce) to 4 hours (for a thick spread), topping up the water as needed.

MIXED NUT PRALINE

Use to decorate cakes and tarts.

To serve four, you will need: 250g (9oz) golden caster sugar, 175g (6oz) mixed nuts, such as walnuts.

1 Put the sugar into a pan and warm over a gentle heat. Line a baking sheet with baking parchment and fill a bowl with very cold water.
2 Shake the pan gently to dissolve the sugar, keeping a close eye on it when it starts to colour.
3 When the sugar has turned a dark golden brown, pour in the nuts and stir once with a wooden spoon.
4 Dip the base of the pan into cold water to keep the praline from burning, then quickly pour the praline on to the parchment and spread out.
5 Cool for 20 minutes, then break into pieces with a rolling pin. For fine praline, crush in a food processor or coffee grinder.

Mixed nut praline

Dulce de leche

PIPING TECHNIQUES

MAKING A PAPER ICING BAG

Reusable and disposable icing bags are available from all good cake decorating shops but it's just as easy to make your own from greaseproof paper. Once you have mastered the technique, make a batch so that you can swap between different coloured icing as you're working.

1 Cut out a rectangle of greaseproof paper 25.5 × 20.5cm (10 × 8 inch) – for smaller bags, cut a proportionally smaller rectangle. Fold in half diagonally, then tear or cut along the crease.

2 Put the paper on the worksurface with the apex of the triangle nearest to you. Bring the top left-hand point round to line up with the bottom point. Hold in place with your thumb and index finger.

3 Bring the right-hand point, over and round the back, meeting at the bottom point. Pull together slightly to tighten the point.

4 Fold over the points of the paper nearest to you to secure the bag. To use, snip the point of the bag with scissors for different icing techniques (see below) or fit with metal nozzles for more intricate designs.

USING A PAPER ICING BAG WITHOUT A NOZZLE

The shape and size of the icing bag point will produce different effects.

- **Lines and dots** Snip off the tip of the point; the smaller the hole the finer the piping will be.
- **Fluted and petals and leaves** Make V-shaped cuts in the bag.

Filling a piping bag

FILLING A PIPING BAG

Drop a nozzle into the end of the piping bag. If using a plastic piping bag, fold over the top to make a collar and, holding it in one hand, fill two-thirds with the icing. Fold over the top and gently press at the top to remove air bubbles and start the icing flowing.

HOLDING THE PIPING BAG

Hold the end of the bag in one hand. Squeeze from the top with your thumb. Rest the nozzle end in your other hand, using it to guide the bag. Squeeze gently for fine work, apply slightly more pressure for thicker lines. To finish a line of piping cleanly, stop squeezing and pull away sharply.

Making a paper icing bag

PIPING WITH ROYAL ICING

Before tackling an ambitious project, such as a wedding cake, practise your icing skills on a board first – the wrong consistency of icing or a shaky hand could ruin your design. It's also worth bearing in mind the following pointers to ensure success:

1 Don't overfill the piping bag, otherwise icing will spill over the top. Messy hands will disturb your concentration and blobs of icing could fall on your design.
2 Keep the work area as clean as possible to avoid mess or blemishes on the cake. Wipe down as you finish each section.
3 Cover the bowl of icing with a damp teatowel or kitchen paper to stop it drying out while piping.
4 Plan your pattern before piping. Prick out the design with a pin to give you a template to follow.

PIPING DIRECTLY ON TO A CAKE

Use royal icing for intricate and delicate cake decorating work, as it sets hard and lasts for months.

Lines and borders are best piped directly on to the cake, while more intricate shapes can be piped on to silicone paper, left to dry then, fixed on to the cake with a dab of royal icing.

For lacework, draw your design on a paper template, then pipe on silicone paper laid over the top. Leave to dry completely before moving. Whole sheets of decorations can be piped on to silicone paper and stored like this in an airtight container for several weeks.

Piping a scalloped design on to a cake

THE STAR NOZZLE

The star nozzle is the most versatile of all the metal nozzles. By varying the pressure and angle, you can produce many designs, including scallops, fluted lines, rosettes and shells.

FLUTED LINE

Holding the piping bag at a 45-degree angle and 5mm (¼ inch) above the surface, pipe towards yourself, raising the bag slightly as the icing flows on to the surface. Pull away sharply to finish.

ROSETTE

Holding the piping bag vertically and just above the surface, squeeze the bag gently until you have the sized rosette you need, then lift away.

CABLE

Holding the piping bag at a 45-degree angle and 5mm (¼ inch) above the surface, pipe to the left then right in a slight zigzag motion.

SPIRAL

Holding the piping bag at a 45-degree angle and 5mm (¼ inch) above the surface, pipe a short line towards yourself, then lift the nozzle up and over the previous line in an arc. Continue piping in arcs, gradually increasing in size as you reach the middle and decreasing in size towards the end.

SHELLS

Holding the piping bag at a 45-degree angle and 5mm (¼ inch) above the surface, pipe a small blob of icing, then bring the bag up and towards you and back down to the surface. Pull away sharply. Pipe the next shell over the end of the previous one.

LATTICE

Pipe straight vertical and horizontal lines in a crisscross pattern.

OTHER NOZZLES

Once you have mastered the basic techniques of icing, you might want to experiment with other nozzles that can produce ribbon, frills, ruffles and leaves.

Fluted line

Rosette

Cable

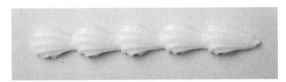

Spiral

Shells

Lattice (with a fine nozzle)

Piping – what went wrong?

Before using any piping equipment, it is essential to have the cream, buttercream, chocolate or icing at the correct consistency. When a wooden spoon is drawn out of royal icing or buttercream, it should form a fine but sharp point. If the icing is too stiff it will be very difficult to pipe; if too soft, the icing will be difficult to control and the piped shapes will lose their definition.

Always remember, the larger the nozzle the stiffer the icing, and for a very fine nozzle the consistency needs to be slightly softer.

THE LINES HAVE BROKEN
- The icing was too stiff.

- The icing was pulled along rather than allowed to flow from the piping bag.

- There were too many bubbles in the icing.

THE LINES ARE WOBBLY
- The bag was squeezed too hard.

- The icing was too runny.

THE LINES ARE FLAT
- The icing was too runny.

- The nozzle was held to near the surface of the icing.

RUN OUT AND CRIMPING TECHNIQUES

TECHNIQUES OF RUN OUT

Flooding icing is used to fill out shapes that have been piped with royal icing on cakes or bisuits.

To make flooding icing, thin down royal icing with a little tepid water. Add a drop at a time, stirring between each addition until the desired consistency is reached. Don't beat, as this adds air bubbles that will appear in the design. When using different colours on one design, allow each one to dry before adding the next.

1 Using royal icing thick enough for piping writing, pipe your chosen design on to a cake, biscuit or a piece of silicone paper – if the latter, work somewhere you can leave the designs to dry completely before moving.
2 Fill another piping bag with the flooding icing (a nozzle isn't necessary), snip off the end and fill in the piped shapes, ensuring the icing floods up to the edges.
3 Leave to dry for 48 hours before moving.

CRIMPING

Crimping is a simple way to give a decorative finish to the edges of fondant icing-covered cakes. It should be done while the icing is still soft. Crimpers look like a large pair of tweezers, come in a variety of crimping styles, such as scallops, hearts, zigzags and curved lines, and can be obtained from good cake decorating shops and websites. Dust the ends with cornflour to stop the crimpers sticking as you work.

1 To crimp the top edge of a cake, put the open crimpers around the icing and gently squeeze together.
2 Put the crimper end next to the previously crimped edge to ensure a continuous pattern. Repeat around the entire cake.

If you don't want to pipe royal icing around the base of the cake, you can crimp instead.
1 Dampen the base edge of the icing with water. Roll out two long pieces of fondant that will together reach around the bottom of the cake.
2 Fix around the base, gently pressing in place. Fit the two pieces together, smoothing over the join.
3 Place the crimpers around the sausage shape and gently squeeze together to make the pattern. Continue around the base of the cake.

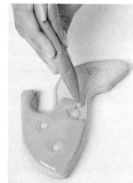

Piping and then flooding the design

Biscuit decorated with run out icing

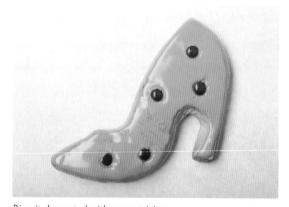

Crimping the edge of a cake

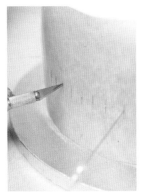
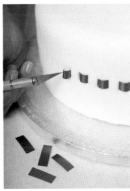

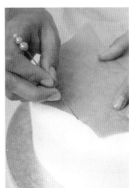

Cutting slits into the cake and then inserting ribbon

Making and using a template

RIBBON INSERTION

Ribbon insertion is a simple but impressive way of decorating a cake covered in fondant icing. It can be used to edge the top or sides of a cake.

1 Cut a strip of narrow coloured ribbon into 1cm (½ inch) long pieces.
2 Next make a template. Cut a strip of greaseproof paper and mark pairs of slots 1cm (½ inch) apart that are slightly wider than the width of your ribbon. Or you can use a ribbon insertion tool.
3 Carefully fix the greaseproof paper to the sides of the cake using pins, then gently cut slots into the cake with a small sharp knife following the template marks.
4 Remove the paper and, using tweezers, insert one end of a strip of ribbon into a slot. Bend the ribbon and push into the paired slot using the point of a knife. Repeat around the cake.

RICE PAPER

Personal photographs can be printed on to rice paper or directly on to icing (see below) and fixed to the top of a cake for an unusual decorative effect. Printer-friendly rice paper and edible ink for use in home printers can be obtained from specialist websites. Thin edible icing sheets can also be printed with safe edible food colourings and can then be applied to sugarpaste or royal icing. Special printers are needed for this technique, or there are companies who will do it for you.

MAKING AND USING TEMPLATES

To avoid mistakes and to ensure your design is symmetrical, it's best to make a template first.

1 Draw a pattern on greaseproof paper cut to the same size as the top of the cake (draw around the cake tin). If you are making a tiered wedding cake, remember you will need a proportionally sized template for each cake. To make a scalloped edge, fold your circular template several times, as shown above, and use a compass (or the bottom of a jar) to mark the curved edge, then cut it out.
2 Attach the template to the surface of the cake with a pin, or hold in place with your hand, then prick the surface with another pin following the lines of your design.
3 Remove the paper and pipe over the pin marks.

MAKING A GARLAND TEMPLATE FOR THE SIDES OF A CAKE

1 Cut a strip of greaseproof paper that fits around the circumference. Measure equal points along the strip and fold the paper over at each mark. Once folded, draw a semi-circle from fold to edge, then cut it out.
2 Unfold the paper and fix around the cake with the straight edge along the base. Pin each point to the cake. Using a pin, prick around the edges of the template.
3 Remove the paper and pipe your chosen decoration using the pin marks as your guide.

SHORTCUT DECORATING

SHORTCUT DECORATING

If you don't have the time to decorate a cake with hand-piped icing there are a plenty of appealing alternatives.

- Fresh flowers make a simple and beautiful decoration for plain iced celebration cakes. A cluster of gerbera, a scattering of primroses or violets or a spray of roses are particularly striking and easy to set aside before slicing the cake. Ensure the flowers have not been sprayed with chemicals before decorating.

- Ready-made sugar flowers are available from all good cake decorating shops and websites. Simply fix on to your cake with a dab of royal icing.

- Fresh ribbons of coconut can look very pretty. Using a potato peeler, peel off thin ribbons of fresh coconut and arrange in loops around the base of the cake, or on top of the icing.

- Ribbons are an effective finishing touch and can be colour themed to the rest of the cake. With the flat edge of the ribbon sitting along the base, fix one cut end to the cake with a spot of royal icing. Smooth the ribbon around the circumference of the cake and fix the other end on top of the first cut end with another dab of icing.

- Decorate an un-iced cake with a layer of nuts and glacé fruits. Brush the surface of the cake with apricot glaze (see page 320), then arrange a selection of nuts, such as walnuts, brazil nuts and whole blanched almonds, and glacé fruits on top. Brush all over the fruit and nuts with more glaze and fix a ribbon around the sides. This decoration will keep for up to two weeks.

Decorate with fresh flowers

Decorate with ready-made sugar flowers

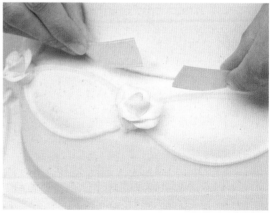

Decorate with ribbon

HAND-MADE DECORATIONS

With a little practise and patience, you can provide small finishing touches that will give your cake a professional touch. Some decorations can be made several weeks in advance and placed on the cake when needed. (For chocolate decorations, see page 327–8.)

MODELLING WITH KNEADED READY-TO-FOLL (FONDANT) ICING

Ready-to-foll icing can be bought ready-made in a variety of colours from cake decorating shops and used to cover cakes or model figures and animals. Knead before using to soften and make more pliable. To colour white icing, knead until pliable then smear on a little food colouring paste with the tip of a cocktail stick. Continue kneading until evenly distributed.

MOULDED FIGURES

Moulding figures requires care and patience. They need two key factors to make them come alive. One is proportion and the other is facial expression. With experience you will learn the feel of the moulding material – to work it until it is soft and perfectly smooth before shaping. You will learn how to handle it, which finger to use and how much pressure to apply to form the right shapes.

Ready-to-roll (fondant) icing can be rolled wafer thin without cracking and dries quickly. It is available in pure white – which can be coloured – or in various colours.

It is a good idea to allow at least 24 hours for figures to dry – they will be easier to handle when you are decorating with them. However, do assemble them while the fondant is still soft, as heads and limbs can be eased into natural positions.

Most moulded figures are made from three basic shapes: a ball, a sausage and a pear. They take between 25g (1oz) and 75g (3oz) of moulding material (fondant or almond paste), depending on the size needed. It is important to gauge that the figures are in proportion with each other and with the cake.

Modelling tools are available to shape and mark patterns. However, there are usually kitchen utensils to hand that will do a similar job. Wooden skewers, small spatulas and sharp knives are all useful. It is worth buying a fine sable brush for painting features and patterns, using food colourings.

Eyes are usually piped and are an essential part of the character. You will find that with practise you can spot the right angle of a head, quiver of a lip or flash of an eyeball that simply brings the character you have modelled to life.

MODELLING ANIMALS AND INSECTS

You can have fun with this type of modelling – use your imagination to make wonderful creatures.

HEDGEHOGS, LADYBIRDS AND TORTOISES

To make ladybirds Roll out 75g (3oz) red fondant icing thinly and cover cold cake buns. Using black writing icing, pipe wings, spots and a smile on the ladybirds and use chocolate drops for eyes.

To make tortoises Cover buns with the same quantity of green fondant icing. Use brown writing icing to draw 'shell' markings and add white chocolate drops. Make the heads, legs and tails from brown icing, and attach to the body with a little jam. Add silver balls for eyes.

To make hedgehogs Cover buns with chocolate buttercream, shaping to form a snout. Decorate with chocolate sprinkles, silver or gold balls for eyes and a dolly mixture sweet for the nose.

Hedgehogs, ladybirds and tortoises

Fondant penguins

PENGUINS

1 Take a small piece of black icing and roll into an egg shape. Roll a small piece of white icing into a ball and flatten into an oval. Mould the oval around the front of the penguin's body.

2 Roll a small piece of black icing into a ball and place on top of the body, moulding it to form the head. Using a cocktail stick, make two small holes for the eyes. Shape a small piece of red icing into a cone shape and press gently on to the head to form a beak.

3 Using a sharp knife or scalpel, cut each side, about a quarter of the way from the top, and pull each side out to form the penguin's wings.

4 Roll out a small piece of red icing and cut out two ovals for the feet; press gently on to the body. Repeat this process to make different-sized penguins.

5 To make a scarf, roll out a piece of coloured icing, cut a long thin strip and place around the penguin's neck. To make a hat, roll out a small thin circle of coloured icing, carefully push a small hollow in the centre and place on the penguin's head. Add a contrasting bobble and press gently into place.

MODELLING FLOWERS

Specific flower, petal and leaf cutters are available from cake decorating suppliers, which make modelling flowers a rewarding task.

Either tint the fondant in several shades of the required colour or brush with coloured dust when the flower has dried. Have photographs handy of the flowers you want to make, for easy reference.

DAISIES

Colour a little fondant icing or petal paste yellow or green for the centres and stalks. Colour the remainder pink, orange or leave white. Roll out thinly and cut into small rectangles. Make a line of cuts or snips along one long edge of each rectangle. Open out to a fan shape. Roll pieces of the yellow or green icing into small balls for the centres and larger balls for the stalks. Pinch out and mould the stalks. Brush the uncut edge of each fan-shaped piece of icing with water and wrap around each stalk, then place a centre in the middle. Open out the fan into petals and pull down slightly.

PANSIES

Divide fondant icing into two halves, then colour one half yellow and one mauve. Roll out thinly. Using a plain cocktail cutter or the base of an icing nozzle, cut five petals for each flower. Place a petal in the palm of your hand, press with your thumb to flatten and lift the outside edge. Make one petal a little larger than the other four. Arrange the petals with the larger petal at the top and the four smaller petals grouped underneath. Mark in the petal lines with a pointed knife. Carefully paint in the details with brown food colouring.

FONDANT ROSES

You will need: sifted cornflour or icing sugar, petal paste in shades of pink, small, medium and large rose-petal cutters, cocktail stick, sponge block.

1 Lightly dust the worksurface with cornflour or icing sugar. Using the pale pink for the outer petals, roll out a small piece of petal paste very thinly. Keep the rest of the paste covered with clingfilm.

2 Dust the petal cutters with icing sugar and cut out 3–4 petals in various sizes. Gently roll a cocktail stick over the round edge of the petal to make a thinner, slightly frilled edge. Repeat with different shades of paste, using the small cutters and darker shade of paste for the inner petals. To make rose buds, cut out small petals in different shades, as shown opposite.

3 Place each petal on the sponge block and gently curl each one to give a shallow cup shape. Curl the petals that will make up the centre of the rose into cones. Cover each petal loosely with clingfilm to stop it drying out.

Fondant roses

Attaching a rose to the cake

4 Brush one side of the inner petal cone with water, then put the next petal in position, overlapping the edges. Continue to add more petals, working around the rose and using all the shades of paste. Dust your fingers with icing sugar or cornflour, cup the half-assembled flower and put the last petal in position so that it overlaps the previous petal and tucks under the first to form a rose. Repeat to make more roses. Leave to dry for 1 hour.

5 Store in an airtight container for up to 3 months.

CHRISTMAS ROSES

You will need: sifted cornflour or icing sugar, petal paste, medium rose-petal cutter, sponge block, yellow dusting powder, stamens, fine paintbrushes.

1 Lightly dust the worksurface with cornflour or icing sugar. Roll out a small piece of petal paste very thinly. Keep the rest of the paste covered with clingfilm.

2 Dust the petal cutter with icing sugar and cut out 5 petals. Gently roll a cocktail stick over the round edge of the petal to make a thinner, slightly frilled edge.

3 Place each petal on the sponge block and gently curl each one to give a shallow cup shape. Cover each petal loosely with clingfilm to stop it drying out.

4 Brush one side of the first petal with water, then put the next petal in position, overlapping the edges. Repeat, adding two more petals.

5 Dust your fingers with icing sugar or cornflour and cup the half-assembled flower. Put the last petal in position so that it overlaps the fourth petal and tucks under the first to form a rose. Repeat to make more roses. Leave to dry for 1 hour.

6 Using a dry brush, dust the insides of the flower with yellow dusting powder, brushing from the centre outwards for a graduated effect.

7 Using the end of a teaspoon, put a blob of royal icing in the centre of the flower. Cut 4–5 stamens in half to make 8–10 heads, trim to size and position in the icing.

MODELLING WITH ALMOND PASTE

Almond paste can be used to make decorations such as flowers, fruit and figurines. First, knead a small amount until soft and pliable, then roll or mould into shapes with your hands. To colour, smear a little food colouring paste with the tip of a cocktail stick and knead until evenly distributed.

MARZIPAN CARROTS

1 Knead 60g (2½oz) almond paste until pliable. Add a dab of orange food paste and knead until evenly distributed. Divide into 15 evenly sized pieces and roll into small carrot shapes.

2 Mark ridges down the sides with a cocktail stick. Cut angelica into small strips and push into the top of each carrot to make a stalk.

CRYSTALLISING FLOWERS AND LEAVES

Edible flowers make a stunning individual decoration for cup cakes or clustered en masse on celebration cakes: rose petals and buds, daisies, pansies, violas and lavender sprigs are all suitable. Herbs, such as rosemary and mint, bay leaves and sweet geranium leaves and fruit, such as grapes and redcurrants, can also be crystallised. They will keep for up to a week in a cool, dry place. Always use flowers and leaves that have not been sprayed with chemicals.

1 Lightly beat an egg white until slightly frothy. Using a small paintbrush, coat the flowers, leaves or fruit with the egg white. Sprinkle with caster sugar to coat lightly and shake off the excess.

2 Leave to dry on baking parchment for two days in a cool, dry place – an airing cupboard or pantry is ideal – where they will crisp and harden.

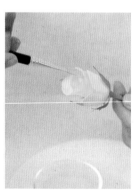
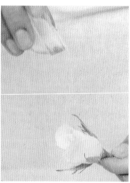

Crystallised roses

FESTIVE DECORATIONS

Christmas cookies *Mini christmas cake*

CHRISTMAS COOKIES

1 Cover Christmas-themed cookies, such as trees, baubles and angels, with coloured flooding icing (see page 334). Leave to dry until set.

2 Colour royal icing and pipe on your design. Leave to set.

MINI CHRISTMAS CAKES

1 Divide a large square fruit cake into individual portions 5–6.5cm (2–2½ inch) square. Brush the top with apricot glaze (see page 320).

2 Roll out white fondant icing to a thickness of 3mm (⅛ inch). Put the cakes, glazed-side down, on to the icing and cut around the edges with a sharp knife. Set aside, icing-side up.

3 Roll out white fondant icing to the same thickness. Using Christmas cookie cutters, such as stars, Christmas trees, bells, and so on, stamp out shapes and brush the underside with water.

4 Position on top of the icing and gently firm in place.

5 Decorate with edible gold balls.

Making Christmas holly and berries

CHRISTMAS HOLLY AND BERRIES

You will need: icing sugar, red and green ready-made fondant icing, holly leaf cutter, cocktail stick, royal icing.

1 Lightly dust a worksurface with icing sugar. Roll out the green icing thinly. Cut out holly leaves with the cutter.
2 Using a cocktail stick, mark a central vein down the middle of the leaf, with smaller veins marked off at an angle. Twist the leaves slightly to make a holly leaf shape and dry over the handle of a wooden spoon for 24 hours to create a curved shape.
3 Roll out berries from the red icing. Fix the leaves and berries to your cake with a blob of royal icing.

WHITE AND GOLD CHRISTMAS HOLLY

1 Use white ready-made fondant icing to cut out the holly leaves and proceed as above.
2 Dip the edges of the leaves in edible gold glitter or gold leaf to finish.

CHOCOLATE CHRISTMAS TREES

1 Draw your Christmas tree designs on a piece of card or paper. Tape a large piece of silicone paper over it – work on a flat surface where your decorations can be left to dry completely before moving.
2 Using a small paintbrush, paint over your designs with cooled, melted chocolate – you could use plain, milk or white. Leave to set completely before removing with a metal palette knife. Store in the fridge in an airtight container between sheets of silicone paper for up to a month.

SNOWFLAKE CAKE

To cover the top and sides of an 18cm (7 inch) square or 20.5cm (8 inch) round cake, you will need: 2 × 300g tubs ready-made royal icing, piping bag with plain nozzle, icing sugar to dust, 1m (40 inch) silver string.

1 Spoon 3 tbsp of the icing into the piping bag. Spoon the remaining icing on top of the cake and use a palette knife to spread over the top and sides in an even layer, swirling the icing with the knife.
2 Using the icing in the piping bag, mark six points, spaced at equal distances apart, towards the outer edge of the top of the cake; use these points as a guideline to pipe a snowflake pattern. Leave the icing to dry overnight.
3 Dust the cake with icing sugar and tie the string around the cake, finishing with a bow.

Snowflake cake

DECORATING CUPCAKES

PIPING ICING ON TO CUPCAKES

Half fill the piping bag with buttercream or frosting and hold the bag vertically as you pipe, squeezing gently from the top. Choose from the shapes below, or use your imagination.

SWIRL

Fit a piping bag with a large star or plain nozzle, depending on the desired effect. Starting from the edge, pipe an ever-decreasing circle on to the cupcake ending with a point at the top. For a multi-coloured effect, fill the icing bag with two or three differently coloured icings, then pipe swirls as above.

SMALL SWIRLS

Insert a star nozzle into a piping bag and pipe in small swirls around the edge of the cake, circling into the centre. Alternatively, pipe around the cake in a zigzag pattern.

BLOBS

Using a large plain nozzle, pipe a large blob of buttercream on to the cupcake. Lift the nozzle slightly and pipe a second smaller blob on top.

FLOODING CUPCAKES WITH ICING

Use a little less cake mixture for each cupcake so that they don't quite reach the top of the muffin cases when they are baked and risen. Spoon a little glacé icing on top of the cooled cakes so that it floods out to the sides of the cases.

Flooded icing

Multi-coloured swirl and small swirls

ALTERNATIVES TO ICING

Dust cupcakes with flavoured sugar, such as vanilla, or coloured icing sugar – draw a design on a piece of card, such as a heart or star. Cut out the centre. Place on top of the cake and dust over the hole with icing sugar. Alternatively, use paper doilies as templates. Apply edible gold and silver leaf, dusts and pollens (see page 323). Top with thin slices of fruit; drizzle with melted chocolate or dulce de leche.

COCONUT BUTTERFLY CAKES

1 Spread fairy cakes with coloured glacé icing, then dip straightaway into desiccated coconut. Leave to set.
2 Slice a circle off the top of each cake and cut in half. Fill the hole with buttercream.
3 Position the cut slices as wings on top of the buttercream.

VALENTINE CUPCAKES

1 Slice the tops off the cakes if they are domed. Discard. Brush the cake tops with apricot glaze.
2 Roll out ready-to-roll white icing to a thickness of 5mm (¼ inch). Cut out circles the same size as the cake tops.
3 Using a heart cutter, cut out the centre of each circle. Discard the hearts.
4 Roll out ready-to-roll red icing to a thickness of 5mm (¼ inch). Cut out heart shapes using the same-sized cutter.
5 Put the red hearts into the white heart-shaped holes. Roll very gently to ensure a snug fit without distorting the shape of the circle. Position on top of the cakes.

QUICK IDEAS FOR DECORATING SMALL CAKES

Let your imagination run wild with decorations for fairy and cupcakes. Colour-theme them for wedding, birthdays and parties. They look particularly striking arranged on tiered cake stands

- Top cupcakes with whipped cream, summer berries and a dusting of icing sugar.

- Spread small cakes with buttercream and decorate with a ready-made sugar flower or a crystallised violet or rose petal.

- A single homemade crystallised rose petal is a simple but stunning decoration for an individual iced cake (see page 340).

- For a triple chocolate treat, spread or pipe chocolate buttercream on top of similarly flavoured fairy cakes and decorate with piped chocolate shapes.

- Shop-bought sweets make easy, fun decorations. Spread cakes with buttercream first, then arrange in patterns.

- Look in the baking aisle of your nearest supermarket for ready-made decorations.

- Spread cupcakes with vanilla buttercream and top with a grating of chocolate.

- Sprinkle buttercream-iced cakes with coloured granulated sugar. To make, put the sugar in a plastic bag with a dab of food colouring. Massage the bag to work in the colour. The sugar keeps indefinitely in an airtight container.

Decorate with crystallised violets

Decorate with shop-bought sweets

Decorate with coloured sugar or edible glitter

GLOSSARY

All-in-one One of several basic methods for making cakes. Ingredients – usually sugar, eggs, flour and baking powder – are mixed together in a bowl, all in one go.

Almond paste A thick paste made from ground almonds, caster sugar and icing sugar. Often used to cover fruit cakes, it provides a flat surface for icing. Almond paste is also known as marzipan, although products labelled 'marzipan' tend to have a higher sugar content.

Baking blind Pre-baking a pastry case before filling. The pastry case is lined with greaseproof paper and weighted down with dried beans or ceramic baking beans.

Baking powder A raising agent consisting of an acid, usually cream of tartar and an alkali, such as bicarbonate of soda, which react to produce carbon dioxide. This expands during baking and makes cakes and breads rise.

Beat To incorporate air into an ingredient or mixture by agitating it vigorously with a spoon, fork, whisk or electric mixer. The technique is also used to soften ingredients.

Bind To mix beaten egg or other liquid into a dry mixture to hold it together.

Blanch To immerse food briefly in fast-boiling water to loosen skins, such as peaches, or to remove bitterness.

Buttercream A soft icing used to cover and fill cakes, made by creaming together butter and sugar.

Calorie Strictly a kilocalorie, this is used in dietetics to measure the energy value of foods.

Caramelise To heat sugar or sugar syrup slowly until it is brown in colour; that is, it forms a caramel.

Chill To cool food in the fridge.

Choux Soft, light pastry, either sweet or savoury, baked as profiteroles, eclairs or buns. It is very moist, creating steam when cooked and causing the pastry to puff up.

Combine To stir two or more ingredients together until mixed.

Compote Mixture of fresh or dried fruit stewed in sugar syrup. Served hot or cold.

Coulis A smooth fruit purée, thinned if necessary to a pouring consistency.

Consistency Term used to describe the texture of a mixture, for example, firm, dropping or soft.

Cream (ingredient) Made from the butterfat layer skimmed off the top of milk. Different types contain different percentages of butterfat, the higher the percentage, the easier the cream is to whip: **Single cream** (18% fat) has the thinnest consistency. It is not suitable for whipping and is used for pouring and in cooking. **Whipping cream** (at least 38% fat) can be whipped to twice its original volume. **Double cream** (48% fat) can be poured or whipped. **Extra thick cream** is single or double cream that has been homogenized to give it a thicker consistency, generally used only for spooning. **Clotted cream** (55% fat) does not need to be whipped and is generally not used during cooking as it separates when heated. **Sour cream** (18% fat) is single cream treated with a bacteria culture to give it a slightly sour taste and a thick texture. **Crème fraîche** (39% fat) is similar to sour cream, but slightly milder and softer. Creams with a fat content of 35% or above are suitable for freezing for up to 2 months.

Cream (technique) To beat together fat and sugar until the mixture is pale and fluffy and resembles whipped cream in texture and colour. The method is used in cakes and puddings that contain a high proportion of fat and require the incorporation of a lot of air.

Cream of tartar Also known as tartaric acid, this is a raising agent that is also an ingredient of baking powder and self-raising flour.

Crème pâtissière A rich egg custard that is often used to fill cakes and pastries, such as profiteroles and éclairs.

Crêpe French term for a pancake.

Crimp To decorate the edge of a pie, tart, shortbread or cake by pinching it at regular intervals to give a fluted effect. Special crimping tools are used to give a decorative edge to fondant-iced cakes.

Crystallise To preserve edible flowers or fruit in sugar.

Curdle To cause sauces or creamed mixtures to separate once the egg is added, usually by overheating or over-beating.

Dredge To sprinkle food generously with flour, sugar, icing sugar, and so on.

Dropping consistency Term used to describe the required texture of a cake or pudding mixture just before cooking.

Test for it by taking a spoonful of the mixture and holding the spoon on its side above the bowl. The mixture should fall of its own accord within 5 seconds.

Dust To sprinkle lightly with flour, cornflour, icing sugar, and so on.

Extract Concentrated flavouring, which is used in small quantities; for example, vanilla extract.

Ferment Chemical change deliberately or accidentally brought about by fermenting agents, such as yeast or bacteria. Fermentation is utilised for making bread, yogurt, beer and wine.

Filo Delicate sheet pastry used to make fruit or savoury parcels, scrunched up as a topping on pies, and layered to create desserts such as baklava.

Flour Generally made from grinding wheat, this is the basis for breads, cakes and pasta, among other basic recipes. **White or plain flour** has had most of the wheat germ removed and is commonly used in cakes, in conjunction with a raising agent such as baking powder, as well as in biscuits, pastry and some breads. **Self-raising flour** is plain flour with a raising agent included. **Wholemeal flour** contains the whole of the wheatgerm, producing a denser result, which is higher in fibre. **Strong flour** is made from high-gluten wheat varieties, which helps dough to expand and rise. It is often used for bread-making. **Gluten-free flour** is usually made from a combination of ground rice, potato, buckwheat and maize.

Folding in Method of combining a whisked or creamed mixture with other ingredients by cutting and folding so that it retains its lightness. A large metal spoon or plastic-bladed spatula is used.

Fondant icing Pliable, all-purpose icing made from icing sugar, egg white and glucose, used to cover cakes and for modelling decorations. Also known as 'ready-to-roll icing'.

Frosting To coat leaves and flowers with a fine layer of sugar to use as a decoration. Also an American term for icing cakes.

Galette Cooked savoury or sweet mixture shaped into a round.

Ganache A rich filling or coating for cakes, choux buns and biscuits, made from chocolate and double cream.

Gelatine An animal-derived gelling agent, sold in powdered form and as leaf gelatine.

Gelazone A vegetarian gelling agent sold in powdered form in sachets, and used as a substitute for gelatine.

Glaze A glossy coating given to sweet and savoury dishes to improve their appearance and sometimes flavour. Ingredients for glazes include beaten egg, egg white, milk and syrup.

Gluten A protein constituent of grains, such as wheat and rye, which develops when the flour is mixed with water to give the dough elasticity.

Griddle A flat, heavy, metal plate used on the hob for cooking scones or for searing ingredients.

Grind To reduce foods such as coffee beans, nuts and whole spices to small particles using a food mill, pestle and mortar, electric grinder or food processor.

Hull To remove the stalk and calyx from soft fruits, such as strawberries.

Infuse To immerse flavourings, such as aromatic vegetables, herbs, spices and vanilla, in a liquid to impart flavour. Usually the infused liquid is brought to the boil, then left to stand for a while.

Knead To work dough by pummelling with the heel of the hand.

Knock back To knead yeast dough a second time after rising, to ensure an even texture.

Kugelhopf mould Tube-shaped, deep container with fluted sides, used for baking a traditional Austrian yeast cake of the same name.

Macerate To soften and flavour raw or dried foods by soaking in a liquid; for example, soaking fruit in alcohol.

Madeleine tray A baking tin with 12 shell-shaped indentations for baking traditional French madeleines.

Mandolin A flat wooden or metal frame with adjustable blades for slicing vegetables.

Mocha Term which has come to mean a blend of chocolate and coffee.

Muffin case Paper casing for cooking cupcakes and muffins.

Muffin tin Tray of cup-shaped moulds for cooking small cakes and deep tartlets. Also called a bun tin.

Parboil To boil a vegetable or other food for part of its cooking time before finishing it by another method.

Pare To finely peel the skin or zest from fruit.

Pâte The French word for pastry, familiar in pâte sucrée, a sweet flan pastry.

Patty tin Tray of cup-shaped moulds for cooking small cakes and deep tartlets. Also called a bun tin.

Pectin A naturally occurring substance found in most varieties of fruit and some vegetables, which is necessary for setting jams and jellies. Commercial pectin and sugar with pectin are also available for preserve-making.

Pestle and mortar Heavy marble or porcelain bowl with a heavy grinding tool for grinding herbs, spices, nuts, and so on.

Pith The bitter white skin under the thin zest of citrus fruit.

Pizza stone A clay stone for pizza baking, which reproduces the intense heat of a professional pizza oven.

Prove To leave bread dough to rise (usually for a second time) after shaping.

Puff A light, flaky pastry, made by repeatedly layering and rolling fat and pastry dough.

Purée To pound, sieve or liquidise fruit to a smooth pulp. Purées often form the basis for sauces.

Reduce To fast-boil stock or other liquid in an uncovered pan to evaporate water and concentrate the flavour.

Roulade Soufflé or sponge mixture rolled around a savoury or sweet filling.

Royal icing A traditional white icing made from sugar, lemon juice and egg whites, which dries to a hard finish. It is used for covering fruit cakes and also for piping decorations.

Rub-in Method of incorporating fat into flour by rubbing between the fingertips, used when a short texture is required. Used for pastry, cakes, scones and biscuits.

Run out Method of icing biscuits or cupcakes by piping a shape with royal icing and then 'flooding' it with thinned icing.

Shortcrust The simplest and quickest of the pastries to prepare at home, used for making tarts and pies. Sweet shortcrust pastry and rich shortcrust pastry can be made by adding sugar and egg yolk.

Sieve To press food through a perforated sieve to obtain a smooth texture.

Sift To shake dry ingredients through a sieve to remove lumps.

Simmer To keep a liquid just below boiling point.

Skim To remove froth or scum from the surface of jam, and so on. Use either a skimmer, a spoon or kitchen paper.

Spring-release tin Also known as a springform pan, this is a round cake tin with a spring-release side and removable base, which is clamped in. Used for cakes and desserts that are not to be inverted.

Steam To cook food in steam, usually in a steamer over rapidly boiling water.

Steep To immerse food in warm or cold liquid to soften it, and sometimes to draw out strong flavours.

Suet Hard fat of animal origin used in pastry and steamed puddings. A vegetarian alternative is readily available.

Sugar syrup A concentrated solution of sugar in water used to poach fruit and make sorbets, granitas, fruit juices.

Swiss roll tin Shallow, rectangular tin, available in several different sizes, used for baking sponges that are filled and rolled after baking – such as roulades.

Torte Rich cake made with little or no flour.

Tepid The term used to describe temperature at approximately blood heat, ie 37°C (98.7°F).

Thermometer, Sugar/Fat Used for accurately checking the temperature of boiling sugar syrups.

Unleavened Flat bread, such as pitta, made without a raising agent.

Vanilla sugar Sugar in which a vanilla pod has been stored to impart its flavour.

Whipping (whisking) Beating air rapidly into a mixture with a manual or electric whisk. Whipping usually refers to cream. Whisking can also refer to the basic cake-making technique, in which the sugar and eggs are whisked together over a pan of simmering water. Melted butter and flour are then folded into the mixture.

Zest The thin coloured outer layer of citrus fruit, which can be removed in fine strips with a zester.

INDEX

pandolce 230

panettone 231

panettone pudding 263

pansies 338

Parmesan and olive grissini 222

pasties, Cornish 143

pastries 182–8, 238

pastry 126–8, 310–15

pâte sucrée 313

pavlova: strawberry pavlova with rosewater syrup 268

peaches: peach brulee 250

raspberry and peach cake 28

roasted fruit 248

peanut and raisin cookies 92

pears: pear and blackberry crumble 252

pear and ginger steamed puddings 257

pear, cranberry and frangipane tart 162

pecan nuts: banana and butterscotch loaf 25

chocolate pecan bars 81

double-chocolate brownies 86

maple syrup and pecan muffins 57

pecan pie 155

spiced pecan, apple and cranberry cake 26

sultana and pecan cookies 93

penguins 338

pepperoni sausages: cheat's goat's cheese and sausage pizza 217

pepper and pancetta buns 223

Peshawari nan 214

pies 310–11

savoury pies 130–43

sweet pies 150–59

pinenut and honey tart 163

pink cupcakes 68

piping techniques 331–3

pistachio nuts: chocolate and pistachio biscotti 105

gluten-free pistachio and polenta cupcakes 72

pistachio and rosewater stollen 235

pistachio baklava 187

pitta bread 215

pizza 129, 216–17

plums: American-style plum cobbler 254

plum and almond tart 161

plum and cardamom pie 152

polenta: corn bread 205

gluten-free pistachio and polenta cupcakes 72

sticky lemon polenta cake 23

poppy seed and honey bagels 218

praline: creamy coffee and praline gateau 43

mixed nut praline 330

prawn tartlets 146

puff pastry 128, 313

pumpkin: sweet pumpkin cake with toffee sauce 19

Q

quiches 148–9

R

raisins: Italian rosemary and raisin loaf 209

kugelhopf 245

peanut and raisin cookies 92

raspberries: chocolate and raspberry torte 115

raspberry and cream cheese chocolate brownies 88

raspberry and peach cake 28

raspberry and white chocolate tarts 180

raspberry cheesecake 113

raspberry coulis 317

raspberry millefeuilles 183

raspberry ripple cupcakes 63

ready-to-roll icing 325, 337

red velvet cake 53

refrigerator cake 121

rhubarb: rhubarb and cinnamon pie 153

rhubarb and ginger cheesecake 109

ribbon insertion 335

rice paper 335

rice pudding 267

rich shortcrust pastry 127

ricotta tart, sweet 173

rock buns 34

rocket: roasted vegetable and rocket tartlets 145

rolls 212–13

rosebud wedding cake 274

roses, fondant 338–9

rough puff pastry 127

roulades 37, 295

royal icing 320, 325, 332

rum babas 244

run outs 334

rye bread, dark 201

S

Sachertorte 119

salmon and asparagus pie 132

salt, bread-making 305

salt and pepper rolls 212

sauces: easy pizza sauce 216

toffee sauce 19

sausage rolls 142

sausages: cheat's goat's cheese and sausage pizza 217

savarin, strawberry 244

scones 190–91

Scotch pancakes 189

seeds: gluten-free seed loaf 203

toasted seed and nut bread 204

seven-minute frosting 321

shortbread 99–102

shortcrust pastry 126, 312

Simnel cake 280

Sleeping Beauty's castle 282

small cakes 33–5

snowflake cake 341

snowy Yule log 278

soda bread, oatmeal 200

sourdough starter 304

spinach: Moroccan filo pie 137

spinach and feta pie 130

spotted Dick 260

steak and kidney pie 135

steamed puddings 258–61

stollen 235–6

Picture Credits

Photographers: Marie-Louise Avery (pages 32, 194, 198, 199, 203, 204, 208, 209, 210, 211, 213, 220, 221, 222, 223, 224, 226, 228, 229, 230, 233, 234, 235, 240 and 241); Neil Barclay (page 77); Steve Baxter (pages 144 and 171); Martin Brigdale (pages 11, 37, 91, 99, 119 and 180); Peter Cassidy (page 137); Jean Cazals (page 217); Stephen Conroy (page 123); Nicki Dowey (pages 19, 20, 25, 28, 29, 30, 38, 39, 43, 44, 45, 46, 51, 54, 55, 56, 57, 59, 62, 73, 76, 80, 81, 84, 85, 86, 87, 89, 92, 93, 94, 96, 102, 104, 105, 113, 116, 117, 118, 122, 132, 138, 139, 150, 151, 152, 158, 174, 177, 183, 186, 205, 206, 207, 212, 225, 227, 245, 249, 254, 258, 263, 264, 266, 279, 283, 284, 285, 286, 287, 337, 338 and 341 bottom); Will Heap (page 31); Emma Lee (page 41); Gareth Morgans (page 216); Myles New (page 149); Craig Robertson (pages 112, 131, 133, 135, 136, 141, 142, 145, 147, 148, 153, 154, 155, 156, 160, 161, 163, 164, 165, 167, 168, 169, 173, 175, 179, 181, 182, 187, 252, 255, 256, 262, 267, 290, 291, 292, 293, 294, 295, 296, 298, 300, 303, 304, 305, 306, 307, 310, 311, 314, 315, 316, 317, 319, 324, 325, 326, 327, 328, 329 and 330); Brett Stevens (page 134); Lucinda Symons (pages 12, 13, 14, 15, 17, 18, 22, 23, 27, 33, 34, 35, 36, 42, 49, 58, 60, 61, 63, 64, 65, 66, 67, 68, 69, 70, 71, 72, 78, 88, 95, 98, 101, 103, 108, 111, 120, 121, 143, 157, 162, 166, 172, 185, 188, 189, 190, 191, 195, 196, 197, 200, 201, 202, 214, 215, 218, 219, 231, 232, 236, 239, 242, 243, 244, 250, 251, 253, 257, 259, 260, 265, 273, 275, 278, 281, 297, 318, 331, 332, 333, 334, 335, 336, 339, 340 right and 341) Martin Thompson (pages 10 and 277); Philip Webb (pages 26, 47, 50, 90, 106, 248 and 261); Kate Whitaker (pages 24, 52, 53, 82, 83, 114, 115, 178, 237 and 269); Tim Winter (page 159)

Home Economists for Anova Books: Joanna Farrow, Emma Jane Frost, Teresa Goldfinch, Alice Hart, Lucy McKelvie, Kim Morphew, Aya Nishimura, Bridget Sargeson and Mari Mererid Williams

Stylists for Anova Books: Wei Tang, Helen Trent and Fanny Ward